THE ROMANTIC ECONOMIST

Since economies are dynamic processes driven by creativity, social norms and emotions, as well as rational calculation, why do economists largely study them through the prism of static equilibrium models and narrow rationalistic assumptions? Economic activity is as much a function of imagination and social sentiments as of the rational optimisation of given preferences and goods. Richard Bronk argues that economists can best model and explain these creative and social aspects of markets by using new structuring assumptions and metaphors derived from the poetry and philosophy of the Romantics. By bridging the divide between literature and science, and between Romanticism and narrow forms of rationalism, economists can access grounding assumptions, models and research methods suitable for comprehending the creativity and social dimensions of economic activity. This is a guide to how economists and other social scientists can broaden their analytical repertoire to encompass the vital role of sentiments, language and imagination.

Educated at Merton College, Oxford, Richard Bronk gained a first class degree in Classics and Philosophy. He spent the first seventeen years of his career working in the City of London, where he acquired a wide expertise in international economics, business and politics. His first book, *Progress and the Invisible Hand* (1998) was well received critically, and anticipated millennial angst about the increasingly strained relationship between economic growth and progress in welfare. Having returned to academic life in 2000, Bronk is now a writer and part-time academic.

RICHARD BRONK is currently a Visiting Fellow in the European Institute at the London School of Economics and Political Science.

THE ROMANTIC ECONOMIST

Imagination in Economics

RICHARD BRONK

London School of Economics and Political Science

CAMBRIDGE UNIVERSITY PRESS
Cambridge, New York, Melbourne, Madrid, Cape Town, Singapore, São Paulo, Delhi

Cambridge University Press
The Edinburgh Building, Cambridge CB2 8RU, UK

Published in the United States of America by Cambridge University Press, New York

www.cambridge.org
Information on this title: www.cambridge.org/9780521735155

First published 2009

Printed in the United Kingdom at the University Press, Cambridge

A catalogue record for this publication is available from the British Library

Library of Congress Cataloguing in Publication data
Bronk, Richard.
The romantic economist : imagination in economics / Richard Bronk.
p.   cm.
Includes bibliographical references and index.
ISBN 978-0-521-51384-5
1. Economics.   2. Romanticism – Economic aspects.
3. Economics – Philosophy.   I. Title.
HB71.B7786   2009
330–dc22
2008041688

ISBN 978-0-521-51384-5 hardback
ISBN 978-0-521-73515-5 paperback

In memory of my father
John Ramsey Bronk (1929–2007)

The histories and political economy of the present and preceding century partake in the general contagion of its mechanic philosophy, and are the product of an unenlivened generalizing understanding.

Samuel Taylor Coleridge, The Statesman's Manual (1816)

> In weakness we create distinctions, then
> Believe that all our puny boundaries are things
> Which we perceive and not which we have made.

William Wordsworth, Fragment (c. 1799)

Strange as it may seem, if we read History with any degree of thoughtfulness, we shall find, that the checks and balances of Profit and Loss have never been the grand agents with men; that they have never been roused into deep, thorough, all-pervading efforts by any computable prospect of Profit and Loss, for any visible, finite object; but always for some invisible and infinite one.

Thomas Carlyle, Signs of the Times (1829)

Valuation is expectation and expectation is imagination.

George Shackle, Epistemics and Economics (1972)

Contents

ix

Preface

Our understanding of the world is structured and limited by the language and metaphors we use. Each individual's vision is partly socially constructed by shared frameworks of interpretation; but it is also the product of particular life-experiences and an imaginative capacity to invent new perspectives.

The Romantic Economist is inevitably shaped by my background, which has given me a somewhat unusual combination of perspectives on the great discipline of economics. For much of the last eight years, I have been privileged to work at the London School of Economics and Political Science, teaching postgraduate courses in applied and theoretical political economy – the sister discipline of economics. My own university training was, however, in philosophy and classical literature. Despite or because of that, I spent the first seventeen years of my career in international finance – as a pension fund manager and subsequently an adviser at two investment banks and the Bank of England on European Monetary Union and supply-side reform in Europe. While in the City of London, I was lucky enough to have access to many of the best and brightest in the economics profession. I also gained an insight into what motivates entrepreneurs and structures the behaviour of operators in financial markets. At the same time, I retained a strong interest in philosophy and literature, and became especially fascinated by the Romantic thinkers and poets who wrote around two centuries ago. This fascination resulted largely from a growing conviction that the Romantic outlook is very relevant to economics and markets.

The longer I worked in the financial and business world, the more intrigued I became by the intermittent power of economics to explain and predict, and also by the frequent mismatch between the way economists model economies and the way markets actually work in practice. Why do economists rely on relatively static equilibrium models to make predictions, when markets and economies are so clearly dynamic and characterised by massive uncertainty, relentless innovation and perpetual novelty? And why do economists make the assumption that economic agents are motivated only to maximise (within given constraints) the satisfaction of their preferences and optimise their trading possibilities on the basis of rational expectations? For the most part, the entrepreneurs and investors I met seemed to know so little about the future to which their preferences and expectations related that they had no real way of optimising anything but their own salaries. It increasingly struck me that successful investors are not merely rational calculating machines; they must also have a good intuitive grasp of emerging patterns. Likewise, successful entrepreneurs require more than careful rational analysis of the markets they are in; they need, above all, to have fertile imaginations in the constant quest to create new goods, new techniques and new strategies for dealing with new eventualities. They also need plenty of self-belief, a determination to win and even a dose of arrogance. No wonder the best sometimes resemble Byron's heroes – self-creative, assertive and proud – rather than the anaemic 'economic man' found in textbooks.

My experience as a European investment manager also taught me two other lessons that economics sometimes seemed at a loss to explain. The first was that national institutions and history matter to economic performance, and that there is no such thing as a universal template for competitiveness or economic growth. For example, the most successful countries are often the ones whose firms best exploit their own particular institutional and cultural advantages, whatever they happen to be. Secondly, I learned that, in the non-academic world of business and policy-making, it is seen as self-evident that values and goals other than efficiency sometimes provide an important motivation for economic actors. Moral sentiments like loyalty and trust, the goal of excellence for its own sake, and dreams bordering on delusional obsessions, all play their part. It was in trying to understand such factors that I found a rich source of insights in the criticisms of rationalist disciplines (such as economics) made by Romantic philosophers and writers – insights that I suspected were either unknown to most economists or ignored by them. What, I began to wonder, would be the impact of applying these Romantic insights to the contemporary practice of economics?

On returning to academia, my respect for the academic discipline of economics increased. I quickly learned that at the cutting edge of the discipline there is already a lot of exciting work being done to incorporate more psychological realism into economic models, and to examine the role of national institutions and norms in explaining behaviour. There is also more focus than in old economics textbooks on the role of creativity and innovation in driving economic growth, and much more attention paid to the problem of uncertainty about the future. Despite this, I remained convinced that certain important adjustments, particularly at the edge of the discipline, to the research practices and assumptions used by most economists could make an enormous difference to their success in helping us explain the real world and make practical decisions. In particular, I felt that clearer boundaries of applicability should be established for both standard equilibrium-based models and the narrow definitions of economic rationality on which they depend. It was from this conviction that my ideas for *The Romantic Economist* germinated.

Throughout the book I develop what I see as the most crucial implications of Romantic thought for economics. The first is that successful explanations of the behaviour of economic agents often need to take as much account of the roles played by imagination and sentiment as of those played by deductive reasoning and optimisation calculations. The second is that we should acknowledge how far utilitarian philosophy and mechanical metaphors from physics structure and bias the way economists currently see the world. My central thesis is that economists can gain new insights and develop more successful models by borrowing alternative metaphors and assumptions from the philosophy and literature of Romanticism. The success or otherwise of this project should be of more than esoteric interest. How economists see and analyse the world matters to us all, since it increasingly helps to structure government policy and the behaviour of firms and consumers. Incorporating lessons from Romanticism therefore has potentially wide implications for the nature of the society we live in, as well as for the discipline of economics.

It is my hope that, by providing a novel history of ideas and philosophical framework, *The Romantic Economist* generates a narrative that makes sense of many of the more exciting but disparate developments in modern economics. I do not claim any great originality for my discussion of the 'two cultures' divide, nor for the synoptic history of economics and Romantic thought, in the book's early chapters; rather my aim there is to introduce this history of ideas to those unfamiliar with some or all of it. My focus in later chapters, though, is a more original one: to make instrumental use of this history of ideas to suggest a new set of grounding assumptions and models that might be helpful to economists. My aim is to offer a road map for how practitioners – whether in academia or applied business and policy analysis – could in future combine more systematically the strengths of standard economics with lessons from Romanticism. Such a synthesis has, I believe, never been more necessary than today. For creativity, imagination and the organic interdependence of people – all emphasised by Romantics – have become as central to our future prosperity and happiness as the rational optimisation of trading possibilities and efficiency highlighted by standard economic theory. If economics is truly to show us the path towards the wealth of nations and the poverty of none, we require new and more imaginative ways of analysing our socio-economic predicament.

In writing this book, I have had several audiences in mind: first, academic economists and other social scientists who are interested in placing contemporary methodological debates in their history of ideas context, and are receptive to unorthodox pointers for developing new research techniques and models that answer valid parts of the Romantic critique of rationalism. The second targeted audience is university students, who I hope will find accessible the modular style of the book, with each chapter written as a stand-alone argument and introduction to an area of thought. Thirdly, I aim to interest business and professional users of economics who want to understand the root causes of lacunae in the armoury of standard economics (particularly when dealing with uncertainty, incommensurable values and innovation). Finally, I believe there is a much wider audience possessing some academic background in either literature or economics, who may be interested in what the history of ideas can tell us about the necessary role of imagination, creativity and perspective in economics. With this broader audience in mind, I have tried to use a minimum of jargon and no mathematics, and assume little prior academic knowledge.

The opening chapter of *The Romantic Economist* takes some of its inspiration from William Wordsworth's *Preface* to the *Lyrical Ballads*, often seen as a manifesto of the Romantic Movement, and introduces the main arguments. The rest of the book falls naturally into two parts. Part I is called 'The Prelude' (as a tribute to Wordsworth's great poem explaining his intellectual development), and explains how the Romantic Economist relates to the history of ideas. Chapters 2 and 3 place standard economics and the most important critiques of it in the context of the 'two cultures' schism that opened up between rationalism and Romanticism in the nineteenth century; and they discuss previous attempts by economists and others to reach across this great cultural divide. Chapter 4 outlines some of the main lessons from Romanticism that I believe are relevant to economics.

Part II of the book then uses these lessons to develop key aspects of a more Romantic approach to economics, and suggests how they might be put into practice. This part is called 'Fragments of unity' to reflect the impossibility of finding any one holistic explanatory system or set of synthetic models that can encompass all the crucial facets of economic behaviour and all the perspectives relevant to studying them, including those missing from standard economics. For while we should always try to provide a more unified and organic picture of human nature and social reality, we have also to acknowledge that only fragmentary insight is ultimately possible. Indeed, it is, I believe, the false hope of finding a single unified theory capable of explaining everything in our social and economic predicament that has kept economists so loyal to the rational actor and equilibrium models of standard economics. If only one theoretical framework is allowed, then these models may represent as good a pretender to universal explanatory power as any other. But if economics is to reach its true potential, it needs always to keep in mind that radically different models and perspectives may be required for studying different kinds of question and problem.

Some commentators will argue that my proposed new vision for the discipline of economics is really an advertisement for political economy rather than economics – for a broader, more interdisciplinary approach to studying economic behaviour and creativity embedded in their social and political context. To some extent, this is true. My focus on economics itself, though, is justified by the huge pretensions of many economists to explain ever more in the fields of markets, politics, social interaction and technological innovation. It is also worth remembering that economics grew out of the wider discipline of 'political economy' as practised by Adam Smith, Robert Malthus and John Stuart Mill. Smith is often co-opted by economists as one of their own; but he knew, as modern economists have generally forgotten, that imagination plays a role in science, and sentiment drives economic behaviour.

Acknowledgements

While writing this book, I have been helped by so many people that, despite long hours alone in my study, it feels almost like a collaborative project. Only stubborn shortcomings are entirely my own. In particular, I am more grateful than I can say for the constant intellectual and moral support of my wife, Vyvian. She has read and commented upon every chapter, and even been willing to engage in long discussions on abstruse questions of philosophy and economic methodology at the end of a day in the office. I am indebted also to my colleagues in the interdisciplinary European Institute at the London School of Economics and Political Science who, together with my students, have enabled me to develop a much clearer conception of my argument. My thanks go to Nicholas Barr, Kevin Featherstone, Simon Glendinning, Michel Goyer, Abby Innes, Jennifer Jackson-Preece, Waltraud Schelkle and Paul Taylor for their very helpful suggestions at the research seminar where I first presented my outline argument in 2004, and for their support since. I am also particularly grateful to my former student, Dora Husz, for her many insightful comments and suggestions.

Five friends and colleagues kindly agreed to read particular chapters of the book: Fred Bridgham, John Gray, Bob Hancké, Nicola Lacey and David Soskice. I am indebted to them for being so characteristically generous with their time and judicious in their advice. I would also like to thank Deirdre McCloskey and the anonymous reviewers who took the trouble to give me such perceptive and constructive comments on *The Romantic Economist*. I have benefited enormously, too, from discussions with Jane Darcy, Michael Drolet, Stephen Harrison, Douglas Hedley, Christopher Tanfield and Neil Vickers, and from their reading suggestions. Over a longer timescale, I am grateful to David Bowers and Christopher Potts for showing me, when we worked together, how economics should be used to chart the unknown future. As an undergraduate at Merton College, Oxford, more than a quarter of a century ago, I was also lucky to be taught by John Lucas, who has remained a friend and philosophical mentor ever since.

I am very grateful to him for many wonderful discussions on this and other subjects over the years.

The Romantic Economist would not have been the book that it is without the intellectual help of all the above, but it might never have seen the light of day without the contribution of the following: Ros Edwards, who has been everything an author might want of an agent; Richard Fisher, my broad-minded and supportive editor; Teresa Lewis, Jodie Barnes and the rest of the team at Cambridge University Press, who guided the book through production with great care; Barbara Docherty, my superb copy-editor; Nick Wetton, who displayed skill and tenacity in obtaining the copyright permissions for the passages quoted; and Kerrina Commins, who typed much of the original draft with her usual efficiency and good humour. My warmest thanks to them all. Finally, thanks to my sons Justin and Philip for being so encouraging, and for making some typically perceptive suggestions of how to frame certain key points; and my mother for being understanding about the time I needed to spend on this project.

The book is dedicated to my father, Ramsey, who sadly died just as I completed the text. As a scientist in a very different field, he always stressed the importance of maintaining an overview of the intellectual context and practical implications of research. I hope that *The Romantic Economist* is worthy of his memory. In any case, I will forever remember his wisdom and his kindness.

For permission to publish copyright material in this book grateful acknowledgement is made to the following:

M. H. Abrams: extracts from *The Mirror and the Lamp – Romantic Theory and the Critical Tradition* (Oxford University Press, 1953), reprinted by permission of the publisher.

Isaiah Berlin: extracts from *The Crooked Timber of Humanity – Chapters in the History of Ideas* (John Murray, 1990), reprinted by permission of the publisher and Curtis Brown Group Ltd.

Philip Connell: extracts from *Romanticism, Economics and the Question of 'Culture'* (Oxford University Press, 2001), reprinted by permission of the publisher.

Milton Friedman: extracts from *Essays in Positive Economics* (University of Chicago Press, 1953), copyright © 1953 by the University of Chicago, reprinted by permission of the publisher.

John Gray: extracts from *Two Faces of Liberalism* (Polity Press, 2000), reprinted by permission of Polity Press.

J. G. Herder: extracts from *J. G. Herder on Social and Political Culture*, trans. F. M. Barnard (Cambridge University Press, 1969), reprinted by permission of the publisher.

Geoffrey M. Hodgson: extracts from *Economics and Utopia – Why the Learning Economy is not the End of History* (Routledge, 1999), reprinted by permission of Taylor & Francis Books (UK).

John Maynard Keynes: extracts from *The General Theory of Employment, Interest and Money* (Macmillan, 1936), reprinted by permission of Palgrave Macmillan.

Paul Krugman: extracts from *Development, Geography, and Economic Theory* (MIT Press, 1997), reprinted by permission of the publisher.

Thomas S. Kuhn: extracts from *The Structure of Scientific Revolutions*, 3rd edn. (University of Chicago Press, 1996), reprinted by permission of the publisher.

Gareth Morgan: extracts from *Images of Organization* (Sage, 2006), reprinted by permission of Sage Publications.

Lionel Robbins: extracts from *An Essay on the Nature and Significance of Economic Science*, 2nd edn. (Macmillan, 1935), reprinted by permission of Palgrave Macmillan.

Joseph A. Schumpeter: extracts from *Capitalism, Socialism and Democracy* (Routledge, 1994), reprinted by permission of Taylor & Francis Books (UK).

George Shackle: extracts from *Epistemics and Economics – A Critique of Economic Doctrines* (Transaction Publishers, 1992), reprinted by permission of the publisher.

William Stafford: extract from *John Stuart Mill* (Macmillan, 1998), reprinted by permission of Palgrave Macmillan.

Richard Tarnas: extracts from *The Passion of the Western Mind – Understanding the Ideas that have Shaped our World View* (Ballantine Books, 1993), copyright © 1991 by Richard Tarnas, reprinted by permission of Harmony Books, a division of Random House, Inc. and Frederick Hill Bonnie Nadell, Inc. on behalf of the author.

M. Mitchell Waldrop: extracts from *Complexity – The Emerging Science at the Edge of Order and Chaos* (Penguin, 1994), copyright © M. Mitchell Waldrop, 1992, reprinted by permission of SLL/Sterling Lord Literistic, Inc.

CHAPTER I

Preface to The Romantic Economist

I THE ROMANTIC AND IMAGINATIVE ASPECTS OF ECONOMICS

Romanticism and economics may seem strange intellectual bedfellows. Romanticism is a loose collection of philosophical beliefs and artistic creeds which celebrate the role of imagination, creativity and emotion, while being generally sceptical of the ability of scientific reason to provide a coherent set of universally applicable answers to human problems. Economics is a self-styled 'social science', proud of its mathematical modelling and dedicated to the analysis and prediction of the market behaviour of rational agents seeking to optimise their wealth or utility. To many, Romanticism and economics seem to be quintessential polar opposites, perfect embodiments of C. P. Snow's 'two cultures', separated by a 'gulf of mutual incomprehension'.[1] On this view, the Romantic Economist is at best an oxymoron – an apparent contradiction in terms; at worst he or she must be suffering from intellectual schizophrenia.

By contrast, I outline in this book a new approach to economics in which the Romantic Economist plays an important role both within the economics profession and in the interpretation of economic analysis for policy-makers and entrepreneurs, by providing a vital third way between extreme forms of Romanticism and neoclassical economics. For, on reflection, it is surely odd that the Romantic emphasis on imagination, creative vision and sentiment should be seen as alien to the capitalist activity and market behaviour that economists seek to explain. It is likewise strange to view economists as simply generalising from the observed nature of economic behaviour when, in General Equilibrium Theory, for example, they have created a metaphorical system of great imaginative as well as mathematical power. It is my contention that imagination and reason often need to go hand in hand in both economic behaviour and the discipline of economics.

In the chapters that follow, I outline a number of Romantic attributes that are central to market behaviour and should therefore be of interest to economists. In particular, imagination and creativity are as necessary to economic actors as to artists. Economic actors do not simply rationally optimise their trading possibilities according to given preferences, given goods and given constraints. They continually create new goods, new options and new preferences; they imagine new goals and, in the vast space of possibilities opened up by the complexity of creative interaction over time, they must imagine new possible strategies and act on them. As George Shackle has argued, imagination is what agents must 'substitute for knowledge in that vital and limitless area where we are eternally denied it, "tomorrow"'.[2] In a world of perpetual novelty, creative choice and large degrees of freedom, economic expectations cannot be purely the product of reason; your decisions must also be based on how you imagine the future and how you will it to be.

In such a dynamic world, success depends on an intuitive grasp of emerging patterns, and on creative experiments in viewing problems according to different perspectives. It also depends on understanding that social interaction is often better modelled according to the organic and biological metaphors favoured by Romantics than the mechanical equilibrium metaphors used by neoclassical economists. For social and economic activity is characterised by a complex interdependence of agents, institutions and culture, in which integrated units (firms, markets, or societies) are more than the simple sum of their parts. Preferences, choices and even modes of vision and thought are interdependent and to some extent socially formed. Institutions and economic specialisations are mutually reinforcing. Moreover, many types of economic activity exhibit not diminishing returns and a tendency to equilibrium (as generally assumed in neoclassical economics) but increasing returns and an unpredictable and dynamic reaction to small changes in conditions. History matters.

Economists normally use the simplifying assumption that economic agents can make and reveal consistent preference rankings in all the areas of choice featured in markets. Implicitly, they often go further and assume that measures of economic growth, or cost-benefit analysis, can measure overall changes in welfare. But the Romantics remind us that we cannot easily reduce everything to a single scale of value; they baulk at measuring the environment, human suffering, freedom, love and art according to the calculus of money. They insist that there is no single right answer and no optimal trade-off to be made in the choices between such incommensurable values. If this is so, how much store can we set by exclusively monetary measures of welfare? And how much as economists should we see the consistency of preferences as the hallmark of rationality?

Economists also usually make the simplifying assumption that economic agents are predictable folk: they will always maximise their utility or self-interest within the constraints of given goods, income and information. But the Romantics remind us that motivation is much more complex: while we do sometimes rationally calculate how to maximise our self-interest, we are also driven by an array of sentiments as well as creative intuition. Moreover, in Romantic philosophy, even the basic utilitarian notion of pursuing our self-interest mutates into something more nebulous. For on the organic view of us as social beings, the concept of the self whose interests we care for may be extended to include our community; and, as William Hazlitt made clear, our interest in our own future involves not merely rational prediction but an imaginative anticipation of the future pleasure of our imaginatively projected future selves.[3] Consumers, we may note, constantly seek to reinvent their identities; they also project idealised visions onto holidays, or life with a new car, and come to identify themselves with a look or an image that is for sale. Nor are entrepreneurs guided only by rational expectations, probability analysis and a desire to maximise their own happiness: to be good at their job, they often must imaginatively empathise with the needs of their workforce and the longings of consumers; and they need constantly to create new markets, products and methods. At times, they may even strut the stage of commerce like Nietzsche's Superman – self-creative, assertive and exhibiting an unusually strong 'will to power'. Workers, too, are not just commodified units of production, their services traded in the marketplace; like their bosses, they typically seek self-esteem from their job, identify with colleagues and their firm and take a pride in their work. As John Ruskin noted after making similar observations about economic motivation: 'All which sounds very strange: the only real strangeness in the matter being, nevertheless, that it should so sound.'[4]

Economists, of course, recognise that much of this is true. The central question is whether or not these Romantic features of economic activity are just 'noise' around the edges of basically rational and predictable behaviour that is otherwise well catered for by neoclassical models. Standard economics assumes that economic agents are perfectly rational; that is the basis of its predictive equilibrium-based models. Modern versions generally allow for certain types of information problem and market failure, and recognise that institutions and even history play a role; but they still assume that these factors do not call into question the underlying model of agents as rational utility maximisers within these constraints. Now if, as I argue in this book, economic agents actually have no way of optimising their utility, at least in certain types of situation, and must instead imagine their futures, while being prey to sentiments, phobias, delusions and dreams, then these Romantic aspects of behaviour suggest a more systematic challenge to some of the standard assumptions made in economics.

The implication of these arguments is that we may have much to learn from Romanticism about the nature of economic behaviour. In many cases, economic activity is as much a function of creativity, imagination and sentiment as is the act of writing a poem or painting a picture. Furthermore, it is my contention that Romanticism can also teach us a lot about the nature of the discipline of economics itself, helping us elucidate some of the prerequisites of good economic analysis. For, in their work, economists are surprisingly dependent on imagination and creative ways of looking at the world. As Beatrice Webb – the famous pioneer of social sciences and joint founder of the London School of Economics and Political Science – stressed, sympathy and 'analytical imagination' play an important role in understanding the dynamics of human behaviour. F. R. Leavis ascribed to Webb the view that, for this reason, a literary training should be seen as a good qualification and resource for sociologists and other social scientists.[5] More centrally still for the argument here, Adam Smith was surely correct when he noted that all scientific systems are 'inventions of the imagination, to connect together the otherwise disjointed and discordant phenomena of nature'.[6] By contrast, modern economists are often bemused by such an apparently Romantic emphasis on the role of imagination in the conduct of their scientific profession.

In his iconoclastic book, *The Economics of the Imagination* (published in 1980), Kurt Heinzelman went much further than Webb and Smith. Arguing that the economist is 'a poet, a maker of fictions', he proceeded to study 'the poetics of economic discourse'. In particular, he noted that economics provides us with a 'resonant system of metaphor'.[7] D. N. McCloskey followed suit in an important book, *The Rhetoric of Economics*, saying that: 'Economists are poets/But don't know it.' Pointing out that economists generally fail to acknowledge the 'metaphorical saturation of economic theories', she added:

To say that markets can be represented by supply and demand 'curves' is no less a metaphor than to say that the west wind is 'the breath of autumn's being'. A more obvious example is 'game theory', the very name being a metaphor.[8]

Aristotle argued that, while fine for poets and politicians, metaphor should be avoided by scientists and philosophers;[9] but in fact science is riddled, and necessarily riddled, with metaphors – economics being a prime example of this. Economic theories and models are never a direct encapsulation of some unbiased and unmediated vision and analysis; rather, they (and the hypotheses, metaphors and assumptions contained within them) behave like giant metaphors, actively structuring our vision and analysis. Furthermore, imaginatively changing the models or metaphors we use changes the way we structure our perception and thought – changes, in a very real sense, the way we see the world. For this reason, as McCloskey argues, we will do better economics if we understand fully the structuring role of the metaphors, models and assumptions used by economists. Most economic theory is currently constructed around the metaphor of mechanical equilibrium (borrowed from nineteenth-century physics) together with the assumption (borrowed from utilitarianism) that agents are self-interested maximisers; and the symbiosis between this metaphor and this assumption has profound effects on the way economists see and understand the factors they study.

The Post-Modernist thinker, Jacques Derrida, argued that philosophers usually try to ignore the textual and literary aspects of their trade,[10] and we might add that the same is true of economists. For this reason, there is merit in deconstructing economics to uncover the hidden influence of metaphor and of other essentially literary devices such as the use of allegory and the persuasive impact of the beauty and symmetry of its mathematical models. In this and other ways, Romantic and Post-Modernist philosophy's contribution to literary criticism is surprisingly relevant to understanding the nature of economics and other social sciences. Many of the issues are at least parallel. Does economics, like art, *imitate* actual or 'ideal' reality? Or does its choice of dominant metaphor, assumptions and perspective structure – and, in a sense, *create* – the picture it paints? And is economics, like art, to be judged for its own sake or for its relevance to a broader audience?[11]

Before more practical readers are tempted to close this book for good, it is important to underline why the project of the Romantic Economist matters to us all. The way that economists structure their vision and thought reads across to the policies they promote and therefore to the very economic behaviour they study. The dominant metaphors and philosophical assumptions of economics do more than structure the discipline, its texts and its vision; for these in turn influence policy and the self-conception of economic agents. As a result, the metaphors and assumptions used by economists may come to structure social reality itself. As John Stuart Mill wisely noted, 'speculative philosophy, which … appears a thing so remote from the business of life and the outward interests of men, is in reality the thing on earth which most influences them'.[12]

A similar belief that particular perspectives or 'discourses' structure both thought and practice led Post-Modernists like Foucault and Lyotard to be wary of 'totalising discourses', or 'grand narratives', and emphasise their relationship with ideology and power.[13] To enforce a dominant 'discourse' is to enforce a way of life as well as thought. The argument surrounding the 'Washington consensus' approach to economic reform in Eastern Europe in the period following 1989 should perhaps be seen in this light. The economist, Joseph Stiglitz, has argued that it is possible to trace the origins of the Washington consensus recommendations for extreme versions of 'shock therapy' throughout the region (including very rapid price deregulation and privatisation and large public spending cuts) to the simplified 'textbook models' with which many of the neoclassical economists and advisers concerned structured their view of the world. The poverty of these models ensured a failure to see how important to the success of reforms in these 'transition' countries were social norms and 'organisational capital', and the specific local institutions which support them.[14] Whether the dominant models or metaphors used in such economic discourse are adopted for ideological reasons or merely have ideological implications is, of course, a moot point.

Another more general example of a social science discourse having significant practical and ideological implications is Public Choice Theory. Public Choice Theory is a widespread application in the social sciences of Rational Choice Theory – a central part of the neoclassical economic paradigm. It starts with the utilitarian assumption that all individuals (even politicians and bureaucrats) are essentially self-interested utility maximisers. As a result the theory predicts that politicians and bureaucrats will further the public interest only if it is also in their individual interests to do so – because the voting public knows what they are up to, or other constraints apply. This theory has had huge success in explaining many examples of 'government failure' where public accountability or information is low. It is far from clear, however, that it provides a successful model for explaining or predicting the behaviour of most public officials most of the time. Perhaps more importantly still, the widespread acceptance by opinion formers of its cynical assumption (that those in government are not motivated by anything but their own interest) has helped corrode the social norm of 'public service' and consequently trust in government. The question of whether this model is full enough to give correct explanations in most situations is considered later in this book; and the answer matters not only to the predictive success of social scientists' models but also to public policy and ideology concerning the nature and role of government.

2 ROMANTIC ECONOMIST: NEITHER REVOLUTIONARY NOR MAINSTREAM

At first sight, it might seem self-evident that the project of injecting into economic discourse new grounding assumptions and metaphors derived from Romanticism represents a wholesale attack on current economic methodology. But this would be to misrepresent both the constructive intent of the Romantic Economist and the pluralism and sophistication of modern economics.

The Romantic Economist proposes a joint venture between standard economics (with its neoclassical model of rational behaviour) and more Romantic approaches that allow for the organic interdependence of agents and institutions, and an important role for imagination, creativity and sentiment in decision-making. With such a joint venture in mind, there is nothing to be gained from descending into another 'anti-economics' rant of the sort William Coleman deplores.[15] My intention is, therefore, that this book should, like the Romantic Economist it promotes, engage seriously and respectfully with the principles of standard economics, while suggesting some specific practical ways to improve the discipline. This can best be achieved precisely by not setting up an Aunt Sally in the form of a funda-mentalist economics that is deaf to all Romantic concerns. As Coleman argues, constructive criticism of economics is not well served by misrepre-senting economics as a monolithic and simplistic discipline that has never taken account of any criticisms directed at it. From its inception, there have in fact been huge debates within economics about the nature of the discipline. Indeed, it would be fair to say that if no great economist, past or present, has acknowledged or articulated a problem, this is likely to be important evidence that the problem does not really exist. Many of the best critiques of econom-ics, as Partha Dasgupta has noted, come from thoughtful practitioners[16] – those who are aware of the intricacies of the latest techniques and the practical problems of framing research, but also alive to what are essentially Romantic concerns.

The argument in this book builds initially on criticism of standard neoclassical economics made by key historical figures within the discipline – including Mill, List, Schmoller, Marshall, Veblen, Keynes, Schumpeter and Hayek – as well as on Romantic critiques from beyond economics. Furthermore, *The Romantic Economist* stands firmly on the shoulders of recent figures in the discipline, in each area where a more Romantic approach to economics is outlined. For many of the most exciting develop-ments in economics in recent years – a period Diane Coyle justifiably calls 'a new golden age' for the discipline[17] – have gone some way to operation-alising what is implicitly a more Romantic approach to economics. So, for example, among the economists discussed in later chapters, Brian Arthur and the Complexity theorists develop what is essentially an organic model of economic interaction, while Douglass North's insights into the role of institutions in structuring beliefs and behaviour echo the views of many Romantic thinkers. The pioneering work of Peter Hall and David Soskice in establishing the new school of Varieties of Capitalism also takes seriously a number of quintessentially Romantic concerns, especially on the role of national difference. Likewise, the development by David Weimer and Aidan Vining of a multigoal approach to cost-benefit analysis is an example of how a Romantic emphasis on incommensurable values can be incorpo-rated into disciplined policy analysis; while the work of James Buchanan and Viktor Vanberg, and of Endogenous Growth theorists, makes good progress in understanding and modelling the dynamic creativity of an eco-nomy. One of the most important recent attempts to improve the behav-ioural assumptions on which economic models depend is research by Daniel Kahneman and Amos Tversky into the different ways in which people frame the information and options at their disposal, and how this impacts on the decisions they make and the preferences they have; and this research also implicitly builds on Romantic concerns, this time about the creative role of perspective.

For all the virtues of these attempts to reform the discipline from within, there remain, I believe, two vital and original roles for *The Romantic Economist* and the new type of economist it champions. The first is to demonstrate that many of these existing critiques of standard economics can be better articu-lated and further illuminated by embedding them within the historical context of Romantic responses to Enlightenment rationalism. For this is the lost conceptual and metaphorical framework for many of the adjustments and caveats to economic theory already proposed by leading economists past and present. Only by understanding this framework can we fully appreciate the import and significance of much cutting-edge theory, and hope to solve the many riddles that remain. The second related and pragmatic purpose of *The Romantic Economist* is to promote experimentation with Romantic metaphors and assumptions, as alternatives to the mechanical metaphors and utilitarian assumptions that still for the most part structure and constrain economists' vision. Romantic philosophy and literature is probably the last place most social scientists would think of looking for new ideas and per-spectives, or for help in understanding what links the seemingly disparate critiques they take seriously; but I will argue that it is, in fact, one of the most exciting potential sources of alternative grounding assumptions and meta-phors available to economists. For example, it is there we can learn the central importance of imagination as well as rational calculation in the formation of an individual's expectations, strategies and options, and the resulting need for more profound changes to the microfoundations of some models than most economists currently envisage. In ways such as this, *The Romantic Economist* can provide suggestions for how experts in each field might, in due course, incorporate new assumptions into their existing analysis or develop new models that can provide complementary insights. In this sense, the book is envisaged as 'work in progress' – a source of partially elaborated new ideas for the hard-pressed practitioner who does not have the time to study cultural history, philosophy, or the economists of old, for herself.

The proposal that economists should consider building imagination into the foundations of their models alongside calculating reason, or use organic models that deny the possibility of optimisation or equilibrium, may lead some to reply that such recommendations ignore the boundary between economics and other disciplines. Joseph Schumpeter noted in his *History of Economic Analysis* that economics is an 'agglomeration of ill-coordinated and overlapping fields of research', its frontiers (like that of all sciences) 'incessantly shifting';[18] and there are some who argue that economics should be defined as the study (by whatever method) of a set of topics or problems relating to economic activity. In general, though, it has become fashionable of late to argue that what delimits economics is its reliance on a particular set of methods and assumptions – not least that you can explain outcomes in terms of individuals rationally optimising their utility within given con-straints. Clearly, if economics is so defined, it can have no place for other (more psychologically plausible) assumptions and models that take account of the role of imagination and sentiment, even when studying those areas of the economy and markets where anecdotal evidence suggests they are highly relevant. If, as I will argue, these areas include all those where innovation and creativity are central, as well as some aspects of labour markets and of consumer behaviour, and many attributes of financial markets, then such a narrow methodological definition of the discipline may preclude econo-mists from having the necessary tools at their disposal in some important areas of research. The more Romantic approach to economics advocated in this book requires acceptance of greater methodological pluralism in the study of economies and markets.

A similar debate is also relevant to the contentious question of how to define 'political economy' and its relationship to economics. Historically speaking, 'political economy' is the name given both to the genetic parent of modern economics and to its younger stepsister, Public Choice Theory. Economics emerged as a 'scientific' discipline out of 'political economy' towards the end of the nineteenth century, as it gradually abstracted from political concerns and adopted the metaphors and techniques of physics. But the 'political economy' of early figures like Adam Smith still represents a tradition alive today among those who define (as I do) 'political economy' as the intersection of political and economic substance and different relevant methodologies. By contrast, the standard current use of the term refers much more narrowly to Public Choice Theory and other pure applications of the neoclassical economic methodology (of rational choice) to political subjects.[19] This limited definition would again preclude the use of more Romantic assumptions and models.

There are two possible reactions to the many serious attempts within recent versions of standard economics and Public Choice Theory to model the role of institutions, the impact of innovation and the importance of increasing returns, information problems and other features of the organic interdependence of agents, all the while sticking religiously to rational choice microfoundations. We can be impressed at the ingenuity of the theory-saving adjustments made to take account of these challenges to old neoclassical theory – adjustments that appear to succeed in preserving the essential microfoundations of a predictive science. Alternatively, we can be reminded of Thomas Kuhn's famous example of such paradigm mending. He pointed out that, by the time Ptolemaic astronomy had finished (at the time of Copernicus) coping with all the exceptions to the predictions produced by its core model (of an earth-centred universe), it was a monstrous system 'of compounded circles', whose 'complexity was increasing far more rapidly than its accuracy'.[20] For Kuhn this was a tell-tale sign of paradigm 'crisis' and an impending 'paradigm shift' to a new mode of vision and analysis. In this book, I suggest that economics would, in relation to some issues, likewise be best served by giving up ever-more prodigious attempts at theory mending in the vain attempt to preserve the universal applicability of its central rational choice models. I also argue, however, that in the case of economics what is needed is not a complete paradigm revolution, but rather a recognition that no one paradigm (or set of structuring assumptions, models and metaphors) can ever explain everything important in the economic sphere. Instead, the choice of paradigm or theory should depend on the nature of the problem studied; and sometimes we need to use several paradigms side by side. There are many problems that standard rational choice and equilibrium models explain very well; but there are others far more cogently and simply explained by different more Romantic metaphors and models.

3 USING THE HISTORY OF IDEAS

It is often supposed that today's economists have little to learn from the history of economics that is useful to their practical research. This is because it is assumed that current practice embodies all the important lessons of the past. This assumption arises from an erroneous view of the history of intellectual disciplines – that there is a linear progression in which the latest versions always incorporate all that was good in previous versions. In fact, as Kuhn so well articulated, while new paradigms are generally superior in solving key problems of the day, they necessarily imply some analytical losses as well as gains. All new structuring sets of metaphors and assumptions restrict our vision in important ways as well as revealing new insights. Moreover, to some extent at least (as Kuhn argued), paradigms are 'incommensurable' – that is, they cannot be completely combined into one super perspective that makes everything clear.[21] These then are the fundamental justifications for studying the history of economics: it can help us keep alert to the possibility of bias in the way we currently frame problems by seeing them through the eyes of earlier generations of economists; and it can be a resource for suggesting different approaches to current problems – enabling us to see how previous intellectual dead-ends might now open up new vistas given the application of modern techniques.

While this book incorporates many lessons from the history of economics, its main focus – as should now be clear – is on two much broader uses of the history of ideas. The most important is using the general Romantic challenge to Enlightenment rationalism as a suggestive commentary on lacunae in the modern discipline of economics; the aim here is the radical one of using the philosophy and literature of Romanticism as a source of new perspectives and a new language with which to analyse economics and economic activity. The other connected aim is to help elucidate past and present methodological debates about economics by placing them within the intellectual context of the philosophical and literary conversation between Romanticism and rationalism that took place roughly two centuries ago. One justification for doing so is that this was the period when political economy was emerging as a separate discipline; and many of the concerns and disputes raging then at a time of revolutionary change and emerging global capitalism have strong contemporary appeal.

The first and most obvious way of pursuing this project is to examine what Romantic thinkers had to say directly about economics. So, for example, chapter 6 will focus on the so-called 'Romantic economics' movement in nineteenth-century Germany and, in particular, on Friedrich List and his stress on the importance of national rather than universal answers to economic problems. From time to time, I will also highlight interesting comments about political economy in the poetry of Wordsworth and his contemporaries. One such comment is William Wordsworth's famous argument in *The Prelude* that by applying the test of 'solid life' – that is imaginative and perceptive observation of real-life experiences – he could perceive the 'utter hollowness' of political economy. He believed that Malthus, in particular, saw 'by artificial lights', and he decried his tendency to 'level down the truth/To certain general notions'.[22] Nevertheless, while comments like this are certainly suggestive, it is fair to say that relatively few incisive insights can be derived from the direct comments on economics made by the English Romantic poets and critics. Indeed, it was with some justification that (despite otherwise lionising him) J. S. Mill labelled another such poet, Samuel Taylor Coleridge, an 'arrant driveller' on the subject of political economy.[23]

The failure of many English Romantics to engage constructively with economics hardly comes as a surprise given the often-noted schism that opened up between Romantics and those of a more rationalist and scientific persuasion. Political economy attracted growing antipathy among Romantics as a result of its association with harsh social reforms, the utilitarian philosophy of Bentham and the negative social and environmental impact of industrialisation. Wordsworth and Thomas Carlyle are often best remembered now in relation to economics for their strong emphasis on the dehumanising and deadening effect on man of becoming a mere cog in the machinery of industry and living 'mid the din/Of towns and cities'.[24] It may have been partly this sort of negative reaction to industrialisation that led most Romantic writers, quite as much as economists, to overlook the crucial role of imagination, creativity, self-expression and emotion in economic behaviour. It is for this reason that most of the important implications that Romantic thought can have for economics must be gleaned indirectly from what the Romantics had to say about other matters, including the role of imagination in the writing of poetry.

I am aware that in seeking to draw lessons for contemporary economics not only from a different discipline but also from a different historical period I am in danger of offending against some of the widely accepted norms of modern academia: to some, applying insights from poetry and philosophy to the seemingly distant discipline of economics will appear to be an example of intellectual dilettanteism; and others may be particularly uncomfortable about any discussion of historical ideas that is not a history of ideas. This book proposes that we should use historical ideas instrumentally to suggest new theoretical and practical ways of thinking in a seemingly unrelated area; but critics may argue that this flies in the face of the impossibility of understanding historical ideas properly except by way of a thorough understanding of the structuring assumptions, textual linkages and social contexts of the time in which they were situated. In other words, it may be argued that by using past ideas in current debates, I run the risk of anachronistic meaning being applied to texts when they are removed from the social, linguistic and literary contexts that structured their meaning.

My response to such methodological concerns is twofold: first, I try hard to avoid the worst pitfalls of anachronism in my treatment of past thinkers and to give, where appropriate, some flavour of the original context and meaning; secondly, I am otherwise intellectually unapologetic about my approach. It is precisely because there is a certain incommensurability of outlooks and narratives over time (as well as over the range of disciplines) that the borrowing of metaphors and perspectives is so stimulating of new and unexpected insights of a philosophical and practical nature. Moreover, I hope to demonstrate that the theoretical and practical gains to be had from a dialectic between old and new views of the world far outweigh the dangers of inadvertent misrepresentation of past ideas. Carefully researched and contextually grounded history of ideas is, of course, a vital academic discipline – and one that has informed many of the ideas in this book; but a historical approach to past ideas is not the only valid one. Ideas do not die; and we should not be limited, as academics or otherwise, to treating old ideas as fossils correctly labelled in the museum cases of past thought. There is as much to be gained from a dialogue between living and dead thinkers as between different contemporary disciplines and modes of discourse. Indeed, the strongest message of this book is that the most surprising and useful new insights often come from making connections between old and new ideas as well as between diverse disciplines.

One obvious potential anachronism I must take note of is the concept of Romanticism itself. The poets we now call 'Romantic' did not generally think that they belonged to such a group. Romanticism was defined as a movement to be contrasted with the classical or neoclassical (pitting, for example, organic against mechanical metaphors) by the German critic A. W. Schlegel in famous lectures given in the first decade of the nineteenth century, and Coleridge was aware of this; but the term did not gain common currency as a label for the English poets of Coleridge's day until the second half of that century.[25] As M. H. Abrams put it, the 'romantic "movement" in England is largely a convenient fiction of the historian'.[26]

Moreover, this is not the only danger with the term 'Romanticism'. As Marilyn Butler has observed, Romanticism 'is not a single intellectual movement but a complex of responses to certain conditions which Western society has experienced and continues to experience'.[27] In other words, the posthumous labelling of certain poets and thinkers as 'Romantic' does not in practice designate a self-consistent body of thought and doctrine. Some Romantic poets, for example, were politically conservative (like Southey) while others were radical (like Shelley).

I argue in chapter 4 that it is perhaps the best to view 'Romanticism' as a classic 'family resemblance' word in the Wittgensteinian sense; in other words, while no single essence or set of characteristics is designated by all uses of the term, and there is no coherent set of rules with which all uses of the word must comply, the different uses of the term do form what Kuhn calls a natural family, 'constituted by a network of overlapping and crisscross resemblances'.[28] To back up this view, I outline some important family resemblance links between key aspects of the thought we label 'Romantic' – between, for example, the emphasis on organic metaphors, incommensurable values and the primacy of imagination over reason. In later chapters, these same links (somewhere between suggestive and logically necessary) help connect together various suggested 'Romantic' critiques of standard economics under the umbrella title of the 'Romantic Economist'; in other words, they suggest a family resemblance between the fragments I present of a new more holistic and Romantic approach to economics and political economy.

If Romanticism is an anachronistic (though still useful) umbrella concept, then there are, of course, clear dangers that its use may suggest a greater degree of coherence and consistency than is warranted by the facts in the challenge it is said to represent to neoclassical, Enlightenment and rationalist thought. This is not least because 'Enlightenment' is a similar broad umbrella designation; and because there is plenty of overlap between some of the actual thinkers and thoughts referred to when we use the terms 'Enlightenment' and 'Romantic'. There is a sense, however, in which the very lack of total coherence of Romanticism as a putative 'system of thought' suggests the greatest lesson it can bequeath us. Isaiah Berlin argued that the most important message coming from the vast corpus of Romantic literature and philosophy is that there is no monist, overarching and objective explanatory or value system, and that there is no single ideal and self-consistent template for mankind discoverable by reason.[29] It is clear that some Romantics – particularly those of a strongly Idealist and religious persuasion – would not have agreed with Berlin; but his argument is supported by more than the breathtaking variety of perspectives adopted, and ways of life promoted or evoked, by the thinkers classified as 'Romantic'. Most of them shared an interest in the structuring role of language and imagination in perception and thought; and most of them refused to countenance the reduction of all values to the single scale of utility or money. For these reasons, the majority shared a healthy reluctance to believe either in the universality of any system giving answers to moral and practical questions or in the inalienable truth-status of science. Coleridge, for example, expressed relief that he had avoided being 'imprisoned within the outline of any single dogmatic system'.[30] The Romantic Economist will likewise try to avoid being confined to the 'single dogmatic system' favoured by standard or neoclassical economics.

4 WORDSWORTH AND MARSHALL

Wordsworth's famous 1800 *Preface* to the *Lyrical Ballads* has come to be seen, in the words of Abrams, as having 'something of the aspect of a romantic manifesto'.[31] There are a number of reasons why this treatise on the nature and methods of his new poetry can also serve as a suitable mascot for this opening chapter to *The Romantic Economist*.

First of all, as Aidan Day and others have observed, the *Lyrical Ballads* and its *Preface* were less revolutionary in technique, subject matter and intent than many subsequent critics have tended to assume. While Wordsworth, of course, claimed novelty for his co-production with Coleridge, his *Preface* did not in fact suggest an extreme rejection of all earlier poetic techniques, Enlightenment values, or reason. Indeed, in many respects, the works of Wordsworth (and Coleridge) are as much products of the Enlightenment as reactions to it.[32] This mirrors the relationship to economics I propose for the Romantic Economist – as much child of this Enlightenment discipline as rebellious critic of it. Wordsworth argues in his *Preface* that the poet should be 'ready to follow the steps of the Man of Science' and 'be at his side'[33] – hardly an extreme Romantic rejection of reason. In this book, I argue that the Romantic Economist similarly should refuse to believe that there is an inevitable conflict between a scientific approach to economics and a Romantic emphasis on the importance of emotion and imagination; rather, the two approaches should inform each other and be complementary.

Wordsworth does note that one advantage the poet has over the scientist is a more holistic view of the world. This was to become a general motif of Wordsworth – that a rationalist approach 'sacrificed/The exactness of a comprehensive mind/To scrupulous and microscopic views'. Scientific reason led in his view to 'narrow estimates of things' and to superficiality. The poet, on the other hand, had a much more comprehensive knowledge, not least of human nature and the interdependence of men with their environment.[34] In this also, the Romantic Economist should follow Wordsworth's example, and advocate a more holistic view of economic activity as interdependent with its social and natural environment, combined with a broader understanding of the motivational and emotional make-up of economic actors.

In the 1802 amendment to his *Preface*, Wordsworth explains that his principal aim in the *Lyrical Ballads* is:

> to chuse incidents and situations from common life, and to relate or describe them, throughout, as far as possible, in a selection of language really used by men; and, at the same time, to throw over them a certain colouring of imagination, whereby ordinary things should be presented to the mind in an unusual way.[35]

The emphasis here on the important role of the imagination in presenting things in a different light was to become one of the dominant themes of Romanticism. Wordsworth elsewhere speaks of the 'modifying powers of the imagination' – which he explicitly links to the use of metaphor – and stresses the creative role of mind in perception.[36] Herein lies perhaps the most important message of Romanticism for economics, too: the need to make use of imaginative shifts of perspective and metaphor to present things in a new light and thus gain new and surprising insights, while having a strong general understanding of the ways in which the metaphors we use create and structure what we see.

The *Preface* passage quoted above is also relevant to economists in its insistence on writing in a 'language really used by men'. Wordsworth claimed that he could best capture people's real thoughts and emotions by using everyday language and focusing on everyday incidents. He believed that it is impossible fully to articulate the feelings that motivate ordinary people in an artificial language that is completely alien to that in which they think and feel. He would therefore take great pains to avoid the specialised 'poetic diction' and 'false refinement' generally favoured by the poets of his day, 'who think that they are conferring honour upon themselves and their art in proportion as they separate themselves from the sympathies of men'. Wordsworth's other concern was to reach a broader audience: 'Poets do not write for Poets alone, but for men.' This, he believed, also demands that they express themselves 'as other men express themselves', and not in the artificial 'family language' of the poetic fraternity.[37]

The lessons here for economists are not hard to find. In economics, too, there is much to be said for analysing market behaviour in the language used by the actors themselves since it is most likely to reflect the concepts and feelings with which they structure their experience. To use a specialist language – and so structure our vision according to a different conceptual and metaphorical framework – may be very useful in giving us a different perspective on the same situation. But to avoid completely the 'language really used by men', as much economic analysis does, runs the risk of missing what, from the actors' point of view, are the key elements of the situation or problem being analysed. Economists should therefore follow Wordsworth's example and avoid an over-reliance on specialist economic terminology and the dehumanised language of mathematics and algebra, except in situations where their use yields important analytical gains in relation to a particular problem. In other words, the choice of language should always be driven by the nature of the problem being analysed; and, crucially, the true nature of the problem can often be best assessed in the first instance in the multifaceted language of everyday usage. All too often, economists write and think in maths, not for the valid reason that to do so encapsulates and explains a problem more quickly, clearly and precisely, but because, in Wordsworth's words, they 'think that they are conferring honour upon themselves and their art'. They relish speaking in the 'family language' of the economics fraternity, in part at least, because the audience they care about is other economists who may be impressed by the orna-ments of refined mathematical notation and algebra. Mitchell Waldrop makes this point beautifully in his book on complexity:

Theoretical economists use their mathematical prowess the way the great stags of the forest use their antlers: to do battle with one another and to establish domi-nance. A stag who doesn't use his antlers is nothing.[38]

The cost of this strategy is that economists for the most part work in a language that struggles to capture aspects of economic life not easily expressed mathematically. They also make their work inaccessible to a wider audience, thereby often cutting themselves off from a fruitful two-way discourse with those using other perspectives structured in ordinary language.

To be fair, economists are by no means alone in operating in a specialist language that is quite alien to everyday experience and a barrier to wider comprehension. Wordsworth's contemporary, the essayist William Hazlitt, attacked the writing style of the philosopher Jeremy Bentham for its 'barbarous philosophical jargon' and for being 'a curious framework with pegs and hooks to hang his thoughts upon, for his own use and guidance, but almost out of the reach of everybody else'.[39] For Hazlitt, the problem was not only that such prose is a barrier to its being read by non-specialists, but also that the very precision and abstraction it represents helps preclude a more comprehensive understanding of the human predicament.[40] This reminds us that the beauty of language in its everyday form is that by being less precise and abstract than philosophical or economic language – that is, by being more fluid, suggestive and yet grounded in common experience – it is, paradoxically, less apt to drain away the complex significance of a situation. There is, of course, a trade-off here between precision and logic on the one hand and fertile suggestiveness on the other. The ideal situation for an economist or philosopher is, therefore, often to make use of both types of medium – in particular, to assess the nature of a problem in the fluid and grounded language 'really used by men', the better to be able to decide which specialised language, if any, can then help us analyse that problem more effectively.

To any historian of economics who considered it, the Wordsworth passage discussed here would have obvious parallels to the comments made a hundred years or so later by the famous economist, Alfred Marshall, on the use of the specialist language of mathematics in his discipline. In a series of letters to his pupil Arthur Lyon Bowley, Marshall expressed an increasing scepticism about the value of mathematical formulae used by economists who, he thought, had come to resemble 'highly specialised calculating machines'. He regarded algebraic techniques as 'mathematical toys' providing abstract models rife with unrealistic assumptions and widespread *ceteris paribus* clauses. Given that 'in economics "other things" are so often not equal', such mathematically based models are, he thought, much less useful in gaining insight into the complex problems of real life than 'a level headed observation of life'. He argued that 'the application of exact mathematical methods' is 'nearly always a waste of time' when used to study the complex world of interdependent causal factors and numerous relevant variables that can neither be isolated nor expressed numerically. He was particularly scathing of applying 'a varnish of mathematical accuracy to many places of decimals on results the premises of which are not established within 20 or 50 per cent'.[41] Before urging Bowley to do all he could 'to prevent people from using Mathematics in cases in which the English Language is as short as the Mathematical', Marshall set out the rules that he himself used:

(1) Use mathematics as a shorthand language, rather than as an engine of enquiry. (2) Keep to them till you have done. (3) Translate into English. (4) Then illustrate by examples that are important in real life. (5) Burn the mathematics. (6) If you can't succeed in 4, burn 3.[42]

In the Preface to his famous economics textbook, Marshall acknowledged the advantages of precision and brevity that came from expressing economics in mathematical terms, and admitted that mathematics may be very useful to the author of an economics text in getting to the heart of a problem. He was equally adamant, however, that such mathematics is 'laborious to anyone but the writer himself' and a waste of time for the reader of economics. Marshall resolved to banish all his mathematical workings to the textbook's appendix.[43] In this, of course, he was mindful of his intended audience – students, policy-makers and the public – rather than other professional economists trying to reproduce his findings mathematically.

Among all the critics of the overuse of mathematics in economics, Marshall has perhaps been the most influential within the discipline because he was a brilliant mathematician as well as a fine economist. His were not the sour grapes of artistic types who feel excluded by too much algebra. As A. C. Pigou (Marshall's successor in Cambridge) noted:

Objections from people innocent of mathematics are like objections to Chinese literature by people who cannot read Chinese, and are not worth listening to. But objections from Marshall are in an entirely different class and deserve a most careful and respectful hearing.[44]

Marshall's reasons for distrusting the overuse of mathematics in economics raise a number of issues that are crucial to the argument of this book. First, Marshall was so insistent on translating economics back into everyday language because, just like Wordsworth, he wanted his work to be accessible to a wider audience. Making economics accessible in this way is a necessary condition of policy-makers, entrepreneurs and ordinary readers being able to benefit from economic analysis. It is also crucial to the project of the Romantic Economist in a deeper sense, because it helps ensure that the assumptions and methods used by economists, and the way they frame problems, are open to audit by the broader audience. Making economists speak in everyday language forces them to justify their methods and assumptions in the court of practitioner and informed generalist opinion.

Secondly, Marshall was particularly concerned that mathematics should not become the 'engine of enquiry'. This chimes in with one of the central themes in this book – namely that, in all applied economics, the choice of precise method, technique and even language of analysis (mathematics or English), should be driven by the nature of the real-world problems being analysed, rather than the preferred method and language determining the kind of economic problem deemed worthy of consideration. Applied economics should not be primarily technique-driven but instead make use of the method and language appropriate to each problem.

Marshall's fear that the use of mathematical models would make economists strangers to realism raises the third set of important issues for the Romantic Economist. Marshall was as keen that economists should ground their analysis in real-life examples as Wordsworth was that poets should write about incidents from everyday life; but, as he also recognised, there is a great danger that economists' determination to express themselves mathematically makes them keen to ignore everything that cannot be expressed mathematically. Moreover, the desire to build mathematical models that are complete in themselves encourages economists to abstract from most of the complex messiness of life and in particular the prevalence of multiple concurrent causal factors. As a result, they can end up analysing the logical implications of a theoretical construct that bears little relationship to everyday problems. None of this need matter, of course, if the modelling exercise is being done for its own sake; but, if these models are then applied directly to real-life policy issues, the dangers grow.

Marshall also objected to a mathematical approach to economics because he thought it tends (in Pigou's words) 'to focus attention on mechanical analogies' rather than the 'more important biological analogies in which the organic forces of life and decay are dominant'.[45] As Marshall himself wrote: 'The Mecca of the economist lies in economic biology rather than in economic dynamics',[46] and in this he echoes a key Romantic motif central to much of this book. In one respect, however, Marshall has been proven wrong with hindsight. The new developments in non-linear mathematics and the mathematics of complexity can now model exactly the sort of organic interdependence effects (including increasing returns) that Marshall, with such prescience, realised are crucial to economic systems. The use of mathematics no longer need bias economists against structuring their discipline according to organic metaphors.

For this and other reasons, the Romantic Economist should be less hostile than Marshall was to the use of mathematics in economics, so long as we learn key lessons from Romanticism about its limitations and how to use it. The positive merits of using mathematics are clear: above all, the huge analytical power of mathematical models can often unearth counter-intuitive implications that would be quite impossible for those analysing the same problem purely in the less precise logic of everyday language to grasp. It is also true that the mathematical expression of economic theories, together with statistical analysis, allows for the testing of models and theories with a precision that would otherwise not be possible. Milton Friedman famously argued that the simplification of reality necessary to construct a mathematical model in economics (which so bothered Marshall) does not in fact matter so long as the model produces accurate predictions; for him it was the ability to test a theory's predictions empirically that is key to economics' status as a science.[47] In today's discipline, a whole host of econometric and mathematical techniques, together with vast computing power, ensure that economists' theories and models are indeed tested with apparent rigour.

What Friedman and other economists have often ignored, though, is that the mathematical language and models they use significantly constrain and structure their analysis, interpretation and even perception of data, rendering their testing of theories less objective than they like to believe. The data economists use to test a theory are typically the product of vision that is itself structured by that theory and the mathematical techniques used. Problems and evidence that are not easily expressed in rigorous mathematical terms tend to be overlooked, however central they are to our predicament; or they are framed in formal terms (even when less formal techniques would be more appropriate) with consequent distortion and loss of detail. More widely, the mathematical superstructure of economics has come to dominate the discipline and determine the way economic facts are viewed and analysed. Economists' entire outlook is structured by the requirement of mathematical method: factors must be abstracted from real-world complexity so that they can be standardised within the framework of models; data must be measurable (and usually commensurable in monetary terms) or be ignored as 'noise'. The complaint of the Romantic Economist is not that economists are normally uninterested in the real world, fail to test their theories, or use reductionist models; rather, it is that they are often unaware of how far their vision is structured by the mathematical models they use. Mathematical models are, as Paul Krugman has pointed out, just another form of metaphor – and economists need to be aware of the distortion as well as focus these metaphors imply for the way they look at the world.[48]

To ensure that we get the benefits of mathematical modelling while avoiding its pitfalls, economists should be careful to use both mathematics and everyday language. By expressing themselves in prose as well as mathematics, economists can ensure their research results are open to scrutiny by those outside their own discipline. More generally, to use ordinary language alongside mathematics is to structure our vision in two different ways, and this helps reduce the dangers of bias in the way questions are framed and data are assessed. In particular, we need to use the multifaceted language of everyday usage to assess in an open-minded way what kind of problem is being studied in each case; this is crucial if the nature of the problem is to dictate the method and language eventually used in analysis, and not the other way round. Finally it is important that economists are exposed to new ideas expressed in prose and non-mathematical metaphors, so that they can spot where new kinds of mathematical model and formal technique might be useful.

5 THE STRUCTURING ROLE OF METAPHOR

When economists use mathematical models to represent some aspect of social reality, they are writing or thinking in a metaphorical language; and the particular underlying structure and logic of this language permeates and constrains their vision, so that their reading of social reality may be quite different from those using other metaphors and other languages. This is a fact often overlooked by economists who may assume that they are combining the timeless verities of mathematics with unbiased scientific observations of the facts 'out there' to get at some objective truth. While others may see through a glass darkly, economists often implicitly believe that they can see the world as it really is. One of the most profound lessons of Romanticism explored in this book is that we can in fact never have unmediated access to reality. Even the observations and findings of the supposedly 'objective' sciences are structured by the particular languages, conceptual categorisations and metaphors used. The later Romantics, like Nietzsche, were especially convinced that there is no uniquely valid perspective or interpretation that captures reality beyond doubt and in all its aspects. Instead, there are many different perspectives and interpretations, structured by different languages and battling it out for supremacy. The complex philosophical reasoning behind this Romantic belief that perception and knowledge are perspective-dependent and partially created by language and metaphor can be succinctly captured by the analogy of 'the mirror and the lamp' used by M. H. Abrams in his famous book of that title. The classical view of perception expressed by Locke and others was of the mind as a 'mirror' passively *reflecting* (or registering) images presented to it. Abrams contrasts this unsophisticated and inadequate view of perception with that represented by the Romantic motif of seeing the mind as a 'lamp', which partly *creates* what it sees by the light it sheds.[49] One way in which the Romantics believed the mind can structure or create the world-as-it-appears-to-us is with the use of metaphor.

In considering the role of metaphor in economics, it is useful to start with another crucial distinction made by Abrams, this time between analogies that are *illustrative* and metaphors that *constitute* the very lens through which we view the world.[50] Discussions and textbooks in economics are often peppered with illustrative analogies and similes. For example, as William Tabb points out, economics textbooks have traditionally used Robinson Crusoe on his island to illustrate the problem of allocating scarce resources between competing goals – a rather odd choice of analogy given that he was nowhere near a market nor (initially) other agents.[51] In another example, the economist Brian Arthur has used playing chess as an analogy for the computational implausibility of an economic agent ever working out the optimal move in the complex game of real markets.[52] Such similes and analogies can often profoundly influence the way we think about and model aspects of economic behaviour. The effect on the way we view the world becomes more all-pervasive, however, when a metaphor comes to constitute the very conceptual structure with which we look at and analyse social reality. McCloskey makes another important distinction here: when the structuring metaphor is still, to use her terminology, 'live' – that is, conscious and surprising – we are aware of its structuring effect; but when it becomes 'half-dead' – that is, no longer consciously recognised – we may become oblivious of the extent to which it structures and constrains our vision. McCloskey gives a number of excellent examples of each: Gary Becker's metaphor of children as 'durable goods' is arresting and thought provoking, and causes us to see our relationship to children in a new (if not entirely convincing) light. By contrast, 'half-dead metaphors' such as the 'elasticity' or 'velocity' of money, market 'equilibrium', or 'production functions' no longer surprise us as economists, and we tend not to appreciate how far they influence our thought.[53]

When metaphors become buried in this way and cease to be questioned, there are two inevitable dangers. The first is that there may be important distortions and deficiencies in our vision and analysis because of the structuring effect of the conceptual and logical framework implied by the metaphor. As Coleridge famously said: 'No simile runs on all four legs';[54] and the imperfect nature of an analogy becomes potentially a source of considerable inadvertent distortion in our vision if simile mutates into metaphor and then becomes unconscious. The second danger is that when a metaphor hardens into one of the implicit and unquestioned metaphors of everyday or specialist language, it starts to have an impact not only on the way we see social or market reality but also on the way we structure that reality through our behaviour and the policies we advocate. As Thomas Carlyle said when discussing the 'Machine of Society' metaphor prevalent in his day:

Considered merely as a metaphor, all this is well enough; but here, as in so many other cases, the 'foam hardens itself into a shell', and the shadow we have wantonly evoked stands terrible before us, and will not depart at our bidding.

Carlyle was convinced that grave moral and social consequences flow from understanding society as a machine. He was also concerned that such a guiding metaphor, once hardened, may imprison us 'like some glass bell', forcing us into an 'unwise mode of *viewing* Nature'. As he pointed out, though, since 'the bell is but of glass', we have it in our power to break it, and so free ourselves from metaphorical bondage. Carlyle's vivid prose serves, if nothing else, to remind us of the liberating effect on our vision and action of experimenting with different metaphors.[55]

The danger that hidden metaphors may distort both our vision and social reality itself makes it imperative that – as economists, policy-makers, entrepreneurs and voters – we remain conscious of the metaphorical structuring of economic vision and analysis. As Philip Mirowski has shown convincingly in *More Heat than Light*, standard economics is almost entirely structured according to metaphors from nineteenth-century energy physics; this implies a central focus on the 'static physics model of equilibrium', with utility playing a role in a 'field theory of value' analogous to that of potential energy in a field of force. Mirowski advocates engaging in 'metaphorical reasoning' to establish the 'dissonances as well as resonances' that flow from applying this 'social physics' metaphor to markets;[56] and it is to this end that I outline in the following chapters some of the main positive and (often forgotten) negative implications of using this metaphor.

My more general argument is that metaphorical reasoning should be extended to include open-minded experimentation with different similes and metaphors to yield complementary insights and alternative ways of modelling and simulating economic activity. For example, Coleridge likened the spread of bankruptcies to 'a fever, at once contagious and epidemic';[57] and this illustrative simile, in his day merely suggestive, could now be used to suggest how the dynamics of default risk and market panic might be modelled and simulated using equations from the analogous field of epidemiology. The application of new constitutive metaphors can also give us alternative ways of framing particular problems and, by suggesting new ways of structuring our vision and analysis of social reality, it can prevent us being imprisoned by one dominant metaphor or paradigm. Indeed, borrowing metaphors from other disciplines (even literature) is an important source of intellectual cross-fertilisation for economists. Schumpeter was, of course, right to point out that cross-fertilisation can all too easily lead to 'cross-sterilisation'[58] if, for example, structuring metaphors become so mixed that the resulting manner of viewing or analysing social reality is internally incoherent; but there is no intrinsic reason why confusion should result from careful experimentation with different metaphors in parallel to give us access to two or more intellectual perspectives on a problem at once.

The Romantic Economist focuses in particular on the insights to be gained from structuring our analysis of social and economic reality according to quintessentially Romantic organic (and biological) metaphors, just as Marshall advocated. It also examines the use of metaphors derived from modern non-linear physics, and explores how markets and economies are often best modelled by seeing them as analogous to complex and dynamic physical or biological systems rather than mechanical systems in equilibrium. This 'complexity' analogy emphasises threshold effects, positive feedback and dynamic uncertainty; and when our view of the economy and markets is structured by expectations that we might see such phenomena, they suddenly seem to apply all over the place where we failed to see them before. We need to remember, however, that no metaphor gives us perfect vision. Different metaphors highlight different aspects of reality; and while some metaphors may provide a way of structuring our vision and analysis that is more useful or intuitively seems to make more sense of a particular problem, we should always regard the observations and findings so structured as provisional, pending the possible discovery of a new or complementary metaphor.

6 ROMANTIC ECONOMICS PREFIGURED

The mission of the Romantic Economist is now clear – to find 'a third way' between the narrow version of rationalism still entertained by many economists and the wilder excesses of Romanticism. This involves developing models of the behaviour of economic agents that recognise the vital roles played by imagination and sentiment as well as reason; and, when considering the prerequisites for good economic analysis, it involves championing the use of analytical imagination, metaphorical reasoning and open-mindedness as a complement to mathematical rigour and logic. Part II of this book indicates how these two related aims can be put into practice.

Chapters 5–9 explain how economists could more comprehensively than hitherto introduce structuring assumptions and metaphors borrowed from Romanticism into their analysis and models. The aim is not to dispute the enormous analytical power of standard economics and its neoclassical and rationalist assumptions; rather it is to help understand why it sometimes succeeds magnificently and at other times fails lamentably, and so to elucidate more clearly the boundaries of applicability of standard models. The central thesis is that standard equilibrium-based models and associated microfoundations based on the assumption of rationally optimising individuals cannot work well when applied to problems involving a significant role for moral sentiments, the organic interdependence of agents, incommensurable values, or the radical uncertainty of choice in situations where creativity and increasing returns make the future unknowable. Since economic problems fairly frequently involve such features, these chapters present an attempt to reformulate some of the key philosophical assumptions underpinning the discipline at its current boundaries, and suggest new kinds of practical model that could enable economists to tackle such problems with confidence. These include more organic models of economic interaction, new approaches to the measurement of welfare and the introduction of *homo romanticus* as a model of motivation. Innovative models like these, based on lessons from Romanticism, can complement standard economic models, and carry greater explanatory load in relation to certain types of problem.

Chapters 10 and 11 switch from a substantive focus on explaining the Romantic and imaginative aspects of economic activity to providing a new vision for the discipline and how it should operate. In particular, chapter 10 suggests some new research formulation procedures that should make it easier for economists and political economists to approach a new problem initially in a more open-minded and multiperspective manner, and so establish its nature free from the structuring bias of a particular paradigm, perspective, or model. This should help ensure that the theory, model, or language then used for analysis is driven by the nature of the problem, rather than the preferred theoretical approach determining both the type of problem considered and the way a question is framed. An audit of research after it is complete is also proposed, in order to ensure that its conclusions are not undermined by bias in the selection and interpretation of data resulting from the vision of the researchers being structured according to one particular analytical and metaphorical language.

The new template for the discipline of economics proposed in this book is likely to be adopted only if several preconditions are met. One is the relaxation of a commonly accepted standard of what counts as a 'scientific' explanation. When Friedman argued that economics' status as a 'positive' science depends on its ability to produce theories that can make precise predictions capable of being tested and falsified, he was expressing a widespread view of the nature of all good scientific hypotheses.[59] In practice, though, this sets up an entirely unrealistic standard for judging explanatory hypotheses in relation to many kinds of economic and market behaviour – one which restricts the kind of problem that can be 'explained', and at the same time threatens to make a laughing stock of economists on the many occasions their predictions are (for understandable reasons) poor. It is worth noting that there are in fact many branches of 'science' (such as the study of evolution or weather systems) where the goal is only to model patterns at a general level (or simulate possible outcomes), and to explain actual outcomes after the event but not to predict them with any precision. It is my contention that many kinds of economic problem (those involving creativity and increasing returns) lend themselves to precisely this lower standard of explanation. The capacity to make predictions should not be the holy grail of good economic theory. All explanatory hypotheses should, of course, still be falsifiable in some sense, but the falsification in these cases cannot be by the rigorous testing of *ex ante* predictions. Instead it must involve looser standards of intuitive judgement of 'fit' and careful assessment of the reasonableness of a model's assumptions. In short, I am arguing for a much broader definition of the 'science' of economics than Friedman entertained, one more akin to the 'tooled knowledge' or 'refined common sense' promoted by Schumpeter.[60] Such a science will still – as all science must – rely on models that try to bring order to the apparent chaos of events by the judicious choice of simplifying assumptions. But it will allow for eclecticism in the choice of model (and type of model), so long as this eclecticism is driven by an open-minded assessment of the nature of the problems being studied.

If the economics discipline is to welcome the inclusion of the Romantic Economist in its midst, another precondition may be some changes to the institutional incentive structure of the profession. David Colander and others have focused in recent years on the need for more open-minded economic journal policies and promotion criteria.[61] Such changes may indeed be required if we are to see the creation of more broadly based research teams in economics departments that are not afraid to include mavericks and even some from other disciplines who can help standard economists to think outside the box. Changing the incentive structure of any discipline is, of course, notoriously difficult, and I will be content if I convince at least a few economists that it is necessary. The wider aim is therefore to convince the users and funders of economic research – entrepreneurs, policy-makers, students and voters – that certain changes already occurring in economics should be encouraged and deepened, to ensure that the discipline can fulfil its potential to help us, to a greater extent than it has already, create a better future.

PART I

The Prelude: the Romantic Economist and the history of ideas

CHAPTER 2

The great divide

It is often suggested that a large and growing chasm separates scientists (including economists) from literary and artistic types (including Romantics) – a great divide in methodology, vision and values. On this view, scientists try to establish the truth through rational and objective analysis of evidence, while artists create visions out of their imaginations, and prefer intuition and inspiration to reason. Whereas the dispassionate observation of the scientist seems predisposed to present a world that is explicable and predictable in terms of universal laws of nature, this is anathema to the artist who may, as John Keats famously did, deplore the scientist for being determined to 'clip an angel's wings', 'empty the haunted air' and 'unweave a rainbow'.[1] When it comes to our depiction of social reality, the contrast appears no less stark between those who seek to explain it objectively in terms of the rational and therefore predictable calculations of utility-maximising agents acting within constraints and those who emphasise the less predictable influence of custom, feelings, imagination, chance events and the transforming role of particular perspective. This chapter examines the historical origins of this supposed schism – particularly between a rationalist and a Romantic outlook – and assesses how far it is, or has been, a reality. To the extent that the great divide is fact rather than fiction, it then considers how far it is possible or desirable to bridge the gap, with a view to producing a more Romantic approach to the predominantly rationalist discipline of economics. The principle protagonist in the story presented here is John Stuart Mill, the renowned English philosopher and economist of the mid nineteenth century, who did so much to set the parameters of this debate.

I MILL ON BENTHAM AND COLERIDGE

In 1838 and 1840, Mill wrote two essays that, as a pair, were to become hugely influential. The first was on Jeremy Bentham (the famous utilitarian philosopher and legal reformer); the second was on Samuel Taylor Coleridge (the Romantic poet, essayist, lecturer and devotee of German philosophy). Mill claimed that these men had been 'the two great seminal minds of England in their age'.[2] Crucially, though, he saw them as resembling 'inhabitants of different worlds', noting: 'They seem to have scarcely a principle or a premise in common. Each of them sees scarcely anything but what the other does not see.'[3] Both Bentham and Coleridge may have had enormous influence on their followers but, Mill argued, 'the two systems of concentric circles which the shock given by them is spreading over the ocean of mind, have only just begun to meet and intersect'.[4] Here is a classic statement of the great divide in thought and outlook between the paragon of rationalist social theory and the quintessential Romantic. Moreover, the divide Mill painted had obvious implications at the time for economics: Bentham was not himself an economist, but his utilitarian philosophy had a powerful influence on the emerging discipline, particularly through the writings of Mill's father, James Mill; and the Lake poets like Coleridge were already strongly associated with attacks on political economy and the utilitarianism that increasingly underpinned it.

Mill outlined, in the essays, three main limitations and weaknesses of Bentham's philosophy that are still relevant to a modern critique of standard economics. First, he criticised Bentham's very limited understanding of the complexity of human motivation, which translated in his social theories into 'an unusually slender stock of premises', chiefly that people pursue their own personal interests or pleasure, subject only to certain constraints or 'sanctions'.[5] This is still the main motivational assumption in both utilitarianism and economics, and Bentham foreshadowed modern Public Choice Theory by seeing those in government, in particular, as motivated only by calculations of their own self-interest, unless constrained to act otherwise.[6] Mill complained that Bentham failed to recognise the importance in much of human motivation of the pursuit of personal excellence or 'any other ideal end for its own sake', and overlooked the influence of 'the sense of *honour*', 'the love of *beauty*', 'the love of *power*', and 'the love of *action*'.[7] These are all important attributes of the *homo romanticus* proposed in this book as a key player on the economic and political stage, alongside the familiar 'economic man' of the textbooks.

Mill's second concern was over Bentham's narrow view of institutions and laws, and his neglect of their role 'as an instrument of national culture'. Bentham, he argued, took 'next to no account of national character and the causes which form and maintain it'. For Mill, 'A philosophy of laws and institutions, not founded on a philosophy of national character, is an absurdity'.[8] Mill was interested here in far more than national and geo-graphical differences in institutional inheritance. He believed that Bentham and other philosophers ignored the vital contribution to the success of civil society made by national institutions and education systems, and by feelings of allegiance, loyalty and something held 'sacred', together with 'a strong and active principle of cohesion'. By 'attempting to new-model society without the binding forces which hold society together', they were guilty of championing reforms that could only end in failure.[9] This was, of course, in essence the argument employed by Edmund Burke in the 1790s against revolutionary political change of the sort seen in France at the time, and it remains the basis of many critiques of *tabula rasa* or 'shock therapy' reforms of economic and political institutions to this day.

It was in this area that Mill believed Coleridge provided his most vital lesson. Like the German philosopher J. G. Herder (whose theories he introduced to Britain), Coleridge focused on 'culture', 'the causes influencing the formation of national character', and the 'growth of human society'. In particular, he saw 'in the character of the national education existing in any political society, at once the principal cause of its permanence as a society, and the chief source of its progressiveness'. Coleridge's vision of a national education system as 'the *nisus formativus* of the body politic', its 'shaping and informing spirit', was all part of an organic vision of society ignored by Bentham's reductionist methodology. Coleridge believed that the 'cultivation of learning', together with a national constitution, helps maintain an essential balance between preserving traditional knowledge and social values, on the one hand, and providing the prerequisites for social progress, innovation and growth, on the other.[10] Philip Connell, in his book *Romanticism, Economics and the Question of 'Culture'*, shows that Coleridge's antipathy to political economy and the French economists of the eighteenth century was driven primarily by his rejection of the view that 'universal ideas of reason' can 'dictate the organising principles of a given community' on their own[11] – without, that is, due account being taken of national history and the specific social factors integral to the organic development of any society. Appreciation of the role of national institutions and cultures in determining economic outcomes and policy solutions remains among the most important lessons of Romanticism for economics.

The third set of criticisms that Mill made of Bentham related to his method of analysis. For one thing, Bentham's method was reductionist – 'treating wholes by separating them into their parts' – whereas Mill saw value in Coleridge's more organic 'philosophy of society'.[12] Moreover,

Bentham was, Mill argued, too dismissive of 'vague generalities', because he 'did not heed, or rather the nature of his mind prevented it from occurring to him, that these generalities contained the whole unanalysed experience of the human race'.[13] Many of the most telling criticisms of the methods of modern economics take a similar line to Mill here, and focus on both its reductionist methodology (explaining everything in society in terms of the behaviour of individuals) and on the tendency of those in the discipline to ignore (or dismiss as 'noise') anything that cannot be precisely quantified and modelled. These were not, though, Mill's most damning criticisms of Bentham's method. Much more seriously, he argued that Bentham suffered from 'a deficiency of Imagination', which meant that he had no sympathy with, or understanding of, most of 'the strongest feelings of human nature'. It was this lack of imagination which was responsible for his limited under-standing of human motivation.[14] Beatrice Webb would later agree with Mill that 'analytical imagination' is essential to any sociologist wanting to gain a clear conception of human nature.[15] But whereas Webb would come to believe that novelists and poets have much to teach the budding sociologist, Bentham was notoriously hostile to poetry. He argued that 'all poetry is misrepresentation', a perversion of 'precise logical truth'; and he famously stated that, for any given quantity of pleasure produced, 'push-pin is as good as poetry'.[16] This Benthamite hostility to the art of poetry, and the denigration or dismissal of imagination and culture it implied, was to become a *cause célèbre* in the great divide between extreme rationalism and Romanticism. The schism it represented was to haunt Mill to the point of psychological instability.

Mill was not, of course, uniformly hostile to Bentham. Indeed as a utilitarian philosopher himself, by upbringing and profession, he was strongly influenced by him. Mill's most considered assessment of Bentham was that he 'could, with close and accurate logic, hunt half-truths to their consequences and practical applications, on a scale both of greatness and minuteness not previously exemplified'. Moreover, Mill argued that to reject Bentham's 'half of the truth because he overlooked the other half, would be to fall into his error without having his excuse'. After all, Bentham had the virtue of being a 'systematic half-thinker' (unlike Coleridge who produced 'no systematic work', only 'fragments'), and he produced 'frac-tional truths' of great value.[17]

At this point in the essays, Mill developed his central thesis that 'no whole truth is possible but by combining the points of view of all the fractional truths'. It is this, he believed, that makes the juxtaposition of Bentham and Coleridge so important:

In every respect the two men are each other's 'completing counterpart': the strong points of each correspond to the weak points of the other. Whoever could master the premises and combine the methods of both, would possess the entire English philosophy of his age.

Mill looked forward to a time when 'the noisy conflict of half-truths, angrily denying one another, has subsided, and ideas which seemed mutually incompatible, have been found only to require mutual limitations'.[18] Mill, in other words, did far more than articulate the great divide between Bentham and Coleridge as archetypes of complementary half-truths. He also pointed to the need to combine these half-truths in a new synthesis that could overcome the intellectual schism between Enlightenment rationalism and Romanticism. Indeed, while Mill ostensibly discussed 'the two great seminal minds' of their age, as the perfectly complementary pair of half-thinkers, a 'third man' appears in Mill's account – the synthesiser of half-truths. As Leavis puts it, 'as we follow Mill's analysis, exposition and evaluation of this pair of opposites we are at the same time, we realise, forming a close acquaintance with a mind different from either – the mind that appreciates both and sees them as both necessary'.[19] Mill's philosophical mission in life became, in essence, to reconcile these two complementary outlooks. In this way, he foreshadowed many of the specific projects central to *The Romantic Economist*.

The philosophical theory behind Mill's synthesising vision was derived from contemporary German and French philosophy, as he makes explicit in this passage:

For, among the truths long recognised by Continental philosophers, but which very few Englishmen have yet arrived at, one is, the importance, in the present imperfect state of mental and social science, of antagonistic modes of thought: which, it will one day be felt, are as necessary to one another in speculation, as mutually checking powers are in a political constitution.[20]

The most famous Continental exponent of such a view was G. W. F. Hegel, with his 'idealist' dialectical model of intellectual progress – moving from thesis to antithesis, and then to a synthesis of the two that can in turn serve as a new thesis (and so on), in a never-ending development of the human Mind or Spirit. Mill was particularly drawn to a philosophy of history bearing similarities to this – that of the French Saint-Simonian philosophers, especially Auguste Comte. It was from them that Mill derived the notion of 'natural' or 'organic' periods of history, followed by 'transitional' or 'critical' periods that cast doubt on all the old certainties and allow for the development of a new higher 'organic' phase.[21]

It is useful at this point to distinguish two quite distinct aspects of Mill's thought in this regard. The first is a philosophical understanding that most systems of thought are not right or wrong *per se* but rather they embody partial truths or perspectives; from this it follows that synthesising such systems – or using them in parallel with other partial truths – can lead to more complete truth or vision. As Mill put it:

All students of man and society who possess that first requisite for so difficult a study, a due sense of its difficulties, are aware that the besetting danger is not so much of embracing falsehood for truth, as of mistaking part of the truth for the whole. It might be plausibly maintained that in almost every one of the leading controversies, past or present, in social philosophy, both sides were in the right in what they affirmed, though wrong in what they denied; and that if either could have been made to take the other's views in addition to its own, little more would have been needed to make its doctrine correct.[22]

This sort of learning from complementary schools of thought is what Mill had in mind when he argued that Coleridge's 'writings, and those of his school of thinkers, are the richest mine from whence the opposite school can draw the materials for what has yet to be done to perfect their own theory'.[23] A contemporary example may help elucidate Mill's thesis here. Many models in neo-classical economics or Rational and Public Choice Theory (which assume that agents are self-interested utility maximisers) are clearly valuable as part of the truth – as what might be called 'systematic fragments'. The error comes from treating such models – such fragments – as able to represent the whole truth of socio-economic interaction. Instead, we should stand ready to combine such models with other partial truths derived perhaps from sociology or Romanticism – with their emphasis on the role of social norms and imagination. Such a combination of competing social philosophies may help us see calculating rationality as necessarily intertwined with social conditioning and creativity.

It is important to remember, however, that a second aspect of Mill's thought goes well beyond this general a-temporal philosophical presumption in favour of a synthesis of half-truths. Following the Saint-Simonians, Mill adopted a philosophy of history that identified particular historical periods of thought as stages in an ongoing historical dialectic that leads to a progressive improvement in our grasp of the truth. Specifically, Mill saw the eighteenth-century philosophy of the Enlightenment as in a dialectical thesis – antithesis relationship with the Romantic or German philosophy represented in England by Coleridge:

Thus it is in regard to every important partial truth; there are always two conflicting modes of thought, one tending to give to that truth too large, the other to give it too small, a place: and the history of opinion is generally an oscillation between these extremes … Thus every excess in either direction determines a corresponding reaction; improvement consisting only in this, that the oscillation, each time, departs rather less widely from the centre, and an ever-increasing tendency is manifested to settle finally in it. Now the Germano-Coleridgean doctrine is, in our view of the matter, the result of such a reaction. It expresses the revolt of the human mind against the philosophy of the eighteenth century.[24]

In these few lines, Mill did much to cement the standard view that Romanticism represents a revolution in thought against the cold reductionist rationalism of the Enlightenment. There is in Mill's account a tendency to shoehorn eighteenth-century Enlightenment thinkers into one 'spirit of the age', one side of a dialectic or schism in thought, and to see Coleridge's 'reactionary school' as providing the elements missing in their excessively rationalist vision. The eighteenth-century philosophers, according to Mill, underestimated all the institutional, cultural, normative and sentimental prerequisites of an ordered society; and, thankfully, Coleridge and his friends filled these lacunae. In fact, this simplified historical version of the great divide was to pose considerable problems. Much of Romantic thinking may be antithetical to many strands of rationalism, and many Romantic thinkers may have been reacting against specific rationalist doctrines; but this does not mean that there was ever a monolithic eighteenth-century Enlightenment against which the Romantics rebelled at a specific point in time.

2 NERVOUS BREAKDOWN OF AN ECONOMIST

Mill's philosophy of history owed much to his own unusual intellectual development. This is captured in his famous *Autobiography*, published in 1873, in which he described a crisis that we would now call a 'nervous breakdown'. Mill had been educated by his father James Mill on strict Benthamite principles; but, at the age of twenty, he tells us, 'the whole foundation on which [his] life was constructed fell down', and he suddenly awoke from his Benthamite illusions.[25] His crisis included the onset of three related doubts: first, he began to see that rational 'analytical habits' can dissolve feelings and act as 'a perpetual worm at the root both of the passions and of the virtues'. His life to date had been bereft of the 'culture of the feelings' necessary for true virtue, good analysis and the formation of a rounded character. Secondly, he recognised that Bentham's utilitarianism could not provide anything like a full enough account of either happiness itself or how we attain it. And, lastly, he came to realise that the premises his father had used in his utilitarian theory of politics and government 'were really too narrow, and included but a small number of the general truths, on which, in politics, the important consequences depend'.[26]

Mill's *Autobiography* is famous not merely because it articulates the sort of crippling doubts that so many students and others share when presented with a utilitarianism-based version of political economy (such as modern Rational or Public Choice Theory), which purports to explain everything analytically in terms of interests, constraints and incentives. What is so special about the *Autobiography* is that it outlines Mill's lifelong attempt to resolve these doubts in his own philosophy. So, for example, it reveals how he came to understand that the 'practice of analysis' must be balanced by 'the internal culture of the individual' – including specifically a 'cultivation of the feelings' through the imagination. No sooner had the 'medicine' of Wordsworth's poetry provided him with this 'culture of the feelings' than Mill realised that it is a necessary complement to purely rational analysis in the quest to understand and improve our social predicament.[27] Moreover the culture of feelings is also an essential element of the good life itself. Again it was Wordsworth that helped Mill see just how limited is the Benthamite conception of happiness as simple pleasure sensations: from his poems Mill learned that the aesthetic pleasures of the imagination and of 'thought coloured by feeling' can be 'perennial' or higher sources of happiness.[28] In his own version of utilitarianism, Mill was later to develop a complex theory of 'higher' and 'lower' pleasures, in direct contravention of Bentham's dictum that the pleasures of push-pin are equal in moral value to those derived from poetry. More generally, he would maintain, contrary to Bentham, that people attain happiness precisely by not aiming to maximise it, but rather by fixing 'on some object other than their own happiness; on the happiness of others', or 'even on some art' pursued for its own sake.[29]

Mill learned from Wordsworth and other Romantics that 'imaginative emotion' is 'not an illusion but a fact, as real as any of the other qualities of objects'.[30] This is a fundamental point, and one that represents another important lesson of Romanticism for modern economics. For example, the imaginative projection of visions of future happiness onto new goods, services and jobs is itself a source of current (anticipatory) pleasure; and it also drives our desire to possess these goods. This helps explain why advertising (by helping to conjure pleasing associations in our minds between new goods and idealised dreams or imagined feelings) has come to play such a crucial role in stoking consumer demand. It may also account for the fact that, while very few English graduates become economists or sociologists (as Webb would have liked), many do become key players in the advertising industry; for they are trained in the commercially crucial arts of imaginatively cultivating (and projecting) feelings, and creating (and communicating) dreams.

In Mill's *Autobiography*, we see another quintessential Romantic theme emerge – that of personal self-development or self-creation – and this was to become a central feature of his philosophy, foreshadowing Nietzsche. In Mill's account of his own self-development there is, as William Stafford has pointed out, a strongly dialectical flavour: if the thesis was the narrow rationalism of logical analysis and Benthamite utilitarianism, the antithesis was the Romantic influence of Wordsworth, Coleridge and Carlyle; and from this Mill attempts to fashion his own synthesis.[31] As Stafford goes on to articulate:

This journey is also a process of *Bildung*, of self-development both emotional and intellectual. It is the story of how a man, with pain and travail of soul, created his own character. It has a Saint-Simonian pattern, from narrow certainty through doubt to an enriched certainty. It gains added significance by being described as going hand-in-hand with, and helping along, the evolution of European thought and culture. Mill's revolt against Benthamism is not narrated as a mere private affair; it purports to symbolize and give voice to the protest of a whole generation against the aridities of the Enlightenment. If we buy Mill's story, then we accept him as a cultural leader, a bellwether, one who lived and experienced the travails of the European soul as it took the next step forward; a representative man who articulated the issues of the age with peculiar insight and incisiveness.[32]

In the *Autobiography*, Mill consistently argued for a synthesis of half-truths, claiming that he never participated in the reaction against eighteenth-century thought, 'but kept as firm hold of one side of the truth as [he] took of the other'. It becomes clear that, in aiming to learn the positive lessons of Coleridge's eclecticism and Goethe's 'many-sidedness', Mill saw his project as nothing less than reconciling rationalist eighteenth-century thought with the nineteenth-century Romantic reaction to it.[33] The symbolism of an intellectual chasm or great divide is clear in his gratitude to John Sterling (a follower of Coleridge) for 'joining hands with me across the gulf which as yet divided our opinions'; but Mill's account then charts his own mental 'transition', as he sought to weave anew the fabric of his thoughts, until both sides of the divide had modified each other to produce in him a stronger unifying mental tapestry.[34] It is for the nobility of this synthesising objective that I count Mill as the patron saint of today's Romantic Economists.

Mill's project of synthesising half-truths was based on two related philosophical propositions: first, an assumption that half-truths can be added together in a meaningful way to produce something closer to the whole truth; and, second, the supposition that antithetical debate between 'antagonistic modes of thought' (which are complementary to each other) can help us clarify the nature of the eventual synthesis needed to produce the whole truth. To this was added a historical proposition that this thesis–antithesis–synthesis pattern can be seen in the history of ideas, together with a tendency for the oscillations between extremes to get narrower and tend towards synthesis. Mill was, in other words, optimistic that the great divide would (as well as should) be overcome. All three of these propositions deserve further analysis.

While Mill assumes that a full synthesis of half-truths is logically possible, even if he had failed to achieve it, it is on reflection far from clear that half-truths can always be added together to produce whole truths in any such systematic way. For one thing, the behavioural tendencies (such as the pursuit of self-interest) isolated by one theoretical model may turn out to be not even half-applicable in practice when some other tendencies (such as following social norms) isolated by another theoretical model are important. Tendency 'A' plus tendency 'B' may often not produce a combined tendency 'A *plus* B', but rather a compound tendency 'C' different from either; and this compound may be unstable and, with the catalyst of some small additional factor, change into something quite different again and perhaps exhibiting no systematic tendency at all. As a result, the whole truth can often be established (if at all) only by observation in relation to some very particular fragment of social reality where all factors are known. It is often impossible to arrive at systematic and testable holistic explanations in cases of multiple causation. Just as importantly, any one model or theoretical approach represents a unique way of viewing the world – a way of simplifying what is 'out there' and reading order into it. By combining different approaches there is, therefore, a danger that we may lose focus even as we diversify our perspectives. It is for this reason that the Romantic Economist must often be content with using different modes of vision side by side rather than trying to combine them into one. Contrary to Mill, we can often best bridge the chasm between rationalist and Romantic approaches by giving up the hope that a complete systematic synthesis of the two is possible.

Mill's confidence that it is the clarity of antithetical debate that can help deliver a new improved synthesis may also have been too optimistic. As he himself recognised, those on either side of a dialectical debate often parody their opponents, and are unable or unwilling to see the best in each other's arguments: 'Disputants are rarely sufficiently masters of each other's doctrines, to be good judges what is fairly deducible from them.'[35] The psychological implausibility of fair treatment of opposing modes of vision or thought becomes all the greater when the antithetical debate is subject to a rhetoric of extremes – usually involving *reductio ad absurdum* arguments. As C. P. Snow acknowledges, the division of outlooks or approach into a binary dialectic is in intellectual terms 'a dangerous process', because it generally entails an oversimplification of the nature of arguments on both sides.[36] For all these reasons, fiercely contested dialectical argument, especially when combined with the increasing specialisation of intellectual endeavour, may render the emergence of a Mill-like 'third man' dedicated to synthesising extremes less, rather than more, likely.

In the end, the question of whether antithetical debate tends to widen an intellectual schism or allow for synthesis is an empirical question as much as a philosophical one. Does history suggest that the vigorous pursuit of each respective logic makes an eventual superior synthesis more likely because more obviously necessary, as Mill seemed to believe? Or does the cut and thrust of dialectical debate render resolution less likely by progressively corroding faith that there is any intellectual framework or middle ground possible that can convincingly claim to embrace both sides of the divide? To help answer these questions, it is useful to consider whether historical evidence bears out Mill's particular theory of history – that there is a *diminishing* oscillation between dialectical extremes and a tendency to synthesis – or whether it suggests instead that there has in fact been a *widening* schism between rationalist and Romantic approaches. The latter hypothesis is well expressed by Richard Tarnas in his book, *The Passion of the Western Mind*. He argues that the 'medieval dichotomy between reason and faith' had mutated by the nineteenth century into a more general and unbridgeable schism between scientific rationalism and the Romantic outlook:

Because both temperaments were deeply and simultaneously expressive of Western attitudes and yet were largely incompatible, a complex bifurcation of the Western outlook resulted. With the modern psyche so affected by the Romantic sensibility and in some sense identified with it, yet with the truth claims of science so formidable, modern man experienced in effect an intractable division between his mind and his soul.

For Tarnas, the great divide between the Romantic and scientific outlooks produced a 'profound incoherence' in modern thought, with the two cultures 'present in varying proportion in every reflective individual'.[37]

Tarnas, in short, argues (contrary to Mill) that the schism gradually widened, and that the two outlooks could never be fully synthesised because they were ultimately incompatible. In his pessimistic view, our cultures and even our individual outlooks have become hopelessly divided between the external world of science and the internal world of imagination.

Mill's greater optimism about the potential for a substantial narrowing of the cultural divide in his own day rested in part on his oversimplification of both Enlightenment thought and the Romantic reaction to it, and on his exaggeration of the early stages of the dialectic between them. In particular, Mill underestimated the complexity and nuances of eighteenth-century thought. The extreme rationalism and radicalism of Bentham and James Mill were not as typical of earlier Enlightenment thought as he seemed to suppose. The Enlightenment is correctly associated with a growing belief in the power of reason to resolve man's problems; but the widespread emphasis on rational analysis did not lead in all cases to a monochrome and mechanistic vision of human nature and society acting according to universal Newtonian-style laws of nature and the cold logic of self-interested reason. Take, for example, the 'cult of sensibility' associated with the Earl of Shaftesbury, which stressed the role of sentiment, feeling and sympathy. This emphasis on sentiment was a widespread feature of eighteenth-century thought – with especial prominence in the writings of the Scottish philosopher and economist Adam Smith. The importance of a culture of feeling was not a discovery of the Romantic poets, even if it was from them that Mill discovered it.

Two other key figures in the Scottish Enlightenment serve also to work against Mill's simplified picture. As Connell points out, the philosopher Dugald Stewart emphasised the importance of 'the cultivated imagination' for a successful prosecution of political economy in the service of progressive government.[38] More influentially still, David Hume's penetrating rational analysis of the human predicament took an unexpected and disconcerting turn when he produced his famous theory of scepticism. This cast doubt on our ability to know anything beyond the contents of our own minds. Hume argued, for example, that we can never know (by means of observation or rational analysis) that, in the world of objects, A causes B. Instead all we have is a constant conjunction (so far) of sense impressions of B following A, which leads to a corresponding association of ideas of B and A in our minds, and a resulting mental tendency (or habit) of expecting such a conjunction to continue. Hume argued that we erroneously take this habitual mental expectation as experiencing a causal link in the world of objects and knowing it exists. Radically, he also maintained that it is through the operation of the imagination that the mind creates a belief in causal connections, and then projects this belief onto external objects.[39] The detail of Hume's view is not important here. Suffice it to say that Hume – a key Enlightenment figure – was very subversive of the claims of reason and the truth-status of science, and he posited a large and important role for the imagination. In both respects, he prefigured much of the Romantic philosophy that was to follow.

In her book, *Economic Sentiments*, Emma Rothschild demonstrates that another equally famous Enlightenment thinker, the French philosopher the Marquis de Condorcet, should be seen as 'a visionary of the enlightenment and also of the counter-enlightenment'. She shows that Condorcet was deeply opposed to much utilitarian thinking and emphasised the role of sentiments as well as reason; he also stressed the diversity of human nature and values alongside the uniformity and universality of some aspects of both. Rothschild argues that by belonging in this way to both sides of the putative divide in the 1790s between the French Enlightenment and its critics, 'Condorcet's work suggests … that the frontier between the two sides is quite difficult to find'.[40]

These examples are enough to establish that the Enlightenment was not a monolithic rationalist enterprise: instead, it contained significant internal dialogue and debate and, indeed, many specific antecedents of Romantic thought. From this it follows directly that the opening salvos of the 'Romantic reaction' were less revolutionary than Mill and others have supposed. Isaiah Berlin would later argue that the Romantic movement represents 'the greatest single shift in the consciousness of the West that has occurred' – a shift away from the universalist and rationalist dogma of the Enlightenment.[41] But it is neither clear that its early protagonists would have seen it that way, nor that their work constituted something entirely novel.

Much recent scholarship on the works of Wordsworth and Coleridge, for example, has stressed that they were building on themes well aired in the decades before (the role of sentiments, fragments and so on);[42] and that the poets were not – initially at least – entirely antipathetic to scientific rationalism and the world of commerce. Wordsworth was adamant that the poet should work with, not against, the 'Man of Science'; and, in *The Prelude* (his great poetic account of intellectual self-discovery), he revealed his admiration for Isaac Newton as well as his initial enthusiasm for the rationalist political philosophy of William Godwin. It is true that Wordsworth was explicit that he quickly came to distrust the latter's tendency both to 'abstract the hopes of man/Out of his feelings' and to ignore the 'accidents of nature, time, and place'. He also made clear in *The Prelude* his dislike of many aspects of Robert Malthus' political economy doctrines (in particular the latter's tendency to blame Nature, rather than the dislocation from it, for the vice and misery of mankind).[43] Nevertheless, Connell shows convincingly that, in the early years at least, Wordsworth's engagement with political economy was constructive and his attitude to Malthus (and even Godwin) ambivalent.[44] Connell also demonstrates that, however hostile Coleridge may have been to political economy as a discipline, he was not as opposed to commerce and trade as many have later assumed. In his 1817 'Lay Sermon', Coleridge argued that it is not the 'spirit of barter', nor 'the extent or magnitude of the commerce' *per se* that cause problems, but rather the lack of suitable 'correctives of the commercial spirit' in the form of religion and respect for tradition that can act as a 'countercharm to the sorcery of wealth'.[45] This plea for balance in the socio-economic state to prevent the worst excesses of speculation was part of Coleridge's overall passion for synthesis and the reconciliation of opposites. In his psychological theories, for example, Coleridge did not see imagination as in opposition to reason, but instead as the faculty that can heal the division in men's minds and souls.[46]

From these examples we can see that in early Romantic thought there continued to be a dialogue and attempted synthesis between the rival claims of imagination and reason, feeling and calculation, and religion and commerce. Not all Romantics were antipathetic even to the abstract political economy of the Ricardian school. Wordsworth's friend Thomas de Quincey explicitly tried to reconcile admiration for the economics of David Ricardo with a Romantic vision, producing in his writings on political economy a strange blend of mechanical and organic imagery, and trying to inject into Ricardo's system a much-needed focus on the role of consumer desire (and debt) in driving an economy.[47] At the same time, some political economists were alive to at least some Romantic concerns. In particular, the school of 'Christian Political Economy' complemented a scientific approach to economics with an insistence on the important role played by the moral and institutional framework within which an economy operates.[48]

Nevertheless, any student of the early to mid nineteenth century inevitably comes away with a strong sense of this middle ground crumbling or being overshadowed by an increasingly virulent rhetoric of extremes. The dialectical debates now fashionable through the influence of German philosophy on Coleridge, Carlyle and others seem to become ever-more polarised. William Blake had already dubbed art 'the Tree of Life' and science 'the Tree of Death', while the politician and Romantic philosopher Edmund Burke had mourned the passing of the 'age of chivalry' and its replacement by 'that of sophisters, oeconomists, and calculators'.[49] The growing alliance between the Ricardian school of economics and the avowedly anti-poetry Utilitarianism of Bentham, as well as Malthus' support for harsh poor law reform, did not help the temper of the debate between poets and economists. Coleridge saw economists as 'colder-hearted' and 'glib'; and Wordsworth, who firmly rejected the corrosive mind-set of utilitarian calculus – 'of nicely calculated less or more' – was by the 1840s referring to political economists as irremediably 'heartless'.[50] Attacks such as this could not go unanswered. When another Lake poet, Robert Southey, wrote his polemics against the new world of commerce and materialism, Thomas Macaulay ridiculed him as suggesting that England would be better off with 'rosebushes' and pretty cottages than 'steam engines' and health.[51] In another polemical tract, Thomas Love Peacock aped Bentham's attack on poetry and the imagination. This, in turn, prompted the poet Percy Bysshe Shelley (who in other respects had little in common with the cloying, nostalgic conservatism of Southey and some other Romantics) to leap to the defence of poetry and the moral, aesthetic and practical value of the imagination. In his *A Defence of Poetry*, Shelley launched a sustained attack on the limitations of political economy, science and utilitarianism – 'the selfish and calculating principle' – when divorced from 'the creative faculty'. Poets, he argued, should be acknowledged as 'legislators of the world', and the poetic imagination should be seen as 'the root and the blossom of all other systems of thought'; for imagination alone can ensure that we do not succumb to the limitations implied by the 'unmitigated exercise of the calculating faculty' and 'the mechanical arts' that characterise utilitarianism and so much of economic discourse.[52]

In 1831 (just a few years before Mill wrote his 'Bentham' and 'Coleridge' essays), Peacock included a satirical version of this increasingly ill-tempered dialectic in his novel *Crotchet Castle*, which featured a thinly disguised Coleridge arguing with a dry professor of political economy. Connell sums up the significance of the work as follows:

Peacock ultimately appears not so much to have been taking sides as attempting to depict, through the lens of fictional satire, a rapidly widening fault line within British intellectual life. Like Carlyle, albeit rather more even-handedly, he was responding to an important new set of distinctions within political and literary discourse, centred in the first instance upon the confrontational claims of moral imagination and economic science, but broadening into a more fundamental opposition between literature, aesthetics, and feeling, on the one hand; and science, utility, and reason, on the other. During the late 1820s these antitheses became peculiarly intransigent, resulting in an influential rhetoric of ideological and attitudinal disjunction – or 'two cultures', as it has sometimes been described – that would form an enduring element of British intellectual life until well into the twentieth century (and perhaps beyond).[53]

Connell is undoubtedly correct to insist that the origins of this deepening schism were 'equivocal' and 'complex', since the Enlightenment contained many seeds of later Romantic doubt, and early Romanticism still owed much to Enlightenment thinking. Moreover, there is plenty of evidence to support Connell's thesis that even by the 1820s there was no 'simple binary opposition' between the scientific culture (of political economy and utilitarianism) and the culture of feeling and imagination.[54] And yet, despite all this, a bifurcated convergence on two broad but sharply differentiated 'cultures' did undoubtedly take an increasing hold on British, and Continental European, thought. As a result, by the time Mill wrote his essays and *Autobiography* (and even more by the late twentieth century, when Berlin wrote), it appeared in retrospect that the Romantic outlook was indeed the polar opposite of the dry rationalism of both Benthamite Utilitarianism and the scientific temperament, which together formed the main nineteenth-century legacies of the Enlightenment project. What is more, the schism seemed to gain even more intellectual and cultural potency as the twentieth and twenty-first centuries approached. It remained true, of course, that some of the finest minds on either side of the divide continued to subvert such intellectual dichotomies, and tried, like Mill, to bridge the divide; but to do so became increasingly difficult, and Mill's hope that the two sides would come closer together has remained elusive.

There are, I believe, two principal reasons for the continued widening of the dialectical schism between the rationalist and Romantic outlooks. The first relates to the dichotomy between mechanical and organic metaphors, and was highlighted by the Romantic essayist Thomas Carlyle in *Signs of the Times*. Carlyle was alarmed by the pervasive power of the metaphors of mechanism used by rationalist thinkers, particularly metaphors of the 'Machine of Society' and the mind as machine. He complained that 'faith in Mechanism has now struck its roots down into man's most intimate, primary sources of conviction' and, as a result, has come to structure our analysis, our moral and religious beliefs and even our vision. He believed that the widespread use of the metaphor of mechanism (in what he called 'the science of Mechanics'), together with the related utilitarian emphasis on moral calculation, was insidiously altering and constraining our whole way of looking at the world. Carlyle was particularly troubled by the moral and political consequences of this – for example, the tendency always to take the 'Body-politic' more seriously than the 'Soul-politic'.[55] At a more general level, though, Carlyle was pointing to the most important truth about such dominant structuring metaphors – that those who have internalised them cease to have access to the same evidence and the same yardsticks in debate as those using different metaphorical schemas would have. To use Carlyle's own image, unless we break free from the metaphorical chains we have made for ourselves, our outlooks remain forever imprisoned by them and hence divided from the outlooks of those captured by other metaphors.[56] It is this which makes it so significant that the dominant metaphors and assumptions we use to construct our vision of social reality have tended to coalesce into two groupings – one around the metaphors of mechanism (associated with Newtonian physics), the other around organic metaphors (associated with Romanticism). The result has been that our entire outlooks have tended similarly to a binary division.

The organic metaphors emphasised by Romantic writers do, it is true, closely resemble models used currently by some scientists in the study, for example, of evolutionary biology and weather systems. James Lovelock's Gaia hypothesis is a well-known example of this. In this sense the split between the use of mechanical and organic metaphors is not identical with a more general split between a scientific and a literary outlook. The crucial theoretical distinction here is not between science and reason, on the one hand, and literature and imagination, on the other; it is between a narrow mechanical model of scientific explanation and rationality (focusing on formal calculus, precise prediction and the constrained optimisation of given factors and preferences) and a more holistic, dynamic and indeterminate explanatory framework (focusing on organic interdependence and the role of creativity). In practice, however, there are two reasons why the dichotomy between the two sets of dominant metaphors – mechanical and organic – has undoubtedly contributed to a broader 'two cultures' schism between science and art: first, because both sides have so often failed to appreciate the relevance of organic models to a fruitful scientific understanding of the mind and of the social and economic world; and, secondly, because most scientists, in particular, have not appreciated how far their vision is structured and constrained by the primarily mechanical metaphors and models they use. As a result, they are frequently unaware that they may actually see different aspects of the world from those seen by artistic people who use different structuring languages, assumptions and metaphors.

The second general factor that has reinforced the great divide between scientific rationalism and the Romantic outlook is the increasing and inevitable specialisation of practical, analytical and intellectual endeavour. Gone are the days when poets could dabble in scientific experiments. Gone, too, are the days when scientists aspiring to be at the cutting edge of their disciplines could spare much time to read literature or philosophy. It is largely for this reason that, more than a century and a half after Mill wrote his essays, his vision of a synthesis between Romanticism and rationalism is in many important respects further away than ever from fruition. Indeed, C. P. Snow, in his famous book *The Two Cultures*, published in 1959, claimed that there are now in a more general sense two cultures – the literary and the scientific – divided by an 'ocean' or a 'gulf of mutual incomprehension', with 'no place where the cultures meet'. Snow was clear that specialisation in the education system is to blame for this schism. He was certain, too, that the polarisation between the two cultures is a 'sheer loss to us all'. It deprives scientists of 'imaginative understanding', while making literary culture 'tone-deaf' to the potential of science. Worst of all, the lack of contact between the two groups deprives society of the creative sparks that fly from the interaction of opposite poles:

The clashing point of two subjects, two disciplines, two cultures – of two galaxies, so far as that goes – ought to produce creative chances. In the history of mental activity that has been where some of the breakthroughs came. The chances are there now. But they are there, as it were, in a vacuum, because those in the two cultures can't talk to each other.[57]

Sadly, Snow's plea for renewed efforts to bridge the chasm between the world of imagination and literary culture, on the one hand, and the world of science and commerce, on the other, has so far had relatively little effect. Nowhere is this more evident than in the discipline of economics, where many of the vital insights of Romantic thinkers have, as a result, gone unheeded. The disdain many literary people feel for economists and vice versa has led to insufficient intellectual cross-fertilisation. In particular, there remains little focus on the role of imagination and creativity in economics and economic activity.

The growing schism between the two cultures over the last 180 years or so may help explain the curious puzzle which John Hope Mason poses at the beginning of his book, *The Value of Creativity*. Mason maintains that creativity emerged as a value in the nineteenth century and became seen, in Matthew Arnold's words, as 'the true function of man'; and this seems easily explicable given the wonders of scientific, technological and economic progress from around 1700 onwards, and the consequent modern need continuously to innovate and adapt, in order to avoid falling victim to the process of change. This leads Mason, however, to the following conundrum:

If it was the case that it was mainly these factors which enabled human beings to regard themselves as not being dependent on a Creator, but as being themselves 'creative', why did the value which subsequently appeared have nothing to do with technology or economics? Why was it applied instead to the non-material realm of aesthetic activity, with the paradigm of the 'creative' individual being not an inventor or an entrepreneur but a poet or artist?

Mason's own answer to this puzzle is fascinating. He argues that creativity was seen in two radically different ways by Romantic and other writers: either – for example, in Mary Shelley's *Frankenstein* – as potentially 'amoral, dangerous and disruptive'; or – for example, in Coleridge – with neo-Platonic overtones, as a means to transcend all that is base and ugly in the material world with a spiritual and aesthetic vision of harmony.[58] In essence, therefore, creativity was either considered disruptive and unpredictable – a far cry from the harmonious economic equilibrium posited by political economy and a dubious value for entrepreneurs to trumpet; or it was treated as an aesthetic means of escape from the mundane world of economics to the higher verities – in which case it was in scientific and business terms irrelevant, however valuable in other ways.

The 'two cultures' hypothesis can, I believe, complement the solutions offered by Mason to his own puzzle – especially in relation to several other factors he highlights as partly responsible for the failure of artists to see and appreciate as valuable the role of creativity in the world of economics and science. For many writers of Romantic persuasion, industrialism and economic growth had disfigured their landscape, cut the traditional bond between man and nature and caused untold squalor, poverty and ugliness in the slums and cities. This made them recoil from industrial innovation and entrepreneurial activity on aesthetic and moral grounds. At the same time, in part because the apparent philistinism of Benthamite utilitarianism (with its narrow understanding of human motivation and values) read across to the discipline of political economy (with its strong reliance on utilitarian premises), these same writers distrusted economists and their discipline too. Increasingly, therefore, literary and aesthetic culture (which championed the imagination and creativity) was defined in opposition to industrial activities and the materialist concerns of economics. Moreover, a certain cultural snobbery played its part. For example, as Mason notes, the late-Romantic philosopher Friedrich Nietzsche may have done much to establish a secular and individualistic conception of creativity, and indeed to encourage us to relish rather than shun its disruptive and heroic qualities; but he also exhibited in his writings 'contempt for financial, commercial or industrial activities'. As a result, he completely failed to see that his vision of the creative Superman is in practice much more often realised in the cut and

thrust of the business world than in the grand heroics of Byronic outcasts –
a point cogently made more recently by Francis Fukuyama.[59] Furthermore,
this cultural and aesthetic schism has not only prevented artists and poets
from seeing or appreciating the role of creativity and imagination in economics and economic activity; it has also, all too often, prevented economists and
entrepreneurs from wanting even to be associated with such soft, unstable and
avowedly anti-scientific attributes. The more the criticism aimed at them by
literary types becomes shrill (and often unreasonable), the more economists
and businessmen stress the virtues of dispassionate and calculating reason.
They are proud to operate in a world of logical analysis, probability forecasts
and carefully calibrated plans. The idea of analytical imagination or the
entrepreneur as artist is anathema.

There have, of course, been some economists open to at least some
Romantic concerns and metaphors. I will argue in chapter 3, however, that
very few of them have sought to introduce into economics a full appreciation of the implications for economic activity of creativity or imagination, let alone incommensurable values. Only rarely has an economist
reached right across the schism between rationalism and Romanticism to
introduce as central ideas that are at variance with the dominant faith
in rational calculation. For all the differences of emphasis and approach
between different schools of economics, the centre of gravity in the
discipline has remained so firmly in the rationalist camp that the very
idea of a Romantic Economist seems, to many, like a contradiction in
terms. This is what makes it so important to continue Mill's triangulation
project of trying to find a 'third way' between the opposing cultural poles,
or at least to open up channels of conversation between them. It is
accordingly the Romantic Economist's mission to help economists bridge
the divide, and so learn from (rather than ignore) the most challenging
elements of the Romantic critique of narrow rationalism. For there are
many practical ways in which economics can benefit from acknowledging
the role of analytical imagination and metaphor in their discipline, and of
imagination, incommensurable values and sentiment in economic activity
and motivation.

4   MILL AND A BRIDGE TOO SHORT

In an interesting article on the political economy of the period, Donald
Winch argues that Mill was 'the one person to attempt a bridge-building
exercise based on his knowledge of both sides' of the schism between
Romanticism and the rationalist project, but that he ultimately failed in

this endeavour. He concludes: 'Mill's diagnosis of what divided the two camps did not … result in any bridge being built that was capable of bearing traffic across the divide.'[60] It is useful to consider briefly both the validity of this verdict and what we can learn in relation to economics from Mill's efforts to reach across the cultural divide.

Despite his rebellion against the philosophy of Bentham and his father, Mill remained a utilitarian – believing still that the greatest happiness of the greatest number is the ultimate moral good. He made two highly significant amendments, however, to the Benthamite version of this doctrine. First, he argued that people do not gain happiness by aiming directly at it; instead they find happiness by pursuing some other goal for its own sake. This is part of what John Gray calls Mill's 'indirect utilitarianism'; it allowed him to argue that it is consistent with the utilitarian principle to derive from it certain other moral principles or rules (for example, his principle of liberty) that may on occasions prevent the direct pursuit of happiness but would on the whole improve the average level of happiness.[61] This indirect utilitarianism also helped Mill find room for his second key amendment to utilitarianism – his concept of 'higher' versus 'lower' pleasures. This distinction was crucial to his attempt to reconcile utilitarianism with a more Romantic appreciation of the value of both artistic endeavour for its own sake and individual self-creation. His argument was that in civilised countries, individuals increasingly derive happiness not from carnal or physical pleasure sensations (that is, 'lower pleasures') but from 'higher pleasures', including the aesthetic pleasures of the imagination, and those derived from the autonomous pursuit of their own private dreams and the development of their own inner potential. This is what made the principle of liberty so important in Mill's vision: it is liberty that allows each individual to find her own preferred way of life, and act it out without undue hindrance from others.[62]

Many still applaud Mill's attempt to deepen our conception of pleasure and happiness, not least by allowing for the importance of autonomous self-creation and the imaginative pleasures of art and poetry. Mill's amendments undoubtedly presented philosophical problems, however, which are generally thought to have rendered his utilitarianism ultimately confused. Quite apart from the empirical question of whether Mill was right that higher pleasures are always preferred by agents, given an informed choice, there is the problem of the commensurability of higher and lower pleasures. Mill saw higher pleasures as superior in some *qualitative* way (and not merely in relation to theoretically calculable and *quantitative* attributes, such as duration and intensity of feeling). In doing so, he sacrificed what many see as the main advantage of utilitarianism, namely that it purports to provide a single scale of value as the basis of moral calculus, and therefore to provide clear answers to moral dilemmas by allowing respective amounts of happiness to be measured. Without such a single scale of value, how are we supposed to weigh higher pleasures against each other, or against lower pleasures, if we must choose between them? Moreover, if higher pleasures really involve, as Mill seemed to suggest, everyone pursuing their own chosen goals, is this not really a form of value pluralism that suggests there may be no common touchstone of value at all? If so, Mill's attempt to build in a more Romantic conception of the value of art, self-creation and different incompatible ways of life appears to have left his utilitarianism unworkable.[63] I will return to the implications for economics of this problem of the incommensurability of values in chapter 7. Suffice it to say here that Mill did not solve the problems his theory raised; nor did he realise its relevance to economics.

Mill may be more famous today as a moral and political philosopher, but in his own day he was equally famous as an economist. Indeed, his *Principles of Political Economy* (1848) served as the main textbook of the discipline for at least three decades. Mill's attempted settlement in relation to economics between the rival claims of Romanticism and Benthamite rationalism is therefore of particular interest. In many of his writings, Mill was happy to emphasise that Bentham's picture of human motivation is woefully inadequate and needs to be complemented by such Romantic attributes as the love of honour, power and beauty. He was also drawn to the idea of a broader social philosophy – one that takes into account the development of societies and the important role played by national character and the institutions that support it. It can come as something of a disappointment, then, to read Mill's conception of political economy, which seems largely to abstract from these issues. Indeed, the economics historian Eric Roll thought that Mill 'never allowed romantic illusion to invade the citadel of industrial capitalism – its economic theory'.[64] It is certainly true that Mill did more than anyone else in the history of the discipline to establish *homo economicus* or 'economic man' as the standard model of the motivation of economic agents.

In his famous 'Essay on the Definition of Political Economy', Mill argued that economics is concerned with the conduct of man 'solely as a being who desires to possess wealth, and who is capable of judging of the comparative efficacy of means for obtaining that end'. He went on to describe the nature of economics as follows:

It predicts only such of the phenomena of the social state as take place in consequence of the pursuit of wealth. It makes entire abstraction of every other human passion or motive; except those which may be regarded as perpetually antagonising principles to the desire of wealth, namely, aversion to labour, and desire of the present enjoyment of costly indulgences.[65]

The irony then is that Mill – who was otherwise so critical of Bentham's limited model of human motivation – helped ensure that economics would henceforth use precisely this model and consider the economic agent solely as a maximiser of his own wealth or utility. Mill did add the caveat to the above definition that no 'political economist was ever so absurd as to suppose that mankind are really thus constituted'; but he argued that the simplifying assumption was still necessary 'because this is the mode in which science must necessarily proceed'.[66] This remains the position of most thoughtful economists to this day.

Despite this purely Benthamite aspect of Mill's economics, and his retention of many key aspects of abstract Ricardian economics, it is nevertheless important not to underestimate the extent to which Mill qualified his understanding of the status and nature of economics in line with the Romantic critique. Indeed, the influence of this critique is clear in a number of important areas. First, Mill never deviated from the position that his Benthamite model of 'economic man' could be useful only as a first approximation when dealing with the 'business part' of social affairs.[67] He would have been quite opposed to the modern use of this model in Rational or Public Choice Theory to explain the dynamics of government, political pressure groups and democratic voting systems. Such an extension of the economic method to the study of politics would have been anathema to Mill because he always saw economics as just one branch of a broader 'Social Philosophy', in most branches of which more complex motivational and other causal factors would have to be taken into account. It was in this broader social philosophy, he believed, that most of the lessons of Romanticism were relevant. For example, he always intended to work out (as the basis of his social philosophy) a new science of 'ethology' (which would explain the development of human nature in all its diversity) and 'political ethology' (which would deal with the formation of national character). This new science would have echoed the key Romantic insistence on the importance of national factors in limiting the validity of universal models and prescriptions in the area of social affairs.[68]

Mill also fully appreciated that the conclusions of the economic science he describes are true only 'in the abstract' – that is, are 'true without qualification, only in a case which is purely imaginary'.[69] As a consequence, Mill was not guilty of what Schumpeter later called the 'Ricardian vice' (namely, applying universal abstract models directly to real policy issues to generate policy advice on the basis of these models alone). In his *Autobiography*, Mill claimed that his *Principles of Political Economy* always treated economics as a 'fragment of a greater whole; a branch of Social Philosophy, so interlinked with all the other branches, that its conclusions, even in its own peculiar province, are only true conditionally, subject to interference and counteraction from causes not directly within its scope: while to the character of a practical guide it has no pretension, apart from other classes of considerations'. Mill was explicit that pure abstract economics can produce only fragmentary and provisional half-truths, and should never be used to give practical advice 'with no lights but its own'.[70] When applied to policy issues, there is, according to Mill, a need to combine economics with other social sciences and take account of other relevant factors or 'disturbing causes' outside the remit of economics. It is also necessary to have local knowledge about the specific context. Universal laws are not enough on their own, as Mill made clear in his 'Essay':

No one who attempts to lay down propositions for the guidance of mankind, however perfect his scientific acquirements, can dispense with a practical knowledge of the actual modes in which the affairs of the world are carried on, and an extensive personal experience of the actual ideas, feelings, and intellectual and moral tendencies of his own country and of his own age.[71]

One respect in which Mill's 'Essay' strongly anticipates the Romantic Economist is his understanding of the extent to which our vision and analysis of evidence may be clouded by the models we use. Mill believed that 'long and accurate observation' is necessary to ensure that social scientists do not fall foul of a biased 'preconception' about which causal factors matter in a particular case; and he was under no illusion about the dangers of selective vision. Particularly dangerous, as he noted, is the tendency for social scientists to fall in love with their own theories, and to take the 'coherence' and neatness of their models as 'evidence of their truth'. As Mill concluded with typical succinctness: 'In these complex matters, men see with their preconceived opinions, not with their eyes: an interested or passionate man's statistics are of little worth.'[72]

Despite these significant and sometimes overlooked concessions to the Romantic critique (especially in relation to *applied* economics), I think it is fair to conclude that Mill failed to absorb fully some of the most important lessons Romanticism can have for economics. In particular, he wrongly believed that national characteristics and institutions need play no part in the theoretical study of economic 'laws of production';[73] and he assumed that motivation other than the pursuit of self-interest could safely be ignored by economics as a pure science. There is no evidence that he appreciated in any way the role that imagination plays in economic motivation and expectations; and, if he did understand the role of sentiments such as loyalty and trust, he would have seen them only as 'disturbing causes' whose impact should be studied outside the remit of economics and then added back into the equation. Indeed, Mill's most important failure in a theoretical sense may have been precisely that he overestimated how often it is possible to study tendencies or causal factors separately in this way, and then meaningfully and systematically add their effects together to produce a composite explanation.

Mill believed that the assumptions made by economists (constituting the 'general laws' of economic behaviour) can be used to predict at least a significant part of the truth in the real world; and he believed that the effects of other relevant causal factors ('disturbing causes') could be predicted on the basis of laws from other relevant social sciences, and then 'added to, or subtracted from,' these economic partial truths to produce the whole truth.[74] In short, he saw the different causal factors operating in societies (and captured by different social sciences) as like the different forces in a Newtonian force field that, when combined, behave in an entirely predictable and systematic manner. John Ruskin realised the error of this in *Unto this Last* – his late-Romantic diatribe against Mill's political economy. Ruskin noted that in human social affairs, disturbing causes 'operate, not mathematically, but chemically'; that is, they alter the essence of what is going on.[75] To use a practical example close to Ruskin's concerns, the actions of an otherwise self-interested agent who has trust in his colleagues, is loyal to his company, or is dedicated to the pursuit of excellence in his work, cannot be predicted in any systematic manner by combining pure theoretical 'laws' of behaviour. It is not possible to derive a precise prediction of behaviour by simply adding together the effects of the general 'economic' tendency to self-interested behaviour (including opportunism and doing as little as possible to achieve one's goal) and the effects of the more Romantic social tendencies (or 'disturbing causes') of trust, loyalty and the pursuit of excellence (which imply the suspension of self-interest). The particular cultural compounds of (or trade-offs between) such conflicting motivational factors are forged by tradition, norms and leadership. They will vary from place to place, and they can be revealed only by observation.

Ruskin's disgust at Mill's failure to understand this, or appreciate the central importance of wider motivational factors (such as loyalty and the pursuit of excellence) in commerce and economic behaviour, led him to deride Mill's economics as an abstract 'science deficient only in applicability'.[76] Mill ultimately failed to convince his Romantic critics that he had done enough to bridge the great divide and produce an economic science that truly reflects the practical and theoretical importance of *homo romanticus*.

CHAPTER 3

Debates within political economy

The fashion for a simplified dialectical representation of the history of ideas and contemporary culture has waned somewhat since the 1950s when F. R. Leavis, C. P. Snow and others followed the lead of J. S. Mill and nineteenth-century German philosophy. Nevertheless, there is plenty of evidence to suggest that in many important respects the modern outlook is still riven by a cultural and intellectual schism between Romanticism and most scientific versions of rationalism. There remains an important dissonance between visions structured according to organic metaphors and those structured by mechanical metaphors; there remains an unresolved tension between models of human motivation that stress the role of sentiment and self-creation and those that reduce it to the constrained but rational optimisation of preferences; and there remains a disjunction between the claims of art and imagination, on the one hand, and formal scientific methods and calculating reason, on the other. It is a key premiss of this book that this great cultural and intellectual divide has impoverished the science of economics by depriving it of full access to the most important lessons of Romanticism, despite the bridge-building efforts of Mill and others. Nevertheless, as this chapter should make clear, it would be quite wrong to underestimate either the range of debate within the emerging discipline of economics over the last two hundred and fifty years or the extent to which it has already taken on board at least some aspects of the Romantic critique of rationalism. Economics is not now, and never has been, a monolithic discipline built solely on metaphors from social physics and utilitarian assumptions, nor has it been entirely focused on formal axiomatic methods and mathematical models. Indeed many of the key figures in the discipline have raised important problems with these standard approaches and have suggested solutions that, often unconsciously, reflect certain central Romantic concerns and assumptions. The Romantic Economist can take heart from the fact that great economists past and present have seen the relevance to the discipline of some quintessentially Romantic approaches.

In his interesting book on the history of economics, *Reconstructing Political Economy*, William Tabb paints the picture of a 'great divide in economic thought' between what he labels 'A mode' and 'B mode' economists; while the former use 'deterministic mathematical models and test their theories by making predictions', and assume universal laws of rational behaviour and a tendency to market equilibrium, the latter take a more historical approach focusing on the importance of institutions and the various particular paths of socio-economic evolution. Tabb even goes so far as to co-opt C. P. Snow's 'two cultures' image to discuss this fracture within the discipline.[1] By using Snow's motif in this way, however, Tabb is overstating both the scale of the very real disagreements within economics and the difficulty of overcoming them. While different approaches to economics did emerge in the decades following Adam Smith's death, the divide between them is in most cases a pale version of the much more comprehensive schism which developed between Romanticism and literature (on the one hand) and rationalism and science (on the other). Very few even of Tabb's 'B mode' economists have sought systematically to apply to economics the main lessons that can be drawn from Romanticism; and few have even inadvertently hit upon the most important of these lessons – namely the crucial role of imagination and structuring metaphor in economics, the role of imagination in economic expectations and strategy formation, and the importance of incommensurable values. There is a structural reason, too, why the gulf between different approaches within the discipline could never get too wide: the increasing trend towards academic specialisation and discipline proliferation has tended to ensure that those whose critiques challenge too fiercely the methodological centre of gravity of the discipline have over time found themselves spun off – at least in the minds of most subsequent economists – into other disciplines such as economic history, sociology, or moral philosophy, where they have ceased to have much influence on economists.

At the same time, the emerging discipline has done much to synthesise, reconcile or, at least, use side by side the contrasting approaches that have remained within the discipline. As Tabb's account makes clear, most of the key figures in the history of economics – Robert Malthus, John Stuart Mill, Alfred Marshall and John Maynard Keynes, to name but a few – have espoused an eclectic mix of both the standard 'social physics' (or abstract 'A mode') approaches and the more historically aware and holistic ('B mode') approaches.[2] Moreover, the ever-increasing number of 'schools' within the discipline in recent years has ensured a considerable pluralism of substantive focus that is fertile ground for new methodological experimentation. The agenda of the Romantic Economist is to build on this pluralism, by ensuring more openness to alternative methodological approaches and models drawn from completely outside the normal framework of scientific culture, and hence greater flexibility in how we characterise economic problems and choose the methods appropriate to solving them.

There is no intention in this chapter to give a comprehensive account of the history of economics or to outline all the main debates within the discipline. The more limited aim is to give a snapshot of some key disagreements over the last two hundred and fifty years, together with a brief assessment of where the centre of gravity in the discipline is now, in order to gauge how far Romanticism can help elucidate the debates and resolve problems seen as central by many economists.

I SMITH AND THE EMERGENCE OF A DISCIPLINE

Adam Smith may be the most famous economist of all time, but he was by today's standards a polymath. As professor of moral philosophy at Glasgow, he published in 1759 *The Theory of Moral Sentiments*, which emphasised the role of sympathy in creating a cohesive society. This was a very influential work in his lifetime, and remains respected by moral philosophers to this day. Smith's enduring fame as an economist, however, rests on his other great work, *The Wealth of Nations* (published in 1776), which played a major part in the emergence of the discipline of economics in the decades that followed. The richness of Smith's vision within *The Wealth of Nations* and his wider writings means that different aspects of his thought have continued to inspire those on both sides of many of the debates that have raged within the discipline over the last two centuries. Tabb, indeed, sees Smith as the 'father' of both his 'A mode' and 'B mode' wings of economics. This, of course, is not always seen as a strength by economists with tidy minds, so that – as Tabb also notes – 'Smith seems from the vantage point of modern economics to be schizophrenic'.[3]

This apparent 'problem' of the two Smiths rests in part on the undoubted switch of emphasis between his two most famous books.[4] *The Theory of Moral Sentiments* stresses, for example, not only the central importance of sympathy and individual conscience but also the crucial role that imagination plays in each: sympathy involves imagining ourselves in someone else's shoes – what Samuel Fleischacker calls 'imaginative projection'; and conscience involves imagining how an impartial spectator would judge our actions if apprised of all the facts. In Smith's vision, imagination is at the core of the socialised sentiments and moral judgements that help lead to a cohesive society.[5] By contrast, the most famous passage in *The Wealth of Nations* stresses the importance of self-interest (rather than benevolence, sympathy and conscience) in driving economic interdependence and co-operative transactions:

It is not from the benevolence of the butcher, the brewer, or the baker, that we expect our dinner, but from their regard to their own interest. We address ourselves, not to their humanity but to their self-love, and never talk to them of our own necessities but of their advantages. Nobody but a beggar chuses to depend chiefly upon the benevolence of his fellow-citizens.

Given the division of labour, it is, according to Smith, in everyone's self-interest to exploit the opportunity for mutually advantageous exchange in a competitive market.[6]

As D. D. Raphael and Fleischacker both note, Smith himself would have seen no contradiction between his emphasis on sympathy-based moral judgements in *The Theory of Moral Sentiments* and on the rational pursuit of self-interest in *The Wealth of Nations*. Smith's interest as a moral philosopher was in how self-interest can lead to co-operative interdependence in the parts of social life where the bonds of sympathy (or, indeed, general benevolence) cannot reach. In the anonymity of market exchange it would be as unwise as it is unnecessary to rely on sympathetic moral judgement and benevolence; the claims of both are too weak in relation to our trading partners to have much effect; and, in any case, in conditions of free market exchange, the public interest is promoted precisely by each person pursuing his own interest. In making this argument in *The Wealth of Nations*, Smith was in no way denying the moral and motivational importance of sympathy outside the market; nor was he denying the need for the market to be firmly embedded in a framework of legal justice. Explicitly moral judgements and motives were not, in Smith's vision, necessary for morally acceptable outcomes in areas of economic exchange; but that did not mean that moral sentiments and sympathy-based judgements have no role to play in social life more broadly.[7]

Emma Rothschild, in her book *Economic Sentiments*, further resolves the perceived problem of the two Smiths by showing that he belonged to an 'earlier and more open political economy', in which it was natural to mix economic analysis with moral and political philosophy, and it was still recognised that 'the life of cold and rational calculation' is 'intertwined with the life of sentiment and imagination'. In particular, Rothschild demonstrates that Smith's economic agents are driven not only by self-love but also by a wide array of sentiments – by dreams, fears and various carefully enumerated 'economic dispositions'.[8]

Modern economists tend to build a Smith in their own image by quoting very selectively from the relatively infrequent but hugely influential passages in *The Wealth of Nations* where, for example, each agent is said to direct 'industry in such a manner as its produce may be of the greatest value'; or where every individual, although intending 'only his own gain', is 'led by an invisible hand to promote an end which was no part of his intention' and 'to render the annual revenue of the society as great as he can'; or where, by maximising his own investment opportunities, every individual, though studying only 'his own advantage', necessarily prefers 'that employment which is most advantageous to the society'.[9] Here is a glimpse of the rational optimising agent that is the bedrock of the modern economic method; and here, too, seems to be a premonition of the great insight of modern General Equilibrium Theory, namely that a competitive free market can in theory reach an optimal equilibrium outcome which represents the exploitation of all the potential benefits from market exchange by all the participants in the market, so that no further mutually advantageous exchanges are possible.[10]

Such a modern reading, however, goes well beyond the general tenor, and against some of the specific detail, of Smith's own account. Smith made only two explicit references to the invisible hand in relation to economics, and Rothschild judges even these to be 'a mildly ironic joke'. Rothschild also points out that, despite his interest in astronomy, Smith made almost no mention of the mechanical metaphor of equilibrium that would later come to structure so much of economic thinking. Indeed Smith's concern was less to demonstrate the power of the 'invisible hand' of the market than to show that the 'visible hand' of government (to use Rothschild's phrase) is almost always damaging to wealth, order and liberty.[11] Smith's advocacy of both free trade and freedom from government regulatory interference was based (just as Friedrich Hayek's would later be) not on exaggerated claims for the optimality of the market, but rather on a keen understanding of just how little those in government know: 'no human wisdom or knowledge could ever be sufficient', he wrote, to enable government to direct private industry 'towards the employments most suitable to the interests of the society'.[12] Moreover, the behaviour of Smith's economic agents has none of the mechanical and law-like predictability of Mill's *homo economicus*, who will always optimise his trading potential in any given situation. The entrepreneurs in Smith's text are flesh and blood people: they suffer from 'uneasiness', or are driven by 'disgust' or desire for respect; they are motivated by 'folly' and animated by 'chimerical views' – unrealistic dreams of fabulous wealth from gold and diamond mines; even the desire to exchange goods is driven by a 'propensity' that is not necessarily the product of reason.[13]

Writing more than a quarter of a century before the Romantic poets started to fret about the discipline of political economy, Smith did not feel the need to choose in his analysis of economic motivations between the logic of self-interest and the role of sentiments; nor did he abstract (as Wordsworth was later to complain Godwin did) 'the hopes of man/Out of his feelings'.[14] In this sense, at least, Smith is himself a precursor to the Romantic Economist of this book. This is even more the case if we transpose to the realm of economic motivation (to a far greater extent than Smith himself did) his insights, in *The Theory of Moral Sentiments*, on the moral and social role of sympathetic imaginative projection. There are many economic situations in which it is necessary to empathise with customers and their needs, or to imagine how competitors will react by projecting ourselves into their shoes. As Rothschild puts it: 'To think about economic decisions is to think about how other people think'; it is in short 'to feel sympathy'.[15]

There are other important respects, too, in which Smith embraced what would – after the later 'two cultures' schism – be seen as a more Romantic approach to science in general and economics in particular. In his 'History of Astronomy', Smith argued that scientific systems are 'inventions of the imagination, to connect together the otherwise disjointed and discordant phenomena of nature'; such systems are 'imaginary machines' which bring order to the chaos of empirical data and arrange them according to a pleasing structure.[16] Smith here anticipated a quintessentially Romantic belief that we cannot simply derive scientific laws by induction from unmediated empirical observation; rather, we invent metaphors, stories, models and even whole languages that structure our vision and make provisional sense of it. As Fleischacker demonstrates, Smith's stress on the role of imagination in system-building is of a piece with his analytical method in *The Wealth of Nations* and with his understanding of the limits of knowledge. Fleischacker notes that Smith relied for the most part on one rhetorical masterpiece – his famous description of the pin factory – to drive home his point about the benefits of the division of labour; and he argues that, in this way, 'Smith draws on our imaginations, which he considers essential both to good science and to good moral philosophy, rather than giving us a substantial body of evidence or deriving his conclusion from general laws or principles'. Moreover, Smith was sceptical of 'tedious or doubtful calculation' of economic or statistical data, and had 'no great faith in political arithmetick'. Like Hayek two centuries later, he did not believe that we could ever have sufficient knowledge of economic life (in all its complexity and particularity) to enable us to come to definite overall conclusions.

Smith relied instead on a combination of an eye for the telling example, empathetic observations of everyday life and imaginative system-building, to make sense – as best he could – of the causes of economic phenomena.[17] Elements of *The Wealth of Nations* may have inspired much of later standard economic theory and analysis, with its mathematical and predictive models, its deductions from *a priori* and radically simplifying assumptions about human motivation, and its use of statistics, but Smith did not engage in such practices himself.

Less than half a century after *The Wealth of Nations*, a very different type of economics was in the ascendancy. One of the most influential figures in the new economics was Jean-Baptiste Say, who stressed the strict separation of 'political economy' from the study of politics. In his hands, political economy was already beginning its transformation into what is now called 'economics' – a subject carefully abstracted from the art of politics and moral philosophy. Moreover, Say saw this economics as governed by laws – including that subsequently named after him, which states that the supply of goods in an economy creates its own demand. This law entails that, at least in a properly functioning competitive market, there can be no 'general gluts' – no shortage of demand and hence no general underutilisation of goods, capital and labour. A competitive market, in other words, will always return quickly to equilibrium so long as it is left to its own devices.[18]

David Ricardo took a broadly similar approach, and his economics came to typify the emphasis on simplifying abstractions, *a priori* assumptions and deductive rigour ('A mode' economics, in Tabb's terminology) that was from then on to dominate much of the discipline. The methodology he employed is succinctly summarised by Roger Backhouse: 'Ricardo simplified the world he was analysing to the point where he was able to show with strict logic that his conclusions followed.' In particular, Ricardo analysed the economy in terms of the interaction of three general classes or sectors (capitalists, labour and landowners). To explain and predict their interaction, he then built a systematic model that rested on some crucial simplifying assumptions and 'laws' of economic behaviour. The most important of these were the law of diminishing returns and the specific associated assumption of diminishing returns in relation to the agricultural cultivation of land. The analytical model fashioned by Ricardo predicted that economic growth would be choked off by an inevitable rise in the price of food (and hence in landowner 'rents'), as growth in population led to reliance on poorer and poorer land to meet incremental demand.[19]

The detail of Ricardo's theories is not important here, but two key points are worth emphasising about the nature and use of them. First, Ricardo sought to draw key policy conclusions direct from his abstract model, in particular on the need for free trade in corn. Joseph Schumpeter in his *History of Economic Analysis* later called this direct application of the logical output of abstract models to 'the solution of practical problems' the 'Ricardian Vice'; and he was very critical of Ricardo's habit of relying on the near-tautologous deductive results of a theoretical model whose simplifying assumptions 'really settled everything' in advance.[20] The merits or otherwise of this criticism of Ricardo's approach remain one of the key methodological battlegrounds in economics to this day, with no clear consensus on the answers to the questions raised. How far should economics be based on abstract and purely theoretical models? And, whatever the analytical merits of these models in pure theory terms, how useful are such models when applied to practical economic problems? Are economists best able to address practical issues, such as the impact of free trade on the capacity for economic growth, by abstracting from real-life complexity and background 'noise', and by focusing instead on the central long-term relationships and tendencies? Or, are economists who abstract from the complexity of our predicament liable to mislead us and deliver simplistic policy pronouncements, precisely because their models are based on simplistic assumptions?

The second related point to note about Ricardo's theories is that one of his key assumptions – namely that the law of diminishing returns could be applied to the agricultural use of land – proved to be false in the long run. Ricardo essentially assumed a *given* level of technical expertise. In practice, of course, agricultural productivity has been raised by one technological revolution after another, so that scarcity of land and rising food prices have not, for the most part, been serious constraints on economic growth. This example points to a number of interesting questions about the status of so-called 'universal economic laws'. The law of diminishing returns remains to this day a cornerstone of the mathematics of all equilibrium-based models in economics. But, how do we know when such a law does, or does not, apply in real life? Is it to be seen as merely an *a priori* hypothesis that makes the mathematics work but which may or may not be true in practice? Or, is it a useful generalisation of real-life trends and a useful approximation to reality, at least in some types of circumstance?

In his own day, Ricardo's abstract method was challenged by his lifelong friend Robert Malthus – perhaps the most influential economist of his generation. Malthus, like Ricardo, believed that economics is governed by certain laws, including that of diminishing returns. Indeed, it was his belief that 'misery and vice' are the product of 'necessary and inevitable laws of nature' that earned him the opprobrium of the nature-loving Wordsworth. Malthus is best known for his *Essay on the Principle of Population* (first edition in 1798), which painted the notoriously dismal picture of an inevitable tendency for population growth to outstrip growth in the food supply; the resulting chronic scarcity, misery and vice then naturally kept the population at a subsistence-level equilibrium. Self-consciously aiming to produce a Newtonian-style science, Malthus championed in this way the concepts of scarcity and equilibrium that were to become so central to the mechanical metaphors and models of modern economics.[21]

At the same time, however, there are other facets of Malthus' theories that set him apart from the more abstract modelling tendency in economics typified by Ricardo. Perhaps the most important of these is his much deeper appreciation of the role of institutions, moral codes and institutional incentives. As A. M. C. Waterman shows in his book, *Revolution, Economics and Religion*, Malthus believed that institutions mitigate the natural tendency to misery and vice: by harnessing self-interest, they alleviate poverty and allow civilisation to prosper in a lower-population and higher-food-supply-*per capita* equilibrium than would otherwise occur. In particular, Malthus argued that property rights encourage individuals to save (by allowing them to enjoy the benefits of doing so securely), while the institution of marriage (by assigning the costs of children to parents) gives them every incentive to limit the number of children. In this way, Malthus thought, the institutions of property and marriage ensure that self-interested individuals have a strong incentive to exercise 'moral restraint' (by postponing marriage) and thereby give themselves the chance to improve their financial wealth before having children; such a surplus would then allow society as a whole to rise above the brutish subsistence-level anarchy of nature. Moreover, Malthus was not only interested in institutions that provide positive incentives; he also stressed the danger that the institution of poor relief would provide negative incentives, encourage welfare dependency and, by removing the harsh penalties to any failure to exercise moral restraint, lead to wealth-sapping increases in population. The Poor Laws of his day served only 'to create the poor which they maintain', and Malthus duly argued that they should be replaced by much harsher provision that would be seen as a very unattractive last resort.[22]

There is another respect in which Malthus differed more starkly still from the Ricardian tradition, and that was his interest in reconciling both the laws of economics and his policy conclusions with theology. Malthus sought in particular to establish a theological justification for the harsh laws of nature by showing that they served the will of God by encouraging, and showing the advantages of, moral restraint. Because the law of population, in particular, produced 'a state of moral discipline and pro-bation' that accorded with 'the letter and spirit of revelation', Malthus claimed that 'the ways of God to man with regard to this great law are completely vindicated'.[23] Waterman argues that Malthus was in this way a key figure in the emergence of a clearly discernible school of economics, in the first decades of the nineteenth century, which he dubs 'Christian Political Economy'. This school included many of the key figures of the discipline of economics in English universities in the 1820s and 1830s (such as Edward Coppleston, Richard Whately and Thomas Chalmers), and represented an important counter-weight to Ricardian economics. Not only did these economists stress much more explicitly the central need for moral and educational institutions to provide the necessary social and cultural framework for an economy; they also sought to reconcile the new science of political economy with orthodox theological teaching. Moreover, they argued that both science and theology were necessary for policy formulation. It is true that, despite their plea for theology and economics to work together, these same economists did, as Waterman emphasises, anticipate one aspect of the later sharp division between economics and ethics: for, while insisting that they were both necessary, they argued just as forcefully in favour of a division of labour between the scientific study of *means* to given ends and the theological study of which *ends* are appropriate. In this respect, the leading figures in 'Christian Political Economy' foreshadowed the insistence by modern economists on carefully distinguishing fact and value.[24] Nevertheless, their overall position is much closer to that of the Romantic Economist of this book who, like them, insists that the study of ethics and the study of economics (while not being confused) should go hand in hand: the findings of each must continuously inform (and be carefully reconciled with) the findings of the other, if intellectual endeavour in either field is to be relevant to the way we should live our lives in practice.[25]

   There is a third set of methodological differences between Ricardo and Malthus, which are clearly delineated in a fascinating series of letters they wrote to each other. John Maynard Keynes was later to call these letters 'the most important literary correspondence in the whole development of Political Economy'. According to Keynes, Malthus emerges as an 'inductive and intuitive investigator' interested in 'the real world', whereas Ricardo is revealed as an 'abstract and *a priori* theorist' who investigated the theory of distribution 'in conditions of equilibrium'. Keynes drew special attention to one particular exchange. In his letter of 24 January 1817, Ricardo wrote to Malthus:

It appears to me that one great cause of our difference in opinion … is that you have always in your mind the immediate and temporary effects of particular changes, whereas I put the immediate and temporary effects quite aside, and fix my whole attention on the permanent state of things which will result from them.

Malthus replied two days later, as follows:

I certainly am disposed to refer frequently to things as they are, as the only way of making one's writings practically useful to society, and I think also the only way of being secure from falling into the errors of the taylors of Laputa, and by a slight mistake at the outset arrive at conclusions the most distant from the truth. Besides I really think that the progress of society consists of irregular movements, and that to omit the consideration of causes which for eight or ten years will have a great *stimulus* to production and population, or a great *check* to them, is to omit the causes of the wealth and poverty of nations – the grand object of all enquiries in Political Economy. A writer may, to be sure, make any hypothesis he pleases; but if he supposes what is not at all true practically, he precludes himself from drawing any practical inferences from his hypotheses.[26]

In this exchange we can see features of many of the most crucial debates that were to reverberate through the discipline of economics over the subsequent two centuries. These include, first, the relative merits of abstract models based on *a priori* hypotheses versus contextual and historical study of 'things as they are'; and, secondly, the relative importance of studying long-terms tendencies (to equilibrium) and studying shocks or 'irregular movements' which can have a powerful impact over the short-to-medium term. Keynes sided with Malthus particularly on the second of these – noting elsewhere that short- and medium-term deviation from equilibrium can often be much more important to us than any eventual long-term reversion to equilibrium, because 'in the long run we are all dead'. Keynes also praised Malthus for his doubts about Say's law (that supply creates its own demand), and for taking issue in the same letter with Ricardo's view that 'the wants and tastes of mankind are always ready for the supply'.[27] More than a century before Keynes, Malthus recognised the crucial problem of inspiring adequate demand in an economy. In all these respects, Malthus was keenly aware of problems that the Romantic Economist can agree are central to understanding an economy.

2 RECURRING DISAGREEMENTS

As the discipline of economics has evolved in the two hundred years following Ricardo and Malthus' correspondence, a number of methodological and theoretical debates, and practical problems, have become recurrent features. This section outlines those most central to our story.

Much of modern economics is based around the essentially mechanical notion of *equilibrium*. In economics, an equilibrium is reached when none of the parties to exchange can gain anything by trading further, or by adopting different strategies, within the constraints of a *given* set of endowments, preferences, technologies and available strategies. The market is said to be in equilibrium when it is, in this sense, in balance. For this to occur, it is generally assumed that there must be a unique set of prices which 'clears' the market; this equilibrium point is reached when the ratio of prices at which the goods are exchanged is equal to the ratio of the respective marginal utilities which the agents concerned expect to derive from each good. In this important sense, equilibrium models in economics are based on utilitarian foundations: it is assumed both that agents can rank the utility or pleasure they derive from different goods (and hence rank their preferences) and that they will optimise their trading possibilities so as to maximise their utility (or preference satisfaction) within the constraints of a given set of initial conditions. The reason that economists are so fascinated by the possibilities offered by these foundations is that, if agents can always be relied upon rationally to optimise within a framework of given preferences, endowments, technologies, etc., there is some hope that economists may be able to predict the outcome of changes to any specific elements in this framework of given factors. The essentially utilitarian principle that agents will always maximise their utility or preference satisfaction (within a given set of constraints) entails that, if we can specify fully their preference-sets and the various constraints they face, we can predict in an essentially deterministic manner the outcome of their interaction.

The concept of equilibrium, and the related assumption that agents optimise their trading possibilities within a given set of constraints, permeates most of the models and theories used in modern economics, albeit in various different ways. At one extreme is General Equilibrium Theory, derived initially from the insights of Léon Walras in the 1870s. Walras posited that, if all markets are perfectly competitive, there exists a set of prices that will clear all markets simultaneously. He argued that, by solving a set of simultaneous equations representing the whole economy, economists could in principle reproduce mathematically the equilibrium solution that would be reached through a natural process of trial and error by all the interrelated competitive markets within it. Kenneth Arrow and Gérard Debreu succeeded in the 1950s in showing (with a more sophisticated mathematical model) that in conditions of perfect competition, as defined by a set of wholly unrealistic conditions (including no future uncertainty and no monopolies), the economy as a whole would indeed reach such a general equilibrium – an outcome that would furthermore be optimal, or 'Pareto-efficient', in the sense that nobody could become better off without someone else being worse off.[28] Despite the fact that an efficient general equilibrium in perfectly competitive markets can never actually materialise given the unrealistic nature of the conditions for it – so that in a sense it is purely a figment of theorists' imaginations – its realisation in mathematically ingenious theoretical models has nevertheless had a huge influence on the construction of countless applied forecasting models.

Economists, of course, are fully aware of the unreality of the efficient *general* equilibrium of pure theory, and of the practical difficulties of modelling all the interdependent elements of an economy. Most, therefore, follow Marshall's advice to use '*partial*' equilibrium models that look at just one subset of the economy at a time. To help with this, Marshall developed his famous concept of the 'scissors' of supply and demand – with one curve plotting producers' *supply* of a good, and another plotting consumers' *demand* for the same good, and with quantity (*x*-axis) in each case varying in relation to price (*y*-axis). He showed that the two curves intersect like the blades of a pair of scissors at the point where supply and demand are in balance.[29]

Since the time of Walras and Marshall, the sophistication of equilibrium models has risen dramatically. For example, it is now recognised that the equilibrium reached is often suboptimal as a result of either information problems or 'market failures'; the latter include missing markets for the spillover effects of market behaviour, like pollution. It remains the case, however, that in all equilibrium models the assumption is made that individual agents will optimise their trading possibilities and satisfy their preferences as best they can, so that – as long as enough is known about the *given* factors (including the degree of market failure) – apparently precise predictions about economic outcomes can be made. In this sense, the models remain mechanistic and deterministic; they assume that markets are always tending to equilibrium – the point where *all* participants have optimised their trading possibilities.

Although he did much to establish the standard microeconomic tools of partial equilibrium analysis, Marshall himself realised that the fundamental problem with all such equilibrium models is that they fail to take account of the full impact of time. Time has a habit of making a mockery of seeing any factors as 'given', and therefore limits the usefulness of focusing on the market's efficiency in allocating given goods. Time ensures that we live in a dynamic flux. It was for this reason that Marshall believed that 'the Mecca of the economist lies in economic biology'. In the Preface to his *Principles of*

Economics, Marshall argued that 'mechanical analogies' have a large place in economics' textbooks only because they are easier to handle mathematically and conceptually than biological or organic analogies. He thought that the term 'equilibrium' 'suggests something of statical analogy', and that the 'fragmentary statical hypotheses' used in equilibrium analysis should be seen as no more than 'temporary auxiliaries to dynamical – or rather biological – conceptions'. He insisted that 'the central idea of economics … must be that of living force and movement'.[30] Marshall's preferred method in his textbook for dealing with time and change was to introduce into his models different time periods in which different equilibria hold because different factors or constraints apply. So, for example, as Backhouse explains, whereas in the 'market period' the equilibrium price reflects demand and the supply of goods *currently* available, in the subsequent 'short-run' period the level of production can be allowed to vary; in the 'long run', account can be taken of changes in the level of capital investment by companies; and in the 'very long period' certain secular changes in given factors can affect the predicted equilibrium.[31] At each stage, as Marshall himself put it, 'more forces are released from the hypothetical slumber that had been imposed on them' in order to allow changes in conditions to be factored in.[32]

Marshall's ingenious approach, however, does not go far enough for some critics of standard equilibrium theory. George Shackle, for example, in his devastating critique of the 'celestial mechanics' analogy in economics, has argued that equilibrium models represent in reality just 'lightning-flashes in which the scene is stilled to immobility by the brevity of the glimpse'.[33] Marshall's time-period analysis may at least give us a series of strobe-like flashes which reveal a succession of moments in a dynamic process of change; but there is still, as Marshall himself recognised, an unreality about the assumption that the economy can ever reach any sort of equilibrium, and – by corollary – a similar unreality about the assumption that in a dynamic world agents can ever actually optimise their trading possibilities. Equilibrium models do undoubtedly capture something of the awesome self-organising capacity of markets and, in particular, their tendency to allocate factors more efficiently than other forms of exchange. Some economists at the fringes of the discipline have, however, consistently doubted whether such models really capture the essence of a process of change in which mutually reinforcing parameters are in constant flux, driven by choice, creativity and chance.

Five figures particularly stand out in the history of economics over the last century for the challenge they have mounted to the dominant use of the mechanical equilibrium metaphor in economics and the related assumption of optimising agents. All five of them can be seen as the too-often ignored prophets of the more Romantic approach to economics championed in this book, with its focus on organic metaphors that can better explain an economy driven by imaginative and creative agents. The first is the US economist Thorstein B. Veblen (1857–1929), who was sharply critical of the 'teleological' nature of neoclassical theories which seek to explain economic behaviour by assuming that rational optimising agents (acting within given constraints) collectively reach a unique equilibrium point that can be predicted. He argued that economists should be interested in the 'genesis' or 'process' of economic life, and should attempt to understand the underlying 'causes' of change, rather than merely predict the impact of particular changes in 'given' premises on the behaviour of optimising agents. Veblen highlighted the 'habituation' and conditioning of behaviour by institutions, and sought to explain and chart the evolution of this 'institutional fabric'.[34]

The second prophet was the Austrian economist Joseph Schumpeter (1883–1950), who saw the economy as a 'process of change' or as an 'evolutionary process', in which the question of whether or not firms tend to maximise production 'in a perfectly equilibrated stationary condition of the economic process is … almost, though not quite, irrelevant'. He focused instead on the 'Creative Destruction' caused by continuous entrepreneurial innovation – with new goods, new methods and new markets driving out the old – a process which ensures that the given, or 'invariant', conditions of standard economics count for little.[35] Another Austrian, Friedrich Hayek (1899–1992), saw the economy as a spontaneous order (or 'catallaxy' as he called it) which, he was careful to insist, is never in equilibrium. An ardent free-marketeer, he believed that a fully functioning price mechanism provides agents with more information than could otherwise be available in so necessarily decentralised a system as an economy; but Hayek also stressed the pervasiveness of uncertainty, and argued that the competitive market is a 'discovery procedure' – constantly bringing to light new methods, new goods and new needs.[36]

Brian Arthur, and others centred around the Santa Fe Institute in New Mexico in the late 1980s and 1990s, have taken such thinking a stage further, noting the huge importance in economies of increasing returns and threshold effects that render suspect standard equilibrium models based on assumptions of decreasing returns. As Mitchell Waldrop's book *Complexity* explains, Arthur and his colleagues have started to look for new ways to explain and simulate economies and markets as complex systems that display 'spontaneous self-organisation' 'at the edge of order and chaos' and never settle down in a predictable equilibrium. Arthur's aim, in his own words, is to 'portray the economy not as simple but as complex, not as deterministic, predictable and mechanistic but as process-dependent, organic and always evolving'.[37]

The radical insights of Veblen, Schumpeter, Hayek and Arthur, which place uncertainty, creativity and the social formation of preferences at the heart of economics, have important implications for our understanding of the behaviour of economic agents. They imply, in particular, the need for a new model of how economic actors form the expectations and strategies on which their choices depend. The basis of such a new model was provided by our fifth prophet, George Shackle, who argued in the 1970s that time, novelty and freedom of choice entail strict limits on our ability either to know the future or to calculate rationally the optimal course of action. He concluded that economic expectations are not primarily the product of reason but of imagination, and that our decisions must be based on how we imagine the future.[38] Here, finally – in a philosophy of economics tract rarely taught in economics faculties – we can see described the outlines of the creative and imaginative economic agent (*homo romanticus*, as I will call him) that accords much more closely with common-sense notions of the true nature of economic behaviour than does the rational utility maximising agent assumed by most economists.

It was John Maynard Keynes who had paved the way for Shackle's theory, when he noted in *The General Theory* 'the extreme precariousness of the basis of knowledge on which our estimates of prospective yield have to be made'. Keynes had concluded from this that most investment is the product of 'spontaneous optimism' and 'animal spirits' (including the 'spontaneous urge to action') rather than carefully worked-out mathematical predictions of return.[39] However, few of Keynes' disciples realised – and indeed he may not have fully acknowledged it himself – how completely corrosive of mechanistic equilibrium-based analysis such views are. If economic choices are often motivated by sentiments (as Smith thought), convention and habits (as Veblen said), animal spirits (as Keynes supposed), or imagination (as Shackle argued), then there is no reason to posit (in the long or short run) any deterministic tendency to equilibrium on the part of markets. The essentially utilitarian assumptions that individuals seek to maximise their preference satisfaction (with the help of their rational expect-ations of the future), and that there is always one optimal answer out there (within a given set of constraints) to which markets will therefore gravitate, may be plain wrong for much of the time. Maximisation may be neither a psychologically plausible, nor even an objectively rational, strategy for agents to adopt, if the space of possibilities in our dynamic and creative socio-economic world is simply too large for any optimisation calculations or 'rational expectations' to be possible.

Back in the last thirty years of the nineteenth century, there was another famous argument about economic methodology, which still has echoes in today's debates. The main protagonists of the '*Methodenstreit*' were the Austrian Carl Menger and the German Gustav Schmoller. While Menger prefigured Hayek's distrust of equilibrium analysis, he strongly defended the role of idealised pure theory based on universal laws of economic behaviour. He also championed diminishing marginal utility as the basis of value, as well as the standard economic method of explaining social outcomes in terms of individual behaviour (so-called 'methodological individualism').[40] Schmoller, by contrast, argued that there are no universal economic laws, that human motivation is complex and variable and that history and local factors or institutions determine economic motivations and outcomes. As a result, Schmoller (and the 'Historical School' to which he belonged) argued that the appropriate method for explaining economies is empirical and inductive (rather than formally deductive) and, above all, that economics should be both historical and interdisciplinary. As Eric Roll puts it, 'the historical school stressed the unity of social life, the interconnection of individual social processes and the organic, as against the mechanistic, view of society'; Schmoller and his colleagues believed social and economic life to be 'something more than the sum of economic activities of individuals', and they were scathing about the ability of any individual social science on its own 'to understand the entire organism of social life'.[41]

With a few notable exceptions, economics has over the last hundred years largely ignored the explanatory potential of the organic metaphor championed by the Historical School; it has consequently also largely ignored the implications of the organic metaphor both for models of motivation (namely that preferences and behaviour are socially rather than individually formed) and for methodology (the need for historical and interdisciplinary study of the unique development path of each economy). Indeed, in many important respects, Schmoller and his colleagues lost their battle for the soul of economics. As Backhouse points out, by polarising the debate, their quarrel with Menger served only to hasten the divorce of economics and economic history into separate disciplines.[42]

In other respects, however, the methodological debate was always at cross-purposes – a point well made by John Neville Keynes (father of John Maynard). He showed that, in many senses, the two different approaches and methods were trying to do two different things. To help understand why this is so, the elder Keynes went well beyond what would later become the standard distinction in modern economics between a 'positive' science of 'what is' and the normative study of 'what ought to be'. He saw the positive science of economics as a pure, abstract 'science of tendencies only, not of matters of fact' – its laws 'only true hypothetically, that is, in the absence of counteracting agencies'; in this, he followed closely the views of Mill. Crucially, however, the elder Keynes then distinguished this pure, abstract and deductive science (dealing with 'economic uniformities') from what he called 'the art of political economy' which deals with 'practical questions' of *applied* economics. This 'art' cannot simply apply abstract theory; it must also carefully consider ethical aspects and take account of history. The findings of pure abstract theory are 'conditional'; they must not be used to make practical recommendations (or explain particular outturns) without careful consideration of the particularities of the problem, non-economic factors, history and relevant ethical judgements. Having made this distinction between pure theory and applied economics, John Neville Keynes concluded: 'It is because differences of this kind are often overlooked that divergences of view on questions of method become exaggerated.'[43]

Keynes is surely correct here that different methods are needed for pure theoretical analysis than for practical policy advice or historical explanation, and that much of the fury of the *Methodenstreit* came from forgetting this. It is, of course, much harder to argue convincingly that history does not matter, or that we should abstract from national differences and social or ethical considerations, when doing applied economics than when creating theoretical castles in the rarefied air of pure mathematics. Nevertheless, as David Colander argues in *The Lost Art of Economics*, much of contemporary methodological debate and practice continues to blur this distinction between pure theory and the 'art' of applied economics, with the result that there is a continuing tendency to confuse the methodological approaches relevant for each. This blurring has come about largely because – as the elder Keynes well understood – most formal models are in practice not deductive systems based purely on simplified assumptions and 'a few elementary laws of human nature'; instead they mix these simplified assumptions with some additional realistic ad hoc assumptions relevant to specific circumstances, and this makes it fatally easier to forget the still essentially provisional status of the models' conclusions.[44]

There are other reasons, too, why debate has continued to rage about the status and nature of economic theories and their supposedly 'universal laws'. Say viewed political economy as a science built on certain general facts, and as being 'established on unshakable foundations, from the moment when the principles which serve as its basis are rigorous deductions from unquestionable general facts'.[45] Lionel Robbins in the 1930s essentially agreed:

The propositions of economic theory, like all scientific theory, are obviously deductions from a series of postulates. And the chief of these postulates are all assumptions involving in some way simple and indisputable facts of experience relating to the way in which the scarcity of goods which is the subject-matter of our science actually shows itself in the world of reality.[46]

But what are these indisputable facts? Almost all economic theorists agree that they include the ability of economic agents to rank their preferences, the conformity of these same agents to certain postulates of rationality (including the making of consistent choices) and, finally, a tendency on their part to optimise the satisfaction of their revealed preferences within given constraints. There are, though, plenty of reasons to doubt the universal applicability of the utilitarian assumptions underlying both this supposedly self-evident model of motivation and the assumption that consistency of preferences is the hallmark of rationality. Contrary to the utilitarian belief that all values are commensurable in terms of a single scale of value, there are some areas where economic agents have to choose between incommensurable values, with the result that there is no one right answer as to how any individual should rank them – and therefore little reason to expect or privilege consistency of preference ranking. As I shall explore in more detail later in the book, the Romantic critique of utilitarianism reminds us (in this and many other ways) that the foundations of pure economic theory are not indisputable. Some economists, of course, acknowledge this. Marshall, for example, held that pure theory in economics is not a body of universal truths that apply everywhere, other things being equal. Rather, he thought of pure theory as 'an engine for the discovery of concrete truth' or – to use John Sutton's phrase – as a 'diagnostic tool' for teasing out systematic tendencies in the world where they exist;[47] and this is, roughly speaking, my view also of the true role of pure theory. Even this view, however, begs a number of questions – in particular, about the impact of such models on economists' vision. Like metaphors, formal models structure and bias our perception, understanding and analysis; they are not neutral cognitive spectacles.

Many of the internal disagreements within economics have raged over where to draw the boundaries of the discipline, in terms of either the methods used or the subjects studied. Nowhere is this more the case than in the debates over the relationship between economics and ethics. For the most part, modern economists follow the lead of Lionel Robbins, who argued in favour of a strict separation of fact and value. He argued that economics is a positive science studying the 'relationship between ends and scarce means which have alternative uses' and that 'it is incapable of deciding as between the desirability of different ends'. Economics, he insisted, 'is fundamentally distinct from Ethics' – the study of which goals or ends we *should* pursue. Robbins did see economics as providing 'the solvent of knowledge' to ethical choices, by helping us test, for example, for the practical consistency of different goals and informing us about the practical implications of pursuing them. But the ultimate choice between goals or values themselves is, he believed, the province of ethics and not economics.[48]

Robbins' clarity on this issue was exemplary, but in practice several problems tend to remain – two of them flowing from overzealous separation of economics and ethics. First, as Amartya Sen has argued clearly, even when you see economics as simply a methodology for 'engineering' feasible or efficient solutions to problems of achieving given goals with scarce resources, you need to be very careful not to ignore the importance of 'ethical considerations' in explaining the motivation of economic agents and the pattern of economic behaviour.[49] Economic actors are not always simply rational self-interested utility maximisers. They are sometimes, for example, loyal to their colleagues or even act altruistically; and it is, accordingly, necessary to understand more clearly the role that ethics plays in the motivation of economic agents. Secondly, Robbins was undoubtedly correct in identifying that economic analysis can inform us about the implications of pursuing the goals we hold dear (in conjunction with others) and that this rational analysis can, in turn, change our underlying ethical value judgements. Value judgements are best made when fully informed by rational analysis of the implications of these judgements. This means that it is essential for the study of ethics and economics to work side by side, with the frame of reference of each set to reflect the findings and interests of the other. In practice, however, this rarely happens: economists generally assume that the relevant goals are already 'given' and worry no more about them, while moral philosophers see themselves as above mundane questions of efficiency. The Christian Political Economists of the 1820s were a notable exception to this tendency, and the Romantic Economist should be so, too.

One whole field of economics – *welfare economics* – does self-consciously address normative questions of what policy *ought* to be, but it does so using an anaemic variant of utilitarian ethical assumptions. A change is considered uncontroversial if it makes some people better off without making anyone worse off (a so-called 'Pareto improvement'); but, since this is rarely a useful guide in practice (because nearly all reforms or policies make at least a few people worse off), *cost-benefit analysis* then retreats to arguing that a change is beneficial if it brings *net* benefits (because this would in theory allow all losers to be compensated and still leave some net winners).[50] In making these sorts of quasi-value judgements, welfare economists tend to elide the difference in moral terms between actual and potential compensation, and they may also be guilty of ignoring broader moral questions about the correct distribution of goods and income. Even more crucially, by assuming that all important values can be made commensurable in monetary terms, they are making the utilitarian assumption that all values are commensurable according to a single scale of value. In these ways, welfare economists often fail to acknowledge the need in economic policy decisions to make explicit and contested value weighting decisions between such incommensurable values as equity and efficiency, alongside positive analysis of the impacts on efficiency of pursing various goals. They remain embarrassed by the idea of giving any serious role to ethics.

Whenever economists have faced up fully to the need to consider the importance of norms, institutions, culture, history, or the impact of technological creativity, they have tended, since the *Methodenstreit*, to exhibit two kinds of reaction. The first is to acknowledge the demarcation of subject area or method between disciplines – economics, sociology, history and ethics – but then to argue, as Max Weber and Joseph Schumpeter did, for a constant dialogue between the disciplines. Such a dialogue, while avoiding a full synthesis and hence confusion of methods, can bring the benefits of each approach to bear on problems that *de facto* cross narrowly defined discipline boundaries. Weber and Schumpeter both argued that economics, when defined more broadly, should include this dialogue between different methods – between pure economic theory, sociology, economic history and so on.[51] This approach is close to the one promoted by the Romantic Economist; but it has some obvious problems dealing both with mutual distrust and misunderstanding between those trained in different narrow disciplines and with the practical difficulty for any single analyst of mastering several methodologies at once. Economists (and many political scientists) have therefore generally preferred a quite different approach, often called 'economic imperialism'.[52] Economic imperialists openly embrace the need to make a unified study of economic interaction, institutional frameworks and the political elements of choice, but insist that these interlocking facets of socio-economic reality can best be understood by applying one single method to them all – the economic or 'rational choice' approach, with its constrained optimisation models of behaviour, and its associated emphasis on equilibrium.

In the remainder of this chapter, I consider briefly the strange triumph of this single methodological approach, as well as the implications and limitations of its increasingly grandiose and 'imperialist' ambitions to explain everything in the socio-economic sphere.

3 THE TRIUMPH OF SOCIAL PHYSICS AND RATIONAL CHOICE

Any non-economist introduced to economics textbooks, or to articles written by economists for academic journals, is immediately struck by the pervasiveness of both the utilitarian assumption of optimising agents and the mechanical metaphors borrowed from physics. However fierce the methodological debates within economics have been at various points in its history, the centre of gravity in the discipline remains far from the more Romantic outlook championed in this book. Despite the efforts of the Historical School, Arthur and others, organic metaphors are still not generally used to describe the dynamic process of change that characterises most economies and markets; and, despite Shackle's intervention, there is little focus on the use of imagination to form the working hypotheses or create the new strategies that agents must – when they are constructing an unpredetermined future – substitute for (classically defined) 'rational expectations' and 'given' optimising strategies. Instead, as Philip Mirowski has argued in his book *More Heat than Light*, modern economics remains largely structured as 'social physics' around metaphors derived from a now-outdated version of energy physics.[53]

These physics-based metaphors first took a deep hold in the last decades of the nineteenth century, above all through the work of Walras – the inventor of modern General Equilibrium Theory. Mirowski details how Walras, with his training in the physical sciences, systematically applied mathematical techniques derived from contemporary physics to economics; and he quotes Walras asserting that 'the pure theory of economics is a science which resembles the physico-mathematical sciences in every respect'.[54] Vilfredo Pareto, who championed the notion of the 'efficient' equilibrium, followed suit and likened 'the equations which determine equilibrium' in economics to 'the equations of rational mechanics'.[55] Mirowski's exhaustive study of the influence of the physics analogy also discusses a key intervention by the famous US economist Irving Fisher. Writing in the 1920s, Fisher felt able to tabulate the correspondences he saw between economics and mechanics: for example, individual agents in economics correspond to the inanimate particles studied by mechanics; and both economics and mechanics are built around the assumption of a maximising tendency to equilibrium, with marginal utility playing the role of 'vector' in economics that force plays in a mechanical system.[56] Moreover, as Backhouse shows, Fisher made 'persistent use of mechanical analogies' of all sorts in his theories: for example, he modelled the quantity and velocity of money with the aid of the metaphor of scales balanced on a fulcrum, with the different factors represented as either weights or lengths away from the fulcrum; and he modelled bullion flows according to the analogy of a complicated system of cisterns, with the different relevant flows depicted as finding their level.[57] The explicit influence on economics of the metaphors, methods and techniques of physics did not stop there. According to Backhouse, the great mid-twentieth-century economist Paul Samuelson was also heavily influenced by his background in 'mathematical physics', while the pioneering econometrician Jan Tinbergen made heavy use of his physics training in the 1930s to build a model that attempted to predict the behaviour of the whole Dutch economy.[58]

It is still the case to this day that the mechanical metaphors and mathematical techniques imported from nineteenth-century physics have a strong hold over the discipline of economics. The metaphor of 'equilibrium' reigns supreme, sustained by its vital symbiosis with the utilitarian-derived assumption that agents always optimise among consistently ranked preferences within given constraints. It is this assumption which has rendered human agents as apparently predictable as inanimate particles in the deterministic force fields of physics. Together these metaphors and assumptions (and associated techniques) have become the 'family language' of economists, and have increasingly structured and constrained their vision and analysis. Economics, like many other disciplines, has become essentially defined by its methodological approach and hence by the metaphors embedded in this approach. Furthermore, as the techniques used have become more refined and difficult to master, there has been a growing pressure on academics to specialise in one discipline or subdiscipline. This academic specialisation has, in turn, reduced the incentive within economics to listen to methodological outliers: seemingly extreme critiques of the standard economic method have been branded, in William Coleman's terminology, as 'anti-economics', and their exponents safely disposed of as mad, malevolent, corrosive of scientific reason or, at the very least, misguided and ignorant pontificators from other disciplines.[59] Even the clearly more plausible figures arguing for an interdisciplinary or multidisciplinary approach, like Weber and Schumpeter, have generally been ignored by the economics profession, on the grounds that they naively overlook the dangers of being a 'Jack of all trades and a master of none'.

It is important to note, however, that the increasingly homogeneous methodological base of economics has coincided with a new openness about applying this method adventurously to a much wider circle of problems. As David Colander has correctly pointed out, in terms of substantive focus and the sophistication and flexibility of the dominant methodological approach, modern economics often bears little resemblance to the neoclassical economics of Walras, Pareto and Debreu.[60] So, for example, George Akerlof and Joseph Stiglitz, far from assuming perfect information, have built sophisticated models to understand the impact on behaviour of imperfect information caused by asymmetry in the amount of information available to buyers and sellers.[61] Many economists have also endeavoured to build into their models Schumpeter's creative destruction and the manifest importance of increasing returns to certain kinds of investment (such as education) – for example, in 'Endogenous Growth Theory'.[62] Economists are often even willing now to admit that history matters, and to allow for 'multiple equilibria' or 'hysteresis' – where the particular path an economy takes in the short run determines which of many possible long-run equilibria it eventually settles into.[63] In these ways, mainstream economists are beginning to take some steps towards a more Romantic approach to understanding a dynamic economy.

Many of these commendably sophisticated theories, however, effectively add in such factors as technological creativity and the impact of history as merely 'bolt-on' amendments to standard theory, without making any corresponding changes to the old neoclassical 'microfoundations' that still pervade the models they employ. As a result, while such modern economics does indeed build in some lessons of Romanticism as surface amendments to standard theory, it does so without acknowledging what I argue are the devastating consequences of these same lessons for the underlying assumptions and microfoundations on which the amended theory still depends. So, Endogenous Growth Theory may build in creative destruction in a stylised manner, but it still models its effect on the 'steady-state growth rate'; and it still assumes that economic agents are driven by rational probability-calculating expectations and the tendency to maximise expected consumption and profits.[64] Likewise, New Keynesianism may allow for hysteresis to reflect that history matters to the long-run equilibrium level of employment (for example, by destroying skills); but again it does not relax the assumption that agents maximise income and optimise their utility on the basis of rational expectations within these path-dependent constraints.[65] Moreover, while modern economics builds information problems into its models, it still generally assumes 'bounded rationality'. It is very rare, in short, to find in economists' models Keynes' animal spirits or Shackle's imaginative expectations; and yet it is precisely these that necessarily drive much of our behaviour and strategy formation when faced in real life by creative destruction and uncertainty. Indeed, it is my contention that, ironically, the bolder mainstream economists have become in tackling the problems associated with a dynamic and creative economy, the more they have laid themselves open to a comprehensive challenge to the most basic microfoundations of their models. Can it really be appropriate, for example, to continue to assume that agents are rational optimisers in conditions of dynamic uncertainty? What does it even mean to assume that agents maximise expected profits or preference satisfaction, when the future to which these expectations and preferences relate has yet to be created and exists only in the imagination?

The most important single development in economics in recent years may be the return of 'political economy'. Economists in many cases no longer simply abstract from (or take as 'given') the institutional and political framework in which an economy is embedded. Increasingly, they focus explicitly on how economic agents create the institutions that then constrain their behaviour. For example, the modern school of 'Varieties of Capitalism' examines how firms behave as 'regime-makers' as well as 'regime-takers' – creating or reinforcing the institutional framework that best supports their specialisation.[66] Some economists also now take an interest in the dynamics of political voting systems and the formation of a social ordering of preferences, in order to model the extent to which these factors may influence the nature of the constraints facing an economy. Economists are, however, generally only happy to study these institutional and political aspects of socio-economic reality because they feel able to do so using a method – Rational Choice Theory – that is essentially an extension of the economic method.

Rational Choice Theory shares the assumptions made in economics that *group* behaviour can be explained in terms of *individuals* acting rationally to maximise their self-interest (or their own preference satisfaction), and extends this 'methodological individualism' to social and political life. Rational Choice Theory underlies some of the most fruitful models developed in both economics and the wider social sciences, in particular those based on Game Theory. Game Theory models the strategic interaction of rational optimising agents in a 'game' where the 'rules' of the game clearly specify (among other things) the strategies available to each 'player' and the pay-offs of pursuing each strategy. Such games can be either 'co-operative' or 'non-co-operative'; and the theory usually allows for a deterministic and predictable 'equilibrium' solution, which involves each individual adopting the most advantageous strategy available to her within the specified set of available strategies, given the (likely) strategies of the other players. Such models are frequently used to predict behaviour in structured socio-economic situations, such as industrial relations.

Rational Choice Theory is also applied directly to the study of how bureaucracies, governments and democratic voting systems operate – an application called Public Choice Theory. This theory holds that individual voters, politicians and bureaucrats are maximisers of their own utility, and will promote the public interest only if doing so also serves their individual interests. The theory seems to explain, for example, the high incidence of 'government failure' wherever public accountability is low and consequently the voting public has little information about the actions of officials. In this way, the 'economic method' is increasingly being used to explain areas of social and political life that may have nothing to do with wealth creation. This flatly contradicts J. S. Mill's repeated insistence that such non-economic areas of life should always be studied with the help of a wider social philosophy, in which more complex and non-utilitarian motivational factors are taken into account. In Rational and Public Choice Theory, there is generally no attempt to explain the motivation of actors in terms of social norms, national culture, or the pursuit of political ideals. Instead, this modern version of 'political economy' can essentially be defined as the imperial extension of economic method to the study of politics and institutions.[67]

All empires end up being overextended and then become increasingly vulnerable to challenges to their authority. These challenges may start at the exposed fringes of the empire but they typically in time threaten the stability of the centre. The empire of Rational Choice and the economic method is no exception. For all the success of Game Theory and Public Choice Theory in the study of politics, it has failed to suppress radically different conceptions of how best to explain political outturns. One such challenge is a theory called Constructivism, which maintains that social reality is structured by the *social* systems of belief, *collective* modes of vision and *shared* language of the agents who construct that reality. Social reality, in other words, is *socially constructed* by shared vision and values; and if we, as analysts, wish to read the meaning of that reality to the agents who live and create it, and if we wish to understand their reasons for action, we need to understand their collective interpretive structures – the identities, metaphors, norms, language and culture they share.[68] Constructivism builds on many crucial aspects of Romantic philosophy about the structuring role of language and metaphor; and, although it is normally applied to the study of politics and international relations, it also has many important potential applications to economics. Economic agents are not hermetically sealed from the influence of shared identities, beliefs and metaphors. Indeed, economic reality stands little chance of behaving as economists expect unless economic actors are in fact conditioned to think in terms that equate roughly to the models and assumptions economists use.

Thankfully, consumers and entrepreneurs are rarely conditioned to be only self-interested utility maximisers, with no other materially significant motivational impulses. Instead, they are frequently engaged in creating their own identities and opportunities, or in living out socially constructed dreams. Many economic agents have their vision coloured and their motivation structured to a significant degree by culturally specific ideas or norms. It is for this reason that we need to apply lessons of Romanticism to the very microfoundations of economic theory. These lessons include the role of imagination in creating new goods, new preferences, new strategies and new modes of vision; and the role of institutions, language, culture and metaphor in the social formation of preferences, identities and interests. In short, there is a need for the Romantic Economist to challenge the supremacy of standard economic interpretations structured according to purely mechanical metaphors and the universal application of utilitarian motivational assumptions; and to champion instead the interpretation of economic reality according to alternative organic metaphors and Romantic assumptions – especially when these help unlock the way the economic agents themselves envisage that reality.

CHAPTER 4

Lessons from Romanticism

This chapter serves two purposes: it provides an introduction to major aspects of Romantic thought for those previously unfamiliar with them; and it suggests, somewhat controversially, that there is a loose theoretical coherence to an important subset of these aspects, and to the lessons that can be drawn from them. Scholars in the field would never be likely to agree on a definitive encapsulation of the themes and lessons of Romanticism. Accordingly, the attempt here is the more limited one of isolating a set of important themes that have a good claim to be called 'Romantic', and which together suggest a body of interdependent lessons that have the power to transform the way we understand our socio-economic predicament. No apology is offered for mining for linked seams of coherence among the rough-hewn ore of Romanticism.

There are a number of difficulties inherent in any attempt to delineate a definitive set of core Romantic themes and lessons. First, the very concept of Romanticism is an anachronism when applied to the writings of William Wordsworth, Edmund Burke and many of their contemporaries. In Marilyn Butler's words, 'Romanticism, in the full rich sense we now know it, is a posthumous movement'.[1] Most of the poets and philosophers today classed as Romantic did not see themselves as such at the time; indeed, they would not have recognised themselves as belonging to a single movement at all. So, for example, contemporary critics were apt to distinguish the more reactionary and nostalgic 'Lake School' (including Wordsworth, Southey and Coleridge) from the more reformist 'Cockney School' of essayists and poets (including Hazlitt, Keats and Shelley), rather than bracket them together as we now tend to under the label 'Romantic'.[2] Likewise, few of their contemporaries would have seen William Blake or Mary Wollstonecraft (with their attacks on traditional institutions – including marriage – for being instruments of oppression)[3] as having much in common with Burke or Coleridge (with their characteristic faith in the importance of traditional institutions as the guardians of a nation's spirit and accumulated wisdom).

Furthermore, while Coleridge and Carlyle did draw heavily on contemporary German philosophy, English Romanticism (even when posthumously defined) remains in important ways quite distinct from its German cousin. For one thing, German Romanticism was at the time more clearly articulated as an intellectual movement and a style (contradistinguished from classicism), particularly by the Schlegel brothers with their self-consciously programmatic emphasis on organic (as opposed to mechanical) metaphors and on Romantic Irony and fragments.[4] Moreover, the German reaction to the cultural and political universalism implicit in both the French enlightenment and Napoleonic expansionism was (perhaps as a result of greater direct exposure) more extreme and widespread than its English counterpart. The intense interest of the German Romantics in local particularity and the unifying role of language was to be expected in a land still fragmented into a multitude of states sharing little more than a strong linguistic and cultural inheritance; and the often fervent passion for national unity was linked to the topicality of unrealised dreams of nationhood. Even in Germany, however, the boundaries of Romanticism are, in retrospect, far from clear – with some key elements, for example, hard to disentangle from German Idealism, while others are quite distinct from it. Some of the German thinkers we now class as 'Romantic' were advocates of an essentially Christian Idealism, with a neo-Platonic vision of the role of reason (or imagination in creative art) in helping us glimpse the essence or word of God behind mundane reality and, in this way, connecting our own minds with the fundamental reality (divine Mind or the infinite 'I Am') running through all things.[5] By contrast, German Romanticism (when broadly defined) also includes the precursors and followers of Nietzsche,[6] with his secular assertion of self and value creation following the 'death of God', and his radical perspectivism that seems to dissolve knowledge into multiple incommensurable perspectives, each fighting for supremacy.

Another reason it has proved impossible to define a complete and entirely consistent set of ideas called 'Romantic' in a neat dialectical relationship with rationalism, and then locate this set in the history of ideas, is that in reality many different dialectical conflicts coexisted and cut across each other. The convulsions of the French and Industrial Revolutions threw into sharp relief (and rendered more polarised) many different criss-crossing debates already evident during the Enlightenment period. This poses problems for any historian of thought wishing to assign the respective sides of such various debates securely to one side or the other of a 'two cultures' divide:[7] the different conflicts of the period cannot be fully reduced to one super-dialectical divide between rationalism and Romanticism, without considerable distortion.

Moreover, it is in many cases even more problematic to assign individual thinkers and poets completely to one of two camps; not only do they frequently display different combinations of position in relation to the various overlapping debates of the day, but their personal viewpoints were often complex products of their contested age. There are ambiguities and mutations in the thought of most creative geniuses in any period.

For all these reasons, most commentators now have sympathy with A. O. Lovejoy, who famously concluded that we must recognise a 'plurality of Romanticisms'.[8] John Beer, for example, argues as follows:

Instead of searching for and hunting down the great unifying concepts to contain and account for Romanticism, it may be more profitable to consider it as a site of fragmentation.[9]

If Romanticism is really as multifaceted and fragmented as Lovejoy and Beer argue, and if selective readings of it can support diametrically opposite positions, this might suggest that we are unlikely to find in Romanticism a worthy source of lessons for the scientific discipline of economics.

There are two reasons why such a dismissive reaction would be mistaken. The first is articulated by Isaiah Berlin, who argued that the most important lesson of Romanticism is precisely that there is no fully coherent and systematic way of analysing all the facets of our predicament. Berlin argues that the common threads in the different Romanticisms are the affirmation of a 'plurality of ideals' – ideals which are often tragically incompatible and incommensurable – together with recognition of the consequent 'necessity of the will', and rejection of 'the ideal of the jigsaw puzzle solved'. In short, for Berlin, the crucial lesson of Romanticism is that there is no 'universal pattern' or single ideal way of life.[10] Many Romantic thinkers were indeed explicit on these points; but there is a sense in which Berlin was also projecting his own value pluralism (and rejection of universal answers to life's problems) on to the anachronistically defined 'Romantic' corpus, and seeing the lack of full coherence and compatibility between the different ideas, perspectives and values contained therein as a virtue in itself. In any event, Berlin usefully reminds us that incompatibility and incoherence of perspective and value are not always negatives; they give us a choice in how we see and value the world, and the scope to create and imagine further new perspectives and ideals. It would be unwise to conclude that we have nothing to learn from Romanticism simply because it is not a fully coherent, complete and universally applicable system of thought. At the very least, Romantic thought can be a resource for challenging the illusion that any such system is possible.

There is, I believe, a second and rather different reason not to dismiss the robustness and relevance of a Romantic critique. The term 'Romantic' has had such a long and distinguished shelf-life because it is a 'family resemblance' word in the Wittgensteinian sense: while it is true that all the different uses of the term do not refer to a single essence, most of them do share a certain family resemblance and hence form what Kuhn calls a 'natural family'.[11] It is this which enables us to recognise something as 'Romantic' despite the difficulty in defining exactly what is meant by the term. Furthermore, I would argue that the family resemblance between different uses of the 'Romantic' label is, for the most part, a function of there being an important mutually reinforcing interdependence between many of the attributes associated with these different uses. In other words, although some uses of the term 'Romantic' may seem inconsistent in character with some others, many of the different ideas and values that the term is used to designate do in fact comprise a self-reinforcing combination that makes the family resemblance between them strong and compelling. Section 1 of this chapter discusses these links between members of the Romantic family and shows that, while some links are merely suggestive, others are logically necessary. To the extent that these links are established, it suggests that there is a more coherent Romantic challenge to some forms of rationalism than is often credited by modern philosophers and critics.

1 INTERDEPENDENT THEMES AND LESSONS

There are four broad sets of Romantic *themes* highlighted in this book, each of which is common to many, but not all, 'Romantic' writers. These are the importance of organic rather than mechanical metaphors, especially when applied to society or the mind; value pluralism and the absence of any single scale of value; the need for a fuller psychology of human motivation than is allowed for by some versions of rationalism – one that recognises, in particular, the role of imagination and sentiment as well as reason; and, finally, the key roles played by language, perspective, metaphor and imaginative intuition in mediating our perception and understanding of the world we live in. One hypothesis examined here is that these four themes are interdependent and mutually reinforcing in the sense that each one of them is more obviously valid if the others are also recognised as true. A second related hypothesis is that these themes together entail or suggest a number of practical Romantic *lessons* for how we should live out, and understand, our lives. Once again, it is not being claimed that all these lessons are articulated by every Romantic writer; but simply that they are propounded by many of them, and that they are interdependent with each other and with the four broad themes. The principal lessons discussed are the importance of national (or local) as opposed to universal answers to moral and practical problems; the limitations of utilitarianism both as an ethical code and as a model of motivation; the necessity of self-creation and the creation of preferences at an individual and social level; and the crucial role played by imagination as well as reason in reading what is going on in our world and forming expectations or strategies to deal with the unknown future.

Many Romantic writers advocated *organicism* – the use of organic metaphors from biology to understand the nature of social interaction and the workings of the mind. Perhaps the most important of these was the German philosopher J. G. Herder. In stark contrast to the use of mechanical metaphors by most Enlightenment philosophers and scientists, he set out a consistently organic vision of human societies, the human mind and even the physical universe. In each case, Herder used the organic metaphor to signal that the whole is more than the simple sum of the parts – its nature and development being a function of the mutual complementarities and complex self-reinforcing interdependence of the parts; and he used it also to underline that, in each case, the role and function of the constituent parts is determined by their dynamic interrelationship within the organic whole. Above all, the organic metaphor was used by Herder to focus attention on the spontaneous growth of the whole, in a historically continuous process driven by the creative interaction of parts linked by the 'genetic' transmission of a shared principle or spirit.[12]

In his political philosophy, Herder argued that the most natural form of government is the nation state, which is 'as natural a plant as a family'; it develops spontaneously through the organic interdependence and interaction of its citizens, united by the bonds of a shared language and consciousness and by a common history. Herder contrasted the vital organic unity of the nation state with the 'unnatural enlargement of states' and the mixing of nationalities in vast empires, which he thought was doomed to failure:

Such states are but patched-up contraptions, fragile machines, appropriately called state-*machines*, for they are wholly devoid of inner life, and their component parts are connected through mechanical contrivances instead of bonds of sentiment.

Herder rejected the 'scissors-and-paste approach' to both state-building and the abstract classification of types of state, in which different elements are assembled together without careful consideration of either history or the compatibility of the different elements with each other. He distrusted any politics that 'plays with men and nations as if they were inanimate particles', and any philosophy that depicts people as atomised individuals that can be linked by an arbitrary mechanism.[13] Indeed, Herder saw people as quintessentially social animals who could not even survive infancy without social protection and education. 'In this sense', he wrote, 'man is actually formed in and for society'. He believed that we can understand the actions and beliefs of individuals only by understanding their interdependence with other citizens and by getting under the skin of the shared language, traditions and education that structure their outlooks.[14] It followed from this that there can be no general models of human behaviour or templates of action, which – abstracted from local conditions – are universally applicable.

Herder's organic social and political philosophy had a huge influence on later German Romantic thinkers, such as J. G. Fichte and Adam Müller who were keen to nurture the nascent sense of German national identity. Many of his views were also mirrored or echoed by his English contemporary Edmund Burke and by Coleridge. For example, in his *Reflections on the Revolution in France* and in some of his political speeches, Burke championed an essentially organic vision of the nation united by the 'spirit of the English Constitution' and reliant on the accumulated wisdom embodied in its own traditional institutions. As a result, he shared two strong convictions with Herder. The first was that rational analysis can never capture, in Berlin's words, the 'myriad unanalysable strands to which we are loyal' and the spirit unifying a nation, nor reduce them to some form of 'social contract'.[15] In this, Burke pre-empts an important lesson of Romanticism – that we need more than reason to read, play and construct the forward march of social history: abstract rational blueprints will always fail when they ignore local circumstances and the role of shared history, institutions, identity, culture and language. Burke understood that it is our imaginations that help create or sustain our sense of national identity;[16] and, as other Romantics were later to emphasise, we also need to deploy imaginative empathy in order to grasp the spirit of other communities and their language- and tradition-bound identities. Secondly, Burke agreed with Herder that gradual change and natural political evolution are nearly always preferable to revolutionary change, since the latter breaks the traditional bonds of loyalty, drains reserves of accumulated wisdom and disrupts the delicate interdependence of complementary institutions that make up successful evolved regimes. Burke believed that revolutionary change of the sort seen in France in the 1790s, which was aimed at the rapid imposition of a new set of abstract political principles, would inevitably lead to social chaos and a host of unintended consequences.[17] This plea for gradual change, and suspicion of radical blueprints for change that are based on abstract rational principles and ignore the complexity of social organic interdependence, were also to be important lessons of Romanticism, influencing Hayek and Popper among others.

Coleridge, too, propounded an organic vision of the nation state, 'where the integral parts, classes, or orders are so balanced, or interdependent, as to constitute, more or less, a moral unit, an organic whole'; and he echoed Herder closely in his emphasis on the crucial role of education in helping to foster the idea of citizenship and maintain the balance necessary to a successful and dynamic social organism between the forces of 'permanence and of progression'.[18] More broadly, Coleridge shared with Herder and many later Romantics a great distrust of mechanical metaphors to understand social interaction. In one famous passage, he extended this to a discussion of the economy, and attacked the notion that the economy is 'a self-regulating machine', which always reverts quickly to equilibrium after shocks or crashes, making such shocks unimportant in the scheme of things. 'Persons are not things', he thundered, and 'man does not find his level'. The mechanical metaphor, he points out, overstates the likelihood in real life of ever reaching equilibrium; and it also treats people as inanimate commodities, abstracting from the moral, welfare and social-cohesion costs of painful adjustment after an economic shock. For this reason, Coleridge advocated a more organic conception of state and economy – one that stresses the necessary interdependence and balance of different interests.[19]

A key point to note here is that the use of organic rather than mechanical metaphors to understand societies (and the economy) is intimately linked with several other seemingly discrete Romantic themes and lessons. In particular, Herder's organic vision of the nation state is strongly related to the insistence throughout his work on the pivotal role of language in mediating our experience of social life. The ability to speak, Herder wrote, is the 'rudder of our reason',[20] and his lifelong emphasis on how language structures the way we think and experience the world was to be as influential in its own right as his organicism; indeed, it would help form the basis of the last of the four sets of Romantic themes considered in this chapter, namely the role of perspective and language in structuring thought and action. Herder himself saw the two themes (social organicism and the structuring role of language) as integral to each other, because language provides, in the words of F. M. Barnard, the 'psychological matrix' within which an individual relates to society; as a result, language in a very real sense provides the unifying principle of an organic social whole.[21] Herder argued that a nation's language, together with its mythology, reflect the way its people have acted and understood the world in the past; but they also integrate a people going forward by providing a 'distinctive way of viewing nature', a distinctive medium of transmission for culture and tradition from one generation to the next, and a unique way of thinking. Language is a nation's 'collective treasure, the source of its social wisdom and communal self-respect'.[22] Herder taught us that different nations evolve differently in part because their people think and see the world through different cognitive spectacles provided by their own distinct languages and inherited conceptual frameworks.

Herder's social organicism also implied an ethical stance of *value pluralism*, which is the second of the four broad themes I wish to highlight within the corpus of Romanticism. John Gray has defined value pluralism, in his book *Two Faces of Liberalism*, as 'the proposition that there are many kinds of good life', some of which are 'incommensurable' in the sense that their worth cannot be reduced to a single scale of value. Crucially, when values are incommensurable in this way, there is no one right answer in decisions about the trade-offs to be made when the values conflict with one another. In Herder's vision, as Gray notes, the incommensurability of values is 'an anthropological or historical truth': [23] each nation develops its own set of ideals or goals; indeed, the vitality and unique quality of each nation, or *Volk*, rests precisely on its ability to make its own creative choices between different incompatible values in the light of the circumstances it faces. Moreover, Herder did not share the linear conception of human progress that was widespread in the eighteenth century, but rather believed that we should judge historical societies in terms of their own particular values and standards, which are neither necessarily inferior to, nor even commensurable with, those of the present day.[24] Berlin sums up the significance of this aspect of Herder's Romantic philosophy as follows:

Herder upholds the value of variety and spontaneity, of the different, idiosyncratic paths pursued by peoples, each with its own style, ways of feeling and expression, and denounces the measuring of everything by the same timeless standards – in effect, those of the dominant French culture, which pretends that its values are valid for all time, universal, immutable. One culture is no mere step to another. Greece is not an antechamber to Rome …. This has revolutionary implications. If each culture expresses its own vision and is entitled to do so, and if the goals and values of different societies and ways of life are not commensurable, then it follows that there is no single set of principles, no universal truth for all men and times and places. The values of one civilization will be different from, and perhaps incompatible with, the values of another.[25]

Many other Romantic writers also advocated value pluralism, and this was often explicitly evident, as Laurence Lockridge puts it in his book

The Ethics of Romanticism, in 'their fierce opposition to the utilitarian and bourgeois commodification of value'.[26] Most Romantics were highly antipathetic to utilitarianism – the reduction of all value to quantifiable units of pleasure or utility – and even more so to the economic version of it – the reduction of everything to monetary value. For example, Coleridge criticised secular utilitarian rationalism and its influence on political economy in 'The Statesman's Manual':

> As ethical philosophy, it recognised no duties which it could not reduce into debtor and creditor accounts on the ledgers of self-love, where no coin was sterling which could not be rendered into agreeable sensations.[27]

A few years earlier, William Hazlitt had argued carefully that 'all good is not to be resolved into one simple principle or essence', and that there is not some 'fixed invariable standard of good or evil'; he was convinced that it is impossible 'to arrive at some one simple principle, the same in all cases, and which determines by its quantity alone the precise degree of good or evil in any sensation'.[28] P. B. Shelley, too, attacked Benthamite utilitarianism in his *Defence of Poetry*, foreshadowing Mill's famous distinction between higher and lower pleasures. Shelley pointed out that the satisfaction of animal wants (for food and so on) is qualitatively different from the pleasure derived from art, friendship, or the reading of Shakespeare – with 'utility' or 'pleasure in this highest sense' being literally incalculable and therefore incommensurable with the lower animal pleasures.[29]

   These explicit statements of value pluralism are less frequent, of course, than the implicit recognition of it in the artistic output of Romantic poets and novelists. Most obviously perhaps, the celebration by the Romantic poets of the transcendent and all-consuming power of love questioned, by implication, the unfeeling utilitarian philosophy of a 'nicely-calculated less or more'.[30] Berlin argues that value pluralism was also the implicit message of the immensely popular novels of Walter Scott, because his imaginative and attractive portrayals of the medieval past 'shattered the monopoly' of contemporary values.[31] Moreover, the Romantic idealisation of Nature and the rural world, at the very moment their existence was starting to be threatened by the relentless advance of the industrial age, pitted the timeless values of the countryside and of natural beauty against the value system inherent in modern wealth-creation. William Blake, for example, undoubtedly saw the 'dark Satanic mills' (which his poetry ironically came to immortalise) as a threat to both 'England's green and pleasant land' and its way of life, enslaving its people in a machine-like existence from hell.[32] In his *Preface* to the *Lyrical Ballads*, Wordsworth argued that the 'increasing

accumulation of men in cities' and the 'uniformity of their occupations' –
the two inevitable consequences of industrialisation and the division of
labour – were leading to a 'degrading thirst after outrageous stimulation'
and acting to 'blunt the discriminating powers of the mind'.[33] A few years
later, he expressed the same fear of the enervating effect of industrialisation
and consumerism in the famous lines:

> The world is too much with us; late and soon,
> Getting and spending, we lay waste our powers.[34]

Wordsworth's answer to this threat was to stress the incalculable value of
the revitalising power of communion with Nature, as in these lines from
'Tintern Abbey':

> Once again
> Do I behold these steep and lofty cliffs,
> Which on a wild secluded scene impress
> Thoughts of more deep seclusion, and connect
> The landscape with the quiet of the sky.
>
> … Once again I see
> These hedgerows – hardly hedgerows, little lines
> Of sportive wood run wild; these pastoral farms
> Green to the very door; and wreaths of smoke
> Sent up in silence from among the trees, …
>
> Though absent long,
> These forms of beauty have not been to me
> As is a landscape to a blind man's eye;
> But oft, in lonely rooms, and mid the din
> Of towns and cities, I have owed to them,
> In hours of weariness, sensations sweet,
> Felt in the blood, and felt along the heart,
> And passing even into my purer mind
> With tranquil restoration;[35]

Mill was perhaps thinking of this passage when, in the famous chapter of
his *Principles of Political Economy* in which he looks forward to a time when
economic growth will give way to a pleasing 'stationary state', he wrote:

A population may be too crowded, though all be amply supplied with food and
raiment. It is not good for man to be kept perforce at all times in the presence of his
species. A world from which solitude is extirpated, is a very poor ideal. Solitude, in
the sense of being often alone, is essential to any depth of meditation or of
character; and solitude in the presence of natural beauty and grandeur, is the cradle
of thoughts and aspirations which are not only good for the individual, but which
society could ill do without. Nor is there much satisfaction in contemplating

the world with nothing left to the spontaneous activity of nature; with … every hedgerow or superfluous tree rooted out, and scarcely a place left where a wild shrub or flower could grow without being eradicated as a weed in the name of improved agriculture. If the earth must lose that great portion of its pleasantness which it owes to things that the unlimited increase of wealth and population would extirpate from it, for the mere purpose of enabling it to support a larger, but not a better or a happier population, I sincerely hope, for the sake of posterity, that they will be content to be stationary, long before necessity compels them to it.[36]

Mill – the English economist most influenced by the Romantics – was under no illusion that economic growth might snuff out values it does not comprehend. He had heard the cry of the Romantics for the affirmation of values that may be both incompatible with wealth-creation and beyond calculation. He had heard what Jonathan Bate, in his book *The Song of the Earth*, has more recently called 'a cry against the commodification and instrumentalisation that characterise modernity'.[37]

We are now in a position to spell out two Romantic lessons that flow jointly from the themes of organicism and value pluralism. The first is that there are often no universally applicable answers to the practical or ethical problems of life. If national history, character and perspective matter (structuring our outlooks and behaviour); if the effect of our actions is determined by complex social interdependence with others; and if different nations and individuals create their own identities and preferences through the choices they make between incommensurable values; then a science that abstracts from all this – as economics often does – must be of limited use. It is for this reason that I will argue in chapter 6 that there is a strong need for locally or nationally specific economic and political explanatory models and policy templates. Secondly, if we accept the Romantic case for value pluralism, then we cannot have much faith in the moral calculus proposed by utilitarianism that seeks to reduce all ethical value choices to calculations using a single scale of utility, pleasure, or wealth. I will examine the important implications of this for economics in chapter 7.

Utilitarianism enters economics, of course, as more than an implicit value system. It also provides economics (and some strains of political philosophy) with the motivational assumption that economic (and political) actors are purely utility maximisers, rationally and predictably optimising their utility within given constraints. The Romantic rejection of this Benthamite assumption that human being are essentially 'pleasure machines', deciding how to act by reference only to what is expected to maximise their own pleasure or utility,[38] was particularly strident. This becomes apparent when considering the third broad set of themes that I argue can be usefully distilled from Romantic literature – namely *the need for a fuller psychology, one that emphasises imagination, creativity and sentiment as well as rational calculation.*

The Romantics opposed all attempts to ascribe to human beings a purely mechanical and therefore predictable psychology. They generally saw both David Hartley's attempt to explain thought by mechanical laws of association and the utilitarian attempt to reduce motivation and practical decision-making to rational self-interest and utility calculations as travesties of the vital creativity and moral freedom of the human mind. Coleridge, for example, somewhat histrionically argued that the 'philosophy of mechanism', when applied to the human intellect, 'strikes *Death*'.[39] Similarly Carlyle, as part of his diatribe against the 'Science of Mechanics' in *Signs of the Times*, inveighed against utilitarianism, bemoaning its wish to 'comprehend the infinitudes of man's soul under formulas of Profit and Loss'.[40] Most of the Romantics were not antipathetic to reason *per se*, but they were deeply suspicious of any attempt to simplify human psychology down to rational calculus and instrumental reasoning alone. In this vein, Coleridge argued that the 'faculty of means to medial ends' (what he calls 'understanding') is fine as far as it goes, but should be subordinate to reasoning about the 'ends' (or goals) of human life.[41] Moreover, he saw imagination as equally central to human thought, playing a central and creative role not only in artistic endeavour but also in everyday psychology and perception, and even in scientific discovery. In Coleridge's writings, imagination complements (rather than replaces) reason and understanding as part of the complete psychology of man; indeed, imagination is 'first put in action by the will and understanding'.[42]

Hazlitt was also critical of the utilitarian tendency to reduce 'the mind of man to a machine'. In his famous essay on 'Jeremy Bentham' in *The Spirit of the Age*, he criticised Bentham for not making 'sufficient allowance for the varieties of human nature, and the caprices and irregularities of the human will', and for ignoring 'the whole mass of fancy, prejudice, passion, sense, whim'. Bentham, he objected, had 'reduced the theory and practice of human life to a *caput mortuum* of reason, and dull, plodding, technical calculation'.[43] Hazlitt argued elsewhere that we should, by contrast, see ourselves as 'creatures of imagination, passion, and self-will more than of reason or even of self-interest';[44] and he further noted:

if poetry is a dream, the business of life is much the same. If it is a fiction, made up of what we wish things to be, and fancy that they are, because we wish them so, there is no other nor better reality.[45]

And so the practical figure of *homo romanticus* appears, clutching at shadows, driven by dreams, and prey to sentiments and feelings. As Mill came to realise after his nervous breakdown, a key lesson provided by the Romantic poets and philosophers is that a 'culture of the feelings' is as necessary as rational analysis to the way we live and understand our lives, and that 'imaginative emotion' is a fact of social life as real as any other.[46]

Not surprisingly, in their antipathy to the mechanical model of the mind, Coleridge and his Romantic colleagues turned to organicism to explain both the interdependence of mental faculties one with another and the dynamic vitality of the whole. Herder had already made use of the organic metaphor in his own philosophy of the mind. For example, he had argued that reason is just one among many processes of the mind, and that its workings cannot be understood by treating it as an 'isolated faculty'. As Barnard puts it, Herder saw the mind not as a mechanical 'assembly of separate faculties' (reason, the senses, feeling, willing and so on), but rather as an integrated 'creative process', with each faculty interdependent with the others.[47] In his organic theory of the mind, Herder emphasised the 'complex inter-connections of all our ideas, senses and perceptions'. He also crucially saw the imagination as 'the basic and connecting link of all the finer mental powers'.[48] Coleridge partially echoed Herder's views on the unifying role of imagination and the appropriateness of organic metaphors of the mind. For example, in his *Biographia Literaria*, he wrote:

The poet, described in *ideal* perfection, brings the whole soul of man into activity, with the subordination of its faculties to each other, according to their relative worth and dignity. He diffuses a tone and spirit of unity, that blends, and (as it were) *fuses*, each into each, by that synthetic and magical power, to which we have exclusively appropriated the name of imagination.[49]

By applying the organic metaphor to the mind, Herder and Coleridge did not just make clear that the operation of each mental faculty is dependent for its nature and impact on the operation of other faculties. They also underlined the creativity and dynamism of the self-organising whole, under the influence of the imagination. Coleridge made this explicit when he wrote: 'The *rules* of the IMAGINATION are themselves the very powers of growth and production.'[50]

Herder's social organicism also had direct implications for the Romantic understanding of human psychology: because individuals, however diverse, are dependent on others for the language in which they think, and for their daily bread and function in life, their psychology necessarily reflects their social dependence. Herder insisted that human reason is not 'an innate automaton' but 'something *formed by experience*' and fashioned by our 'mode of life'. In his vision, it is not just our preferences and language that are socially formed, but our very way of thinking.[51] Moreover, he argued that, because 'the natural state of man is society', human beings all share two basic instincts – '*self-preservation* and *sympathy*'. Indeed, he believed that 'man was chosen by Nature' to possess the emotions of sympathy and empathy 'to the highest degree'.[52] The importance of this 'organic sensibility'[53] was to be the constant refrain of most Romantics, and they were horrified by the increasing tendency in both political economy and utilitarianism to downplay sympathy as a key element of motivation.

The emphasis placed by many Romantics on value pluralism also had significant implications for their picture of human psychology. This was particularly true among those late Romantics who rejected the implicit Idealism and neo-Platonism of Coleridge and Wordsworth, and hence rejected their faith that imagination (and reason) can access objective and transcendent – if plural – values and help us resolve through quasi-religious intuition the dilemmas that face us. Friedrich Nietzsche spelt out in often shocking terms the implications of value pluralism taken to extremes in a context where there is no ultimate appeal possible to some divine or natural order, and no single, rational perspective that must command assent. In *The Gay Science*, Nietzsche's view of how the heroic at least should respond to their predicament is clear:

Let us therefore *limit* ourselves to the purification of our opinions and evaluations and to the *creation of our own new tables of values* … We, however, *want to be those who we are* – the new, the unique, the incomparable, those who give themselves their own law, those who create themselves![54]

Nietzsche famously proclaimed that God is dead, and looked for the coming of 'Superman', who would exult in the affirmation of his own supreme 'will to power' and create his own set of values. Indeed, Nietzsche welcomed the fracturing of all supposedly universal value systems that hold out the false promise of solving value dilemmas – as he made clear in this maxim at the beginning of *The Twilight of the Idols*:

I distrust all systematisers, and avoid them. The will to a system shows a lack of honesty.[55]

Freed of systems, Nietzsche suggested that we should make self-creating choices to settle the value dilemmas we face, as an act of unconstrained will to power, and as an expression of the character we wish to be. Creativity and ambitious self-assertion is at the centre of his conception of what it is to be human: 'Our very essence is to create a being higher than ourselves. We must create beyond ourselves. That is the instinct of procreation, that is the instinct of action and of work.'[56]

Nietzsche did not shy away from the implications of the untrammelled assertion of will and self-creation that he advocates, as we can see in this passage from *Thus Spake Zarathustra*:

Overcome, you higher men, the petty virtues, the petty prudences, the sand-grain discretion, the ant-swarm inanity, miserable ease, the 'happiness of the greatest number!'[57]

Nietzsche always reserved his particular scorn for the (English) philosophy of Bentham, as in his famous maxim: 'Man does not aspire to happiness; only the Englishman does that.'[58] Nietzsche's very different world is divided between slaves and masters, and he suggests that the latter should act like 'the laughing storm that blows dust in the eyes of all the dim-sighted.'[59]

Nietzsche's Superman is a direct descendant of the heroes of Lord Byron's verse. Byron's heroes, too, exhibit a strong will that breaks the organic bonds of society, and leaves the heroes isolated and proudly dismissive of the crowd below. On their pinnacles of rock or fame, they can secure an unparalleled perspective on the world, but they must also face dangerous storms and tempests with their heads bared. In this famous stanza, Byron is known to have had Napoleon in mind:

> He who ascends to mountain-tops, shall find
> The loftiest peaks most wrapt in clouds and snow;
> He who surpasses or subdues mankind,
> Must look down on the hate of those below.
> Though high *above* the sun of glory glow,
> And far *beneath* the earth and ocean spread,
> *Round* him are icy rocks, and loudly blow
> Contending tempests on his naked head,
> And thus reward the toils which to those summits led.[60]

There is, of course, something deeply distasteful, as well as occasionally exhilarating, about the Byronic and Nietzschean hero – with 'a vital scorn of all', and swayed by 'a secret pride/To do what few or none would do beside'.[61] Over time, the image of an uninhibited will to power and self-creation threatened to obscure, and even obliterate, the gentler lessons of Romanticism. For wherever self-assertion, will and value-creation become overdominant features in the mind of man, the organic interdependence of these with other mental faculties and tendencies (of the sort Herder posited) is broken. In particular, sympathy and constancy are often casualties, leaving humanity at the mercy of cruelty and whim. So, for example, Byron's proud heroes, such as Lara described in the lines that follow, are far from paragons of the 'organic sensibility' that Herder thought was so important to the cohesion of society:

> Too high for common selfishness, he could
> At times resign his own for others' good,
> But not in pity, not because he ought,
> But in some strange perversity of thought.[62]

Byron and Nietzsche showed us how the mental and social landscape is transformed when pity and sympathy are overpowered by will and self-assertion. Opinion remains divided, however, on whether this particular lesson of Romanticism was a direct incitement to the horrific excesses of twentieth-century fascism (and even corporate crime), or a warning from two brilliant (if, in one case, increasingly mentally unstable) prophets who, by emphasising the importance to humanity of the will and self-creation, enabled us to understand the implications of not allowing them to be suitably recognised and harnessed. To deny the importance of the will to power and Nietzschean self-creation may be more dangerous than to recognise them as central facets of what it is to be human. For such a recognition is a necessary precursor of designing frameworks that can help ensure these facets are given space to develop in a socially acceptable way, tempered by rational calculation or agreed norms.

While most Romantics thought of *imagination* as only first among a number of equally important mental faculties, there is no doubt that it received their special focus. They were acutely aware that it is often totally ignored by those of more rationalist persuasion – largely because it is so difficult to capture and define – and they were determined to right the balance. There is, not surprisingly, no single Romantic view of the imagination, and the different poets and philosophers often disagreed in important ways. This is, to some extent, simply a reflection of the fact that imagination is an 'umbrella concept' including many different facets of mental creativity; this alone makes it hardly surprising that different poets have a different focus. Moreover, as Mary Warnock has pointed out, poets like Wordsworth and Coleridge were not systematic thinkers, and it is often dangerous to assume that even their own different observations were all intended to cohere into one theory. For this reason, Warnock advises us to distinguish between the often-acute 'psychological observations' these hugely sensitive poets made about the workings of their own minds and the theoretical frameworks they sometimes tried to build.[63] Both are of interest, but even readers who do not agree with the theoretical frameworks should find the observations fascinating.

In *The Prelude*, Wordsworth makes a number of attempts to capture the essence of the imagination by using visual metaphors from the world of nature. These succeed in conveying the disorienting as well as awe-inspiring quality of the imagination at work; and they point to the mysterious and murky sources of imagination deep in the unconscious. In his description of crossing the Alps, Wordsworth wrote:

> Imagination! lifting up itself
> Before the eye and progress of my Song
> Like an unfather'd vapour; here that Power,
> In all the might of its endowments, came
> Athwart me; I was lost as in a cloud,
> Halted, without a struggle to break through.
> And now recovering, to my Soul I say
> I recognise thy glory;[64]

In a later version of the same passage, imagination is explicitly revealed as an 'awful Power', rising from 'the mind's abyss'.[65] Later in *The Prelude*, Wordsworth describes climbing Mount Snowdon on a moonlit night, and finding himself looking down upon 'a huge sea of mist', out of which emerged among the hills:

> a blue chasm; a fracture in the vapour,
> A deep and gloomy breathing-place through which
> Mounted the roar of waters, torrents, streams
> Innumerable, roaring with one voice.
>   … but in that breach
> Through which the homeless voice of waters rose,
> That dark deep thoroughfare had Nature lodg'd
> The Soul, the Imagination of the whole.[66]

In Coleridge's writings, the imagination is seen as less sublimely mysterious and 'unfather'd': describing it as 'put in action by the will and understanding', he adds that it is 'retained under their irremissive, though gentle and unnoticed, controul'.[67] Here Coleridge's acute self-analysis reveals a central truth about the imagination: it is not merely an unconscious source of new connections and insights; rather, it is often a willed attempt to find new connections, to build new colour and significance. It cannot operate, though, if it is too tightly controlled by the will and understanding; it needs space. As Coleridge puts it elsewhere, imagination is best seen as a 'middle state of mind … hovering between images'.[68] Despite this observation, John Keats still thought that Coleridge tried too hard to harness the imagination and control it rationally. For him, the essence of imagination was what he called '*negative capability*'; that is, when man is capable of being in uncertainties, mysteries, doubts, without any irritable reaching after fact and reason'.[69] Keats was more interested in underlining the central importance of an imaginative receptiveness to new ideas flooding from the unconscious than in examining (as Coleridge did) the delicate interface of this receptiveness with rational analysis.

In the following famous passage, Coleridge highlights several other aspects of his conception of imagination, a conception shared in varying degrees by a number of other Romantics:

The primary IMAGINATION I hold to be the living Power and prime Agent of all human Perception, and as a repetition in the finite mind of the eternal act of creation in the infinite I AM. The secondary Imagination I consider as an echo of the former, co-existing with the conscious will, yet still as identical with the primary in the *kind* of its agency, and differing only in *degree*, and in the *mode* of its operation. It dissolves, diffuses, dissipates, in order to re-create; or where this process is rendered impossible, yet still at all events it struggles to idealise and to unify. It is essentially *vital*, even as all objects (*as* objects) are essentially fixed and dead.

FANCY, on the contrary, has no other counters to play with, but fixities and definites … equally with the ordinary memory the Fancy must receive all its materials ready made from the law of association.[70]

Here in one compressed passage, we see three crucial features of Coleridge's philosophy of the imagination. First, he viewed imagination as central to everyday perception. As John Spencer Hill explains in his commentary, Coleridge thought of 'seeing as making'; and he believed that this creative role in perception (primary imagination) differs from the more explicitly creative nature of poetic imagination (secondary imagination) 'in degree but not in kind'.[71] Secondly, there is a clear element of religious Idealism in Coleridge's view of the function of imagination. Both these aspects are discussed more fully in section 2. The third theme to emerge from this quotation is that imagination is 'vital' – forming a key element of the organic, synthesising and creative functioning of the human mind. In this, imagination is said to contrast with mere 'fancy', which operates mechanically according to 'the law of association' between pre-existing ideas and memories. No passage makes clearer Coleridge's insistence that it is imagination that rescues the mind from mechanical determinism and predictability, and allows human thought to develop as a creative process.

A crucial lesson to emerge from the Romantic fascination with the imagination is its role in helping us both understand our social predicament (past and present) and read and construct the unknown future. Coleridge was adamant that to access the truth about the past and present – and see in them more than 'a shadow-fight of things and quantities' – we must free ourselves from 'the general contagion' of 'mechanic philosophy' and 'unenlivened generalising understanding', and substitute 'the living educts of the imagination'.[72] He believed that only imagination and reason acting together can help us glimpse the deeper truth hidden behind the mass of contradictory data. This essentially neo-Platonic view of the role of imagination in Coleridge's writings is quite different from – and in our secular age less attractive than – Herder's more down-to-earth stress on the historical imagination. The latter, as Berlin explains, should be seen as essentially a form of empathy that 'can enable us to "descend to" or "enter" or "feel oneself into" the mentality of remote societies' and so understand the organic nature of the whole.[73] Such empathetic understanding cannot be achieved by relying on abstract analysis alone. Indeed, any such sole reliance would ensure that we, in Wordsworth's famous words, 'murder to dissect'.[74] This is partly because the feelings involved are often beyond the remit of reason alone to comprehend, and partly because we need to make an imaginative leap to understand societies grounded in different linguistic and conceptual structures than our own. It is also because, as Berlin again sums up so well, we are dealing in the case of each society we look at with 'a process of perpetual forward creation', so that 'all schemas, all generalisations, all patterns imposed upon it are forms of distortion, forms of breaking'.[75]

Imaginative empathy is needed for more, of course, than understanding societies remote in time or place. As Herder and others emphasised, sympathy and empathy are equally important for everyday social life in the present; and a central lesson of Romanticism is that such sympathy is also a product of the imagination. This means that the imagination is at the core of human morality and everyday behaviour. Shelley underlines the role of imagination in sympathy and therefore in morality, in *A Defence of Poetry*:

A man, to be greatly good, must imagine intensely and comprehensively; he must put himself in the place of another and of many others; the pains and pleasures of his species must become his own. The great instrument of moral good is the imagination – and poetry administers to the effect by acting on the cause.[76]

Hazlitt takes this argument a stage further in his *Essay on the Principles of Human Action*, where he notes that the faculty of imaginative projection involved in our sympathetic interest in the feelings of others is fundamentally the same as that required to engender and sustain our current interest in the future feelings of our own future selves:

The imagination, by means of which alone I can anticipate future objects, or be interested in them, must carry me out of myself into the feelings of others by one and the same process by which I am thrown forward as it were into my future being, and interested in it.[77]

Imagination, Hazlitt argued, is as central to the pursuit of self-interest as it is to disinterested sympathy. The reason is clear: the pursuit of self-interest is forward-looking and must, therefore, to a great extent involve chasing the shadows cast by our imaginative projection of possible futures and of the pleasures of our imagined future selves. Since we cannot know the future, and can neither predict for sure our future feelings, nor the events or selves to which they will attach – since, in short, the future is 'problematical' and 'undetermined' – our pursuit of self-interest inevitably involves an imaginative and creative element. As Hazlitt put it in a later essay:

The future is a blank and dreary void, like sleep or death, till the imagination brooding over it with wings outspread, impregnates it with life and motion.[78]

It follows from this argument that there can, in reality, be nothing mechanical and law-like even about the rational pursuit of self-interest. Indeed, this is perhaps the single most important lesson of Romanticism: when we act with the future in mind, we must imagine how the unknown future will be for us, and how we want it to be. The remit of rational analysis and optimisation is forever limited when peering into the future – because that future is created, in part, by how we (and others) imagine it could be. As Wordsworth wrote in *The Prelude*, in relation to those who would tame the 'frorward chaos of futurity' with books:

> Sages, who in their prescience would controul
> All accidents, and to the very road
> Which they have fashion'd would confine us down,
> Like engines, when will they be taught
> That in the unreasoning progress of the world
> A wiser Spirit is at work for us,
> A better eye than theirs, more prodigal
> Of blessings, and more studious of our good,
> Even in what seem our most unfruitful hours?[79]

For Wordsworth, as for most Romantics, this 'wiser Spirit' is the imagination, often seen as nothing less than a visionary power.

2 UNITY AND FRAGMENTS

The remainder of this chapter focuses on a final Romantic theme, the *role of imagination, language, perspective and metaphor in structuring our perception and understanding of the world we live in*. As such, it discusses some difficult philosophical ideas concerning the nature of human knowledge and perception. These ideas, in turn, underlie the quintessential Romantic fascination with 'irony' and 'fragments'; and they suggest some of the most important lessons we can draw from Romantic thought about the nature and status of academic disciplines such as economics.

It was two non-Romantic philosophers who provided much of the initial impetus for this revolutionary aspect of Romantic thought: between them David Hume and Immanuel Kant effected a transformation in the standard philosophical conception of human experience and understanding of the world. Hume cast doubt on the rational status of scientific knowledge by arguing that we cannot know, on the basis of the sense data available to us, that causal connections between observed events or properties actually exist; indeed, we cannot even establish beyond doubt the identity of objects or persons through time. In the first case (causation), the only thing that we have incontrovertible access to is the constant conjunction in sequence of discrete sense impressions, which in turn gives rise to a habitual association of related ideas in our minds; and, in the second case (identity), we have merely an association of ideas based on the similarity through time of disconnected sense impressions. On this flimsy basis, Hume argued, our minds *create*, with the help of the imagination, beliefs in causal connections and the continuous identity of objects through time, and then project these beliefs onto the objects of our perception. Hume was pragmatic enough to acknowledge that we must in fact tentatively override such scepticism about our ability to know anything for certain about the world we live in. But, while his sunny disposition may have enabled him to live comfortably with the consequences of doubt about the ultimate basis of most of what passes for empirical knowledge, and to relish the need to treat all scientific theories as provisional figments of the mind, many of his successors were deeply troubled by his sceptical conclusion. For this conclusion seemed to suggest that we can never infer from experience the truth of even such general laws as Newton had proposed.[80]

The late-eighteenth-century German philosopher Kant responded to Hume with a theory that was to complete a revolution in the theory of knowledge every bit as ground-breaking in its field as Copernicus' proposal in astronomy of a sun-centred rather than earth-centred universe. Contrary to Hume, Kant argued that we do in fact have a firm basis of knowledge of the world-as-it-appears-to-us, but only because of certain necessary ways in which all humans experience and understand that world. The very order that is the basis of science is something, according to Kant, that we read *into* the world-as-we-see-it rather than read (or infer) *from* it. In particular, Kant argued that two Forms of Sensibility (space and time) are read into the world we experience as necessary conditions of our experiencing it; space and time, in other words, are automatically presupposed in the way we experience the world through our senses. He further posited that, with the help of 'transcendental' imagination, we apply to our experience of the world certain Forms of Understanding – that is, *a priori* organisational concepts and principles of interpretation (including causality) – as necessary conditions of making it intelligible. So, for example, we are inherently predisposed to see cause and effect relations between attributes constantly experienced in sequence, because it is part of our necessary mental furniture to see the world that way. If we did not all have such *a priori* principles of organisation and interpretation, Kant argued, we could not make sense of the world; to have such principles is a necessary condition of understanding the world and acquiring knowledge.[81] Richard Tarnas sums up the revolutionary nature of Kant's theory as follows:

The order man perceives in his world is thus an order grounded not in that world but in his mind: the mind, as it were, forces the world to obey its own organisation. All sensory experience has been channelled through the filter of human *a priori* structures.[82]

The influence of Kant's thinking on the Romantic movement was immense. In most cases, his particular insistence on necessary forms of human experience and cognition was dropped, but his central thesis that we read into the world certain structuring principles – and that we, therefore, to some extent at least, *create* the world as we experience and understand it – was to remain central.

Two other aspects of Kant's thought were also to inspire and haunt the Romantics. First, Kant ascribed a large role in perception and understanding to the imagination: he saw ('transcendental') imagination as synthesising and making sense of our experience by constructing it in accordance with *a priori* principles or Forms of Understanding; and he also argued that our ('empirical') imagination fleshes out everyday concepts such as house or palace and applies these to manifold sense data so that we can recognise something as a 'house' or something else as a 'palace'.[83] The details of Kant's theory of imagination need not concern us here. The key point is that many Romantics took their cue from Kant and ascribed an even greater and more creative role for imagination in perception and interpretation than Kant himself allowed. In particular, the focus gradually became on creative and contingent rather than necessary and universal ways of seeing and understanding, with the imagination able to colour and structure interpretation and experience of the world in novel and perhaps misleading ways. Secondly, Kant's response to Hume left many Romantics still deeply troubled because, while he claimed to have established (in our necessary modes of sensation and understanding) a firm basis for knowledge of the world-*as-it-appears-to-us*, Kant was himself explicit that we can never know 'things-in-themselves' or the world-*as-it-really-is*. We can, he argued, only ever know the world already mediated by our own concepts and forms of understanding.[84] Many Romantics saw it as their mission to bridge the remaining chasm between subject and object, and to grasp the infinite reality underlying the world-as-we-see-it.

Romantic Idealism was a response to this desire to overcome the dualism between subject (mind) and object (matter). Friedrich Schelling, for example, saw mind and matter (in Bryan Magee's words) as 'two aspects of a single world-process', and held that it is artistic imagination or intuition that can reveal and replicate consciously in its workings the unconscious spirit underlying all Nature.[85] Again the details of Schelling's immensely difficult philosophy are not important to us; but it exemplifies an essentially Christian idealism that sees the world as the working out of the Divine Mind that we – as artists or believers – can occasionally, and with great effort, glimpse.[86] This view influenced Coleridge who, for example in the famous passage on the 'primary imagination' quoted earlier, combined a Kantian belief in imagination's creative and constitutive role in perception with an Idealist belief that imagination acts 'as a repetition in the finite mind of the eternal act of creation in the infinite I AM'.[87] Wordsworth, likewise, combined a belief in the creative role of mind in perception with a form of religious idealism. In *The Prelude*, he describes an infant's attempt to make sense of the world he sees as follows:

> his mind,
> Even as an agent of the one great mind,
> Creates, creator and receiver both,
> Working but in alliance with the works
> Which it beholds.[88]

Wordsworth's insistence here, and also in 'Lines Written a Few Miles above Tintern Abbey', that the mind half-creates what we see[89] is characteristically observant and nuanced. Of course, he reminds us, the mind must work with the material provided by our senses; in this important manner, our experience and knowledge of the world is empirically grounded. But our experience and understanding must also, he claims, be structured and created by our minds, both by the creative colouring bestowed by our imaginations and, where possible, by our fleeting imaginative intuitions of a deeper reality. 'Joy' is the name given by Wordsworth and other Romantics to that moment when the mind suddenly glimpses, with the help of the imagination, the principle or spirit that informs all reality. In 'Tintern Abbey', Wordsworth wrote:

> And I have felt
> A presence that disturbs me with the joy
> Of elevated thoughts, a sense sublime
> Of something far more deeply interfused, …
> A motion and a spirit that impels
> All thinking things, all objects of all thought,
> And rolls through all things.[90]

Not surprisingly this sort of imaginative intuition of a deep spiritual reality – a spirit that can bridge once and for all the gap between human minds (subject) and external reality (object) by informing both – is fleeting at best. Romantic poetry is suffused with a sense of lost communion with ultimate reality, and with the agony of vanished visions of our place in the universe. Furthermore, over the last two increasingly secular centuries, religious idealism has come to be seen by most people as a dead end – a futile attempt to grasp and understand the nature and meaning of reality by attuning ourselves to the Divine Mind underlying it.

Another Romantic response to Kant's philosophy went in a rather different direction: unimpressed by Kant's necessary ways of understanding as a firm basis of ordered experience and knowledge, many writers and painters stressed the ubiquity of doubt about all interpretations even of the world-as-it-appears-to-us. The problem becomes not so much the impossibility of unmediated access to reality-in-itself as our inevitable failure to formulate one universal and all-encompassing perspective or way of structuring our infinitely complex world. In other words, reality may or may not exist, or be intrinsically knowable, in a form that is not in some sense mind-dependent; but, in all events, reality-as-we-experience-it is inexhaustibly large and chaotic. On this view, it is mankind's destiny to be trapped in an endless series of partial perspectives and fragments of knowledge and an endless struggle to combine them into a more complete and successful mode of vision.

It has often been observed that Coleridge, who more than any other Romantic poet strove to reconcile opposites and unify his understanding into one master vision, in practice produced innumerable fragments. Some of these, like the famous poem 'Kubla Khan', were self-consciously presented as polished fragments of a half-vanished vision. Most, however, were brief notebook entries in which Coleridge's continued attempts to clarify and solve the great questions troubling him resulted only in fragmentary insights which he was unable to complete. Ironically, many of these fragments are concerned with the power of imagination and, in particular, with its capacity 'by a sort of *fusion to force many into one*' and thereby produce 'out of many things … a oneness'.[91] John Beer has neatly summed up the significance of Coleridge's frequent expressions of faith that the imagination can unify our fragmented thought and experience:

> Coleridge's intimately related preoccupation with the one and the many … combined a recognition of the fragmentary nature of human experience with a belief that a wholeness of truth was waiting to be found, if only the seeker were sufficiently diligent … If few were willing to join Coleridge in his quixotic ambition to comprehend the whole of knowledge, the larger problems of fragmentation bore in on all his contemporaries, …[92]

It was the German writer Friedrich Schlegel (and his brother) who did most to develop the fragment as a self-conscious form of philosophical writing and as an embodiment of a theoretical position that encompasses both the search for a unified understanding and the impossibility of ever achieving it. Schlegel is most famous as an advocate of the related concept of *Romantic Irony*. This involved introducing, in Schlegel's own words, 'the producer along with the product', so that the finished artistic work can 'hover at the midpoint between the portrayed and the portrayer'.[93] The intrusion of the artist into his own work makes the artist's partial and created perspective part of the picture and, in this way, shatters the illusion of complete or objective vision; it casts doubt on the interpretation presented, and relativises the truth conveyed, while still celebrating the attempt made. The painter Caspar David Friedrich made extensive use of a visual form of this technique. His *Wanderer above the Sea of Mist* (see front cover) may have an unparalleled perspective on the world below, but we (standing behind him) can see that his vision is only partial. Another of Friedrich's paintings – *On a Sailing Boat* – represents the artist and his wife on a voyage to an earthly paradise, but we (the viewing public) also see the scene for what it is, the inevitably illusory perspective of newly wed lovers. The painting is at once a testament to the power of Romantic love and an invitation to a more complete and knowing perspective.[94] In Schlegel's hands, Romantic Irony became associated first and foremost with a form of philosophy that, like Plato's dialogues, is always striving to capture the whole truth but also makes manifest its own limitations and refuses ever to be set in the aspic of a finished system. Irony, Schlegel stated in one of his most celebrated fragments, arouses in us 'a feeling of indissoluble antagonism … between the impossibility and the necessity of complete communication'.[95]

There are several reasons why the fragment was for Schlegel the ideal expression of Romantic Irony and therefore the ideal form of philosophical writing. Above all, it allows for precisely the ironic (or paradoxical) combination he sought of striving for completeness while simultaneously acknowledging limitation. Schlegel encapsulated the central philosophical conundrum as follows:

It is equally fatal for the mind to have a system and to have none. It will simply have to decide to combine the two.[96]

It is this that makes the fragment a valuable device: for it allows the presentation of a system (or systematic approach) in a form that both celebrates and undermines its claim to make sense of the world. Schlegel underscored the value of the fragment as a complete jewel-like and self-sufficient encapsulation of some isolated aspect of the truth in the following lines:

A fragment, like a miniature work of art, has to be entirely isolated from the surrounding world and be complete in itself like a porcupine.[97]

At the same time, Schlegel saw the fragment as an appropriate form because, as Charles Armstrong has put it, it insists on 'the necessarily provisional and incomplete nature of all thought' and 'bears witness to the absence of the system, the absence of the book which would contain the whole'.[98] This was a crucial attribute for Schlegel, because he believed that any systematic approach is dangerously distortionary unless it acknowledges that it is not (and cannot be) a complete encapsulation of the truth.

There are two other important aspects of Schlegel's theory of irony and advocacy of fragmentary discourse which were to find many echoes in later Romantic thought. First, as Ernst Behler has noted, a one-line fragment published by Schlegel in 1800 ties his theory of irony explicitly to an understanding of the inexhaustible and complex nature of reality:

Irony is the clear consciousness of eternal agility, of an infinitely abundant chaos.[99]

Berlin sums up the significance of this view of the world – and the clear implications it has for any attempts at definitive and systematic understanding – as follows:

if *ex hypothesi* the universe is in movement and not at rest, if it is a form of activity and not a lump of stuff, if it is infinite and not finite, if it is constantly varying and never still, never the same (to use these various metaphors which the romantics constantly use), if it is a constant wave (as Friedrich Schlegel says), how can we possibly even try to describe it? … Therefore do not let us attempt to describe it. But you cannot not attempt to describe it, because that means to stop expressing, and to stop expressing is to stop living … Your relation to the universe is inexpressible, but you must nevertheless express it. This is the agony, this is the problem.[100]

Schlegel's careful use of fragments to express his ideas also lent themselves, however, to a reading that is more optimistic than this agonised admission of inevitable failure. As Charles Armstrong writes, 'true fragments can be construed as being fragments *for* the system, building blocks for an as yet unfinished edifice';[101] and, as Andrew Bowie observes in relation to Schlegel's use of often inconsistent fragments in his philosophy: 'Non-systematic contradiction is understood as a means of arriving at new insight.'[102] The great virtue of fragments is that creative space is left open by the crucial acknowledgement of failure to encompass the whole; and in this space we can arrive at new insights by being imaginatively open to new connections suggested by the unsystematic juxtaposition of different fragments. Fragments allow us to have the benefit of clearly delineated and (in their own terms) self-sufficient perspectives or systems of thought; but by simultaneously highlighting their limitations, they also encourage us to step outside the suffocating dogmatism of necessarily limited systems, and to create new syntheses.

Many other thinkers, of course, have been interested in the constructive as well as destructive implications of writing in fragments. For example, Douglas Hedley has shown that Coleridge was perhaps more influenced in his love of fragments and aphorisms by the early-seventeenth-century scientist Francis Bacon, than by Schlegel. Bacon did not (any more than Coleridge) share Schlegel's more extreme doubts about systematic thought; but he did believe that an unsystematic arrangement of fragments or aphorisms can leave us open to new ideas, stimulate creative inquiry and encourage the imaginative search for new connections. Hedley argues that far from Bacon's interest in aphorisms constituting 'a rejection of system per se', he used them with 'systematic intent'; and this may have encouraged Coleridge to share Bacon's 'confidence in the aphorism as a harbinger of systematic insight'.[103] Fragments and aphorisms have been employed to equally notable, but sometimes more corrosive, effect by Nietzsche and, more recently, Wittgenstein. These philosophers believed that we can never escape the role of perspective and language in structuring our vision, and that our vision is fragmented into a large number of incommensurable perspectives. They were also deeply suspicious of any suggestion of a general theoretical framework. In this condition, not surprisingly, they both thought that the suggestiveness of an almost random collocation of different metaphorical aphorisms and discrete fragmentary insights represents the best hope of improving our understanding.

Wittgenstein's appreciation of how far our conception and understanding of the world is conditioned by the structure of the languages we use – and specifically by the socially engendered rules for their use – has a Romantic pedigree going back to Herder. Herder, it could be said, replaced Kant's *necessary* ways of structuring and understanding the world with *socially constructed* structures of interpretation. For Herder, a nation's language and mythology provide its citizens with a distinctive way of making sense of the world; each separate language and culture ensures that those thinking in its terms apply a particular inherited conceptual framework and emotional outlook to their experience.[104] The implications of this view are clear: the citizens of each nation (or language group) actually see the world differently; and, if we want to understand their beliefs and actions, we need first to understand their language and traditions. There can be no universal model for understanding human behaviour that abstracts from language and culture.

Nietzsche took thinking about the role of language- and metaphor-constituted perspective a stage further. He stressed that all thought is a function of particular perspectives and structures of interpretation. Specifically rejecting the idea of an objective science of facts, he wrote 'facts are precisely what there are not, only interpretations';[105] and he famously argued that 'physics too is only an interpretation and arrangement of the world'.[106] Some interpretations might be more influential or pragmatically useful for us to believe in than others; some might distort our vision less than others; but all of them depend on a conceptual grid we have imposed on reality. Nietzsche believed that it is important to use multiple perspectives, and experiment with different metaphors, in order to increase the range of interpretations available to us and so fine-tune our understanding as best we can; but we must also accept that we can never exhaust the range of possible interpretations, nor ever construct the perfect all-encompassing perspective. In *The Gay Science*, Nietzsche wrote:

The world has rather once again become for us 'infinite': insofar as we cannot reject the possibility that *it contains in itself infinite interpretations*.[107]

The Post-Modernists were later to take Nietzschean perspectivism to extremes. Jacques Derrida attempted to show that any text or system of thought might contain within itself a large number of possible interpretations. Michel Foucault claimed to have unearthed a series of incommensurable *a priori* conceptual grids, with which those living in different historical periods were condemned to interpret their experience. Foucault later also argued that any 'totalising discourses' that seek to impose interpretive hegemony on us all are really organs of power; and Jean-François Lyotard, too, saw mankind's predilection for 'grand narratives' that seek to unify our experience as both illusory and ideological in nature.[108] Such a bleak assessment of the nature and status of systems of thought has sometimes threatened, by a sort of *reductio ad absurdum*, to discredit or obscure the central Romantic lesson that our experience is inevitably structured – but only partly created – by language and perspective. Wordsworth intuitively understood – as the Post-Modernists sometimes seemed to ignore – that our minds only *half*-create our experience. Our various perspectives influence and order what we see, but what is 'out there' must also contribute to our experience. Not all interpretive structures fit well with the empirical evidence available to our senses; some are better or more useful than others at focusing on, and making sense of, what is 'out there' and what matters to us. Instead of merely wallowing (or glorying) in doubt about the validity of any interpretation, we should use our imaginations to construct new and better perspectives, and to combine existing ones, to improve our chances of making sense of our multidimensional and unbounded predicament.

It might seem a tall order, at first sight, to make this Romantic philosophising about the status and nature of human knowledge and interpretation applicable to economics. Even if some economists see immediately the possible relevance to their discipline of organicism, incommensurable values and the role of sentiments and imagination in human behaviour, they may baulk at the idea that Romantic Irony and Schlegel's theory of fragments can have important implications for their 'science'. I will argue, however, that Romantic epistemological theory from Kant to Nietzsche can, in fact, teach us a great deal about the nature of economics.

Economists study social and economic interaction with cognitive spectacles that are heavily coloured by the metaphors they employ. Their vision is irremediably and inevitably theory-laden. No social scientist has unmediated access to reality; rather they half-create the reality they study by means of the conceptual and interpretive framework they project upon it. This creative aspect of economics, indeed, is its major achievement – bringing order to the manifold chaos of our socio-economic predicament. Shackle acknowledged this, in his otherwise stinging critique of standard economic theory:

[Economics] gains insights of a peculiar sort, without which the economic world would appear a mere chaos of proliferating and unintelligible detail, reasonable and orderly only in the small, in space and time, and otherwise altogether lacking any sense or architecture. This achievement of broad intelligibility and visible structure, out of so vast a flood of minutiae and such limitless diversity, is a very great and remarkable achievement.[109]

The structured and intelligible order created by economists comes, however, at a price; for the conceptual grid they impose on economic reality to produce this order filters out any recognition of incommensurable values, sentiment and creative flux. Schumpeter is explicit about the dangers that can result from such selective vision. Considering the misleading conclusions of standard equilibrium and competition theory, which abstracts from the 'organic process' of 'Creative Destruction', he wrote:

Both economists and popular writers have once more run away with some fragments of reality they happened to grasp. These fragments themselves were mostly seen correctly. Their formal properties were mostly developed correctly. But no conclusions about capitalist reality as a whole follow from such fragmentary analyses. If we draw them nevertheless, we can be right only by accident. That has been done. And the lucky accident did not happen.[110]

Schlegel would not have been surprised; he reminded us that, while we must have systems of thought (such as economics produces), 'the systematic procedure remains more or less divisive and isolating', whereas 'philosophising in a lyrical manner, devoid of systematic coherence, at least does not ravage the whole of the truth quite so much'.[111] Indeed, it is perhaps not fanciful to see neoclassical economic (and Rational Choice) theory as a good example of Schlegel's famous fragment as porcupine – 'entirely isolated from the surrounding world', 'complete in itself'[112] and, we might add, repelling alternative perspectives with barbs of particular ferocity.

The duty of the Romantic Economist is now clear: he or she should insist that we not only recognise the great value of current systematic procedures in economics but also acknowledge that they are merely fragments – limited perspectives. Rational Choice Theory, for example, can bring a conceptual order to large aspects of social and economic interaction that is breathtaking and self-sufficient; but we must assert its status as a fragment to acknowledge the futility of any claim it may have to the whole truth. Moreover, we should learn from Bacon, Coleridge and others that we can often gain vital new insights by considering different theoretical systems side by side – as fragments juxtaposed – and by being imaginatively receptive to new connections between them. Different paradigms and theories highlight and order different aspects of our world; that is their function. But in the end the socio-economic reality we seek to understand is an organic whole – more than the simple sum of discrete aspects. To deal with the challenge this represents, we should also try to add new depth to our vision by experimenting with new metaphors and combining existing perspectives in new, often less systematic, ways. At the same time, we need to recognise that the goal of a unified vision – an all-encompassing perspective – will always remain a pipe dream.

It would be easy to succumb to the myth of a lost unity – a political economy in the distant past when economists' vision was whole – and harbour the related delusion that we can recover that unity now. We might even subscribe to an economics version of Alasdair MacIntyre's famous 'disquieting suggestion' in relation to moral theory, that we are left with merely the post-catastrophe fragments of a unified conceptual scheme – one that must be pieced together by returning to the past master of a unified theory (in our case, Adam Smith rather than Aristotle).[113] In reality, though, the unity of past theoretical frameworks can be overstated; and the increased fragmentation that has occurred in modern times is not the result of catastrophe, folly or the Fall of Man. It is instead the inevitable result of the complexity of our predicament and the corresponding need for a division of labour and specialisation in ways of observing and analysing it. As Schumpeter has noted, not even Aristotle at the dawn of scientific thinking managed to create a unified 'universal science'; his was a 'compound of sciences', and 'this compound broke to pieces as the exigencies of the division of labour asserted themselves'.[114] Even Adam Smith wrote about moral philosophy and economics in separate books, however subtle the interaction between them; for he understood better than anyone the productivity benefits of a division of labour. Since his time, the number of discrete disciplines has mushroomed and, even within each discipline, there is often now a necessary fragmentation of vision. As Mirowski has pointed out, modern physics has fragmented into 'partially overlapping and yet partially irreconcilable subfields';[115] and there is to date no theoretical framework that can encompass the respective insights of relativity theory, quantum mechanics and chaos or complexity theory. Throughout science, the fragmentation of conceptual frameworks and perspectives has been both inevitable and richly productive of new insights. Fragmentation has been the price of analytical success.

The merits and necessity of fragmentation, however, should never blind us to the costs it imposes. These costs – principally distortion and compartmentalisation of vision – can be allayed only by remaining aware of the fragmentary and partial nature of even our greatest theories, and by striving always to find some new synthesis that will get us closer to understanding our complex and interdependent world.

In part II of this book, I sketch some new fragments that can hopefully point the way to a more unified political economy vision; but I admit at the outset that complete unity must remain as elusive as it is worth aspiring to. When Coleridge decided that he must postpone completion of his grand theory of the imagination (and leave it for inclusion in his never-to-be-completed *magnum opus*), he wrote himself a letter to be included in the interrupted text, in which he sadly concluded:

You have been obliged to omit so many links, from the necessity of compression, that what remains, looks … like the fragments of the winding steps of an old ruined tower.[116]

In attempting to reconstruct a more unified political economy, the Romantic Economist must accept the likelihood of a similar fate.

PART II

Fragments of unity: Romantic economics in practice

CHAPTER 5

Using organic metaphors in economics

The application of organic metaphors to civil society and the human mind (as well as to the natural world and our place in it) forms one of the great legacies of Romantic thought. This chapter begins by examining how far economists have already factored in organic metaphors, consciously or otherwise, before exploring some ways in which we can incorporate more fully the lessons of Herder, Burke, Coleridge and others. The implications of organicism for the role of nation states and value pluralism are considered in chapters 6 and 7.

Herder stands out among the Romantic organicists because he analysed *everything* through the transforming lens of organicism – including the natural world, a national people (or *Volk*), and the human mind. In each case, he saw the integrated whole as more than the simple sum of its parts, with its character and development determined by the self-reinforcing interaction of the parts; and, in each case, he argued that the role of the constituent parts is a function of their place in the unified whole.[1] So, for example, he thought that the roles of reason and perception could not be understood in isolation from each other or from the other interlocking faculties of language, emotion and imagination. As Herder put it: 'No single activity of so complex an organisation of powers as the human mind can be simply resolved into the component parts of the brain.'[2] The biological metaphor of organicism also emphasised, of course, the spontaneous growth of the whole; and, in the case of a *Volk*, Herder saw this development as reflecting both the creative interaction of the individuals within it and the 'genetic' transmission of a unifying culture and language by means of education.

Coleridge also applied the metaphor of organicism to the workings of the human mind and to the life of a nation. He saw the use of mechanical analogies to explain either of them as a travesty of the necessary interdependence and mutual constitution of component parts within each integrated whole, and as failing to account for the dynamic emergence of growth and development from within. Coleridge highlighted the limits of a reductionist explanation of wholes entirely in terms of their parts, as in the following passage quoted by Abrams:

In the world we see everywhere evidences of a Unity, which the component parts are so far from explaining, that they necessarily presuppose it as the cause and condition of their existing *as* those parts; or even of their existing at all.[3]

Elsewhere, Coleridge uses almost sexual imagery to underline the central difference between the mechanical assembly and predictable interaction of atomistic parts (on the one hand) and dynamic synthesis in an organic whole (on the other), namely that the latter is characterised by what modern economists call 'increasing returns' or 'emergent properties': 'The mechanic system', he wrote, 'knows only ... the relations of unproductive particles to each other; so that in every instance the result is the exact sum of the component qualities, as in arithmetical addition ... In life ... the two component counter-powers actually interpenetrate each other, and generate a higher third.'[4] Coleridge was careful (following A. W. Schlegel) to distinguish more generally between mechanical forms deriving their shape and motion from forces outside and organic forms developing spontaneously 'from within'.[5] This is suggestively analogous to the modern-day economists' distinction between 'exogenous' and 'endogenous' growth – depending on whether the key factors determining growth are seen as coming from outside or within the system analysed.

Herder's comprehensively organic vision included an understanding of how different organisms interlock with each other: men (each 'a cosmos in himself')[6] interact with the social organism in which they live, and this in turn interacts with the natural environment, and so on. Everything is interrelated and interdependent, with discrete organisms containing and comprising other discrete but interconnected organisms. This, interestingly, led Herder to see natural ecosystems and our interrelationship with the environment in astonishingly modern terms:

Since climate is a compound of forces and influences to which both plants and animals contribute, serving all that is alive within a relationship of mutual inter-action, it stands to reason that man, too, has a share, nay a dominant role, in altering it through his creativity ... Once Europe was a dark forest and the same was true of other, now cultivated, regions. The forests have been cleared and, as a result, the climate and the inhabitants underwent a change.[7]

Herder not only understood that we can change the environment of which we are part in ways that affect our own welfare, but also that natural ecosystems are delicately balanced organic systems, which can be destabilised by sudden interference from mankind:

> By suddenly cutting down entire forests and cultivating the soil, the whole balance of nature – which ought to be considered with the utmost care – is disturbed … The rapid destruction of the woods and the cultivation of the land in America not only lessened the number of edible birds which were originally found in vast quantities in the forests and on lakes and rivers, and the supply of fish; it not only diminished the lakes, streams and springs, but it also seemed to affect the health and longevity of the inhabitants.[8]

Such dynamic feedback mechanisms are central to modern understanding of the environment and our place in it. Writing two centuries after Herder, for example, James Lovelock sees the earth or 'Gaia' as a great self-regulating organism, and one which is in danger of being destroyed by rapid man-made changes (like global warming) that reach crucial tipping points and cross thresholds, and so cause self-reinforcing disruption that may in turn prove catastrophic for mankind.[9]

Herder's organicism has proved equally prescient of modern concerns in many areas of sociology and philosophy. Herder combined an insistence that every man has a 'uniquely individual internal structure' with the observation that he is 'not an independent entity'. Human beings are social animals, 'formed in and for society'; their role and very survival is a function of their interdependence with others. Even their thought patterns and vision are, at least in part, socially constituted, being governed by the conceptual schemes embodied in the mother-tongue and traditions of a people and transmitted by means of education.[10] Herder argued that all conscious, connected thought involves language, and that 'it is through the language of the parents that a given mode of thinking is perpetuated'.[11] This entails that men and women within a particular *Volk* are united by a common framework of understanding; but it also serves correspondingly to differentiate the thought patterns and behaviour of those growing up in different language groups or cultures. The members of one *Volk* will see and understand the world differently from those in another, since each *Volk* is endowed with a different linguistic and cultural inheritance and a distinct education system.

While economists have so far largely ignored this particular thesis of Herder's, it has – through the philosophy of Wittgenstein and others – already had a large impact on sociological and political theory. But before considering how we might apply it more directly to economics, it is useful to focus first on some ways in which modern economics has (and has not) succeeded in building in other lessons of organicism – especially the complex interdependence of economic agents and the dynamic feedback mechanisms that drive the development, growth and demise of economies and firms.

I ECONOMIC MODELS OF INTERDEPENDENCE AND GROWTH

The organic metaphor was championed by Schmoller and his colleagues in the German Historical School in their famous late-nineteenth-century battle over economic method with Menger and others (the *Methodenstreit*);[12] but they had limited success in getting the discipline of economics in succeeding generations to take seriously the need either for interdisciplinary study of interdependent economic and social phenomena or for a more organic model of individual motivation and behaviour (that is, one that recognises that preferences and beliefs are *socially* formed). Nevertheless, a number of central figures in the subsequent history of economics did come to understand the acute danger involved in focusing purely on static equilibrium analysis or on 'comparative statics'[13] (where the impact of changing a particular parameter is analysed) – namely that they both abstract too much from the crucial dynamic and emergent properties of markets to have much hope of explaining them. As a result, these same figures could see merit in thinking of economies as organic processes in which history matters. For example, John Neville Keynes – influenced by his friend Marshall – was careful to distinguish between the 'statics' and 'dynamics' of political economy: study of the former ('the main body of economic science') assumes that most factors are given and invariant, and concentrates on analysing the impact of a particular change in conditions in determining which equilibrium outcome is reached. By contrast, the equally important focus on the 'dynamics of the subject' – 'the study of economic progress' – must, Keynes thought, involve historical examination of the trajectory of particular economies; and such dynamics are better captured by using 'biological' (rather than mechanical) analogies that can do justice to the 'organic life and growth' of complex economies.[14]

Marshall himself was insistent on the importance of biological analogies. Tabb quotes him as arguing that 'economic problems are imperfectly presented when they are treated as problems of static equilibrium, and not of organic growth'; static analysis should be used only as an 'introduction to a more philosophical treatment of society as an organism'.[15] In his *Principles of Economics*, Marshall was at pains to emphasise increasing returns and economies of scale in explaining the phenomenon of self-reinforcing success in market competition. This crucially involved a realisation that the law of diminishing returns – a prerequisite of reaching equilibrium – is not always applicable to the dynamic determinants of economic success over time. Put simply, companies are often more rather than less profitable as they get bigger, so that the winner takes all – at least for a period. Marshall did not have access to modern non-linear mathematical tools to model economies of scale and increasing returns to successful competition. Instead he made use of a colourful biological metaphor of trees in a forest to explain them: the few young trees that manage successfully to force their way through chinks in the forest canopy 'get a larger share of light and air with every increase of their height, and at last in their turn they tower above their neighbours, and seem as though they would grow on for ever, and for ever become stronger as they grow'. Marshall understood well enough that eventually, of course, even the giants of the forest 'lose vitality'; competition is a continual organic process of growth and decay marked by vastly different and unpredictable rates of success.[16]

If Marshall was ahead of his time in analysing these phenomena (economies of scale and increasing returns), he was even more so in his focus on the dynamic formation of industry clusters. He understood that when by chance an industry has become established in a particular region, there is often a self-reinforcing pattern of investment in that same field by other firms in the locality. This is because of three factors: first, greater economies of scale resulting from increased local intra-industry trade (where there are high fixed costs); secondly, the advantages to all local firms of a strong local base of specialist suppliers and skilled workers; and, thirdly, what would now be called technological spillovers (or 'externalities') from the formal or informal sharing of knowledge (concerning production or sales techniques) through local networks.[17] It is exactly these factors which account for the organic growth of industry clusters like Silicon Valley.

Schumpeter also became increasingly impatient with static equilibrium analysis and the focus on efficient allocation of resources. He argued that the prevalence of monopolies and oligopolies ensures that the concept of equilibrium ('i.e., a determinate state of the economic organism, toward which any given state of it is always gravitating') is often inapplicable:

In the general case of oligopoly there is in fact no determinate equilibrium at all and the possibility presents itself that there may be an endless sequence of moves and countermoves, an indefinite state of warfare between firms.[18]

The concept of equilibrium becomes, he argued, even more irrelevant when we consider that 'in dealing with capitalism we are dealing with an evolutionary process' – an 'organic process' of change.[19] He spelled out the significance of this for economic analysis and business strategy formation as follows:

> Every piece of business strategy acquires its true significance only against the background of that process and within the situation created by it. It must be seen in its role in the perennial gale of creative destruction; it cannot be understood irrespective of it or, in fact, on the hypothesis that there is a perennial lull.[20]

Schumpeter described the constant creation of new markets and processes that drives the capitalist system as a 'process of industrial mutation – if I may use that biological term – that incessantly revolutionises the economic structure *from within*, incessantly destroying the old one, incessantly creating a new one'. Schumpeter was in no doubt that 'this process of Creative Destruction is the essential fact about capitalism'.[21] Here was a challenge that standard economists could not ignore for long. How could they explain the generation of the new ideas, products and processes that drive capitalist development? And how could they model business strategies designed to cope (through 'an endless sequence of moves and countermoves') with the organic process of creative destruction?

John Maynard Keynes, too, was alive to the possible relevance to economics of the organic metaphor. As Robert Skidelsky has argued, the following passage written by Keynes is evidence of his growing scepticism in later life about the use of mathematical models (imported from contemporary physics) to understand what Skidelsky himself calls 'the complexity, and reflexive nature, of social life':

> The atomic hypothesis which has worked so splendidly in physics breaks down in psychics. We are faced at every turn with the problems of organic unity, of discreteness, of discontinuity – the whole is not equal to the sum of the parts, comparisons of quantity fail us, small changes produce large effects, the assumptions of a uniform and homogeneous continuum are not satisfied.[22]

We can see here the dawning realisation of the central importance of the organic metaphor, and its corrosive effect on so many of the assumptions of standard economics: increasing returns replace diminishing returns; and incommensurable units of value replace the commensurable.

Over the last sixty years, there have been a number of increasingly sophisticated attempts to incorporate and build on these organicist insights of Marshall, Schumpeter and Keynes. In particular, economists have formalised the way they think about the interdependence of economic agents and the frequent spillovers of market transactions. To do this, they have developed the concept of *externalities* to model the effect, for example, of pollution or congestion (*negative* externalities) or knowledge spillovers from research or training (*positive* externalities). The essence of externalities (or spillovers) is that they entail costs or benefits that are not reflected in market prices. This means that the full *social* impact of the market transactions that produce these externalities is not normally reflected in the *private* costs or benefits of those involved in the relevant transaction. Given the standard economic assumption that agents maximise their *private* returns (on the basis of market prices), this further suggests that they will produce less in the way of positive externalities (such as knowledge spillovers) than would be optimal for society as a whole, while from the social point of view there will be an overproduction of negative externalities such as pollution.[23] So, for example, economic theory predicts that a firm will not, *ceteris paribus*, take into account the benefits (or positive externalities) that may accrue to other firms in the region when they decide whether to engage in research and development or training their staff. Nor will they take the costs of pollution from their activities into account when deciding the optimal level and method of production, if those costs fall onto people other than themselves.

Economists have used the concept of externalities to great effect. By measuring the scale of them, and by articulating the incentive problems entailed by the divergence between social and private costs (or benefits), economists have been able to suggest solutions to both the overproduction of pollution and congestion and the underprovision of training and research. One solution is to 'internalise' the externality by setting up property rights that give third parties the right, for example, not to suffer pollution, so that they must be compensated through the price mechanism if this right is infringed. Another is to tax the production of environmental bads like pollution, and subsidise the provision of social or public goods like training – all the while calibrating the level of this government intervention to reflect its impact on the level of externalities. Furthermore, economists have used the concept of (positive) externalities to model such phenomena as the geographical clustering effect that interested Marshall. When we take into account the measurable impact of technological or skill spillovers, we can begin to understand why clusters such as Silicon Valley are so vibrant.

Despite these successes, however, there are good reasons to doubt whether the theory of externalities represents a full solution to the problem of understanding the interconnected nature of human activities and interests in an increasingly congested and interdependent world. Many (if not most) externalities refer to impacts of market behaviour that lie outside the remit of economics as a discipline to explain. For example, if economists want to understand the *causes* and *nature* of the environmental feedback mechanisms that threaten to mire economic activity in increasingly negative conditions and despoil our 'given' natural endowments, they need to engage with the logic and findings of environmental science. Likewise, if they wish to understand the conditions in which we get increasing returns to training and research (or knowledge spillovers), economists need to work with those who understand the relevant technologies. As Paul Krugman has noted in *Development, Geography, and Economic Theory*, while treating the reasons for geographic clusters (or urban concentration) as 'externalities' may succeed in making 'the sources of agglomeration safe for neoclassical economics', it may also be a way of evading serious consideration of the causes behind them:

To say that urbanization is the result of localized external economies carries more than a hint of Molière's doctor, who explained that opium induces sleep thanks to its dormitive properties. Or as a sarcastic physicist remarked to an economist at one interdisciplinary meeting, 'So what you're saying is that firms agglomerate because of agglomeration effects'. Moreover, the pure-externality assumption puts these effects into a kind of black box, where nothing more can be said. Oh, you can try to measure them empirically, and there has been some important work along those lines. But you have no deeper structure to examine, no way to relate agglomeration to more micro-level features of the economy.[24]

More troubling still for standard economics as an explanatory framework is the fact that social institutions and norms often play a crucial role in defining agents' interests and ensuring that their preferences (in relation to polluting activities, for example) are 'other-regarding' or co-operative. Social institutions and norms may even cause economic agents to be guided by ethical motivations that involve a complete suspension of the private utility maximisation habits that economists presume always apply in the absence of countervailing constraints and incentives; and they may also colour the way economic actors view the data available to them. All this suggests that, when dealing with these sorts of spillover problems, economic analysis cannot be safely isolated from an appreciation of the organic interdependence of agents with their social as well as physical environment; instead, we may need to employ a truly interdisciplinary approach to understanding these challenges. The full solution to many of the problems tackled by economists under the rubric of 'externalities' may require a research interface with the discipline of sociology, as well as with environmental science, engineering and so on.

Modern macroeconomics has also recently made strenuous efforts to meet the challenge posed by Schumpeter's organic vision of the economy as a dynamic process characterised by both creative destruction and the empirically observed phenomena of knowledge spillovers and increasing (or constant) rather than diminishing returns to education, training, or investment. 'Endogenous Growth Theory' departs from standard growth theory in not being content to take the rate of technological progress either as a given variable determined *outside* the system or as leading to a merely temporary (and necessarily diminishing) impact on the long-term growth rate. Instead it models the growth rate as something that can be explained by other variables *within* the system. In particular, it seeks to model what happens when you do not get diminishing returns to any new investment or discovery. It shows, for example, how increased education or investment at the individual or firm level can – when these produce unintended positive spillovers at the social or full-economy level – lead (in certain circumstances) to a long-term rise in the growth rate. It also shows how higher investment in research and development (in a system in which patents ensure that firms can earn very high profits from any innovations they make and then plough these profits back into research and development) will lead to a permanent rise in the growth rate, if we assume constant (instead of diminishing) returns to this investment.[25]

Such models have certainly improved our understanding of the dynamics of economic growth. It is important, however, to note two salient features of them: first, they do not allow us to predict the rate of economic growth with any precision in the individual case. You can never fully predict the innovation productivity of particular research and development programmes, since this ultimately depends on the vagaries of the creative imagination. You can also never know *ex ante* the exact mix there will be between increasing, constant, and diminishing returns to investment in research or training. Any stylised assumption about this mix will be just that and abstract from the uncertainty of a future not yet created or knowable. Secondly, these models still assume as part of their microfoundations that firms and individuals are rational probability-calculating optimisers of consumption or profit.[26] But how far do these micro-level assumptions sit comfortably with full recognition of the implications of seeing the economy as a genuinely organic process, where the future is so uncertain (because dynamic and creative) that economic agents struggle to optimise anything? How far must economic agents in fact rely on a mixture of socially conditioned behaviour and imaginative guesswork? The suspicion must be that, while standard economics has succeeded in bolting onto its models some of the dynamic and organic features of growth at the macro-level, it has not faced up to what these features mean for the micro-level behaviour of agents.

If theories such as Endogenous Growth Theory have given up any pretence of making firm *ex ante* predictions that can be tested (one of the supposed advantages of the mechanical equilibrium metaphor or model), and if their micro-level behavioural assumptions seem implausible in circumstances of dynamic change, this raises the question of whether there might be a more satisfying approach to modelling economic change and the development by firms or individuals of strategies to meet and harness it.

2 COMPLEXITY THEORY: MOVING TOWARDS A NEW TEMPLATE

Since the late 1980s, a number of economists have begun to experiment with a radical reconceptualisation of economic theory, built on analogies from modern biology and the new physics that focus on the central importance of non-linear reactions and increasing returns. Many of the key figures have been associated with the Santa Fe Institute in New Mexico which has brought together scientists working on evolution, ecology, brain physiology, artificial intelligence and physics with a number of leading economists.[27]

One of the most prominent proponents of the new Complexity Theory in economics is Brian Arthur. In an influential article in *Scientific American* in 1990, Arthur argued that increasing returns are far more prevalent than most economists assume, particularly in high-technology markets; for these markets are typically characterised by high research and development costs (and high barriers to entry) but very low incremental production costs, leading to increasing returns to scale. In addition, high-technology markets (such as that for video or DVD players) display a tendency for one variant of a new technology to gain the status of industry standard, as a result of a self-reinforcing tendency for consumers to sniff out, and flock to, the competitor who initially manages to establish a slight advantage. Arthur emphasised how far such increasing returns destroy the 'familiar world of unique, predictable equilibria', and undermine the notion that the market (by tending to an optimal equilibrium) always knows best.[28] Whereas in a world of diminishing returns and given factors the economy tends towards a single predictable equilibrium (and any changes in given factors have a temporary and diminishing effect), the advent of increasing returns introduces huge uncertainty by magnifying the impact of even very small changes in initial conditions. Moreover, as Arthur puts it: 'once random economic events select a particular path, the choice may become locked-in regardless of the advantages of the alternatives. If one product or nation in a competitive marketplace gets ahead by "chance", it tends to stay ahead and even increase its lead.'[29]

The implications of all this for economics as a discipline, let alone for policy-makers, are huge. First of all, increasing-returns models can be used to explain *after the event* exactly what has transpired; but in so doing they will highlight that the *detail* and *history* of the process being analysed matter as much as the structuring rules in determining the outcome. This limits the role of purely *abstract* analysis. Secondly, where increasing returns are important, the chances that economists can make precise *ex ante* predictions look vanishingly small. As Arthur notes:

To the extent that small events determining the overall path always remain beneath the resolution of the economists' lens, accurate forecasting of an economy's future may be theoretically, not just practically, impossible.[30]

Arthur is surely right, though, not to counsel despair; for, as he concludes, policy-makers can and should have 'a feel' – an intuitive grasp – of those key threshold moments when a change of adaptive strategy would be most important or successful.[31] To this end, they can be helped by economists' models that highlight correctly the principles of dynamic pattern formation in the economy and the likely tipping points and thresholds to non-linear reactions. Economists may not be able to provide a map of the future, but they can provide some basic orienteering skills and useful pointers.

Mitchell Waldrop's book *Complexity* documents the early years of the Santa Fe Institute's ground-breaking work on Complexity Theory. It gives a glimpse of the power of applying to economic problems the full panoply of non-linear mathematical and computer techniques already used by physicists and biologists, in order to produce life-like simulations of the dynamic behaviour of markets; and, above all, it shows the suggestive power of using analogies from the study of other complex processes and systems – including evolution and the weather – where you can observe 'spontaneous self-organisation'. Instead of modelling economies as tending to some 'static, machinelike, and dead' equilibrium, these analogies suggest ways of modelling economies as 'organic' processes that are constantly evolving and 'alive', driven by a mixture of increasing and decreasing returns to constant mutations in preferences and technology.[32] For example, Waldrop describes Arthur realising that different technologies are often so heavily interdependent with each other that they tend to form 'technological webs', which 'undergo bursts of evolutionary creativity and massive extinction events, just like biological ecosystems'.[33] A contemporary example of such bursts of evolutionary creativity is personal computer technology, which is interdependent with the internet and internet shopping, which is in turn interconnected with broadband and other technologies that allow home-working and fast data transmission; and this rapid evolution of a web of new technologies (and cultures) has coincided with a massive extinction event covering high-street travel agents and the outdated technological and cultural webs associated with the typewriter (including carbon copies and secretarial typing pools) and the pen (pen shops, writing paper, ink manufacture and so on).

Among the most radical findings of the scientists based at Santa Fe was that it is often possible to simulate life-like (that is, very complex and constantly surprising) patterns in computer models where simple component parts interact with each other according to 'simple rules of interaction' – as long as these rules constrain the degrees of freedom sufficiently to pattern behaviour but not enough to lock it into one determinate outcome. The fact that scientists can model this sort of dynamism in artificial computer programs shows that in certain conditions (at 'the edge of chaos') machines and living organisms can have very similar features.[34] Coleridge and his Romantic colleagues might have been less antipathetic than they were to the idea that the human mind (or society) is essentially a 'machine' of interlocking inanimate particles if they had seen recent work on artificial intelligence; for, while Coleridge feared that 'the philosophy of mechanism' must strike '*Death*',[35] artificial intelligence machines can, in fact, produce dynamic and constantly evolving patterns that seem almost alive. Correspondingly, though, economists stand to gain little purchase on predicting exact outcomes if they use computer models of the economy that produce this sort of complex self-organising patterns, which never in fact settle into equilibrium. Waldrop reports the artificial intelligence expert Christopher Langton defending the idea that life may be 'a kind of biochemical machine' in terms that underline beautifully the conflation of mechanical and organic metaphors entailed by Complexity Theory:

The fact is that life does transcend mere matter, he said – not because living systems are animated by some vital essence operating outside the laws of physics and chemistry, but because a population of simple things following simple rules of interaction can behave in eternally surprising ways.[36]

The important conclusion is that (contrary to Coleridge's dictum) econo-mists *can* hope to simulate the full dynamic nature of social and economic organisms with mechanical models, but only if they stop trying to make them deterministic and predictive of a unique equilibrium outcome or steady-state; they need to experiment with modelling behaviour according to rules of behaviour and interaction that allow clear (and observed) patterns to form but do not imply a single optimal outcome. Indeed, it may be only by doing this that economists' models can capture the essence of an economy's dynamism; for, as Waldrop's account intriguingly suggests, this dynamism may in real life be a function of the rules of the game producing indeterminate outcomes while keeping the economy at 'the edge of chaos' – that is, at the critical phase where the degrees of freedom are neither so large as to produce chaos nor so few as to produce stasis.[37]

Perhaps the easiest way to understand economies as complex adaptive self-organising systems is to see them as like the weather: both are structured by clear rules of interaction, but in each case the tendency for small changes in initial conditions to be magnified by increasing returns renders all hope of ever reaching a static and predictable equilibrium non-existent. Waldrop reports John Holland of the University of Michigan making just this analogy and drawing out clearly the methodological implications:

Look at meteorology, he told them. The weather never settles down. It never repeats itself exactly. It's essentially unpredictable more than a week or so in advance. And yet we can comprehend and explain almost everything that we see up there. We can identify important features such as weather fronts, jet streams, and high-pressure systems. We can understand their dynamics. We can understand how they interact to produce weather on a local and regional scale. In short, we have a real science of weather – without full prediction. And we can do it because prediction isn't the essence of science. The essence is comprehension and explanation.[38]

This highlights the central clash of cultures between standard economics and a Complexity Theory (or organicist) approach to modelling economies. When Milton Friedman wrote that the task of economics is 'to provide a system of generalisations that can be used to make correct predictions', and that 'its performance is to be judged by the precision, scope, and conformity with experience of the predictions it yields',[39] he was only stating baldly what most economists seem to believe: an explanatory system is not scientific if it does not allow us to make precise *ex ante* predictions of the future (or precise *ex post* predictions of what has happened in unknown areas of the past) that can be tested. It is the longing to be able to predict the future (and then test these predictions) that makes economists so reluctant to give up the neoclassical framework of constrained optimisation models that tend towards a determinate equilibrium outcome. But as Holland pointed out, there are plenty of scientific explanations which have no such aim: in the area of evolution studies or meteorology, explaining outcomes *after* the event, simulating likely patterns in the future, and making very short-range predictions are all we aspire to – not because we wouldn't like to know the future (or test our theories rigorously), but because the complexity of interaction, positive feedback mechanisms and constant mutations (or chance events) make the future unknowable. To those of us who have had a career in financial markets, the only real mystery is why many economists persist in believing that long-term predictions of any precision are possible when – at least in the area of macroeconomics – they so lamentably and repeatedly fail to produce them. Economists are much better advised to concentrate on explaining and modelling the major dynamics and likely emergent patterns of economic systems, and spotting the probable tipping points or 'trip-wires' leading to potentially exponential change – so that, forewarned about them, we can be wisely adaptive to unfolding trends.[40] To achieve this, economists need to go beyond applying to the study of markets more non-linear mathematics and computer simulation techniques – however rich a toolkit these provide. They also need to change many of the structuring assumptions of their models.

To start with, Complexity Theory itself implies a radically new approach to modelling the micro-level behaviour of economic agents. For if we build in the assumptions discussed above – the prevalence of increasing as well as decreasing returns, the often large impact of small changes in conditions, and significant degrees of freedom in the structuring rules of an economy – it is clear that strategy formation and expectations must involve something more than rational optimisation and probability calculations. In Waldrop's book, Arthur argues that the predicament of the economic agent can best be understood by using the analogy of a game of chess[41]: despite a clear set of rules detailing the types of move that can be made, the set of possible moves a chess-player faces at the outset is effectively infinite; and, the impact of any particular move is largely unpredictable because it depends on the creative strategy and reactions of the other player. In such a situation, the player makes use of rules of thumb, and develops imagined scenarios and strategies in his head, but can rarely hope to make an 'optimal' move or calculate the probabilities of success. In economic markets, of course, the game is often more complex, because there tend to be more than two main players, and the rules of the game evolve nearly as quickly as the strategies of the players.

This chess analogy suggests several ways in which economists need to refashion their models if they want to be better able to simulate likely patterns of behaviour and explain the formation of expectations and strategies by economic actors. One element is the need to consider the essential role played in economic activity by imagination and creative choice: first, in deepening the radical uncertainty faced by players in the game of life (since uncertainty about the future is partly a function of the creative choices yet to be made by other people); and, secondly, in allowing individuals to form adaptive strategies that enable them to plot a course through the uncharted waters of the future. These issues are examined in chapters 8 and 9. But even before taking into account the role of imagination, economists can greatly improve the content of their models, by making use of a more organic understanding of the interrelation of economic life with the rest of the social organism. This will enable them to specify the rules of the economic game well enough to capture the main *social* factors, such as language, institutions and norms, which structure people's behaviour in practice; and it will help them capture the *social* element in the formation of individual expectations and strategy. For, as economic agents, we often make use of rules of thumb and route-maps that are socially formed; and we deliberate on our course of action within social networks that shape our beliefs, our expectations and even our preferences. Only by taking such socially formed rules, expectations and strategies into account can economists be fully successful in modelling the dynamic patterns likely to emerge in an economy at the macro-level, and understand at a micro-level how to model individual or firm behaviour. It is therefore to the integration of these lessons of organicism that I now turn.

3 THE LESSONS OF ORGANICISM

Many Romantics followed Herder in believing that language structures our thought and outlook. They argued that the existence of different linguistic inheritances and associated mythologies means that different peoples often differ markedly in their way of thinking, mode of vision and pattern of behaviour. Publication in 1953 of Wittgenstein's famous *Philosophical Investigations* ensured that a modern version of this view became very influential in the social sciences. Wittgenstein also argued that the structure of language provides the conceptual framework with which we analyse and think about the world. He emphasised the social nature of language (governed by socially formed rules), and stressed that language is, in A. C. Grayling's words, 'woven into all human activities and behaviour', into the 'fabric' of life.[42] Here is a truly organic model of language: socially learned language constitutes the very structure of our individual thought and behaviour, and it derives its shared meaning and rules of use from our everyday communal activities, traditional practices and inherited 'forms of life'. As Grayling puts it in his account of Wittgenstein's thought, learning a language is 'learning the outlook, assumptions, and practices with which that language is inseparably bound and from which its expressions get their meaning'.[43]

The Canadian philosopher and political theorist Charles Taylor takes a similar position and spells out some of the implications for the social scientist. He argues that there is a 'mutual dependence' between social reality and the language used by those within it to describe and think about it; language is 'constitutive' of social reality, in the sense that there are certain 'constitutive distinctions, constitutive ranges of language' that are 'inseparable' from specific practices. Crucially, this implies that each society has a unique 'web of intersubjective meanings', which is 'constitutive of the social matrix in which individuals find themselves and act', while providing a framework of mutual understanding within which members of that society can think and argue. 'Intersubjective and common meanings' are the cognitive glue of the social organism.[44] Given this, Taylor maintains that any social science that ignores the differences in intersubjective meanings between societies will be unable to explain what is going on in the terms in which the actors themselves conceived it, and unable to account for either the internal cohesion of societies or divergences between them. He is therefore deeply critical of any use of a 'universal vocabulary of behaviour' that purports to 'present the different forms and practices of different societies in the same conceptual web'. In words that mirror Herder's earlier disdain for any attempt to adopt a single cosmopolitan world view, Taylor underlines the implications of such a supposedly universal and scientific language of social behaviour: 'The inability to recognise the specificity of our intersubjective meanings is … inseparably linked with the belief in the universality of North Atlantic behaviour types or "functions" which vitiates so much of contemporary comparative politics.'[45]

This is a crucial point for the Romantic Economist. To take a contemporary example, let us make the questionable assumption for a moment that the full-blooded version of Rational Choice Theory (explaining actions in terms of the individual maximisation of self-interest or profit)[46] is a fair approximation of the way in which people in some Anglo-Saxon countries and markets conceptualise and structure their own behaviour; even if this assumption were valid, this would not imply that the same theoretical language could explain behaviour universally in all countries and contexts. The particular language and conceptual frameworks we inherit and use play an important role in shaping our beliefs; and these beliefs, in turn, have a bearing on our action. We cannot therefore hope to explain human behaviour fully with models that abstract from particular languages and cultures; and, if we try to do so, we will drain the behaviour of the significance it had for the individuals concerned.

Constructivism is a modern school of political theory that builds on many of these ideas. Most Constructivists take the view that our collective interpretations and shared language structure (at least in part) our perspectives and beliefs about the world; and since we use these perspectives and beliefs in deciding how to act in constructing society, these collective interpretations and language also structure (at least in part) the very social reality and individual behaviour that we as social scientists seek to explain.[47] In most cases, the focus is widened to include the role of shared *identities* and *norms* in influencing behaviour, and the role of *institutions* both as expressions of these identities and norms and as the means of transmitting or creating them. As Emanuel Adler puts it: 'Constructivists understand *institutions* as reified sets of intersubjective constitutive and regulative rules that, in addition to helping coordinate and pattern behaviour and channel it in one direction rather than another, also help establish new collective identities and shared interests and practices.'[48] In other words, institutions are not – as economists sometimes assume – merely 'given' constraints that regulate and pattern our utility-maximising behaviour; nor do they act only as regrettably necessary solutions to collective action problems; rather, they help embody collectively agreed norms, and these norms, in turn, constitute part of the identity and motivational logic of individual actors. To the extent that these Constructivist assumptions are true, it is clear that the social scientist will not be able to explain the social or economic behaviour of individuals without understanding the collective interpretations, normative structures and institutional frameworks that inform it. The researcher will need to become fluent in the particular narratives and discourses of the society studied. This is an interpretive process which requires both an openness to different perspectives and the sort of analytical empathy and imagination advocated by Herder and (later) Beatrice Webb.[49] We need to be able to get under the skin of other cultures to understand why their members behave as they do.

A focus on the importance of institutions and norms in ensuring the cohesion of a social organism and in guiding individual behaviour has a strong Romantic pedigree. Edmund Burke grounded his opposition to the French Revolution in large part on the essential role played by traditional institutions. In modern parlance, he was interested in both 'formal' institutions (such as parliament and church) and 'informal' institutions. The latter include traditional customs and the 'spirit of the English constitution' that, he believed, 'unites, invigorates, vivifies, every part of the empire', and breathes life into the 'dead instruments' of government.[50] Burke believed that institutions help unite a nation and nurture its organic development in three ways: first, they stabilise the *expectations* of citizens and pattern their behaviour in ways that aid social cohesion and stability. Secondly, they embody the collective wisdom and experience of generations and provide a store of *accumulated knowledge* that is the necessary springboard for learning and innovation in the present. In this way, institutions connect a society's past with its future, and help ensure an organic evolution of thought and practice. Lastly, he believed that institutions and customs embody the *spirit* of a country – the unanalysable feeling of belonging and communal identity.[51] These three separate if related functions of institutions are all pertinent to contemporary socio-economic analysis of markets and firms.

Most contemporary economists recognise that institutions play a role in helping us form stable expectations of the future by reducing uncertainty. Keynes highlighted in *The General Theory* the central problem with assuming that expectations of the future are always either rational (in any important sense) or individually formed: he pointed to 'the extreme precariousness of the basis of knowledge on which our estimates of prospective yield have to be made' when taking investment decisions; and he argued that, as a result, such decisions are often driven by 'animal spirits' rather than probability analysis, or depend on little more than conventional assumptions and the unstable 'mass psychology of a large number of ignorant individuals'.[52] His analysis of the havoc wreaked by uncertainty on the stability and rational content of expectations helped pave the way for a better understanding of the importance of institutions that guide and structure our economic expectations – whether at the macroeconomic level (for example, governments targeting full employment, and central banks credibly targeting a stable and low inflation rate) or at the level of a particular industry (for example, business associations adopting common standards).[53] Such expectation-guiding institutions are necessary to rescue us from a chaos of confused and rapidly changing expectations, and from the endemic instability that can result from such chaos. Expectations are, of course, self-reinforcing in two ways: first, because stable expectations often lead to stable outcomes that in turn reinforce the stability of expectations; and, secondly, because we often read our expectations off those of our neighbours and colleagues – leading to the sort of mass psychology swings that concerned Keynes. Complexity models can be very useful in modelling market expectations, which at a macro-level often resemble self-organising systems at the edge of chaos.

Some economists have noted a more profound sort of impact of institutions, closer to that recognised by Constructivists in the field of international relations and political analysis – namely their influence on the motivational make-up of individuals. Veblen, for example, writing nearly a century ago, defined institutions as 'settled habits of thought' or 'an outgrowth of habit', which can vary over time and place. Moreover he believed that 'an adequate theory of economic conduct … cannot be drawn in terms of the individual simply … since the response that goes to make up human conduct takes place under institutional norms and only under stimuli that have an institutional bearing'. For Veblen, 'the phenomena of human life occur only as phenomena of the life of a group or community: only under stimuli due to contact with the group and only under the (habitual) control exercised by canons of conduct imposed by the group's scheme of life'.[54] Such an organicist view is, of course, deeply antipathetic to economists' general preference for 'methodological individualism' – that is, analysing social behaviour entirely in terms of the given preferences and beliefs of individuals.

In his book *Understanding the Process of Economic Change*, Douglass North has also gone beyond the now well-established view that institutions help reduce uncertainty, and has focused on the ways in which beliefs, modes of thought, and even our preferences are socially and culturally formed by our interaction with others and by institutional conditioning. He argues that 'much of what passes for rational choice is not so much individual cogitation as the embeddedness of the thought process in the larger social and institutional context'; this context includes institutions and rules of thumb that reflect accumulated experience. In addition, North maintains that a country's education system results in 'shared beliefs and perceptions', while a 'common cultural heritage … provides a means of reducing the divergent mental models that people in a society possess'; and he emphasises the extent to which this ensures that different cultures and institutional settings produce different responses to new economic opportunities and challenges.[55]

The most arresting aspect of North's account, however, is his use of up-to-date evidence from research into brain physiology. This appears to support the view that social interaction, learning and the gradual assimilation of inherited culture actually affect the way our brains function. For example, North includes the following quotation from Merlin Donald:

Culture can literally reconfigure the use patterns of the brain; and it is probably a safe inference from our current knowledge of cerebral plasticity that those patterns of use determine much about how the exceptionally plastic human central nervous system is ultimately organised, in terms of cognitive structure.[56]

In other words, as we learn from experience and absorb our cultural inheritance of shared language, concepts and beliefs, we actually affect the physiological structure of our brains – strengthening certain pathways and letting others fall into disuse. Indeed, since the possible connections between the neurons of the brain are almost infinite, and less is hard-wired than we might expect, social interaction, education and the learning of languages (including mathematics) are actually necessary to develop the internal architecture of our minds. To the extent this is true physiologically, and to the extent that brain functions and thought processes are therefore socially conditioned rather than genetically determined, there is a manifest need for economists – just as much as sociologists and psychologists – to recognise the existence of *homo sociologicus*, an agent with socially formed preferences, identity and thought patterns. As the economist Geoffrey Hodgson has expressed it: 'The individual is not an atom, but an organic part of society: necessarily gaining interpretations, meanings and values through social interaction with others.'[57] Moreover as North explains, economists cannot hide behind the argument that competition and 'information feedback' will ensure convergence between societies on a uniquely rational form of cognition, because in an uncertain world where nothing ever repeats itself exactly and genuine novelty is rife, there is no optimal set of beliefs or mode of analysis; nor is there a uniquely efficient mode of perception to which we can gravitate.[58] Economists cannot escape the relevance of history and culture in conditioning the behaviour of individuals and firms.

The institutions we find in an economic setting also play crucial roles as repositories of knowledge and technological expertise, and as mechanisms for transmitting this expertise in a usable form to the next generation. Hodgson explains this clearly in *Economics and Utopia*:

These institutions store and support both tacit and explicit knowledge. In customs and traditions, the knowledge of the past is accreted. The idea that this knowledge can be readily extracted from its institutional carriers, and freely codified and processed by a committee or by a computer, perpetrates a fatal error of Enlightenment thought: that such matters can largely be made subject to reason and deliberation; and the mind may soar free of all the habits, preconceptions and institutions – of which in fact it is unavoidably obliged to make extensive use.[59]

The capacity of engineers, scientists and inventors to innovate is likewise largely dependent on the institutional framework within which they operate. This means that the particular institutional inheritance of a country or region – the legacy of its past – affects its development path in the future as well as its current performance. In the economists' jargon, both present and future performance is 'path-dependent'.

In all these ways, institutions, inherited customs and languages shape individual behaviour and beliefs, and ensure that the socio-economic whole is more than the simple sum of autonomous individuals interacting with one another. For this reason the organic metaphor turns out to be very relevant to economic behaviour. But organicism would lead to analysis as dangerously partial in its way as that carried out under the methodological individualism assumptions of Rational Choice Theory if it did not encompass two further important and closely related facets.

First, the individual person should not be understood as the complete creature or clone of the social organism to which he belongs. Social, linguistic and institutional conditioning only *half*-creates and *half*-constrains the individuals and firms that operate within an organic society. In the vision of Herder (though not, it is true, of all organicists of the Romantic period) every person is a unique and creative individual, albeit 'not an independent entity'. Herder's picture of an organic society is not one in which the whole has complete primacy over the individual in explanatory terms; and it is certainly not one in which the individual is subordinate to the whole in value terms. Rather, Herder saw society as the spontaneous organisation of individuals (who have a plurality of interests and capacities) into a whole that both transcends and informs their individual contribution to it. Both individual and social whole are important: each has a life of its own, and each contributes to the nature of the other.[60]

The insistence by modern Constructivists that individual agents and social structures are mutually constitutive represents, in many ways, an updated version of Herder's conception. As Jeffrey Checkel points out, this thesis of the mutual constitution of agent and structure implies that in methodological terms it is just as misleading to overemphasise the conditioning effect of social institutions and norms as it is to try and explain all social outcomes and institutions merely in terms of the actions of autonomous individuals. Mutual constitution is a two-way causal process, and we need to explain both halves of it.[61] While agents sometimes accept the institutional regime they are bequeathed, they often try to alter it according to their own image, conceptions and specific interests. They may do this, as Colin Crouch explains, by exploiting partial conflicts between inherited traditions, and by recombining into new social configurations 'contradictory components … left "lying around" within society' as a result of past compromises.[62] Moreover, individuals are neither mere cognitive creatures of the social organism into which they were born, nor limited to optimising between the different potential scripts it has to offer. Instead, they often learn from other social settings and from foreign languages and traditions to which they are exposed; and they also seek to change traditional norms and shared beliefs to reflect their own original ideas. Individuals sometimes create entirely novel institutional possibilities and new possible social orders through a combination of imaginative intuition and lateral thinking.

This brings us to another key point about any sophisticated view of organicism: it must not replace the determinism of rational choice optimisa- tion (which assumes that in any given situation there is only one equilibrium outcome) with an organic version of determinism whereby the outcome is entailed by the institutional, linguistic and social logic (or 'spirit') of the whole. Organicism in some variants has involved the idea that the 'seed' or 'spirit' of the organism determines the form into which it will grow. But the idea of a seed that determines the *full* outcome is unnecessarily restrictive, and modern organicism is better served by a metaphor of development involving *mutation*. Social organic processes can develop, like biological evolution, by means of mutations; and mutations are by their nature random and not pre-determined. Of course, as in all evolutionary systems, the mutation survives only if it helps the whole adapt and survive better in its constantly changing environment. In this sense, social evolution is path-dependent: whether a mutation survives depends on the existing interdependent features of the social organism and the environment it faces. Crucially, however, the source of mutation in the social organism is the creative imagination of the individual person who (by an often random new connection in the brain) suddenly lights upon a new idea. Moreover there are times when – as Complexity Theory suggests – from small new ideas come hugely unpredict- able and non-linear changes in the social organism as a whole, given the presence of self-reinforcing complementarities between different institutions, products, norms and so on.

Kenneth Boulding, in his book *The Image*, presents an interesting example of this idea of organic mutation and evolution in a social setting. He argues that the 'basic bond of any society, culture, subculture, or organisation is a "public image"' of what the whole should be – an image which is shared (at least to some extent) by the individuals involved.[63] It is such an image that forms, as we might put it now, the DNA of a social organism. Like DNA, such public images change over time, and Boulding maintains that they change as a result of 'viable mutant images' proposed by influential individuals. Without such mutations, he argues, society would stagnate and 'rapidly settle down to an equilibrium'.[64] The metaphor of mutation is not, of course, perfect. The individuals who adopt and propound to others the new idea that has occurred to them may *intend* to change the social whole in a purposive goal-directed way that DNA mutations do not; but given the prevalence of non-linear reactions to small changes, and the impossibility very often of second-guessing the creative decisions of others in response to a new idea, the impact of intentionality in directing social evolution can be overstated. Kenneth Arrow makes a similar point specifically focused on the evolution of institutions: while individuals may intend deliberately to change institutions in a particular way, the success of the venture is far from assured. As a result, he concludes: 'The alleged dichotomy between deliberate change and spontaneous emergence of institutions is a fallacy. They are actually the same process.'[65]

In the evolution of new templates for the future, existing institutions and languages play a further crucial role we have so far largely ignored: they provide a mechanism for individuals to deliberate and converse; to contest accepted norms, doctrines and images; and, finally, to reach at least an element of consensus. Interestingly, it is this crucial role of social institutions as cauldrons of deliberative debate that can explain why Arrow's famous so-called 'Impossibility Theorem' is nothing of the sort. Arrow demonstrated that, on some fairly standard Rational Choice assumptions, there is often no way to aggregate individual preferences into a social ordering of preferences that is anything but arbitrary. But since consistent social or group-level orderings do in practice sometimes occur, this must – as Arrow well understood – show that the Rational Choice assumptions are flawed in at least one respect; there must, in short, be a mechanism by which a social consensus is sometimes reached that helps to form and order individual preferences and values in particular groups.[66] The mechanism is, of course, democratic debate, which prior to (or during) the decision-making process affects the preferences of individuals, and orders them in political party-based clusters of shared vision and values. We influence each other by argument, by exciting sympathy or respect, and by thrashing out together shared images of the sort of society we want to build; but this is possible only because we share a common language, common conceptual reference points and a forum for joint deliberation.

4 SOME APPLICATIONS OF THE ORGANIC METAPHOR

The organic metaphor potentially offers a rich set of new insights into dynamic interdependence: of individuals with social structures; of different social structures with each other; and of social structures with their physical environment. In some sense, of course, this very richness is also the metaphor's weakness in explanatory terms. Barnard notes in relation to Herder's thought that his 'desire for fusion led at times to confusion'.[67] Seeing everything as interrelated with everything else makes it difficult to isolate key variables from less important ones. Indeed, by definition, a full appreciation of the complex interdependence of all the relevant factors would lead to an explanatory model as impenetrable and complex as the reality it seeks to explain. Moreover, even in simplified organic models, if all the key variables are assumed to exist in networks of mutual reinforcement and mutual constitution, then the absence of any independent variables hugely complicates the task of proving the direction or scope of causal relationships. It is for this reason, of course, that economists and social scientists like to abstract from organic interdependence and the mutual constitution of social structures and individual agents whenever possible, and study simpler one-directional causal relationships: so a sociologist may seek to explain (and prove) the impact of different social norms on the motivational structure of individuals; or an economist may seek to explain (and prove) the impact of individual utility-maximising behaviour on the chances of producing a collective outcome (given a certain set of constraints). These 'partial' endeavours may be successful – and more useful than an organic approach – where there are few important feedback mechanisms to complicate the relationship between agent and social structure; but by the same token they will tend to produce incorrect or misleading answers in cases where such feedback mechanisms are important. In these latter cases, it is highly likely that analysis using organicist models will do a better job of understanding the dynamic interdependence of agents with each other and with social institutions.

There are a number of interesting cases in economics where the use of analytical models based on a more organic understanding of the prevalence of positive feedback mechanisms and the interdependence of social and economic factors has already paid handsome dividends. One such is research undertaken by the 'Varieties of Capitalism' school of political economy, which studies the diversity of institutional regimes among capitalist economies, and the mutually reinforcing links between these regimes and each nation's area of economic specialisation. This school has built some quintessentially organic features into its models – in particular an understanding of the 'interlocking complementarities' that often exist between different elements of a nation's institutional matrix. Peter Hall, David Soskice and others have isolated certain self-reinforcing combinations of institutions, where the whole is in a very real sense greater than the simple sum of the parts. Indeed, they have demonstrated that each institutional element (for example, a training regime) may, when considered in isolation, have a quite different impact from the one it has when it is organically interdependent with certain other institutional features (for example, employment protection).[68] Despite these organicist elements to its theory, however, the work of this school is not designed to emphasise the organic particularity of each national system, so much as to distinguish a few stable institutional equilibria based on different types of specialisation and co-ordination between economic actors, under assumptions of a single (rational actor) model of motivation.[69]

Other examples of research where important insights flow from the application of organic metaphors can be found in fields as disparate as corporate governance, business management, economic reform in post-1989 Eastern Europe and the elucidation of the thought of key figures in the history of ideas. Taking corporate governance first, when economists look through the prism of standard economic assumptions and metaphors, they tend to characterise the firm primarily as a bundle of contracts, and as defined (following the ground-breaking analysis of Ronald Coase) by the need to reduce transaction costs. Coase's theoretical model suggests, for example, that the firm will do those things (and only those things) that can be done more efficiently within the employer–employee relationship than by trading at arm's length through the market.[70] The insights generated by such a classical approach are real enough, but they leave out much that is special about the firm. John Kay, in his extensive writings on business economics, has done much to redress the balance in a more organicist direction, with his focus on the 'internal architecture' of a business: he emphasises the crucial importance of collective and co-operative behaviour, 'relational contracts' (depending on an element of trust), 'organisational knowledge' (defined as 'more than the sum of the expertise of those who work in the firm') and 'established routines'.[71] All of these structural and cultural features allow a firm to transcend the individuals within it.

Kay's analysis is just one example of a growing tendency within the literature on corporate governance and management techniques to analyse firms (explicitly or implicitly) through the lens of organicist theory. Nor is this surprising, for firms are the great social organisms of our day. In firms, as Thomas Carlyle might have put it, cash payment is rarely a sufficient nexus to bind employees together.[72] Successful firms usually have an indefinable spirit or co-operative ethic which invigorates and unites their workforce in a way analogous to the role of national spirit in Burke's writings; and, as Burke might have said, it is a spirit you can neither analyse fully nor construct by fiat. It must grow organically and can be destroyed by revolutionary transformations such as corporate takeovers. Firms are also complex repositories of information and of cultural modes of vision and behaviour. As a result, the findings of recent research on labour mobility among investment bankers should come as no surprise: these findings suggest that home-grown talent tends to perform more effectively in firms than external recruits because it instinctively knows how to make use of the informal networks of information that pervade the company.[73] Effective companies typically grow organically, and are rarely constructed on the desk-tops of mergers-and-acquisition and head-hunting professionals.

Within management theory, Gareth Morgan's influential book *Images of Organization* makes a compelling case for complementing analysis structured by mechanical metaphors (seeing organisations as machines) with analysis through the lens of 'organismic' and 'cultural' metaphors (interpreting organisations as organisms or cultures). Morgan shows that very different aspects of firm behaviour are highlighted by the different metaphors, and that different templates for management are implied by them.[74] Some management theories (like those of Frederick Taylor) analyse organisations as if they are machines, with pre-determined functions or goals, specialist and pre-defined component parts (or job functions), and – in each case – one optimally efficient mode of operation; these theories tend to isolate the very machine-like factors they expect to see. Moreover, Morgan argues that such implicit (or explicit) use of the machine metaphor implies that the organisation 'ought to be run like a machine'.[75] By contrast, theories which analyse organisations as 'organic systems' that are 'in a continuous exchange with their environment' and 'conceived of as sets of interacting subsystems', or as cultures with 'shared systems of meaning' and common rituals and norms, open up perspectives on organisations ignored by Taylorist or other machine metaphor-based theories. The use of organic and cultural metaphors also, according to Morgan, implies quite different management priorities – the need for continual adaptation to environment, congruent subsystems and appropriate corporate cultures.[76]

The process of reform in Central and Eastern Europe following the collapse of the Berlin Wall in 1989 was a fascinating experiment in rapid transition from one type of socio-economic organisation to another. In many cases, the economic reform was carried out according to a 'Washington consensus' prescription of 'shock therapy', involving rapid trade and price liberalisation, rapid privatisation, deregulation and a swift end to state subsidies.[77] At the same time, there was a parallel attempt to construct in each ex-communist country a complete framework of government suitable for a fully functioning, market-based and multiparty democracy. To a significant extent this was achieved by the wholesale importation of a regulatory template (the *acquis communautaire*) handed down by the European Union. Scholars, politicians and voters will debate the successes and failures of this mammoth project of state-building and economic reform for years to come. As they do so, it is likely they will make increasing use of organicist themes. One early example of this was Joseph Stiglitz's attack on the Washington consensus approach to such transition reforms in 'Whither Reform?' Stiglitz couches his argument to some extent in organicist terms: he laments the tendency of the 'market Bolsheviks', with their shock-therapy remedies, to forget the lessons of Burke and Hayek about the dangers of revolutionary reforms based on abstract (mechanical) models. Stiglitz emphasises the importance for the success of an economy of what he calls 'social and organisational capital' embodying 'civil norms', implicit contracts and 'social trust'; and he insists in Burkean terms that such a social framework 'cannot be legislated, decreed, or in some other way imposed from above'.[78] Many of the vital organs of the state are informal and take time to grow. As Stiglitz puts it:

> One of the most difficult parts of a transformation, such as the transition from socialism to a market economy, is the transformation of the old 'implicit social contract' to a new one. If 'reformers' simply destroy the old norms and constraints in order to 'clean the slate' without allowing for the time-consuming processes of constructing new norms, then the new legislated institutions may well not take hold.[79]

Turning to the history of ideas, Burke's preference for the natural evolution of national institutions over revolutionary change followed directly from his organicist premises about the important role played by traditional institutions in enshrining the spirit of a country and transmitting its accumulated experience and norms. Herder likewise insisted on a 'gradual, natural, reasonable evolution of things; not revolution',[80] so as to avoid the danger of disrupting the delicate interdependence of complementary institutions and norms making up the fabric of society. More recently, Friedrich Hayek has echoed Burke and Herder in warning that the implementation of rational blueprints for radical change normally leads to a host of unintended consequences; he, too, has championed the *spontaneous* rather than *designed* evolution of the social organism. Andrew Gamble sums up Hayek's essentially organicist reasoning for privileging the retention of traditional and slowly evolving institutions as follows:

> Existing social arrangements are regarded as embodying the accumulated wisdom of many generations, and are therefore not lightly to be set aside or reconstructed. Those who created the institutions are not necessarily wiser than the present generation; nor may they have had the same knowledge. But their creations were not from nothing; they reflect the experiments of many generations and are therefore likely to embody more experience than is available to any individual or group of individuals in the present.[81]

As Gamble has also pointed out, however, Hayek crucially did not extend to the realm of economics his distrust of revolutionary reform; instead, he was quite happy on the basis of general principles to argue for sweeping economic deregulation.[82] In his book on Hayek, John Gray exposes the full extent of this contradiction in Hayek's thinking – between commitment to radical free-market reforms, on the one hand, and faith in the inherited wisdom of traditional institutions and corresponding fear of the unknown consequences of changing them, on the other. For, as Gray argues, 'To sweep away restrictions on free markets that have been in force for generations must be exceedingly risky, since we cannot know what vital social functions they may be performing'.[83] The reason for this inconsistency in Hayek's thought is that, while he believed that the market is a spontaneously evolving order that is never in equilibrium (a notion akin to modern Complexity Theory), he was always insistent that the market could thrive only if it was undiluted and unconstrained – driven solely by the actions of individual agents.[84] His determination to isolate the market from government interference made him blind to the fact that our inherited institutional framework (by embodying necessary knowledge and norms) is often just as important to the economy as it is to the rest of the social organism. The economy cannot operate without being interdependent with a strong framework of government and partly inherited social institutions.

Strangely enough, as Berlin and Rothschild have pointed out, Burke had also seen the economy as immune from his explicitly organicist vision of the nation. In the area of economics, he was quite happy to posit the existence of universal principles or 'laws of Nature', which made *laissez-faire* policies (conveniently) unavoidable.[85] There is thus, it turns out, a considerable irony in Stiglitz citing Burke and Hayek in support of his negative views on the ultra-free-market Washington consensus. In reality, neither historical figure – despite their organicist credentials in other respects – understood the central importance of seeing the economy as organically interdependent with the rest of the social fabric of society. This is an important weakness in their thought since, as the Varieties of Capitalism school has convincingly shown, many countries do, in fact, derive their principal *economic* comparative advantage over other countries from their specific *institutional* endowments.[86]

Another crucial figure in the history of economic thought that can be unmasked by a consistent application of the organic metaphor is Karl Marx. Superficially at least, there is much in Marx's economic philosophy that seems derived from organicism: he was genuinely interested in the interaction between economic activity and social institutions; he focused on the historical process of change; he emphasised the importance of social classes and collective self-determination; and he understood that creativity and self-expression are central to man's nature. Nevertheless, Marx – like the classical economists – thought that organicism has no role to play in understanding the capitalist system itself. Indeed, his invective against capitalism is derived almost entirely from seeing it through the prism of the machine metaphor favoured by classical economists. So, for example, in *Das Kapital*, he wrote that capitalist methods 'mutilate the labourer into a fragment of a man, degrade him to the level of an appendage of a machine';[87] workers, he thought, are alienated from their true nature by the inhuman functioning of the capitalist machine, which turns them into mere commodities. There was, of course, some truth in Marx's diagnosis of the wretched state of the labourer at the time of the early Industrial Revolution. His failure, however, to see that the mechanical metaphor may not be the best template for understanding or realising the potential of the capitalist system contributed significantly, I believe, to the ultimate failure of his doctrine. Despite his organicist leanings when it came to setting out his vision for a communist utopia, Marx never questioned his conviction that the capitalist market is a machine. In fact, of course, the market is an integral part of the social organism of a modern nation. It is also rife (unlike the communist system) with the capacity for individual creativity and self-expression. Indeed, it is the desire of workers in their role as consumers to create themselves through consumption (as well as the creativity of entrepreneurs and engineers) that gives the capitalist system both its extraordinary vitality and its social legitimacy. Marx never understood this individually empowering aspect of the market.

Interestingly, Marx's failure to understand the true nature of the interdependence of economic activity with the inherited framework of the nation state led him to believe that capitalism would become a purely global phenomenon, operating according to truly universal principles. In this passage from the *Manifesto of the Communist Party* (1848), Marx and Engels see capitalism as consigning local and national differences in economic specialisation and consumer taste to the dustbin of history:

The bourgeoisie has through its exploitation of the world market given a cosmopolitan character to production and consumption in every country. To the great chagrin of Reactionists, it has drawn from under the feet of industry the national ground on which it stood. All old-established national industries have been destroyed or are daily being destroyed. They are dislodged by new industries, whose introduction becomes a life and death question for all civilised nations, by industries that no longer work up indigenous raw material, but raw material drawn from the remotest zones; industries whose products are consumed, not only at home, but in every quarter of the globe.[88]

Marx was the prophet of globalisation and relished its supposed effacement of all links between the capitalist machine and local conditions and institutions. Chapter 6 will examine why Marx was largely mistaken about this, as about so much else.

CHAPTER 6

Economics and the nation state

I NATIONAL VERSUS UNIVERSAL SOLUTIONS

Most Romantics were sceptical of any attempt to reduce human thought and social behaviour to a set of universal laws. In large part, this scepticism flowed from their focus on the organic uniqueness, complexity and creativity of each individual mind or society. They believed that neither the human mind nor society could be explained as a sort of Newtonian cosmos or machine operating in a predictable fashion according to universal principles; in each case, the organic interdependence of elements, the fact of creativity and the unique trajectories of development ensure that history matters and that there are few universal laws of any significance. This represented one of the major fault lines between Romantic social philosophy and Enlightenment thought. While Hume, for example, asserted that it is 'universally acknowledged that there is a great uniformity among the actions of men, in all nations and ages',[1] and French Enlightenment figures, such as Chastellux, argued that the same rational principles could solve human problems everywhere given a basic uniformity of interests, Romantic philosophers begged to differ. Herder spearheaded a largely German reaction to the universalist thought and cosmopolitan arrogance associated in the eighteenth century chiefly with France – the dominant cultural and military power of the time.[2] He did not, for example, believe that there is a single optimal type of government that can 'be of use to all nations in the same fashion at one and the same time',[3] especially since different nations have different conceptions of the good life. Herder was particularly scathing about any attempt by European alliances to 'impose their notion of happiness despotically on all the other nations of the earth', and he argued that 'the very thought of a superior European culture is a blatant insult to the majesty of Nature'.[4]

The principal error of Enlightenment universalism was, in Herder's view, its refusal to accept the central importance of the nation state as the natural unit of social and cognitive interaction and value creation. Herder believed that artificial states built on universal principles lack the spiritual and social bonds that unite any people or *Volk* sharing a common language and a unique set of inherited traditions, institutions and perspectives.[5] At the same time, his focus on the organic interdependence of the elements comprising each nation, and its particular spontaneous pattern of development, left him deeply sceptical of attempts to impose universal ideas and templates of reform:

To force upon the traditional outlook and pattern of life of a nation a new set of beliefs and ideas, without considering their compatibility is invariably futile and frequently harmful.[6]

The moral as well as practical reasons given by Herder for nationally specific solutions and policies are summed up by Isaiah Berlin as follows:

If free creation, spontaneous development along one's native lines, not inhibited or suppressed by the dogmatic pronouncements of an elite of self-appointed arbiters, insensitive to history, is to be accorded supreme value; if authenticity and variety are not to be sacrificed to authority, organisation, centralisation, which inexorably tend to uniformity and the destruction of what men hold dearest – their language, their institutions, their habits, their form of life, all that has made them what they are – then the establishment of one world, organised on universally accepted rational principles – the ideal society – is not acceptable.[7]

The Romantic challenge posed here by Herder and Berlin is still pertinent to modern versions of Enlightenment universalism, which include not only Marxism but also – arguably – the so-called Washington consensus of economic liberalism; both these doctrines assume a single rational destiny for mankind and the need to take radical steps according to a largely identikit model to hasten its arrival. Now, even if we assign no moral value to national self-expression and diversity in themselves, there are – if Herder is right – important national differences in outlook and behaviour shaped by national differences in values, language, history and institutions; and this anthropological fact seems to entail the need for markedly different solutions in different places. John Gray makes this point, arguing that the Washington consensus should be seen as part of the misguided 'Enlightenment project' of a 'universal civilisation' – a project which has always, in his view, depended critically on false anthropological assumptions that ignore Herder's insights about cultural diversity.[8] In particular, Gray maintains that the free-market assumption that all forms of capitalism are converging (or should converge) towards a uniquely rational economic system rests on a quasi-religious universalist delusion shared by Marxist philosophy:

The idea that modern societies are much the same everywhere which is still defended by Enlightenment fundamentalists, has scant support in history. Like many of the hopes bequeathed by the Enlightenment, it is a fleeting shadow of monotheism.[9]

It is important to acknowledge, however, that while some economic policy prescriptions made by policy think-tanks and management consultants do peddle one-size-fits-all solutions that ignore local circumstances and value choices, this is not a necessary feature of standard economic analysis. Most economists defend a much narrower and more plausible version of the Enlightenment project: they see economics as informed by a universalist logic to the extent that it is founded upon a single set of basic models of motivation and interaction that accord with the general postulates of rational choice and the optimisation of preferences; but they are equally adamant that these basic models lead to different analytical and policy solutions when applied to different sets of historically given circumstances. Berlin acknowledges that even some Enlightenment philosophers, such as Montesquieu, went beyond the assumption that all men share the same broad goals (including happiness) to recognise that different historical and cultural circumstances imply considerable variation in the way these general goals are pursued.[10] Most modern economists, likewise, recognise that local circumstances colour preferences and imply historically contingent constraints to their optimisation; they accept that applied analysis has little choice but to take these local factors into account. The remainder of this chapter explores whether such pragmatism about the limitations of universal models is enough to inoculate economics against the Romantic critique, or whether a better approach could be developed.

One way of characterising the standard view of the nature of economic models is to see them as capturing universal law-like regularities (or 'tendencies' as Marshall called them) which are in practice subject to more or less important interference from unsystematic 'noise'.[11] Economists advocating this view do not deny the importance of social or cultural differences, but they operate on the assumption that the models they use can tease out systematic (rational) tendencies that are common to all the diverse socio-economic expressions of humanity. Partha Dasgupta, for example, argues (following Jack Goody):

Our societies are obviously not all the same, but as they were 'fired in the same crucible', their differences must be seen as diverging from a common base.[12]

This view, of course, poses several questions. How large is the common base of our humanity? Does systematic understanding of this common base tell you enough about actual behaviour to be useful when abstracted from local difference? Do local factors, when they are taken into account, merely constrain and qualify universal tendencies, or do they subvert their very logic? Most importantly for the argument in this chapter, is there another level of generalisation and regularity that is important in explaining individual behaviour (and designing policy solutions) short of the universal class of all human beings? In other words, is there a causally important class of factors and behavioural tendencies we can generalise about which lies between universal factors or tendencies, on the one hand, and contingent or random noise, on the other? If so, is this level that of the particular culture or nation state?

The response of a number of a growing number of economists to this last question is to allow a weak form of 'nations and cultures matter' to economic analysis: they accept that certain cultural and institutional factors that vary between nations combine with universal economic laws or behavioural tendencies (such as the optimisation of trading possibilities) to produce nationally specific (and often predictable) outcomes. By contrast, only a few economists embrace the stronger version of 'nations and cultures matter' that allows for national and cultural variation in the underlying motivational logic, vision and even rationality of economic actors. For this stronger version suggests, of course, a limit to the remit of some of the most basic microfoundations of standard economics.

Those who follow Herder in seeing nations as organic unities, in which the parts are interdependent and the whole is more than the simple sum of the parts, are clearly predisposed to think of the nation as an important explanatory variable in the social sciences, and one that reduces the scope for universal laws or policy prescriptions. Organic theories of the nation highlight the importance of national spirit and nationally specific education systems, discourses and languages in structuring the behaviour of citizens; they focus on the historically path-dependent nature of institutional development in each nation; and they underline the dangers of universal blueprints for reform that take no account of their impact on the complex interdependence of inherited habits and institutions. Interestingly, though, not all historical proponents of an organic conception of the nation state and national character have seen economics as central to this conception. Indeed, Burke, for example, went out of his way to make clear his view that economics is governed by universal principles or 'laws of Nature'.[13] Mill, likewise, failed to see the relevance of national factors to the economic 'laws of production' (which he saw as universal), despite applauding the emphasis placed by Coleridge and Herder on the role of national character and national institutions and education systems in holding societies together.[14] Mill did strongly reject a universal approach to designing the legal constitutions of countries: 'the same laws', he wrote, 'will not suit the English, who distrust everything which emanates from general principles, and the French, who distrust whatever does not so emanate'.[15] But when it came to modelling 'economic man', Mill's interest in national character evaporated. For the most part, economics has followed Mill's lead on this. However, a number of interesting figures in the history of economics (most notably in Germany) have taken a very different view – in particular, the school of 'Romantic Economics' in the early nineteenth century and the slightly later Historical School. These economists shared the view that economies are central to national organisms, and that the non-market facets of a nation structure the behaviour of its economic agents and the nature of its economy.

Before considering the merits and limitations of these historical versions of national economics (and then examining an interesting modern variant), it may be useful to note two intellectual health warnings and one organising question. The first warning is that the nation is a contested and ambiguous concept and phenomenon. As James Mayall notes, 'linguistic, ethnic, and political criteria have all been proposed, separately and in various combinations', in an effort to define it more clearly.[16] Not surprisingly, many economists and political economists shy away from using such a contentious unit of analysis. Definitive interpretations of the nation and the nature of nationalism are usually suspect, and are certainly not offered here. My intention is simply to build on the broader insights generated by using the organic metaphor to analyse the interdependence of economies with institutional and cultural factors, by showing how often the modern nation state is the key level of this organic interdependence.

The second health warning is that consideration of organic theories of the nation state is often seen as politically and ethically dubious. This is largely because some proponents in the past have envisaged the nation as having a metaphysical or ethical supremacy over the individual citizen (while often also assuming that their own nation is superior to other nations). J. G. Fichte, for example, identified the self with the *Volk* exhibiting a strong common will;[17] while Adam Müller was suspicious of private property, and believed that an individual 'cannot be thought of otherwise than within the state'.[18] Moreover, both these figures proposed the complete isolation of the national (i.e. German) economy to preserve its spiritual cohesion and economic integrity.[19] Such views have strongly distasteful resonances, particularly for generations that have witnessed (or followed) the horrors of mid-twentieth-century fascism; and these resonances account for much of the low esteem in which political economists today tend to hold national organicism in general. It is important to remember, however, that an organic analysis of nation states need not have these implications. If the metaphor is used to stress the interdependence of citizens and institutions, and the mutual constitution of individual and nation (rather than the supremacy of the latter), it is perfectly compatible with liberal views. Herder, for example, would (if alive today) fit into the most politically correct of academic faculties or political parties – being strongly anti-racist, in favour of the abolition of slavery, deeply sympathetic to the plight of the Native American and passionately convinced that only tolerance of diversity, and self-determination for every nation, can lead to international harmony.[20] Friedrich List (whose national economics is considered in section 2) was also a liberal – exiled and sentenced to prison for his democratic views, and a personal friend of Lafayette.[21] These two figures alone suggest that it would be unwise to consign to the dustbin of intellectual history all organic theories of the nation state merely because of horrors committed in the name of certain perverted versions of these theories.

Finally, as we consider different theories that take the national level of economic analysis seriously, we need to confront the question of whether this is only of historical interest, given the increasing internationalisation of markets in recent years. Even if Marx was premature in his diagnosis, there are many economists and politicians today who believe a version of his view that the forces of globalisation are now effacing all national differences or rendering them economically irrelevant and anachronistic. Any modern proponent of national economics needs to be able to show why globalisation neither necessarily erodes national differences nor makes them inevitably problematic.

2 EARLY ADVOCATES OF NATIONAL ECONOMICS

Writing in the early 1800s, Fichte and Müller shared the view that the economy is central to the national organism; and both also saw the growing economic dependence of different nations on each other through international trade as a threat to the integrity of the nation. Their advocacy of economic isolation is the defeatist counterpart of many modern anti-globalisation protestors who similarly fear that international trade will erode cultural and social diversity. Once again, Herder stands out in contrast for the clarity of his liberal organicist vision: however important he thought it is for each country to sing its own song, he believed that the transmission of culture from one nation to another is equally essential – as long as this transmission does not take the form of enforced harmonisation. He was under no illusion that a nation which isolates itself will 'get set in its own ways', retard the development of its own culture and continue in ignorance.[22] Transposed to the realm of economics, Herder's argument would translate into a strong argument in favour of international trade and the constant exchange of cultural, intellectual and technological ideas.

There are two respects in which Müller's writings on economics are of more abiding interest. First, he stressed the importance (alongside material wealth) of 'spiritual capital': by this term he meant roughly what we mean today by the 'intangible assets' or 'human capital' of nations or firms – their group or team spirit, internalised norms, innovative capacity and technical know-how. These are all facets which take time to grow and which cannot be easily measured or valued.[23] Such intangible assets (or spiritual capital) are a key area of focus today when economists, policy-makers or business-men try to nurture, or assess the value of, the creative potential of a nation or firm. Secondly, Müller insisted that Adam Smith had, in Roll's words, 'unduly generalised from English experience' to posit universal principles and solutions that ignore crucial national differences of behaviour and stage of development.[24] Bruno Hildebrand in the Historical School was later to echo Müller in this view;[25] and, while it is somewhat unfair to Smith himself, the view does point to a central danger in much Anglo-Saxon economics – namely that it tends to assume that models that capture the essence of behaviour in the USA or UK necessarily apply elsewhere.[26] Intriguingly, Walter Bagehot – the late-nineteenth-century English editor of *The Economist* – also recognised the same danger: he argued that political economy, as a 'theory of the principle causes affecting wealth', should be seen as germane only to a 'single kind of society – a society of grown-up competitive commerce, such as we have in England'.[27] Here is a grave challenge to the universalist pretensions of economics and one that econo-mists should not dismiss too lightly. In particular, it is not a given fact that the central microfoundational assumptions of standard economic models indisputably apply to all market (let alone political) behaviour in all countries.

The most interesting of the German nineteenth-century figures compris-ing what is sometimes referred to as the school of 'Romantic Economics'[28] is Friedrich List. List was a political activist, whose two principal works – *Outlines of American Political Economy* (1827) and *The National System of Political Economy* (1841) – advocated a form of national economics carefully attuned to the needs of developing industrial economies. He was a German nationalist (in the best sense) who saw industrial and infrastructure development (as well as internal deregulation) as essential not only for economic growth but also for the unification of a vibrant German nation.[29] Several related aspects of List's thought are significant for the themes of this book. First, List insisted on the importance of analysing economics at the level of the nation state, as well as that of the individual actor and the world economy as a whole: a theory of 'national economics' is needed, he thought, to complement 'individual' and 'cosmopolitan' economics.[30] Secondly, he focused above all on the necessary role of the nation state in promoting what he called the 'productive powers' of an economy. Thirdly, he rejected – in terms reminiscent of Müller – the 'dead materialism' of classical economics, which he saw as interested only in the 'exchangeable-value' of financial or trading transactions. For List it was the less quantifiable productive powers of a nation that are central to its economic potential and long-term prosperity.[31] Lastly, as Liah Greenfeld's account of his thought shows, List embraced a version of organicism in which economic factors are interdependent with other social and institutional factors, and individual economic actors and the national economy as a whole are seen as mutually constitutive.[32]

It is List's analysis of both the 'productive powers' of a nation and the state's role in fostering them that was to be very influential over the 150 years following his death. For List, the essence of national economics is that it 'teaches by what means a certain nation, in her particular situation, may direct and regulate the economy of individuals ... to increase the productive powers within herself'.[33] In his book, *Friedrich List: Economist and Visionary*, W. O. Henderson makes clear the refreshing breadth and practical flavour of List's enumeration of the productive powers of a nation, which went far beyond the factors of production normally discussed in economics textbooks. In Henderson's words, List believed that these productive powers include 'political, administrative, and social institutions, natural and human resources, industrial establishments, and public works'; and he proposed a number of key roles for the state – creating a suitable institutional structure for the economy, improving education and training, incentivising inventors and, above all, improving transport infrastructure.[34] (List was himself a very influential promoter of Germany's nascent railway infrastructure.) The emphasis in List's writings on innovation and a national system of education mirrors the central role given to them by Herder, Coleridge and Mill in their Romantic conception of the national organism. More topically still, List's emphasis on the public goods aspect of research, education and infrastructure development anticipates the focus on positive spillovers in relation to these factors in the 'New' or 'Endogenous' Growth Theory of recent years.[35]

List is best remembered today for his argument in favour of tariff protection for the infant industries of developing countries. Free trade, he argued, may be the optimal policy for the most advanced and industrially competitive economies; but it is not appropriate for developing countries, as it risks locking them into a pre-industrial specialisation in agricultural exports. To become industrialised, he believed that nations should safeguard the early development of their manufacturing base; they could best do this by developing their home market, while using temporary tariff measures to protect it from 'dumping' by established giants in the world economy intent on establishing a world-wide monopoly. Tariffs can act, he thought, as 'fortresses' protecting the fledgling industrial sector of a newly industrialising country until such a time as it can compete on equal terms with the world's market leaders.[36] List was here foreshadowing the focus in modern 'development economics' on increasing returns to investment, economies of scale in production and the need for differential trade policy for the developed and developing world.[37] His central concern that laggards in technology and industrialisation can (in the absence of intervention) become locked into poor relative performance (and that established industrial nations often enjoy enormous advantages from economies of scale) has also received much recent attention in the writings of the Complexity theorist Brian Arthur. Arthur's particular focus on the increasing returns to high-technology investment, and his suggestion that trade and industrial policy should be used to 'strengthen the national research base on which high-tech advantages are built', has served to update List's own preoccupations with securing a nation's 'productive powers'.[38]

In the second half of the nineteenth century, the Historical School in Germany led by Hildebrand, Roscher and Schmoller also embraced an organic conception of the economy as interrelated with other facets of national life.[39] This led these writers to doubt the existence of universal economic laws, and to underline the importance of understanding the role of history and local factors (or institutions) in determining economic behaviour and the development path of each national economy. It also encouraged them to stress the importance of an interdisciplinary approach to studying the interconnected aspects of a nation that affect its economy. The Historical School may ultimately have lost its battle over method, in the sense that few economists over the last century have seen economics as essentially a historical discipline where no universal laws apply. However, the influence of two economists (among others) has ensured that the discipline of economics does now largely accept that national institutions and history can sometimes matter: Veblen, who underlined the importance when explaining economic outcomes of understanding the role played by the 'institutional fabric' and 'life-history' of the relevant community or culture;[40] and Schumpeter, with his stress on the limitations of general 'economic laws' in explaining the 'historical or "evolutionary" nature of the economic process'.[41] The choice, of course, has never really been between a total reliance on universally applicable models and laws, on the one hand, and a historical and interdisciplinary analysis of the divergent and evolving institutional frameworks of different national economies, on the other. We clearly need both approaches to some extent. The quarrel is over the right balance between the two, and whether or not a hybrid approach is feasible. Above all, the methodological battle today is between those who seek to unify our understanding of the different interdependent aspects of our various historically contingent national social economies by applying a single universal set of microfoundational assumptions (based on Rational Choice and Game Theory) and those who argue that we are best advised to use different disciplinary approaches, and different nationally-specific micro-level assumptions, side by side.

3 VARIETIES OF CAPITALISM AND BEYOND

In the early to mid 1990s there was a considerable renewal of interest in distinct national systems of capitalism. Michael Porter, Michel Albert, Wolfgang Streek and others underlined the often startling differences, for example, between the ways in which the German and US economic systems operate; and they also noted the marked associated divergence in social outcomes (especially the degree of income inequality).[42] By the end of the decade, a new school of economics had emerged which sought to explain this economic and social divergence by a systematic analysis of the role of distinct national institutional frameworks in determining patterns of economic specialisation and structuring socio-economic behaviour. The canonical statement of this new approach is to be found in the introductory chapter of *Varieties of Capitalism*, by Peter Hall and David Soskice.[43] Interestingly, several of the leading figures in the new school collaborated for a time in the Wissenschaftszentrum in Berlin;[44] and it is not fanciful to see in the school's theoretical stance echoes of the preoccupations of the earlier German organicist economists and philosophers considered above.

The starting point for the 'Varieties of Capitalism' approach is that institutions matter and that the most economically significant institutions, as Hall and Soskice put it, 'depend on the presence of regulatory regimes that are the preserve of the nation-state'. As a result, there are important 'national-level differences' in economic performance.[45] To an extent, the emphasis here is on the influence of history in determining the path of each nation's development: path-dependent institutional frameworks, which reflect past ethical choices and earlier economic policy and political compromises, constrain and alter behaviour in the present and the future. The 'Varieties of Capitalism' approach does not, however, dwell much on history or politics;[46] instead it emphasises the role played by inherited institutions in resolving coordination problems faced by firms in their 'strategic interactions' with other actors.[47] Different institutional frameworks allow for different forms and degrees of coordination. In particular, the German national system of capitalism (and its close relatives in Sweden and Holland) provides firms with *non-market* institutional resources for coordination (such as business associations and works councils); whereas the US and UK systems force firms to rely much more on *market* coordination (through competition, price signals and legal contracts).[48]

To understand the significance of these differences, it is helpful to focus briefly on the lessons of standard economic analysis of so-called 'market failures'. It is now universally accepted that free competitive markets do not always reach an optimal equilibrium; the ability to reach efficient outcomes can be marred in particular by information problems, hold-up problems and externalities. Taking these in turn, information problems involve either *radical uncertainty* (a future that cannot be known or made the subject of probability forecasts) or *information asymmetries* (where one party to a market transaction or contractual arrangement has an information advantage over other parties). Important information asymmetries may exist, for example, between a firm's engineers and its managers, or between firms and their shareholders and creditors; and these asymmetries may lead to opportunistic behaviour by the advantaged party, mispricing in the market, or 'thin' markets characterised by such distrust between relevant parties that trades dry up.[49] *Hold-up problems* occur when one party in a transaction has made a 'relationship-specific investment' that may encourage the other party opportunistically to exploit the loss of bargaining power entailed by 'sunk costs'.[50] An employee who has devoted years to receiving a firm-specific training may, for example, be vulnerable to exploitation by the firm concerned, since it knows that her options for recouping her investment elsewhere are limited. As a result, a rational employee will be reluctant to invest in such relationship-specific training unless the threat of 'hold-up' can be limited. Finally, *externalities* include the positive spillovers for other firms in a sector of an individual firm's research and development or staff training. Since such spillovers (or public goods) are not normally reflected in market prices, each individual firm has no market incentive to produce them. As a result, the market will not ensure an outcome that is optimal for the sector (or society) as a whole.

Two essential insights in relation to these sorts of market failures underlie the 'Varieties of Capitalism' approach. First, it recognises that, while some market failures can be resolved by extending the reach of market mechanisms, others cannot. For example, the positive spillovers of research and development can often by 'internalised' by a market system of patents that allows firms to benefit from the spillover effects of their own research; and the radical uncertainty associated with investing in new technology can be reduced by quoted venture capital funds that diversify their investments across a large number of start-ups and provide liquid vehicles for investors. By contrast, where information asymmetries, hold-up problems and other externalities abound, the search for a market solution to market failure (or for a 'complete' contract that can remove the risk of opportunistic behaviour) is often costly and futile.[51] In these areas, only non-market institutions such as business associations or works councils can provide the degree of trust, information exchange, or sanctions against opportunistic behaviour, that is required for effective coordination. Secondly, there is a recognition that certain types of production and economic specialisation are much more prone to particular market failures than others. For example, in some markets for mass-produced or standardised products (such as clothes or TVs) – marketed chiefly on cost and with features that are clearly defined by a few key and easily observable variables – there are few information asymmetries between a firm and its clients, or between the firm's managers and its shareholders and creditors. Price signals and product or customer surveys give both client and company the information and feedback they need; and frequent publication of easily disseminated and codifiable data keeps shareholders and creditors informed of the company's trading prospects. By contrast, in the case of products that are highly complex, use non-standard technologies, or are very specific in their customer orientation (such as specialised engineering equipment or highly customised software solutions), information asymmetries between firms and clients, or between managers and providers of finance, may be much more prevalent. In these cases, it may be preferable for clients, shareholders and creditors to have the capacity to monitor and control companies through non-market mechanisms, such as board seats allowing privileged information, or business associations providing quality control and 'network reputational monitoring'.[52]

The differential ability of market and non-market institutions to solve particular coordination problems associated with market failures, together with the differential salience of these problems to different types of economic specialisation, ensures that national variations in the boundary between (and efficacy of) market and non-market institutions provide firms with advantages in different types of specialisation. This brings us to one of the central theoretical innovations of the 'Varieties of Capitalism' approach, namely its reformulation of Ricardo's famous theory of comparative advantage. Ricardo argued that each nation will benefit in efficiency terms by specialising in 'producing those commodities for which by its situation, its climate, and its other natural or artificial advantages, it is adapted, and by then exchanging them for the commodities of other countries'.[53] This theory has over the last 180 years provided the basic liberal justification for a global system of free trade, by suggesting that if each nation specialises in those industries in which it enjoys a relative factor advantage, trade should boost the average productivity, and hence the wealth, of every nation.[54] Hall and Soskice argue, however, that the theory is rendered much more plausible as an explanation of the modern pattern of specialisation across nations, if Ricardo's 'artificial' advantages are interpreted as including each nation's institutional framework. To this end, they have coined the concept of *comparative institutional advantage*, which they explain as follows:

The basic idea is that the institutional structure of a particular political economy provides firms with advantages for engaging in specific types of activities there. Firms can perform some types of activities, which allow them to produce some kinds of goods, more efficiently than others because of the institutional support they receive for those activities in the political economy, and the institutions relevant to these activities are not distributed evenly across nations.[55]

There is considerable *prima facie* evidence to support this theory. Hall and Soskice show, for example, that the marked contrast in institutional structure between Germany (with its plethora of non-market coordination mechanisms) and the USA (relying on market coordination) is matched by an equally marked contrast in technological research specialisation, as measured by patent data. Germany is, in relative terms, particularly successful at innovation in the mechanical engineering and machine-tool sectors; while the USA has its new patents disproportionately concentrated in the biotechnology, semiconductor and information technology sectors.[56]

Moreover, Soskice shows that in terms of export share, Germany is relatively competitive in a very large number of different machine-tool industries, while the USA is more competitive in an almost equally large number of service industries.[57]

To explain fully why there is a link between institutional structure and this pattern of specialisation, the 'Varieties of Capitalism' school focuses on the institutional requirements of different innovation strategies. Hall and Soskice argue that many of the USA's areas of specialisation depend for their success on *radical innovation*.[58] Radical (as opposed to incremental) innovation involves what Björn Johnson has called 'creative forgetting',[59] and a clean break with previous products and production methods and even staff; it is often dependent on *codifiable knowledge* or ideas that can be captured in academic papers, technical manuals, or mathematical formulae and, hence, can be transmitted fairly easily between organisations; and it is frequently generated by the pure-research departments of universities. The institutional framework in the USA is conducive to specialisation in radical-innovation-rich areas of production because it has a number of features which help solve the problems facing firms relying on radical innovation: flexibility in the labour market makes it easy to hire and fire research and production staff, and reallocate labour quickly; a high degree of management autonomy allows companies to make rapid decisions as new opportunities emerge; the easy availability of start-up capital and corporate restructuring allows for a rapid reallocation of capital; and large well-endowed university research departments produce a stream of original research.

By contrast, the lion's share of Germany's areas of specialisation rely on *incremental innovation*, where firms strive to update and improve the quality of existing products and technologies in order to increase pricing power and customer loyalty.[60] It is worth adding that much of the incremental innovation to be found in German companies is geared to customer-specific adaptations; and, as Bengt-Åke Lundvall explains, these tend to be triggered by insights generated from 'learning-by-doing' and constant interaction between a firm's engineers and its customers.[61] Geoffrey Hodgson makes the crucial point that such 'countless piecemeal innovations' normally involve the sort of *tacit* or *technical knowledge* that is possessed only by those 'close to the production process'; and he underlines the peculiar difficulties involved in the exploitation of tacit or technical knowledge:

Technical knowledge is highly contextual. It is often difficult to understand the nature or value of an innovation without intimate knowledge of the situation to which it relates. It is often difficult or impossible for one unit to convey to another what precisely is required. Unless there are shared ideas and patterns of experience then agents are unlikely to understand the raw data in the same terms. Because of the lack of these common conceptions, they may not, in effect, speak the same language.[62]

An institutional framework such as that found in Germany helps overcome the difficulties of using and communicating tacit or technical knowledge by providing the conditions for long-term cooperative interaction and group interpretation; in this way, it offers significant advantages for companies engaged in incremental innovation, by allowing them to exploit their engineers' tacit knowledge of their customers' specific and evolving technological needs. In particular, the German system includes safeguards for continuity in the employment of dedicated staff; significant shop-floor autonomy, coupled with works councils that facilitate cooperation, trust, and information exchange between managers and the shop-floor; non-market cooperation (through business associations) between firms in the same sector to provide the necessary specialist vocational training; and strong links between companies and specialist sector-specific research institutes.

By concentrating so much on the institutional prerequisites of innovation and learning – and especially the role of different training regimes (university or vocational-training based) – the 'Varieties of Capitalism' approach mirrors the emphasis placed on 'productive powers' by List. It is also an important contribution to understanding the 'organic process' of economic creativity and 'industrial mutation' that so fascinated Schumpeter.[63] Moreover, these are not the only respects in which the theory has an organicist and Romantic tinge. In terms reminiscent of Romantic theories of the organic and self-reinforcing interdependence of social institutions, the 'Varieties of Capitalism' theory also highlights the prevalence of 'interlocking complementarities' between different parts of a country's institutional framework.[64] As Hall and Soskice explain, 'two institutions can be said to be complementary if the presence (or efficiency) of one increases the returns from (or efficiency of) the other'.[65] So, for example, a vocational training regime (like that in Germany) works more efficiently in the presence of German worker co-determination, collective-wage-bargaining, and employment protection institutions, since these allow the employees being trained to be confident that employers will not opportunistically exploit their relationship-specific 'sunk costs', but will instead offer them long-term and well-paid employment once the training is complete. The vocational training system also works better in the presence of strong business associations; for business associations can reassure employers providing training that other companies will face sanctions if they consistently free-ride by providing no training of their own and instead poaching trained staff from other firms. Without these complementary institutions, neither employers nor employees would have the incentives to invest much in vocational training. As a result of a host of such institutional complementarities within the German (or US) capitalist system, Hall and Soskice conclude that 'the economic returns to the system as a whole are greater than its component parts alone would generate.'[66] In other words, it is not each particular feature of a system in isolation that is effective, but the self-reinforcing combination of complementary features.

This aspect of the 'Varieties of Capitalism' theory mirrors almost exactly the central insights of Herder and Coleridge, who – as examined earlier – insisted that organic unities are more than the simple sum of their parts. It also leads to remarkably similar policy conclusions. For example, Herder's warnings against a 'scissors-and-paste' approach to state-building without regard for the compatibility of the different elements being assembled[67] are matched by warnings within the 'Varieties of Capitalism' school that cherry-picking institutional features from different capitalist systems without due regard for complementarities will often be ineffective and lead to 'institutional inconsistency'.[68] There is no point in the UK trying to copy Germany's vocational training regime in the absence of the supporting institutions that such a regime requires (including employment and wage protection for skilled workers and inter-firm cooperation). At the same time, the frequently mooted liberalisation of labour laws in Germany might jeopardise the vocational training regime that is the main basis of that country's comparative advantage. Nations must carefully consider the impact of any policy changes on the system as a whole.

Another related Romantic feature of the 'Varieties of Capitalism' approach is its refusal to accept a universal template for corporate governance or economic organisation, and its refusal to believe in a common destiny for capitalist economies. It demonstrates clearly that there is no single 'best practice' against which we should benchmark every nation's institutional framework, as the EU's Lisbon agenda and the Washington consensus often seem to assume. Rather, each nation must find its own path to economic efficiency by reinforcing those elements of its institutional structure that give it a comparative advantage, while removing those that are inconsistent with the institutions on which that advantage depends. Furthermore, any general attempt to efface all national differences may not only deprive each country of its distinct competitive advantage; it may also deprive the world economy as a whole of some of its vibrancy and diversity. International trade thrives when companies and consumers can exploit differences between nations in their areas of institutional advantage; and institutional diversity helps underpin an international division of labour that leads to efficiency gains for the world as a whole.[69] We should not, therefore, expect the ever-increasing volume of world trade to lead to convergence on a single model of capitalism; rather it should lead to a renewed determination on the part of national actors to accentuate those elements of their institutional framework that give their country a distinct advantage. As Hall and Soskice put it: 'Because of comparative institutional advantage, nations often prosper, not by becoming more similar, but by building on their institutional differences.'[70] This helps explain why Marx was wrong to expect the demise of 'national industries' and the establishment of a single 'cosmopolitan character' of production.[71] It also provides us with a serious economic argument in favour of Herder's general advice that each nation should develop according to its own distinctive rhythm.

Despite these Romantic features, it would be misleading to present the 'Varieties of Capitalism' school as adopting a fully organicist approach. In particular, it does not – in the microfoundations of its model – allow for fundamental national diversity either in the motivational make-up of economic agents or in their socially learned cognitive patterns and normative goals. It allows for path-dependent differences between countries in their area of specialisation and in what therefore constitutes the optimal institutional configuration; but it still assumes that economic efficiency is the only relevant goal and that the key actors – firms and workers – are seeking to maximise their own economic interests. In other words, the underlying motivational model remains a universal one derived from Rational Choice and Game Theory. Despite occasional mention of different nationally-specific 'cognitive focal points',[72] there is very little organicist emphasis on the role of institutions, discourse and language in structuring beliefs, or on the role of different cultural norms in structuring behaviour.

These impoverished microfoundations become limiting and somewhat implausible as a set of working assumptions when trying to explain, for example, the diverse nature and role of welfare states in the various capitalist systems. There may be distinct economic advantages for firms and their workers of the different welfare and income protection systems, but it is implausible that this is the only reason for their continued existence, let alone for their origins. If we want to understand why France has a very high minimum wage that nearly everyone agrees raises unemployment (or costs the government billions of euros in offsetting tax rebates), we may not find the answer simply by looking at the economic interests of firms or even of the median voter. Instead, we may need to consider the distinctive ethical settlement between the rival claims of economic efficiency, liberty and equality in a country whose foundational motto accords *egalité* and *fraternité* an equal status to *liberté*. The behaviour of individual actors in a nation is often heavily influenced, as Boulding put it, by a shared 'transcript' or 'public image' of what the country should look like.[73] It may also be influenced by what Coleridge called the unifying 'Idea of a Constitution'.[74] Each nation may indeed have a distinct spirit – as Edmund Burke thought – influenced by its foundational texts and inherited discourse.[75] Understanding this spirit and its role should, I would argue, play a part in comparative analysis of different national political economies. For example, a full explanation of the contrasting trade-offs between leisure and working time that we can observe in France (with a thirty-five-hour working week and a statutory minimum of five weeks' holiday) and in the USA (with long working hours and very short holidays) would require us to delve deep into the role of culturally determined norms and distinctive visions of the good life. It cannot be explained merely in terms of the different interests of firms and workers.

In an incisive review of the 'Varieties of Capitalism' approach, Chris Howell argues that, for all its merits, it suffers by offering 'an extremely thin notion of politics' and by using a perspective that 'flattens history'.[76] While it builds into its models a wide array of interdependent social institutions (like education systems and welfare states), it does not seek to understand their evolution or persistence in terms of an historically aware analysis of cultural norms and political contestation. In this sense, it remains impervious to the concerns of the Historical School. Hall, Soskice and their colleagues have developed a fine set of explanations of why institutions matter to firms and may determine their area of specialisation, and why firms may (in turn) try to reinforce those institutions that help them solve the coordination problems central to that area of specialisation. But their theory does not explain how and why the institutions emerge in the first place. Indeed, it is not clear how it could explain their origins when using only rational choice micro-level assumptions (of self-interested actors); for there are well-known collective action problems inherent in setting up cooperative institutions under these assumptions.[77] This analytical lacuna is important because, if cultural norms and political agreements on value trade-offs (between efficiency and equity, for example) were responsible for the institutions emerging in the first place, the influx of new ideologies and the evolution of a new political consensus might sweep them away, regardless of the economic interests of firms and their workers. More seriously still, the 'Varieties of Capitalism' approach assumes that the interests within each capitalist system are as mutually self-reinforcing as its institutions. This overlooks the fact that within all political economies different actors have different and often incompatible interests. Any particular settlement between competing interests is very unlikely to stand for all time; and while the institutional arrangements engendered by the settlement (while it lasts) will shape interests (and economic specialisation) to some extent, they do not remove the possibility of a shift in the balance or perception of interests at a later date.

A significant related criticism of the 'Varieties of Capitalism' approach is that its emphasis on self-reinforcing systems of mutually complementary institutions and firm interests can explain stubborn divergence and stability in economic systems better than it can explain change. Hall and Soskice, for example, argue that 'institutional complementarities generate disincentives to radical change', and that national systems tend to respond to shocks by the 'institutional recreation of comparative advantage'; as a result, any change will normally be limited and path-dependent. They acknowledge that institutional complementarities 'raise the prospect that institutional reform in one sphere of the economy could snowball into changes in other spheres as well', but they assume that this serves to concentrate key actors' minds on the need to preserve the integrity of the system and tread warily in the area of reform.[78] In other words, the theory paints a fairly static picture of what are sometimes called 'punctuated equilibria'[79] in institutional configurations – generally static (because optimal and self-reinforcing) configurations, which are occasionally buffeted by shocks into a new equilibrium.

Bob Hancké and Michel Goyer have underlined the limitations of this model. They accept that inherited institutional frameworks limit the options for change because of the need for institutional compatibility; but they deny that these frameworks determine (even for a time) the optimality and therefore, in rational choice terms, the inevitability of one particular outcome or adjustment path. Instead they argue that capitalist systems are 'caught in an almost permanent process of redefinition', as actors reassess the advantages they gain from the existing institutional configuration, and exploit the 'degrees of freedom' and the 'multiple potential scripts' it has to offer.[80] At the system level, this analysis seems to lead in the direction pointed by Complexity theorists who see societies and markets as constantly evolving and self-organising systems at the boundary between chaos and stasis.[81] At the micro-level, Hancké and Goyer emphasise the capacity of actors to learn about new options, invent new possibilities, deliberate and choose between alternative strategies open to them, and generally to 'do unexpected things that do not necessarily follow directly from the institutional framework'.[82]

This argument represents something of a return to the more open and dynamic version of organicism proposed by Herder. Herder understood that the process of cultural development is the combined product of traditions transmitted from one generation to another (by education) and 'the creative operation of individual minds'.[83] Education, he thought, entails continual assimilation and reappraisal of tradition.[84] In Herder's vision, individuals are not trapped by their national inheritance; they are partly formed by it, and partly enabled by it to reinvent themselves and their nation. He also believed that other countries provide an important source of new ideas and options: indeed, if nations are not to stagnate, they must 'freely learn from one another', and keep an eye on the world about them.[85] Charles Sabel has made a similar point in relation to innovation in economic organisation: economic actors are not fully bounded by inherited cognitive or institutional structures; rather they are 'strategically self-reflective', and scan the world 'to uncover the range of potentially viable strategies'.[86]

4 GLOBALISATION AND NATIONAL ECONOMICS

By showing that growing international trade encourages the exploitation of comparative institutional advantage, the 'Varieties of Capitalism' approach offers a welcome corrective to the Marxist and Washington consensus view that all capitalism systems should, or inevitably will, converge on a single cosmopolitan economic model. There are, however, a number of reasons to expect that the broader process of globalisation (together with so-called 'Europeanisation' at the EU level) does pose at least some threat to the persistence of national differences and therefore to the relative importance of economic analysis at the national level. The negative impact of globalisation (and Europeanisation) on national particularity can manifest itself in two contrasting ways: either as an increase in the homogenisation of cultures and institutions across different nations, or as a fragmentation of the specific cultural and institutional fabric within each nation.

Many commentators have noted the problems posed by the increasing homogenisation of financial markets, which may, for example, make it increasingly difficult for Germany to retain its distinctive structure of cross-shareholdings and 'patient capital' associated with the *Hausbank* system. One set of pressures comes from the new European single currency, which may lead to significant cross-border rationalisation of the banking sector, as well as the creation of a single capital market within the euro area. More generally, companies are increasingly disadvantaged if they cannot tap into global capital markets that operate according to international accounting standards and reporting conventions; these markets, which (normally) offer plentiful cheap arm's-length debt finance, are dominated by savings institutions imbued with an Anglo-Saxon investment culture that is often suspicious of practices such as long-term cross-shareholdings and the involvement of other stakeholders in the decisions of management. At the same time as financial markets are being homogenised in these ways, companies wanting to export are faced with an increasing demand (whether under the auspices of the WTO or the EU) for harmonisation of trading standards and market regulations designed to provide a level playing-field in international trade; such harmonisation may alter the boundary between market and non-market institutions in a way that could destabilise some national models of capitalism which depend on state intervention or regulation.[87]

The main challenge to national economic diversity may, however, come from a different direction. As Howell notes, ideas 'now flow across national borders as freely as capital';[88] and, in some cases, this may represent a far greater threat to the stability or integrity of distinct national capitalist systems than does the homogenisation of capital market rules, financial market conventions, and accounting or trading standards. For if the institutional framework of each capitalist system is partly a reflection of past value choices and established political consensus, a flood of new ideas and visions of alternative life-styles from abroad may weaken the grip of inherited norms and, in Suzanne Berger's words, 're-open old lines of domestic discord';[89] this may, in turn, lead to changes in the system as a whole. It is arguable, for example, that the large number of top-level German students studying for degrees or MBAs in UK and US universities or business schools will eventually undermine the traditional management ethos in Germany; for these graduates return home having absorbed an alternative culture based more on competition than long-term commitment and cooperation, and they may be especially keen to replicate the alluring remuneration packages on offer to managers in Anglo-Saxon economies. The increasing number of talented French students in the same schools may also help to weaken the hold of the traditional 'élite coordination' system in France, based on the primacy in both public and private sectors of graduates from the *Grandes Écoles*. More generally, the pervasiveness of US television, Hollywood films and the world-wide web may serve to homogenise the dreams and preferences of consumers throughout large parts of the world. None of this, of course, means that all national diversity and particularity will disappear. Indeed, the influx of new ideas may serve, as Herder expected, to revitalise and reinvigorate national political economies rather than simply efface national differences. Nevertheless, there is little doubt that, in the age of the internet and mass mobility, we have entered into a state of flux where the boundaries between our common humanity and our national differences are changing.

In recent years, globalisation has also been associated with a rise in migration flows between different nations. This has greatly improved the scope for cultural cross-fertilisation and the emergence of new cultural amalgams at a national level; but it has also led to socio-economic multiculturalism – that is, greater cultural and economic variation *within* nation states. In truth, few nations have ever been culturally monolithic; most have always included differentiated cultures within cultures that are, at least in part, a function of historical waves of immigration. This cultural pluralism can have important economic ramifications. As John Gray notes:

Subject to constraints of geography, competition and power, different societies develop modes of economic life that express their different ways of life. Where, as in most late modern societies, there are several ways of life, there tend to be a number of distinct types of productive enterprise, expressing different family structures, religious beliefs and values.[90]

For example, the inherited family structure and traditional work ethic of many UK citizens who originate from the Indian subcontinent provide them (when combined with other general UK institutional features) with a unique set of 'institutional' advantages for many types of small business. As a result, when explaining the pattern of economic development and specialisation, the 'Varieties of Capitalism' approach increasingly needs to take seriously the comparative institutional and cultural advantages of different groups *within* each national system.

There is little doubt that economic analysis at the national level remains a crucial supplement to standard analysis of economic behaviour at the twin levels of the individual and the world market; and it is likely to remain so for as long as key elements of the institutional, cultural and normative framework within which economic agents operate are a function of national legislation and state power, national tradition and discourse, and national education systems. However, especially in the era of globalisation and mass mobility, the nation is not the only organic unit of social, economic and cognitive interdependence; we must also be alive to the implications of other levels of organic interaction. In practice, each of us belongs to a number of nested and overlapping groupings – family, region, firm, industrial sector, ethnic or religious group, nation, multinational alliance (like the EU), and the 'international community'. Each of these different cultural and institutional groups are characterised by a more or less pronounced degree of organic unity, and they interlock with each other in dynamic and surprising ways. Economists cannot safely ignore any of these levels of analysis when trying to explain some types of economic behaviour. The Romantic tendency to focus on national organisms has proven to be one of its most influential legacies in the modern era, and it remains highly pertinent today. In our post-modern world, however, the Romantic Economist should also make broader and more imaginative use of the analytic framework provided by the organic metaphor to understand the plurality of ways in which cultural and institutional factors can be interdependent with economic activity.

CHAPTER 7

Incommensurable values

I NO SINGLE SCALE OF VALUE

One of the great debates in moral philosophy is between value pluralists and value monists.[1] Pluralists believe that rival values are often inherently plural and incommensurable; by this, they mean that different values cannot be derived from a single self-consistent and universal system of principles (or from some single objective essence of the good), and cannot be compared with one another according to a single scale of ultimate value. As a result, pluralists argue that there is no one right answer as to how we should live our lives. By contrast, monists believe that value conflicts – for example, between equality and liberty or between natural beauty and economic efficiency – can be fully resolved by recourse either to a unique set of foundational principles or to the touchstone of one ultimate value. Utilitarianism is an example of a monist ethical doctrine, since it purports to provide a common currency for moral judgements, and one that can be used to solve all moral dilemmas. It aims to decide between the rival claims of alternative courses of action by weighing their consequences according to the scale of utility. In other words, it renders the consequences of alternative scenarios commensurable (that is, comparable with one another) in a single unit of account. For the most part, the Romantics railed against utilitarianism, and many of them instead supported (often inadvertently) a value-pluralist outlook.

The relevance of this debate to the Romantic Economist arises from the enduring symbiosis between standard economics and utilitarianism. Despite twentieth-century attempts to water down the utilitarian content of their models, the outlook and approach of most economists remains imbued with much of the methodology, analytical content and normative allure of utilitarianism.[2] Utilitarianism bequeathed to economics a model of individual motivation, which assumes that agents seek to maximise their own utility (or wealth). Equally crucially, the utilitarian emphasis on the moral obligation to *maximise* utility or happiness ('the greatest happiness of the greatest number') – rather than merely increase or reach a satisfactory level of happiness – was echoed by the emphasis in economics on the goal of 'Pareto efficiency'. A Pareto-efficient equilibrium is one that allows for the maximisation of the utility (or preference satisfaction) of all market participants within the confines of a system of mutually advantageous trades – that is, within the constraints of an initial distribution of wealth and abilities.[3] Furthermore, economics appears superficially to provide the utilitarian with a ready-made scale of utility, by reducing all manner of complex goods and services to the index of monetary value. As George Shackle noted in *Epistemics and Economics*, the prices established by repeated market transactions 'enable collections of the most diverse objects to be measured in a single dimension and treated as representing a scalar quantity'.[4] Indeed, Shackle continues: 'Economics might almost be defined as the art of reducing incommensurables to common terms.'[5]

Jeremy Bentham's famous formulation of utilitarianism was published in 1789, soon after Adam Smith's *Wealth of Nations* and just prior to the Romantic revolt against certain forms of Enlightenment rationalism. Bentham defined 'the standard of right and wrong' entirely in terms of the quantity of pleasure and pain: the best action, law, or institution is the one which maximises pleasure and minimises pain.[6] The Benthamite moral calculus assumes that all forms of pleasure (or utility) can be reduced to a one-dimensional standard that takes into account only such quantitative aspects as intensity or duration. In this way, the calculus can ensure that there is always a clear and unambiguous answer as to which among several alternative courses of action is morally preferable. This hedonistic version of utilitarianism was always likely to strike the Romantics as an ignoble and limited theory of value, but Bentham went out of his way to excite their ire. In the following passage, written in 1825, he underlined his philistine insistence on the complete commensurability in value terms of what Mill would later dub 'higher' and 'lower' pleasures. Arguing that the value of both is 'exactly in proportion to the pleasure they yield', he wrote:

Prejudice apart, the game of push-pin is of equal value with the arts and sciences of music and poetry. If the game of push-pin furnish more pleasure, it is more valuable than either. Everybody can play at push-pin: poetry and music are relished only by a few.[7]

Most Romantics were appalled by the utilitarian reduction of all value to quantifiable units of pleasure, and deplored the influence of utilitarian thinking on the emerging discipline of political economy. They were also scathing about the growing tendency in a market economy to see everything in terms of monetary value. Coleridge lambasted the reduction of moral claims of duty to 'debtor and creditor accounts on the ledgers of self-love', while Hazlitt insisted that there is no 'fixed invariable standard of good or evil'.[8] As John Whale notes, Hazlitt viewed sympathetic imagination as a better guide to morality – when considering, for example, the slave trade – than cold computation with the help of 'twenty volumes of tables and calculations of the *pros* and *cons* of right and wrong, of utility and inutility, in Mr Bentham's handwriting'. In particular, Hazlitt took issue with the assumption that economic gains and human suffering could be made commensurable: 'an infinite number of lumps of sugar put into Mr Bentham's artificial ethical scales would never weigh against the pounds of human flesh, or drops of human blood, that are sacrificed to produce them.'[9]

In his book *The Ethics of Romanticism*, Laurence Lockridge maintains that, at a more general level, the Romantics consciously attempted 'to revalue a world where value has seemed to be displaced'. Increasingly faced with utilitarian ethical reductionism and the industrial economy's 'commodification of value', they sought (as Lockridge puts it) to 'replenish values'.[10] Many Romantics followed Kant in seeing autonomous human beings as intrinsically valuable.[11] Coleridge, for example, strongly objected to economics' commodifying tendency to treat people as 'things' that find their level in market equilibria.[12] Wordsworth and Coleridge also followed Kant in seeing natural and artistic beauty (especially the sublime) as having particular value as symbols of a deeper reality.[13] Time and again, Romantic writers celebrated values – such as love, beauty, honour, freedom and self-expression – that are neither directly commensurable with pleasure sensations nor, in many cases, compatible with the simple pursuit of material wealth and pleasurable feelings. Usually, of course, the assertion of a plurality of values was implicitly rather than explicitly formulated in their works. Nevertheless, the powerful evocation of the special value of the natural, emotional and aesthetic aspects of life by Wordsworth and others represented an enormous challenge to Bentham's narrow theory of value.

Mill famously tried to incorporate these lessons of Romanticism into his version of utilitarianism by distinguishing between 'higher' and 'lower' pleasures. It was Wordsworth's poems that first awakened Mill to the value of aesthetic pleasures and 'thought coloured by feeling'.[14] But Mill's higher pleasures also include those that come from autonomous self-creation and the freedom to develop one's own character and potential; and it is this that makes liberty so valuable in Mill's conception of utilitarianism. Mill thought that, given the chance, civilised human beings would always choose the autonomous and free pursuit of their own dreams and 'experiments in living' as an essential element of happiness.[15] He also argued that such higher pleasures have a 'superiority in quality, so far out-weighing quantity as to render it, in comparison, of small account'.[16] Two problems with Mill's argument, however, damaged his claim to have produced a workable and more Romantic variant of utilitarianism. First, if some pleasures are *qualitatively* superior in ways that have nothing to do, even indirectly, with the long-term *quantity* of pleasure, then it is impossible to construct the sort of single scale of utilitarian value that is the main appeal of the utilitarian moral calculus to many people. Secondly, higher pleasures of the sort Mill outlines are likely to be so plural in nature as to be incommensurable with each other as well as with lower pleasures; this makes it impossible to derive an unambiguous answer as to how to choose between different types of pleasure when, as inevitably happens, they conflict with each other. A further problem with Mill's account was his conviction that higher pleasures would always be preferred over lower pleasures by agents acquainted with both – a claim that is empirically false, as any university nightclub bouncer could testify.[17]

It is not clear that Mill ever fully appreciated the scale of the damage done to the utilitarian project by his laudable recognition of what are essentially incommensurable and plural values. In part, this was because he erroneously ascribed incomparable superiority (in value terms) to higher pleasures, thereby avoiding the full implications of their incommensurability with mere pleasure sensations. Had he faced up to the incommensurability and frequent incompatibility of different kinds of pleasure, he would have understood the clear implication that there can never be one right answer as to how we should balance them. As John Gray puts it in his important account of plural values in *Two Faces of Liberalism*: 'To say of goods that their value is incommensurable does not mean that one is incomparably more valuable than the other'; rather, the recognition that different values are incommensurable means 'that, when their demands conflict, there is no settlement of the conflict that is uniquely right or best'.[18]

The contribution of Romanticism to understanding the incommensurability of values goes beyond its celebration of a plurality of values and the frequently tragic implications of conflicts between them; and it goes beyond the depiction of agonised choices between conflicting values (where no answer seems right). Equally important is the celebration of the diverse nature of past and contemporary civilisations – whether in the historical novels of Walter Scott or the philosophy of Herder; for this helped establish as anthropological fact that there are many contrasting but perhaps equally reasonable ways of life that, in Gray's words, 'embody different settlements among discordant universal values'.[19] It is a historical fact of great significance that mankind has never been able to agree across different cultures and historical periods on one encompassing and self-consistent value system that gives us a uniquely rational method of deciding on the ideal way of living. Herder was particularly insistent that each nation has its own valid interpretation of the good life.[20] As we might put it now, nations are structured by their own peculiar inheritance of conceptual and ethical traditions, and they continually redefine themselves by a unique series of deliberative social choices between incommensurable and conflicting values. To take a contemporary example, the French consensus on the right trade-off between equality and liberty is different from that in the USA: neither consensus is more rational than the other; and each consensus is an integral (but evolving) part of the social organism of the respective nation. Herder's consistent value pluralism also made him correctly wary of any linear and universal conception of progress. He argued that we should avoid judging societies according to supposedly universal and timeless criteria.[21] For Berlin, this represented one of the central lessons of Romanticism: that there is 'no single set of principles' or standards, nor any 'single ideal', that applies to all men everywhere for all time.[22]

A value-pluralist moral outlook vastly increases the scope for what Gray calls 'self-creation through choice-making'.[23] Nations or societies define their collective identity by the political choices they make about the appropriate trade-off between incommensurable values. How different societies respond, for example, in the post-9/11 world to the conflicting demands of security and liberty determines their character and identity. There is no uniquely rational answer as to how we should balance the rival and incommensurable claims of security and liberty. Any claim that security is really part of liberty (or vice versa) is usually an attempt to hide from (or obscure) the agonising choices to be made. Improved security often comes at the cost of civil liberties, and because there is no fundamental principle that tells us how to balance these values, the choice is collectively ours to make. At the individual level, too, we are constantly making identity-defining choices between incommensurable and conflicting values. When Nietzsche trumpeted 'the Death of God', and argued that there is a plurality of ethical perspectives reflecting particular interests and contexts, he was clear that this left scope for self-creation through 'the creation of our own new tables of values'.[24] He understood that value pluralism allows for the self-defining assertion of our own value choices as a free act of will. Nor in reality is this the privilege only of supermen: moral freedom is the preserve of any individual able and willing to make her own creative and character-defining choices among incommensurable and conflicting values. In the everyday moral judgements we make about how to balance the conflicting demands of incommensurable values – such as loyalty and self-interest, or love for our partner and career success – we slowly but surely define who we are and create our own particular identity.

Self-creating choice among incommensurables is rarely a one-off exercise. Since there is not one uniquely rational trade-off to be made, people often remain ambivalent and undecided; or they display inconsistent preferences over time. For example, it is sometimes seen as a mark of irrationality when voters express a preference for both much lower taxation and a better publicly funded national health service, given that it is rarely possible to meet both demands at once; but the incommensurability of personal wealth and physical health means that voters can quite legitimately possess and express these rival preferences concurrently, since they do not have the wherewithal to fix upon one optimal trade-off between them that settles the issue in their minds. Very often, too, we cope with conflicting and incommensurable demands on our time, energies, money and allegiance by developing split personalities. Because we cannot achieve a full personal resolution between the conflicting demands and perspectives implied by our various competing incommensurable roles (such as housewife, lover, mother, employee and patriot), we often develop multiple identities. As Barry Schwartz argues in *The Paradox of Choice*, this ability to adopt different personas in different situations both 'liberates us' and 'burdens us with the responsibility' of a constant need to choose between them.[25] Schwartz also points out that, in the mundane realm of market choice between different purchasing and spending priorities, we often exploit the incommensurability of these different roles and their corresponding frames of reference, and become 'creative accountants when it comes to keeping our own psychological balance sheet'.[26] We may scrimp and save in our role as housewife only to blow the savings in a profligate fashion as a mother or partner in love. This opens the way for advertisers carefully to reposition the very same goods that do not sell well in one category so that they fall under an incommensurable category more conducive to the suspension of normal budgetary logic.

Gray argues that there are two common misconceptions which make many people reluctant to accept the prevalence and importance of incommensurability.[27] The first misconception is that, if different social ways of life really embodied radically different settlements between incommensurable values (and were structured by what Taylor calls incommensurable 'conceptual webs'[28]), these ways of life would not be mutually intelligible. This idea that incommensurability (if true) would necessarily lock us into particular historical or nationally-specific moral and conceptual outlooks – without any capacity to become culturally bilingual and rationally debate their respective merits – is a post-modern exaggeration that tends to absurdity. As Herder reminded us, we can with the help of historical imagination and empathy understand other moral and conceptual systems and incommensurable ways of life; and those within each way of life can, and should, freely learn the benefits of other perspectives.[29] Incommensurability does not imply mutual unintelligibility or the impossibility of moral progress. Instead, it implies that we can never reduce all moral and conceptual outlooks to one master outlook, without a loss of ethical and cognitive texture.

The second related misconception is that incommensurable values leave no room for reason in ethical debate. As Gray argues, this would be true only if the sole form of reasoning admissible were the deduction of consistent and unambiguous conclusions from a single all-encompassing and harmonious system of moral principles.[30] In fact, of course, reason has a much more flexible role. We can admit that there is an irreducible element of creative or radical choice among incommensurable values – choice that cannot be fully determined by rational argument – without in any way implying that such choices must be made for no reasons. When we make political decisions about how to balance the incommensurable values of security and liberty, for example, there is much room for rational analysis and debate about the full implications of various choices and the actual extent of unavoidable trade-offs. Many tragic choices look less tragic when we have analysed fully all the relevant options and implications. Rational analysis may suggest that we can avoid conflict between the values in certain ways; it may also present us with evidence of so sharp (and inevitable) a trade-off between them that we are minded to change our instinctive moral position. Reasoned argument can in this way alter our initial weighting of incommensurable values and enable us to make more informed choices between them. What it cannot do – if values are genuinely plural – is to render them commensurable according to one harmonious system or scale of values, and so pinpoint one optimal trade-off. It is this remaining element of moral indeterminacy (as well as different rational analysis of the facts) that explains why different countries make different trade-offs between security and liberty, and why these trade-offs change in the light of new events. The destruction of the Twin Towers in New York in 2001 altered the ethical settlement in the USA, partly because it provided new information about threats; but partly, also, because the images of that day so corroded the image that Americans had of their own security and place in the world, and so captured their imaginations, that they collectively chose to redefine the character of their nation by altering the balance of its values. There were other equally rational courses of action. The choices were made for reasons, but they also represented a free choice of political identity.

Value pluralism – and the degree of moral freedom it implies – is often shunned as an idea because, in this age of reason and science, we have come to prefer the certainty of moral absolutes that promise definite answers to the dilemmas we face. Furthermore, some Romantics and other opponents of utilitarianism have taken absolutist positions of their own: they may see art, beauty, honour, or love as incomparably valuable – as supreme values that should never be traded off against other lesser values; or they may hold certain individual rights to be absolute constraints on the behaviour of others that should never be compromised whatever the consequences. The fairly obvious tendency for such moral absolutism to lead to tragic consequences is, of course, one of the main appeals of utilitarianism, since it assesses the relative value of different actions entirely in terms of their overall consequences. The utilitarianism of Bentham and his followers, however, exhibits a different sort of fundamentalism – the absolute conviction that there is only one intrinsic good or ultimate source of value, namely pleasure or utility. Utilitarian fundamentalists argue that all we need to know is which of several options produces the greatest utility or pleasure for the greatest number, and it is then ethically mandatory that we pursue that option; they are content to see individual rights violated – or artistic and cultural icons smashed – if, all things considered, this allows for more utility or pleasure overall.

In practice, of course, many utilitarians are cultured and nuanced thinkers who have sought, like Mill, to build other values into their conception of utility: happiness or utility are said to involve satisfying whatever preferences individuals happen to have (including for autonomy, honour, artistic integrity and so on). This broad-minded conception of utilitarianism is certainly more appealing than Benthamite fundamentalism in one sense; but what it gains in psychological plausibility and moral eclecticism it loses in analytical bite. 'Utility' becomes a vacuous hold-all concept for whatever we desire or value. On this account, utilitarianism becomes little more than a model of rationality focusing on the consistency of preferences and analysis of consequences. It is no longer a substantive doctrine that can give unambiguous answers to moral dilemmas. Moreover, if the main remaining contribution of utilitarianism to moral decision-making is the insistence that rival objects of desire (whatever they are) can and should always be made commensurable in a single unit of account (such as monetary value), then it serves only to obscure the very real ethical dilemmas we face when making choices. As Gray puts it:

It is not impossibly difficult to render the goods that make up happy human lives into a utilitarian notation. The price of doing so, though, is to drain significance from some of the deepest conflicts that ethical life contains.[31]

The incorporation of value pluralism into analysis of economic decision-making and policy choices involves then a rejection of both ethical absolutism and utilitarianism: no values or rights are held to be so supreme as to constitute overriding constraints or goals, whatever the consequences and regardless of other values; and there is no assumption made that we can (or should) reduce all values to one finely calibrated index of ultimate value. Indeed, one of the great lessons of Romanticism for economics is the need to recognise how often we must make agonised choices between conflicting and incommensurable values. The value pluralism promoted by the Romantic Economist also recognises, however, that these agonised choices should, in a sane world, be made following reasoned analysis of the context of choice, and not as some uninhibited and random acts of will. To this end, it is useful to examine how far it is possible for economists to fashion decision-making tools and measures of policy success that combine explicit formulation of necessary value choices with rational analysis of the relevant facts. Many of the practical economic decisions made by individuals, as well as policy decisions taken by government, require radical choice between incommensurable values. All too often at present, these essential character-defining value choices are obscured in a welter of analysis of consequences – consequences that are assumed to be commensurable and measurable according to a pre-agreed system of value. It is a key role of the Romantic Economist to find ways of making explicit the value choices we face in these situations, and then to further the required ethical debate by providing rational analysis of the implications (in relation to each value) of the different possible trade-offs.

2 THE MEASUREMENT AND ETHICAL DEFINITION OF POLICY SUCCESS

It is generally agreed that democratic and liberal governments should aim to promote the welfare of their people. But how should we define welfare or well-being? And, is it the only relevant goal for public policy, or one among several? If welfare is taken axiomatically to be the sole goal of public policy, it often quickly becomes seen as a hold-all concept for everything of value – including wealth, leisure, sensual pleasure, liberty, equality of opportunity, dignity, autonomy, job satisfaction, strong communities, high educational attainment and a vibrant arts sector. There are two problems with such a catch-all definition: first, a unitary measure of success in promoting welfare is clearly impossible across so vast a canvas of essentially incommensurable items; and, secondly, such an umbrella formulation of welfare provides us with no way of deciding the relative importance of the diverse and frequently conflicting values included within it.

There are two theoretically interesting alternatives to such muddled thinking. The first is to revert to an updated version of Benthamite fundamentalism and assert, as Richard Layard does in his book *Happiness*, that we should judge the relative merit of different intermediate moral and practical goals by whether they improve our feelings of pleasure and happiness – as measured by surveys of reported happiness and scientific analysis of brainwave patterns.[32] By settling in advance that there is only one *intrinsically valuable* good – happiness – so that everything else in the above list of welfare-enhancing factors is of purely *instrumental value*, and by producing tolerably successful methods of assessing the level of happiness, this approach promises to give us clear-cut answers as to how we should lead our lives and construct government policy. The second approach championed by the Romantic Economist is radically different: it starts from the assumption that we should recognise – and celebrate – the plurality of intrinsic values (and even a plurality of incommensurable ways of being happy); and it argues that we should therefore dispense both with a unitary all-encompassing concept of welfare and with the mirage of finding a single scale of ultimate value. It then advocates making explicit the variety of incommensurable and often conflicting goals potentially important to us, while underlining the need to make identity-defining choices concerning the relative weights we want to apply to them when making decisions; and, finally, it proposes that we should support and supplement these value choices by analysis of our success in meeting each specific goal under different scenarios. But before we consider how this second (Romantic) approach might be put into practice, it is useful to analyse first the shortcomings of the standard economics attitude to welfare and its measurement: this takes neither the Bentham–Layard nor the Romantic Economist route, but instead assumes a particular version of the muddled 'hold-all' conception of welfare.

Standard economics tries to stay out of ethical debates as much as possible. It takes the path of least ethical resistance by simply assuming that improved welfare is the central goal relevant to economic policy and that welfare is synonymous with the satisfaction of people's preferences (whatever they may be). The usefulness of this formal definition of welfare is twofold: it avoids substantive ethical controversy;[33] and it suggests that efficiency in the satisfaction of market-expressed preferences must be an important contributory goal. Furthermore, to the extent that the satisfaction of market-expressed preferences is a large component of welfare, it would seem to follow that Gross Domestic Product (GDP) measures of growth in the economic output produced to satisfy such preferences should represent a reasonable proxy for progress in welfare. Suddenly, the whole problem of defining welfare, and measuring progress in it, seems resolved. We can assume that the preferences people actually express in the market reveal to us what is important to their well-being; and, since we can render the satisfaction of these various preferences commensurable thanks to the market prices freely paid by consumers, we can measure the aggregate level of well-being by means of GDP statistics.[34]

Most economists (but many fewer policy-makers) are aware that there are huge problems with these loose assumptions, and especially with taking measures of economic growth as proxies for progress in welfare. Shackle is not alone in noting that the general use in economics of 'hold-all variables' such as GDP necessarily abstracts from the rich complexity of economic activity. As he put it:

Economics is the supremely ingenious device for eliciting scalar quantity from vast heterogeneous assemblies of qualitatively incommensurable things. But this trick only serves certain purposes. It submerges detail, not abolishes it.[35]

In many areas, of course, policy-makers need to have a method of gauging the aggregate scale of market output, and for this limited purpose GDP measures (and other such hold-all variables) can fit the bill. What is suspect, however, is the extent to which GDP growth has become seen by policy-makers as a social goal in itself – with little trouble being taken to consider its real make-up and significance.

There are several specific reasons why measures of economic activity are poor proxies for progress in welfare, under any normal definition of welfare or well-being. Some of these relate to the frequently tenuous link between whether something is traded (on the one hand) and its contribution to our well-being (on the other). First, there are many non-traded goods (such as leisure, friendship, or clean air) essential to our well-being but not measured in the GDP series. Secondly, there are many traded goods (such as pornography, gambling, or fashion accessories) that some would argue have a negative or, at best, small positive impact on welfare, but which may well exceed in market-value terms such essentials as clean water or refrigerators. Furthermore, many other traded goods (such as locks for doors and windows, roadside noise barriers, or high-factor sun cream) represent regrettable necessities that are not desired for their own sake, but are needed to deal with the burgeoning costs of social and environmental degradation – costs which are themselves not subtracted from economic growth measures.[36]

It can be argued, however, that this mismatch between market coverage and contribution to welfare is only the beginning of the problem. More seriously still, the weighting of different traded goods in GDP measures is determined by their market price: in other words, the various goods are made commensurable by the prices established for them by repeated trades. While objective in one sense, weighting by market price is highly suspect when used to construct a measure of welfare. This is because the price of goods is determined as much by their scarcity as by their subjective value to consumers, which explains why caviar is usually much more highly priced than fruit in season or clean water. The latter basic necessities of life may be more important to our general well-being but, while plentiful, their price is low; and they consequently count for little in GDP statistics. Furthermore, the weighting given to goods in measures of economic activity is more a function of the wealth of those buying them than of the strength of the desires of those concerned. In this respect, GDP growth is a better measure of increases in the desire-satisfaction of the rich than of the average citizen.[37] As Michael Todaro has shown, in many developing countries the richest 10 per cent of the population capture about 35 per cent of the national income, and the richest 40 per cent enjoy over 70 per cent of the income.[38] The position is similar in the USA: Todaro notes, for example, that between 1977 and 1989, the richest 1 per cent of the US population enjoyed 60 per cent of the *growth* in post-tax income.[39] With such huge inequality, it is quite possible for GDP to rise sharply, with little or no improvement in the real incomes or welfare of even a majority of citizens.

Some economists advocate adjusting GDP growth measures to take account of inequality for utilitarian reasons: they assume (plausibly) that income has a diminishing impact on utility or happiness as it gets larger, and therefore argue that we should give a greater weight (in average welfare terms) to growth in income of the poorest quintile of society than to that of the richest. Such a 'poverty-weighted' index (to use Todaro's terminology) may capture better the rise in average levels of welfare or utility, and it undoubtedly increases the political salience of poverty reduction.[40] The problem with this approach from the point of view of standard economics, however, is that there is in practice no scientific way of deciding what is the right relative weighting to give to increases in the wealth of richer and poorer people; this is because there is (as yet) no agreed way of calibrating the impact of increasing wealth on the level of happiness, welfare, or utility (however defined) of different sections of the population.

The value-pluralist response of the Romantic Economist to the issue of inequality-adjusted indices would, of course, be rather different: first, it would involve asking why we should be limited to relying on a purely utilitarian justification for taking poverty into account, since equality may have an intrinsic value beyond its contribution to levels of happiness or well-being. Secondly, it would involve pointing out that, given the incommensurability of the different values concerned, there is not even in theory one correct answer as to what moral weighting should be given to poverty reduction. The trade-offs between aggregate wealth maximisation, economic liberty and equality of distribution are often violently contested political issues; and the decision of how to balance these incommensurable values helps define the character of a nation. If the job of the economist in such cases is to support the political decision-making process, then this may be best achieved by providing a range of alternative statistical series that analyse the implications for policy priorities of giving different weights to the different values or goals, while also examining the effects of different policies on our success in meeting each of the various goals. So, for example, economists should perhaps, as a matter of course, analyse the impact of different economic policies in terms of both normal wealth-weighted GDP statistics and (what Todaro calls) an 'equal-weights' series (that gives an equal weighting on the basis of share of population to wealth increases of rich and poor); and to these might also be added a range of 'poverty-weighted' measures.[41] Only then can politicians and voters make an informed choice of what value weight they wish to give in their policy deliberations to poverty reduction versus aggregate wealth increases, and decide what are the right policies to reflect their choice of value trade-off.

In general, the Romantic Economist will argue that we should, wherever possible, make available disaggregated data, which analyse the impact of policy in respect of each relevant goal separately – rather than deciding ahead of time how to weight these goals to reflect their notional contribution to some catch-all goal of welfare. Disaggregation enables decision-makers to assign their own relative value weights to the different incommensurable goals in the light of the analysis presented. The self-defining choice of value weighting is often as crucial to policy formation as the analysis of relevant empirical data and factual context. For this reason, the value weighting should never be simply assumed *ex ante*, nor buried in the assumptions of a 'hold-all' statistical series. Instead, the need for value-weighting decisions should be made explicit, and the option given to assign different weights to different components of any composite index.

An example of this in action is the UN *Human Development Index* (HDI). The HDI is formed from three sets of indicators measuring health (based on life expectancy at birth), educational attainment (a combination of literacy rates and school enrolment ratios) and the standard of living (represented by real GDP data *per capita*). The index is usually presented as a simple average of these three dimensions.[42] Since, however, the disaggregated data is also made available, it is straightforward to apply different weightings to the different component variables, thereby creating different series that explicitly reflect different choices of value trade-off between health, education and wealth. This general approach can be extended to other areas, so that we can measure the effectiveness of different policy regimes against various distinct non-market goals (such as civil liberties, gender equality, environmental footprint and artistic opportunities), allowing a separate choice then to be made (informed by this analysis) of what relative value weighting we wish to assign to each goal. In his book *The Green Economy*, Michael Jacobs argues in a similar vein for using disaggregated quality-of-life indicators:

> Economic performance must be assessed using a variety of indicators, each showing in its own terms one aspect of what is considered important. It is true that in many cases these will move in opposite directions, making it difficult to say whether, 'overall', society is getting better or worse off. But this problem is not erased by the use of a single indicator, it is simply hidden within its calculations. It is much better that changes in the different indicators are out in the open, where they can be seen. We can all then make our own judgements on whether any given change from one year to another represents progress or not; and economic policy can be decided accordingly.[43]

It should be emphasised that what is being suggested here is not some deliberate confusion between ethics and scientific analysis, but rather the avoidance of such confusion by ensuring that important ethical decisions of how to weight different goals are neither determined inadvertently by the market weighting and market pricing of different forms of preference satisfaction, nor buried in the working assumptions of statisticians. John Neville Keynes and Lionel Robbins were fully justified in distinguishing carefully between *positive* analysis of facts (what *is*) and *normative* or ethical consideration of goals (what *ought to be*). The problem is that, whenever economics is applied to produce practical policy recommendations, it must combine both positive and normative analysis in some way. As Keynes put it: 'no solution of a practical problem, relating to human conduct, can be regarded as complete, until its ethical aspects have been considered.'[44] Although, economists generally accept this, the standard response within the discipline is still to try to minimise ethical controversy in applied analysis, by assuming that the only goal that matters is improved welfare, and that we can read off what welfare entails from market-expressed preferences. Moreover, loath even to admit the possibility of interpersonal comparison of utility or happiness, the standard approach to *welfare economics* (as normative as most economics gets) fights shy of questions of the distribution of income and wealth, privileging instead the uncontroversial goal of making 'Pareto improvements' – where someone is better off but no one is made worse off. This limits even welfare economics fundamentally to trying to engineer the most efficient market solution to a social problem for any given initial distribution of wealth or abilities.[45] It is true that the goal of market or Pareto efficiency can be conjoined with many different initial distributions of income or other endowments, so that it can be a potentially useful (and uncontroversial) adjunct to politically inspired and controversial redistribution measures.[46] But still little attempt is being made by economists themselves to marry ethical reasoning with economic analysis. This can have disturbing implications if what Amartya Sen dubs the 'engineering approach'[47] to constructing efficient solutions in a market context comes to be seen by policy-makers as providing practical blueprints for what *ought* to be done – without any serious attempt being made at any stage to define the full range of appropriate social goals to be taken into account.[48]

An explanation for the evident disinclination on the part of most economists to engage with serious ethical debates is suggested by an illuminating passage in Milton Friedman's famous essay on 'The Methodology of Positive Economics'. While prepared to admit a role for 'normative economics' – when carefully distinguished from the 'objective science' of 'positive economics' – he ventured the following opinion:

[In] the Western world, and especially in the United States, differences about economic policy among disinterested citizens derive predominantly from different predictions about the economic consequences of taking action – differences that in principle can be eliminated by the progress of positive economics – rather than from fundamental differences in basic values, differences about which men can ultimately only fight.[49]

Friedman assumes that in many cases differences of policy relate to different predictions about what constitutes the most efficient means to reach agreed goals. Clear up such factual questions, and the policy issue will be settled. Friedman may often be right about this; but there is nevertheless something depressingly limited and pessimistic about the vision of politics and social choice that his words betray. Good government is not merely a function of scientifically well-founded and technocratic solutions to agreed goals. Countries (like Sweden and the USA) often define themselves by the radical choices they make between incommensurable and conflicting values. These value choices are the essence of politics – the product of vigorously contested and socially constructed political discourse and debate. Moreover, even if there is no uniquely rational solution to the trade-offs between incommensurable values, there are valid reasons for making particular value choices. It is simply wrong to argue that decisions about the acceptable trade-off between liberty and equality, for example, can be settled only by a fight. Consensus on ultimate values can and does emerge through a process of rational debate, imaginative empathy and democratic voting. The contention of the Romantic Economist is that there is much that economics can do to illuminate this value debate, both by carefully separating factual and value judgements (and making the need for the latter explicit), and by supplying the analytical wherewithal to make informed choices between incommensurable values.

This ethics-support role for economics was, to some extent, foreshadowed in Robbins' famous *Essay on the Nature and Significance of Economic Science*. The essay is most often quoted for its definition of economics as a positive science, and for its declaration that economics is 'fundamentally distinct from Ethics'.[50] What is less often noted is Robbins' equally strong twin insistence that we cannot in any way evade the necessity of ethical choice, and that economics can provide the 'solvent of knowledge' to help us make such choices. As he put it:

There is nothing in Economics which relieves *us* of the obligation to choose. There is nothing in any kind of science which can decide the ultimate problem of preference. But, to be completely rational, we must know what it is we prefer. We must be aware of the implications of the alternatives. For rationality in choice is nothing more and nothing less than choice with complete awareness of the alternatives rejected. And it is just here that Economics acquires its practical significance. It can make clear to us the implications of the different ends we may choose.[51]

It is sad that, in the seventy years since Robbins wrote, this noble call for economics to inform our ethical choices has largely been ignored by economists determined to insulate their science from ethical controversy by treating preferences and goals as simply 'given'. To see an example of how this could be rectified, and how positive analysis and ethics can work side by side – each informing the other – it is instructive to consider a non-standard approach to cost-benefit analysis.

The standard approach to cost-benefit analysis starts from the core assumptions of welfare economics: it treats welfare as a unitary concept – its content defined by revealed preferences and its components weighted by market valuations – and it takes Pareto efficiency as the central goal of policy. Cost-benefit analysis involves, however, two important extensions of welfare economics: first, it dispenses with the restrictive criterion of *actual* 'Pareto improvements' (where the alternative chosen over the status quo must make someone better off without making anyone worse off), and instead adopts the so-called 'Kaldor–Hicks' or *potential* 'Pareto-improvement' criterion (where something should be done if the aggregate gains are large enough that they could in theory be used to compensate all the losers and still leave some better off).[52] In other words, a policy is recommended if it produces *net* benefits, even if there are some losers, and even if potential compensation to them is not actually paid. Secondly, cost-benefit analysis extends the practice of rendering goods commensurable according to monetary price to *non*-market goods, in an attempt to determine the full *social* (that is, market and non-market) costs and benefits of particular policies. It does this by various methods, chiefly by assigning a notional 'willingness-to-pay' value to non-market goods on the basis of how much it is estimated people would pay (given the chance) – for example, how much they would be willing to pay to retain an area of outstanding natural beauty or be free of aircraft noise.

It will be quickly apparent that standard cost-benefit analysis of this form has many of the same flaws as a decision tool that GDP statistics have when used as measures of welfare. Most importantly, standard cost-benefit analysis ignores all ethical goals other than welfare, and assumes that all forms of welfare are commensurable in value terms according to the single scale of monetary value. What is more, this commensurability assumption is now applied even to items (such as natural beauty or absence of aircraft noise) often considered incommensurable with each other (and with money) and not normally traded in markets. This is despite the psychological implausibility of the idea that people can pick a unique 'willingness-to-pay' price out of the air without the informational context provided by repeated market transactions. In addition, cost-benefit analysis (as normally constructed) is a rich person's charter: for as Daniel Hausman and Michael McPherson point out, the poor will be willing to pay less than the rich to avoid airport noise or a road through their neighbourhood because they have less money to spend.[53] This matters since a potentially Pareto-efficient outcome (the highest net benefits available) recommended by cost-benefit analysis may in fact cause considerable losses for some (often the poorest) in society. In these ways, cost-benefit analysis can produce answers that are highly debatable from an ethical point of view – making significant claims about how we ought to balance incommensurable values, while effectively recommending redistribution of benefits in the name of aggregate gains. As a result, I would argue that we should not pretend that cost-benefit analysis can remain aloof from ethical debates.

Fortunately, it is possible to take on board many of these problems through a more nuanced (and Romantic) approach to cost-benefit analysis, specifically designed to support policy decisions that involve choices between incommensurable and conflicting values. In their book *Policy Analysis*, David Weimer and Aidan Vining outline what they call 'multigoal analysis'.[54] This involves specification of the different *values* that society may wish to take into account (for example, equality, liberty, human dignity and natural or artistic beauty); the specification of particular *goals* designed to embody these values (for example, equality of opportunity, preservation of civil liberties, poverty reduction and environmental or artistic heritage preservation); and the design of specific *criteria* for judging success in respect of these goals. Armed with such criteria, the policy analyst can gauge the advantages and disadvantages of each policy alternative in relation to each of the goals. Unless one alternative is better in relation to all the goals specified, the analyst can then show how different weightings attached to the different values (and implied goals) will give different answers as to which policy should be chosen. In this way, there is no attempt to render incommensurable values commensurable to produce one 'right answer'; and there is full account taken of a plurality of values. At the same time, the need for identity-defining choices of how to balance values (and goals), and so weight the costs and benefits in relation to each of them, is made explicit.

Multigoal analysis recognises that, when choosing among different policies, we need a combination of *scientific analysis* of positive and negative implications in relation to each relevant goal and *pure ethical choice* of what relative value weighting to assign to the various incommensurable goals (especially when they conflict with each other). Moreover, multigoal analysis has a further advantage for policy-makers and society: by not taking values as already 'given', it recognises that, in the words of Weimer and Vining, '*specifying the appropriate weights for goals is more commonly an output of, rather than an input to, policy analysis*'.[55] As Robbins argued in his *Essay*, we often cannot rationally decide what weighting we wish to attach to different values and goals until we have applied the 'solvent of knowledge' to the debate. For example, we may instinctively think, as good environmentalists, that all the remaining Amazonian rainforest should be sacrosanct, or that no more whales should be killed, because of the intrinsic value of these endangered habitats and species. When presented with information, however, showing that a small controlled loss or cull could produce huge benefits in relation to some conflicting goal that we have previously ignored or to which we have assigned a low weight, we might adjust our value preferences and downgrade a strong constraint to a highly weighted goal. There remains, of course, no optimal trade-off between such incommensurable goals. Knowledge does not remove the obligation to make a radical choice; but it is only rational to make such identity-defining choices for reasons we have considered.

3 CONSISTENCY AND INDIFFERENCE

Those who see GDP statistics as measures of social progress, or use the standard version of cost-benefit analysis as a decision tool, are guilty of assuming that welfare is the only relevant value and that its components can be made commensurable with each other according to the scale of monetary value. But is the rest of standard economics similarly guilty of ignoring problems raised by the plurality and incommensurability of values and preferences?

On the face of it, it seems that great pains have been taken to inoculate the main body of economic theory against the virus of value pluralism and incommensurability. After all, as Robbins made clear in his famous *Essay*, most modern economists start from the assumption that we have no practical way of making comparisons between people of the amount of happiness (or utility) they receive even from the same good or the same amount of money. As a result, these economists avoid all *cardinal* measurement of magnitudes of utility, and ensure that their theories depend only on the less controversial *ordinal* ranking of preferences.[56] Robbins argued that 'the fact that individuals can arrange their preferences in an order' is one of the 'indisputable facts of experience', and one which forms the very 'foundation of the theory of value'.[57] He continued:

From this elementary fact of experience we can derive the idea of the substitutability of different goods, of the demand for one good in terms of another, of an equilibrium distribution of goods between different uses, of equilibrium of exchange and of the formation of prices.[58]

It is indeed the case that upon the simple assumption that each individual can rank his preferences (whatever they are) according to an individual scale of relative valuation, and that these ordinal rankings can be compared between people, rests much of the edifice of modern economic theory – from indifference analysis and demand curves to Rational Choice Theory. The assumptions are supplemented by some supposedly self-evident axioms of rationality designed to ensure the consistency of preferences: for example, it is assumed that preferences are *transitive* so that, if I prefer A to B and B to C, I logically must also prefer A to C.

One of the central applications in economics of the ordinal ranking of preferences (combined with the consistency axioms of rationality) is the construction of *indifference curves*. An indifference curve represents a continuous series of possible combinations (of two goods) among which a consumer is indifferent. It is assumed that the consumer can rank in order the value to him of all the different potential combinations of the two goods, and thereby reveal a number of distinct 'indifference' series of combinations – with the consumer indifferent in each series between all the combinations (of the two goods) it represents. Each series is assumed to form a line or curve – and all combinations on that line provide the consumer with the same overall preference-satisfaction (or utility). It is assumed that a complete *indifference map* can be constructed showing different (parallel) curves, each representing a different amount of total preference satisfaction or utility. A consumer will always prefer to be at any point on the indifference curve (or series of combinations) that provides him with the most overall preference-satisfaction or utility available. When combined with a budget line (defined by the total size of the budget and the ratio of the prices of the two goods), the full set of indifference curves can be used to predict the optimal choice for the consumer – which will lie at the point at which the most attractive indifference curve (from an overall utility point of view) just intersects with the budget line.

The question of interest to us is whether this sort of analysis based on the ordinal ranking of preferences is compatible with a value-pluralist conception of markets in which the preferences revealed by each agent are both incommensurable with those of other agents and (sometimes) incommensurable with each other. As Gray correctly argues, one of the virtues of markets is precisely that they allow economic agents 'with different or incompatible goals', and 'animated by rival and (in part) incommensurable values', to engage in mutually advantageous trades.[59] Moreover, providing that each individual can still produce a consistent ordering of her own market-expressed preferences (whatever they may be) according to her own particular value scale, standard economic models based on ordinal preference rankings seem to have no problem accommodating an *interpersonal* plurality of values. Problems do start to emerge, though, when we realise that each agent is often having to work with a plurality of conflicting and incommensurable values or objectives of her own: for this implies that there is no uniquely rational trade-off between the values from the individual's point of view, and no one rational answer as to how she should rank her relevant preferences. The incommensurability of values or preferences does not, as we have seen, preclude an individual from comparing them loosely with each other, and making choices between them for reasons. It does, however, imply that she is very unlikely to have the sort of finely calibrated personal scale of relative valuation that the complete and consistent preference rankings used in indifference analysis would require. The choices we have to make are often agonised, and there may be equally good reasons for making quite different choices, given that there is no single scale of ultimate value to which we have access. Moreover, there are times when we are literally unable to make choices between conflicting incommensurable values – paralysed by our inability to decide and our unwillingness to accept the tragic losses involved in choosing any particular option, since the losses are not compensated *in kind* by the advantages of that option.

Suppose, for example, that a parent is trying to decide between continuing to earn a salary in her chosen profession and looking after an infant for zero, one, two, three, or four years – with salary received now, and salary per year on return, falling in proportion to the time spent on parental leave. Stripped of the tacit assumption underlying ordinal preference rankings, that the person concerned has a single ultimate touchstone of value (such as pleasure) that can provide one right answer as to the correct trade-off ratio between salary and time with the child, it is likely that the parent will find it very difficult to articulate an ordinal ranking of all potential combinations. The choice between the incommensurable values of parental duty and income is likely to be agonised, and the boundary of 'indifference' between levels of salary and amounts of time with the child may well not form a precise line. There may be combinations the parent knows she would not accept (fairly little time off and a much lower return salary) and other potential choices she knows she would accept (lots of time off and a still high return salary); but there may also be a large range in the middle where she is unsure of what self-defining trade-off she would wish to make. It may, in other words, be impossible to draw an indifference curve with any precision since the boundary of indifference – or rather indecision – is wide. The word 'indecision' is more appropriate than 'indifference' here because, when choosing between incommensurables, there is often no choice of trade-offs to which we are indifferent; instead we are agonised by any choice we make, and may regret and immediately want to revise it. Indeed, if we are truly indifferent in the normal sense of the word, it is usually through a sort of Existentialist resignation that any actual choice we make is random rather than precisely calculated, in the sense that we could equally rationally have made a number of dramatically different choices. Moreover, it is important to note that in the case of incommensurable values, there are often important minimum thresholds (in this case, of time with children or of salary) below which we are unwilling to make any further trade-offs. As a result, such indifference curves as we can draw may well exhibit the sort of kinks that make it even less likely that there is one optimal choice, or a unique equilibrium, when we know the budget line (or in this case, the conditions of employment determining the actual substitution ratio of time off and salary).

One response to this argument would be to allow that consistent and continuous rank-ordering of preferences may be difficult in the few areas of severe incommensurability involving such values as a parental duty to spend time with one's children, which by definition involve the agent being unwilling to substitute the value freely for money or traded goods. But, a defender of standard economics might continue, it is unlikely that such problems would occur in the case of most frequently traded goods, which we are used to thinking of as substitutable in the context of market exchange, and used to rendering commensurable in value terms according to the scale of market price. This defence might be illustrated, for example, by a market including sea tuna and fish-farmed salmon: here presumably it is plausible that we can introspectively have a good idea of our substitution ratio between the two types of fish based on our taste, so that indifference curves could be drawn. With a budget line known (based on the total money available and the price ratio of the fish), we could then derive the best available outcome in terms of a particular combination of tuna and salmon to maximise the satisfaction of our preferences for the two fish taken together. In such a case, surely, it is also reasonable to expect that preferences are consistent (and transitive) and that indifference curves will form clear-cut lines allowing us to predict the effects of changing the budget line. It seems obvious that there can be no question here of moral indeterminacy – of needing to make self-creative choices between incommensurable values. If we are in two minds about this question, it must be because we haven't done our homework; for there is a right answer out there. Furthermore, it is surely reasonable to expect some consistency over time: we don't change our preferences for one fish over the other from one day to the next, either randomly or because we are in agonies of indecision; or, rather, if we do, the changes will average out over time – so that across a population the indifference curve will be steady for long enough to allow us to make useful predictions.

Even in such inhospitable territory, however, I would argue that value pluralism can rock the edifice of consistent preference rankings and indifference analysis to its foundations. It may be true that fish are subjectively commensurable in taste terms and objectively commensurable in price terms, but incommensurable values can still attach to them. Suppose, for example, that some individuals are exercised about the impact of fishing the tuna on dolphin populations or on the survival of indigenous Pacific peoples who depend on them for subsistence-level fishing; and suppose that fish-farmed salmon becomes tainted by scares about radiation fallout from Chernobyl; and suppose, further, that a new fashion dictates that all the best hosts must serve tuna tartar. In these cases, the actual preferences we reveal by our market choices are a product of a series of complex self-defining trade-offs between incommensurable, and often conflicting, environmental, health, status and taste concerns. Revealed preferences and current price tags may provide mere snapshots of a maelstrom of unstable incommensurable value trade-offs. There may be no reason to expect consistency of preferences over time or even at a particular moment. For if the essence of incommensurable and conflicting values is that there is no one right trade-off ratio between them, why should we expect a fully consistent and complete ordering of preferences to exist at all? And – even if one does miraculously appear – why should it last for more than a moment in time?

If this analysis is correct, value pluralism seems to present a significant problem for much standard economic theory wherever important incommensurable and conflicting values attach to market-traded goods. Even the central axioms of rationality – consistency (including transitivity) of preferences – used in economics and Rational Choice Theory begin to look questionable. Unless we make the 'utilitarianism-lite' assumption that each individual has access to a single internal and incontrovertible scale of value that can render all his preferences part of a self-consistent system, it is not clear why we should privilege the consistency (and transitivity) of preferences as a hallmark of rationality. And, even if – by theoretical fiat – we insist on consistency at any moment in time, it is still not clear why we should expect revealed indifference curves to tell us anything more than the state of play at one moment. Unless there is some external evidence of stability in the trade-offs made between the relevant incommensurable (and conflicting) values, despite the absence of a uniquely rational answer for each individual as to what those trade-offs should be, it seems unwise to expect indifference curves to provide any basis for predicting consumer behaviour. Indeed, the suspicion must be that much of the dynamism and unpredictability of markets is caused by the constant redefinition of desired trade-offs between incommensurable and conflicting values.

It might be argued that instability in the trade-offs made by *individuals* between the incommensurable values attaching to market-traded goods is perfectly compatible with the relative stability over time of indifference curves at *group level*. The assumption might be that changes from the status quo are likely to be random and that, since random variations in large groups cancel each other out, an indifference curve based on a snapshot of the current average trade-off between two values across a population may be a reasonable guide to future behaviour. If, however, the presumed consistency of ordinal rankings over time is based simply on the law of large numbers, it is hardly a robust criterion for prediction. For it makes the highly unrealistic assumption that there are no society-wide or market-wide influences on the formation of values or on the construction of reasons for changes in preferences. In fact, of course, it is precisely the *social* formation of value-weighting decisions between incommensurables that helps give both the impetus for change and some stability in preferences over time. In addition, market actors themselves try to influence others in making these self-defining choices through image-based marketing and advertising. In this sense, value choices and the creation of preferences become endogenous to the social or market system being studied. We cannot simply assume that the preferences are 'given', because they are constantly being formed and reformed – in part by the very processes we seek to explain.

In conclusion, moral indeterminacy in a world of plural and incommensurable values introduces indeterminacy in consumer preferences and behaviour; and it also gives great scope for the social and market construction of value trade-offs and preferences. Economic analysis needs to be as alive as advertising agents and marketing directors are to the role of images, fashions, debates and socially constructed norms in redefining (and stabilising) our preferences. The individual creation of identity through consumer choice between incommensurable items, and the creation of social preference structures by social actors and market firms, must both fall within the scope of economic analysis. For the complaint made by Kenneth Boulding in a speech nearly forty years ago (and quoted by Tabb) remains highly pertinent:

One of the most peculiar illusions of economists is a doctrine that might be called the Immaculate Conception of the Indifference Curve, that is, that tastes are simply given, and that we cannot inquire into the process by which they are formed.[60]

CHAPTER 8

Imagination and creativity in markets

At the dawn of the Romantic era, Herder wrote: 'Of all the powers of the human mind the imagination has been the least explored, probably because it is the most difficult to explore.'[1] The Romantics who followed did their best to remedy this, with brave if unsystematic attempts to elucidate the nature of imagination – the faculty they saw as central to our very humanity. Coleridge, for example, asserted that the imagination is 'the distinguishing characteristic of man as a progressive being', and 'the indispensable means and instrument of continued amelioration'.[2] He described the imagination as a divine gift, which 'stimulates to the attainment of *real* excellence by the contemplation of splendid Possibilities … and fixing our eye on the glittering Summits that rise one above the other in Alpine endlessness still urges us up the ascent of Being'.[3] Some 150 years later, Bronowski was to speak in somewhat similar terms in his book, *The Ascent of Man*. For him, 'cultural evolution is essentially a constant growing and widening of the human imagination'; art and science both 'derive from the same human faculty: the ability to visualise the future, to foresee what may happen and plan to anticipate it'.[4] Imagination is, of course, more than this power to visualise and anticipate a different (often idealised) future and be motivated by it. It is also, as Shelley articulated, the basis of sympathy – of our ability to transpose ourselves into 'the place of another and of many others', to see the world from their point of view, and feel their pleasure or pain.[5] Equally importantly, the imagination is the source of human creativity: it is, in Coleridge's words, the 'true inward Creatrix', building something entirely original – whether nightmare or dream, implausible or quite possible – 'out of the chaos of the elements or shattered fragments of Memory'.[6]

In the mid-nineteenth century, Matthew Arnold expressed an increasingly widespread view that 'free creative activity' – the business of the imagination – 'is the true function of man'.[7] By this time, however, the 'two cultures' divide had become pervasive – exacerbated by the narrow rationalism of Bentham and his political economy followers, with their infamous antipathy to the imagination, and by the equally immoderate counter-offensive against political economy mounted by Coleridge, Carlyle and others. The most damaging legacy of this divide has been the tendency of those on both sides to undervalue the role of imagination and creativity in the practical world of economics and business.[8] This chapter makes a sustained attempt to counter this tendency, by building on the insights of Schumpeter, and Buchanan and Vanberg, into the economy as a 'creative process',[9] and then exploring how to make imagination central to the microfoundations of economics – central, that is, to our analysis of how individual economic actors construct choices, form expectations and create strategies.

The argument developed here owes much to George Shackle's philosophy of economics. As Shackle notes, 'Imagination and Reason are the two faculties that make us human', and yet economics has almost entirely ignored imagination in favour of the predictability of instrumental rationality.[10] This denial of the central importance of creativity and imagination at the level of the individual economic actor is intimately related to the mechanical conception of markets at the system level as allocative mechanisms tending towards equilibrium. Standard economics relies on equilibrium-based models that are, in the words of Waldrop, 'static, machinelike, and dead';[11] and this reliance is implied by (and implies) a similar mechanical model of human reasoning on the part of *homo economicus* in the microfoundations of these models. *Homo economicus* employs cold deductive (and instrumental) logic to optimise within a closed system of given factors and preferences; and his (or her) interface with the uncertain future is largely limited to the rational calculation of risk in the form of historically determined probabilities. System and individual, on this account, both behave predictably – tending to the rational optimisation of given factors. By contrast, the moment we highlight the creative and imaginative vitality of much of the everyday thinking of individuals in an economic environment – the role of creative perspectives, the creation of new ideas, preferences and blueprints, and the creative delineation of possible strategies and outcomes for the future – it is clear that we need to model economic interaction at the system level as a dynamic and evolving process, with radical uncertainty about the yet-to-be-created future at its centre. Likewise, fully appreciating that the economy is a dynamic and creative process implies the need to recognise the importance for economic agents within that process of using their imaginations to plot a course across the uncharted waters of the future.

In order to understand the role of imagination in our economic interaction – and its equally important role in the study by economists of that interaction – it is useful to begin by outlining a working definition or account of imagination. This is no easy task; for despite the efforts of the Romantics, the imagination remains the ghost at the banquet of philosophy, psychology and neurophysiology. A look at standard textbooks in these fields will reveal entries on the imagination far smaller than might be expected. In large part, this is because, as John Whale puts it, the word 'imagination' is commonly used to refer to a 'bewilderingly diffuse set of ideas'.[12] Wittgenstein was explicit that to inquire into the nature of the imagination is essentially to ask how 'imagination' as a word is used in various contexts;[13] and it is certainly tempting to use his 'family resemblance' notion to describe the relationship between the different uses.[14] There is no single faculty of the mind that is denoted by 'imagination'; but equally the different attributes associated with different uses of the word do share a family likeness. Mary Warnock has argued that this Wittgensteinian approach understates the 'common elements' in the concept of imagination in its different manifestations.[15] On this debate I shall remain agnostic. It seems clear that imagination is an umbrella concept used to denote a wide variety of crucial mental and cognitive faculties and processes; and, for our purposes, the structure and shape of the umbrella are less important than the identification of mental functions ascribed to the imagination by the Romantics and their followers. In particular, it is not my intention to engage in endless semantic debate about the boundary between imagination and certain forms of reasoning and lateral thinking. Instead, I want to use the ideas of the Romantics to focus on the creative elements missing from the narrow rationalist psychology implicit in economic models, and to explore what they tell us about the behaviour of economic agents and the subject matter of political economy.

I THE NATURE OF IMAGINATION

One notable feature of the Romantic account of imagination is the role accorded to the imagination in perception. For Coleridge, the 'primary Imagination' is the 'prime Agent of all human Perception': the imagination actually helps construct the world, as we perceive it. This creative role of the mind in perception – which in Wordsworth's terminology 'half-creates' the world we see – is, Coleridge believed, different only in degree from the more consciously creative role of the poetic imagination.[16] The Romantics were influenced (directly or otherwise) by Kant's account of the mind reading into the world certain structuring principles as a necessary condition of our experiencing and making sense of it, and particularly by the large role he ascribed to the imagination in both perception and understanding. This role includes fleshing out the everyday concepts we apply to the chaos of sense data so that we are able to recognise something as a 'house' or as 'money'.[17] Warnock argues that the special contribution of the Romantic poets has been to help us discern a link between this Kantian role of 'the image-forming faculty' in everyday perception and the equally important part played by the imagination in creating new and surprising interpretations of the world we experience.[18]

Wordsworth, in the 1802 *Preface* to the *Lyrical Ballads*, emphasised a 'colouring' role for the imagination, by which ordinary things could be 'presented to the mind in an unusual way';[19] and for Abrams this becomes a quintessential aspect of the Romantic theory of the mind. It is the imagination which enables us to self-generate an emotional or metaphorical colouring that illuminates the world we see in a creative manner: the mind's role in perception becomes, Abrams argues, that of a 'lamp' projecting meaning and value, and not merely a 'mirror' reflecting reality.[20] For the Romantic Economist, the imaginative use of metaphor duly becomes central to a more open-minded approach to the scientific study of economics; but, equally importantly, the creative structuring and colouring of perception and analysis should be recognised as an everyday feature of economic agents' attempts to make sense of the world and invest it with emotional and moral value. As Iris Murdoch observed, the world we face when deciding how to act is 'not just a world of "facts" but a world upon which our imagination has, at any given moment, already worked'.[21] This is one creative function of the imagination that both economists and entrepreneurs need to bear in mind.

At a basic level, the imagination is also crucially involved in the visualisation of what cannot be seen. 'Visualisation' here should not be understood as narrowly pictorial, but can encompass acoustic, sensual and even emotional representation of something not immediately engaging our senses. Imaginative visualisation is more than mechanical memory: it may include the construction of counterfactual worlds in the past, or the creation of new possible worlds in the future; and it may include the investment of these images of an alternative past or possible future – as well as mere remembered moments (Wordsworth's 'spots of time'[22]) – with particular significance and emotional value. Imaginative visualisation may also involve placing ourselves in the shoes of others, visualising their feelings and empathising with them. Whether in the created visions of significant remembered moment, 'might-have-been', idealised anticipation, or sympathetic identification, the mind visualises a scene that is often built up, enhanced and extrapolated from mere suggestions. Imagination allows us to construct a significant vision out of shards of memory, and it enables us to join up the suggestive dots of evidence before us, and so visualise or anticipate something we can neither know for sure nor see at present. Above all, it provides us with a set of created images that can affect our behaviour, particularly when they engage our current emotions. This then is a further reason why the imagination is important for our understanding of social and economic interaction. As J. S. Mill noted, 'the imaginative emotion which an idea when vividly conceived excites in us, is not an illusion but a fact, as real as any of the other qualities of objects'.[23] Such imaginative emotion can attach as much to visualisations of what is absent, or only in the possible future, as to imaginatively coloured perception of the present.

In the Romantic period, William Hazlitt spelled out clearly the full importance of imagination as 'the immediate spring and guide of action': he saw imagination as necessarily involved in transposing ourselves into 'the feelings of others' and so feeling action-guiding sympathy; and he argued that it is also imagination which allows each person 'to throw himself forward into the future, to anticipate unreal events and to be affected by his own imaginary interest'.[24] Indeed, Hazlitt saw imagination as the means whereby anyone is able to identify with his future self, and take an interest in the feelings he imaginatively projects that his future self would experience when faced with some imagined future event. Since 'the individual is never the same for two moments together', even the projection of 'continued personal identity' into the future is, in Hazlitt's account, an act of imagination. As he puts it, 'this very circumstance of his identifying himself with his future being, of feeling for this imaginary self as if it were incorporated with his actual substance … is itself the strongest instance that can be given of the force of the imagination'.[25] In Hazlitt's hands, therefore, even the standard utilitarian notion of individuals pursuing their own self-interest dissolves into a quintessentially imaginative enterprise: all rational purposive action (whether for the benefit of ourselves or others) 'must relate to the future'; and, since the future is yet to be created by the choices we make and is 'problematical' and 'undetermined', it can affect us only 'by means of the imagination'.[26] We must imagine the interest that our imagined future selves would feel for this imagined future; and it is this imagined future interest in the imagined future consequences of action today that excites in us a current 'emotion of interest' sufficient to motivate us now.[27] This revolutionary incursion of the imagination into the citadel of rational goal-directed and self-interested action was to find an important echo in the later economic philosophy of Shackle.

We have concentrated so far on the constructive role of imagination in perception, interpretation and emotional colouring, and on its equally central role in visualising what is absent and anticipating possible futures in a way that can excite our emotions and engage our will. The especial fascination of the Romantics with the imagination centred, however, on its perceived role as the source of genuine creativity and novelty, and as the locus of existential freedom from scientific determinism. It is now generally accepted that the imagination involves the making of new connections between parts of the brain not previously linked.[28] The establishment of new pathways across the synapses may start from a stream of essentially random and often unconscious new connections; but if the instrumental or artistic significance of any of these weak new connections is spotted, then the mind can consciously reinforce them into new dominant pathways in the brain – new ways of thinking. Since the potential combinations of neurons or existing pathways are almost infinite, so is the potential for human creativity. The imagination is indeed a 'limitless ocean', as Herder supposed;[29] It is also a source of mental agility and freedom – giving us the wherewithal to move beyond inherited thought-patterns and categories. The imagination enables us – if we are receptive to significant new connections – to think outside the box and make intuitive leaps; and it allows us to transcend the conditioning of our thoughts by our social and personal past, and to escape the parameters of deductive rationality. The imagination is both subversive of established order in our ideas and the means of generating a newly emerging and creative synthesis. Coleridge famously said of the poetic (or 'secondary') imagination: 'It dissolves, diffuses, dissipates, in order to recreate';[30] and elsewhere he spoke of the imagination as at once a 'restless faculty' – a 'middle state of mind … hovering between images', the source of mental fluidity and receptiveness[31] – and a 'synthetic and magical power' that blends, fuses and shapes our ideas into a new unity.[32]

It was another Romantic poet, John Keats, who underlined the central importance of an open-minded receptiveness to new aspects of experience, new ideas and new perspectives. For Keats, the quality most necessary to creative literary genius is '*negative capability*; that is when man is capable of being in uncertainties, mysteries, doubts, without any irritable reaching after fact and reason'.[33] Following Keats, we might say that a full openness to unexpected and unlooked-for promptings of our imagination – to significant new connections arising from our unconscious – comes from 'remaining content with half-knowledge'[34] and not straining to impose our own particular interpretation. The great virtue of a poetic sensibility, as Shelley observed in similar tone, is that it 'awakens and enlarges the mind itself by rendering it the receptacle of a thousand unapprehended combinations of thought'.[35] This sort of imaginative receptiveness is denied all those who are prematurely determined to adopt one perspective on experience or to encase their thoughts in the certainties of established fact and the restrictive logic of deductive rationality. This represents another important lesson for entrepreneur and economist alike.

Open-minded receptiveness to unconsciously generated new connections is not, however, a full enough account of creativity and imagination in action. Two other facets are usually important: first, the ability to scan the promptings of the imagination for significance, while consciously encouraging the search for new connections in pertinent areas; and, secondly, the ability to build a more complete and lasting version of a significant new vision. One of the dangers for the creative person is that she may be swamped by new connections and suggestions, and unable to spot the significant wood for the innumerable trees. Hazlitt observed of Coleridge that his imaginative powers were often positively debilitating: 'he has only to draw the sliders of his imagination, and a thousand subjects expand before him, startling him with their brilliancy, or losing themselves in endless obscurity.'[36] It was perhaps because Coleridge was frequently so distracted by his prolific receptiveness to ideas and images from his unconscious that he was adamant that the poetic imagination should be seen as a 'power, first put in action by the will and understanding, and retained under their irremissive, though gentle and unnoticed, controul'.[37] For Coleridge, the imagination must, to some extent at least, be a conscious, willed activity, proceeding in concert with reason and understanding. Wordsworth presented a typically balanced account of the required mix between receptiveness and consciously directed effort when, in *The Prelude* (1805), he wrote of minds imbued with the power of imagination:

> they build up greatest things
> From least suggestions, ever on the watch,
> Willing to work and to be wrought upon,
> They need not extraordinary calls
> To rouze them …[38]

Wordsworth was also, of course, touching here upon the crucial constructive role of the imagination in transforming the germ of a new idea ('least suggestions') into a more comprehensive insight or vision.

In her essay 'The Darkness of Practical Reason', Iris Murdoch has more recently explored the balance required in creative thinking between passive receptiveness, conscious direction and constructive enhancement. She takes issue with Stuart Hampshire for relegating imagination, in her words, to 'the passive side of the mind', and for 'regarding it as an isolated non-responsible faculty which makes potentially valuable discoveries which reason may inspect and adopt'. For Murdoch, 'imaginings' are neither 'just drifting ideas' nor 'unwilled, isolated, passive'. They are not, as an economist might now put it, just exogenous shocks to our mental system. Rather, Murdoch argues, 'Imagining is *doing*, it is a sort of personal exploring'; it 'builds detail, adds colour, conjures up possibilities in ways which go beyond what could be said to be strictly factual'; and it is an activity in which we are 'all constantly engaged'.[39]

One particular aspect of such willed and largely conscious exploration of new possibilities that is very relevant to scientists and entrepreneurs is what is usually called 'lateral thinking'. Edward de Bono argues that creative problem-solving frequently involves lateral thinking – in the sense of 'new conceptual jumps' which allow us to generate new hypotheses and see things differently. As he explains, these intuitive jumps can often be sparked by 'deliberate habits of provocation': with a problem in mind, we intentionally play with the random juxtaposition of existing ideas as 'provocative stepping-stones' to new patterns of thought.[40] To put it another way, we consciously try to trigger the imaginative firing of new connections in our brains by placing side by side discrete and unrelated fragments, aphorisms and ideas;[41] and we carefully monitor the new pathways that appear, so that we can reinforce those with instrumental or creative significance. This is, of course, only the first stage of deliberate creative thinking. As the new idea or use-pattern grows in our minds, we also – unconsciously and consciously – feed it and shape it with a stream of old and new connections, combined with emotional colouring, sustained attempts at visualisation and renewed bouts of lateral thinking.

Murdoch's emphasis on the 'active' and well as 'passive' aspects of the imagination at work was a clear echo of Coleridge's own attempts to articulate its characteristics. In a famous passage in the *Biographia Literaria*, Coleridge described the process of creative thinking as follows:

Most of my readers will have observed a small water-insect on the surface of rivulets, which throws a cinque-spotted shadow fringed with prismatic colours on the sunny bottom of the brook; and will have noticed, how the little animal *wins* its way up against the stream, by alternate pulses of active and passive motion, now resisting the current, and now yielding to it in order to gather strength and a momentary *fulcrum* for a further propulsion. This is no unapt emblem of the mind's self-experience in the act of thinking. There are evidently two powers at work, which relatively to each other are active and passive; and this is not possible without an intermediate faculty, which is at once both active and passive.

(In philosophical language, we must denominate this intermediate faculty in all its degrees and determinations, the IMAGINATION …)[42]

As Richard Holmes has observed, the psychology of this account of creativity seems 'remarkably modern', with its 'model of the engagement between the conscious forward drive of intellectual effort ("propulsion"), and the drifting backwards into unconscious materials ("yielding to [the current]"), constantly repeated in a natural diastolic movement like breathing or heartbeat'.[43] In more anachronistic terms, we might even interpret Coleridge's image here as a reference to the pulse of conscious effort he thought required to spark new ideas and search for new connections that can modify, or allow us partially to escape, established (and often unconscious) pathways and use-patterns in the brain.

The relative importance in creativity of our conscious and unconscious resources was contested by Romantics, and remains a very pertinent issue to this day. Wordsworth saw the imagination as an 'unfathered vapour' and as emanating from 'the mind's abyss' – a clear reference to the unconscious.[44] He would no doubt have agreed with his German contemporary A. W. Schlegel that genius is 'the most intimate union of unconscious and self-conscious activity'.[45] Interestingly, though, while Schlegel linked the unconscious with intellectual freedom, Coleridge instead seemed to see conscious and willed creativity as both essential to poetic imagination and the basis of freedom from mechanical determinism.[46] Coleridge's main concern was to liberate poetic creativity from the mechanistic mental determinism of Hartley's associationism; and, to this end, he carefully distinguished 'imagination in its passive sense' – which he called 'Fancy' – from the poetic Imagination, which he saw as 'co-existing with the conscious will'.[47] Whereas Fancy derived 'all its materials ready made from the law of association', and could merely (consciously or unconsciously) rearrange and aggregate together established ideas, the poetic Imagination was seen as 'essentially *vital*' – producing synthetic combinations that could grow into something entirely new.[48]

Today, armed with advances in neuroscience and Complexity Theory, we might want to disentangle three issues that Coleridge mixes up here, namely freedom from mental determinism, the vitality of new ideas and the divide between the conscious and unconscious. In modern terms, it is tempting to see Coleridge's Fancy as corresponding to travelling along – and simply reordering – the established pathways of the brain built up by frequent associations; and, by contrast, to see his active poetic Imagination as the creative potential released when new pathways are triggered and reinforced – opening up whole new emerging use-patterns in our brains.

Coleridge's use of organic imagery to describe the imagination at work recognises the central fact about creativity – that it is not a mere rearrangement of existing thoughts but the self-reinforcing growth of new patterns of thought. As we might put it now: from a random new connection (whether conscious or unconscious) between existing ideas grows a whole new way of thinking. This growth may happen slowly and laboriously, or it may resemble a flash of complete intuition – the sudden emergence of a new vision, a new order. Interestingly, had Coleridge had access to such modern ideas, he might have been less insistent that genuine creativity must be in large part a willed and conscious faculty, and less worried that reliance on the unconscious might trap us in a deterministic and moribund view of the world. As John Howkins makes clear in his book *The Creative Economy*, we now understand that the new creative connections which take us beyond normal patterns of thought (and grow into substantially new ideas) can be a feature of either 'heightened consciousness' or a 'more dreamlike state' involving 'a loss of control of consciousness'.[49] Indeed, it is now generally agreed that a high proportion of all thought – including creative and problem-solving thought – takes the form of unconscious rather than conscious activity.[50] Ironically, of course, Coleridge – the master dreamer – was himself prolific in both states. The creative use of imagination by entrepreneurs and economists is no different: it also typically involves combining conscious with unconscious resources, and willed exploration with open-minded receptiveness to sudden unexpected revelation.

It is a commonplace today (outside standard economics) that any policy-maker, entrepreneur, or scientist who wants to be both creative and effective should combine imaginative and intuitive thought (on the one hand) with logic and disciplined rationality (on the other). Weimer and Vining, for example, argue that the good policy analyst should combine logic with intuition, and 'linear' with 'nonlinear' thinking;[51] and Howkins argues that the creative entrepreneur needs to mix 'intuitive jumps' with 'cold-blooded calculation' and 'reality checks'.[52] Likewise, Einstein may have needed a flash of inspiration before he could develop his theory of relativity, but this was only the necessary catalyst in a process of thought that also necessarily involved huge amounts of logical analysis intertwined with imaginative experiment with metaphor. Most Romantics recognised this necessity for imagination and reason to act in concert: however much they were champions of the imagination, and antipathetic to a narrow reliance on deductive logic, they were rarely hostile to reason itself. Hazlitt, for example, was adamant that he did not see imagination as 'contradistinguished from or opposed to reason'; indeed, he spoke of the need for 'a reasoning imagination',[53] which he saw (in Lockridge's words) as 'the sole faculty that adapts previous experience to possible eventualities'.[54] This is an important idea. We have many creative moments, but they solidify into an action-guiding vision of a possible future (or a projected solution to a problem) only if we judge them rationally as likely to be feasible and pertinent in the light of experience. Imagined futures and creative solutions often go way beyond what can be rationally deduced from today's facts and hypotheses; but these potential futures or solutions must be stress-tested (so far as possible) by a rational and ethical audit, if they are not to lead us unnecessarily astray. Imagination on its own may lead to nightmare and delusion; and only when conjoined with rational analysis and ethical judgement does it make progress likely. But, similarly, reason without imagination is of limited use, since it is ultimately confined to the elucidation of given modes of understanding. To expand the empire of knowledge and human endeavour, we need to be imaginative as well as rational.

The Romantics had huge faith in the power of the imagination. Wordsworth, for example, described it in *The Prelude* (1805) as a faculty that can transform our capacity for insight and extend the remit of reason:

> … Imagination, which, in truth,
> Is but another name for absolute strength
> And clearest insight, amplitude of mind,
> And reason in her most exalted mood.[55]

There is a strong religious and even Millenarian tone to Wordsworth's account of the imagination's ability to grant us intuitive glimpses of the principle or spirit that informs all reality. It is this that seems, in his vision, to assure us of a better future:

> Our destiny, our nature, and our home
> Is with infinitude, and only there;
> With hope it is, hope that can never die,
> Effort, and expectation, and desire,
> And something evermore about to be.[56]

In 'Tintern Abbey', Wordsworth spoke also of 'the deep power of joy' associated with grasping intuitively the 'motion' or 'spirit' that pervades everything mental and material. This deep religious feeling of joy was for Wordsworth (as for Coleridge) the true gift of the imaginative mind's communion with 'the life of things'.[57]

If we strip away the religious idealism from Wordsworth's account, there remains here a widely experienced phenomenon. As Howkins notes, an 'upsurge of emotion and joy' is a common adjunct to 'eureka moments'.[58]

Our minds are continually engaged in trying to match existing use-patterns in the brain to our unfolding predicament, and in creating new patterns where the existing ones do not seem to apply. The sudden intuitive sense that a new pattern forming in our minds (or a new application of an existing pattern by way of analogy or metaphor) 'clicks' with the pattern latent in natural or social reality – and rings true as an explication of the principles underlying that reality – can produce a feeling of elation that is the immediate emotional reward of creative thinking. Waldrop, in his book *Complexity*, gives an example of this. He relates the scientist Stuart Kauffman's joyous and quasi-religious reaction to realising he had produced a model that seemed to explain how life first emerged from the primordial soup: 'I had a holy sense of a knowing universe, a universe unfolding, a universe of which we are privileged to be a part … I felt God would reveal how the world works to anyone who cared to listen.'[59]

2 THE ECONOMY AS CREATIVE PROCESS

When Isaiah Berlin came to sum up what he saw as the main lessons of Romanticism, he emphasised two closely related themes: the first was the central importance of individual creativity, including the creation of new values, goals and visions; the second was the 'endless self-creativity of the universe', the impossibility of nailing down with laws and formulae this 'unceasing flow', and the unfathomable depth and complexity of the 'process of perpetual forward creation' central to social life.[60] Both these lessons are relevant to economics. To adapt the second one first, it is clear that the most important attributes of capitalist economies at the system level are their boundless creativity and their complex mix of regular ebb and flow with course-altering surprise events.

It is Schumpeter who has underlined most eloquently that a capitalist economy is 'first and last a process of change' – 'an evolutionary process' that 'not only never is but never can be stationary'.[61] Insisting that the 'process of Creative Destruction is the essential fact about capitalism', he showed how creativity is at the heart of this process of endless renewal:

The fundamental impulse that sets and keeps the capitalist engine in motion comes from the new consumers' goods, the new methods of production or transportation, the new markets, the new forms of industrial organisation that capitalist enterprise creates.[62]

Schumpeter also did much to spell out the analytical, policy and business implications of this insight: it calls into question the relevance of 'static equilibrium' analysis focused on the optimisation of *given* factors; and it suggests that maximising efficiency in a static allocation sense (that is, at any given moment) may even be antipathetic to long-run success in the endless dynamic struggle to create the next generation of goods and technologies.[63] Schumpeter carefully contrasted the 'textbook picture' of 'competition within a rigid pattern of invariant conditions, methods of production and forms of industrial organisation', with the 'kind of competition which counts' in the real world, namely 'competition from the new commodity, the new technology, the new source of supply, the new type of organisa-tion'. His conclusion was stark and uncompromising: 'In other words, the problem that is usually being visualised is how capitalism administers existing structures, whereas the relevant problem is how it creates and destroys them.'[64]

On this Schumpeterian view, the creation of imaginative new products, markets, production strategies and organisational structures is key to the competitiveness and dynamism of an economy. Nurturing the capacity for generating innovative ideas, and for being individually and institutionally receptive to these new ideas when created, therefore becomes central to the success of an economy or firm; and understanding the institutional require-ments of different innovation strategies becomes correspondingly central to economic and policy analysis. So, for example, innovation may be *radical* (involving substantially new product-types and wholesale changes in pro-duction methods and conceptual approach) or *incremental* (involving piece-meal adjustments to existing methods, products and mind-sets); and these two types of innovation are fostered by different cultural and institutional environments.[65] Radical innovation usually thrives in fluid and iconoclastic environments, favourable to the creative rejection of established techni-ques,[66] and tolerant of lone mavericks prepared to think outside the box and recast problems entirely. It is also encouraged by a loose aggregation of people from widely diverse backgrounds (as in Silicon Valley), since this makes significant new connections between previously unrelated ideas more likely. Incremental innovation, by contrast, tends to be more prevalent in teamwork environments where engineers can build successfully on the collaborative mining of a deep seam of shared tacit knowledge of existing processes and customer requirements, by experimenting cooperatively (as in many German mechanical engineering companies). As Hodgson puts it: 'The creative spark is often a result of the striking of intuition upon the flintstone of tacit skills';[67] and a shared understanding of these tacit skills, and the group ability to spark new ideas from them, require supportive institutions.

Most innovation (whether radical or incremental) relies on an imaginative and open-minded approach to problems, and involves new developments that could not have been rationally deduced *ex ante* from the problem faced and given knowledge. Innovation is rarely the mere logical drawing of conclusions from available evidence; instead it usually requires the imaginative injection of inherently unpredictable novelty. For this reason, the pace and direction of innovation depends ultimately on the vagaries of the human imagination, the salience of its promptings and the receptiveness of key individuals to new ideas. Nevertheless, innovation does not simply arrive on the scene unexpectedly and randomly, as economists frequently assume, like a *deus ex machina* or an 'exogenous shock'. Rather the type and prevalence of innovative ideas (or mutations in thought) depends to a significant degree on the institutional framework in which innovators operate; and the ability of new ideas to take root likewise depends on the institutional environment. In this sense, innovation is endogenous to the system. Moreover, innovation is often a function of the directed and carefully financed search by individuals or firms for new solutions and ideas, as well as of more diffuse imaginative exploration of existing problems.

Crucially, Schumpeter was right to suggest that the institutional and financial requirements of successful innovation cultures might clash with the requirements of short-term allocative efficiency. For example, the chances of radical innovation may be enhanced by the employment of eccentric individuals in universities and companies, but this is likely to be costly in the short term, and there is little guarantee that it will produce any dividends from one year to the next. Similarly, incremental innovation through teamwork may be encouraged by employment protection for engineers, since it assures those who might generate improvements to existing methods and products that their insights would not simply lead to the loss of their jobs; and yet, as economists and politicians daily remind us, such employment protection may be efficiency-sapping in the meantime. Incentivising the imagination is not, of course, an exact science, but it usually involves more than clearly articulated problems and financial incentives. Equally important are tolerance of diversity and failure, a balance between rivalry and communication, and – above all – the intellectual space for creative thinking.

In a paper published in 1991, Nobel prize-winner James Buchanan and his colleague Viktor Vanberg provide a useful update on thinking about 'the market as a creative process'.[68] Given the evident importance of creativity, they take issue with the 'residual teleology' of standard conceptions of the market, which assume that there is 'a conceptually definable equilibrium

toward which the process of socioeconomic change could be expected
to gravitate'; and they are equally critical of the idea of the market as a
'discovery process', which suggests that there is an improved future 'out
there' waiting to be discovered through suitable hard work and error-
elimination techniques. Instead, they argue, 'which future will come into
existence will depend on choices that are yet to be made'.[69] Buchanan and
Vanberg underpin their attack on 'the tenuousness of the whole notion of
equilibrium, defined as the exhaustion of gains from trade' by emphasising
that in reality there is rarely a given pre-defined 'set of goods to be allocated'.
Instead, they argue, economic actors are engaged in a constant quest to
imagine '*new trading prospects*' and '*create* new goods that are expected to be
of potential exchangeable value'.[70] When Buchanan and Vanberg also insist
on replacing the word 'discovery' with 'creative' to describe the dynamic and
inventive process that is an economy, it might be thought they are splitting
semantic hairs. After all, as they admit, Hayek's discussion of 'Competition as
a Discovery Procedure' acknowledged the central importance of the market as
a means of discovering new methods and new goods; and Hayek himself
never assumed that markets tend toward any sort of optimal equilibrium
position.[71] It is undoubtedly the case, however, that an emphasis on *discovery* suggests that market participants are faced primarily with *information
problems*, and that performance can be improved by better knowledge. If,
by contrast, the future is, as Buchanan and Vanberg maintain, 'yet to be
created',[72] then market participants are faced primarily with the challenge
of *creating* a future to their liking, as well as *adapting* skilfully to the
unpredictable novelty introduced by other creative individuals.

Buchanan and Vanberg's article explicitly draws on two major modern
developments in the theory and philosophy of economics, which they
correctly identify as complementary to each other. The first is the new
scientific understanding of 'nonlinear systems' exhibiting 'spontaneous self-
organisation' – an approach associated in economics with Complexity
theorists like Brian Arthur.[73] This new school has shown how economies
can be modelled as self-organising systems, producing dynamic, constantly
evolving and often novel patterns, and driven by a mixture of increasing and
decreasing returns to frequent mutations in technology and taste.[74] The
significance of Complexity Theory (and its variants) is, as Buchanan and
Vanberg note, that it appears to account for 'the coordinative properties
of markets'[75] in a way that does not involve assuming that the rules of
interaction lock them into determinate and predictable outcomes or
steady-states. The second development is centred on the philosophical
contribution of Shackle. Shackle deepened our understanding of the

uncertainty faced by economic actors, by pointing out that it depends above all on the fact that the future will be (in Buchanan and Vanberg's words) '"created" in the process of choice'.[76] The future depends on how we imagine it could be, the novel ideas we introduce into the equation and the non-pre-determined choices we make. Shackle also emphasises the necessary role of imagination (as well as reason) in forming expectations and constructing the framework of choice in such an uncertain environment. Imagination becomes both a source of novelty and mutation in the economic process and a tool for coping with the uncertainty created by that novelty. Such a central role for imagination contrasts sharply with the focus of standard economics on agents rationally and predictably optimising given factors and preferences. As Shackle himself puts it in his book *Epistemics and Economics*:

> Not everything that economics touches is fit to be turned to certainty and pure reason. By tacitly assuming that the right conduct can always be discovered by taking orderly thought, and that this is how men's conduct is formed, economics has precluded itself from understanding the vast area of human enterprise where disorder is the essence of the situation, the areas of break-away, of origination, of poetic creation or innovation in elevated contexts or in the mundane one of business, and of conflict and cut-throat struggle.[77]

We will explore in section 3 how far Shackle's emphasis on both the radical uncertainty created by choice and the creative role of imagination can provide the basis of a new set of microfoundations for understanding the behaviour of actors within an economy that is a self-organising and creative process. Of more immediate relevance is Shackle's eloquent insistence on the inappropriateness of modelling the creative process of economic invention and choice according to the metaphor of 'celestial mechanics' as manifested in the 'neo-classical conception of general equilibrium'. For Shackle, equilibrium-based models can at best give us 'lightning-flashes in which the scene is stilled to immobility by the brevity of the glimpse'.[78] Such models inevitably miss the dynamic essence of what is going on. As Shackle wrote:

> To acknowledge that there is novelty, in the sense of fundamentally undeducible things, waiting to be encountered for the first time, is to acknowledge that we cannot build models that will exhibit the course of a society's history over even a limited span of time.[79]

Writing before the new science of complexity, Shackle was not aware of the capacity of mathematics to model non-linear reactions to novelty *after the event* or simulate likely patterns in the future; but his central point remains valid, that – where innovation and creative choice is important – long-term prediction is impossible and there is no determinate outcome or steady-state to which an economy will tend.

To understand the extent to which an economy is a creative process, we must consider more than the creation of new products, new technologies and even new conceptual frameworks. A free-market economy is also a dynamic process because, as Hodgson points out, it allows for the creation of new preferences, new goals and new identities on the part of self-creating consumers and entrepreneurs.[80] Markets provide a space where individuals can experiment with self-defining trade-offs between incommensurable values. We define who we are, in part, by the market choices we make. Markets also allow individuals to chase their private dreams and attempt to bring their guiding visions to pass. Indeed, much of our demand for increased income and new goods comes from our idealised anticipation of a life enriched by them – by our action-guiding visualisation (as Hazlitt would put it) of the imagined feelings of our imagined future selves.

In his book, *The Romantic Ethic and the Spirit of Modern Consumerism*, Colin Campbell argues that economic historians studying the Industrial Revolution in the eighteenth and nineteenth centuries need to explain the revolution on the demand-side quite as much as that evident on the supply-side. The transformation was not merely a function of new technologies and an increased propensity (helped by Max Weber's famous 'Protestant ethic') to save and invest; it was also, Campbell argues, a function of a revolutionary modern attitude to consumption, which saw consumers on an ever-quickening treadmill of new desires, with a seemingly insatiable demand for new goods.[81] Campbell's explanation of this phenomenon is that the consumer became imbued with a 'Romantic ethic' – 'ever-casting his day-dreams forward in time', and 'attaching them' to particular 'objects of desire'. From now on, the consumer continually employed 'imagination to perfect pleasures and project these on to future experience'. Such dreaming is pleasurable in itself, of course; but crucially it also encourages consumers to believe that if they can only attain the new product (such as a holiday or a car) onto which they have projected their idealised expectations, they will be happier still. In practice, though, given the disillusionment that follows attainment of the inevitably less-than-perfect product, modern consumers are, Campbell argues, forever left to project their dreams onto the next generation of new goods.[82]

For all its power, Campbell's thesis can explain only part of the dynamic of modern consumer demand. Companies and their advertising agents also play a proactive and complementary role. As Brown, Doherty and Clarke note in *Romancing the Market*, marketing and product-design departments do more than 'reflect' consumers' wants and exploit their dreams; they also stoke and even create them.[83] Jeremy Rifkin quotes Charles Kettering of General Motors making this point beautifully in the 1920s: '"The key to economic prosperity", said Kettering, "is the organised creation of dissatisfaction."'[84] The continual creation of new models of car, or new fashions of clothing, enables and encourages us as consumers to dream new idealised dreams associated with products carefully differentiated from those we have now; and this, in turn, creates demand for otherwise unnecessary upgrades to the latest versions of each product. In addition, our idealised dreams themselves are not purely internally generated; they are usually social phenomena as well – constructed, in part, by the power of advertising-propelled myths. The creation of new models and fashions also, of course, fuels the competitive instinct to establish social dominance and status recognition through having the latest product; and here, too, advertising plays its part by creating the social definition of what constitutes status.

As Buchanan and Vanberg acknowledge, recognition that a modern economy is intrinsically a '*creative process*' does not preclude there being analytical mileage in viewing it also (with standard economics) as an '*allocative process*' or (with Hayek) as a '*discovery process*'.[85] The three different characterisations can provide complementary insights, with each one enabling us to focus on different important features within our complex socio-economic predicament. Which one is most suitable depends on the particular problem or situation being analysed. Whenever the structures of preferences, goods and technologies are relatively stable, the most analytically interesting features of any particular market may well be the relative efficiency of its allocation of resources, and the relative suitability of its institutional structure of incentives. It is indeed the case, as Paul Krugman has suggested, that the tendency to allocative efficiency can be one of the most important 'emergent properties' of markets;[86] and it therefore makes perfect sense to study the market as an allocative process, especially when endowments, factors and consumer tastes are stable, and relevant information is easily available. At other times, though, when markets are characterised by ill-informed agents and highly dispersed information, the role of the price mechanism as a signal may be the most important aspect to study – and the 'discovery' paradigm may be more appropriate. Likewise, when the main focus is on explaining the dynamic behaviour of fast-changing markets, rife with creative consumers and producers, and with increasing returns to successful innovation, we need to switch metaphors again, and view the economy as a creative or evolutionary process.

3 IMAGINATION AND THE MICROFOUNDATIONS
OF ECONOMICS

The remainder of this chapter examines the basic building blocks of an explicitly Romantic set of microfoundations, suitable for a new theory of choice and economic interaction that does not rely exclusively on equilibrium and optimisation models. This involves understanding the role played by novelty and individual choice in creating uncertainty in a social setting; the importance of imagination in structuring choice; and the central contribution of imagination (as well as reason) to the formation by individuals of the expectations and strategies that guide their behaviour.

Uncertainty

Ever since the interventions of Frank Knight and John Maynard Keynes, economists have been unable to ignore the importance of uncertainty. Knight made the now classic distinction between *risk* – where it is possible to define measurable probabilities over a large number of cases that the unexpected will occur (for example, fire or death from driving) – and fundamental *uncertainty*, which is not amenable to measurement in probabilistic terms.[87] (Probability estimates cannot be made in cases of uncertainty because, for example, the various possible outcomes cannot be defined in advance, or because the case under consideration is a complete one-off and there are no observable statistical regularities in our past on which to base such estimates.) The implications of risk and uncertainty contrast sharply. Risk poses relatively few problems for economic actors and for economists modelling their behaviour: despite the problems of moral hazard and adverse selection, there are insurance markets for pooling measurable risk; and economic actors can be safely assumed to adopt rules of thumb that ensure that they do not systematically make large errors in their probability forecasts (since, if they do, other market operators will exploit their failure). For this reason, the existence of risk does not broadly speaking call into question the prevalence either of rational expectations and optimisation strategies on the part of individual actors, or of predictable behaviour at the system level. By contrast, radical uncertainty about the future makes attempts by economic actors to deduce an optimal course of action from known (or estimated) factors problematic, and therefore strikes at the heart of attempts by economists to model economic behaviour as tending towards some determinate outcome. The crucial question, therefore, is how important uncertainty is. If it merely represents an occasional problem, it may at a system level constitute a form of random 'noise' around the basically predictable outcomes of rational choice and the optimisation of given preferences, factors and estimated probabilities. If, on the other hand, uncertainty is pervasive, it calls into question the very microfoundations and theoretical superstructure of standard economics.

Keynes famously asserted 'the extreme precariousness of the basis of knowledge' on which our expectations of return on investment must depend; and he argued that many of our economic decisions are, therefore, not taken as 'the outcome of a weighted average of quantitative benefits multiplied by quantitative probabilities'.[88] Uncertainty was, for Keynes, a major cause of both economic instability and the failure of markets to 'clear' to an optimal equilibrium. As Stephen Dunn notes, however, Keynes did not theorise extensively about the ultimate cause of economic uncertainty, focusing instead on the reactions to it, and the tendency of ill-informed speculators to make it worse. In particular, according to Dunn, Keynes failed to appreciate the extent to which the uncertainty faced by investors and other economic actors is the inevitable result of 'the emergent novelty associated with enterprise' and the 'creative acts' of entrepreneurs. Indeed, Dunn argues, 'the creative aspect of the competitive process, and its connection with uncertainty, lie dormant in Keynes'.[89] It is here that Shackle's contribution is so important. For it is he, above all, who has made explicit the central and ubiquitous role of imagination and individual choice in creating the 'unforeknowable' and unpredictable nature of the future.

In his book *Imagination and the Nature of Choice*, Shackle analyses the imaginative genesis of much of the uncertainty we face. He writes of each chooser's 'own original, ungoverned novelties of imagination … injecting, in some respect *ex nihilo*, the unforeknowable arrangement of elements'; and he suggests that 'originative perpetual creation of history by the pursuit of works of imagination into the sphere of action is a cutting into the fabric of governance of time-to-come by time past and thus a cutting of the deductive process based on knowledge of what has been the case'.[90] But this is not all: 'the sequel of any present choice of action' by an agent is 'partly shaped by choices made, by others or himself, in time-to-come'. As a result, the future (or 'history-to-come') facing any decision-maker 'waits to be created, to be *originated*, by choices to be made, now and in time-to-come, by himself and others';[91] and, as Shackle states elsewhere, 'we cannot know what choices will be made at moments still to come'.[92] The significance of this should be clear: if economic decisions are often made as part of a long sequence of choices (where the decisions could go either way without impugning the rationality of the chooser), and if imagined novelties in the economic sphere can be both genuinely novel and feasible, then the existence of choice and imagination in itself necessarily implies that the future is often uncertain.

Shackle, of course, is not alone in realising the impact of novelty and imagination on the prevalence of uncertainty. Douglass North, for example, has pointed out that 'uncertainty is not an unusual condition; it has been the underlying condition responsible for the evolving structure of human organisation throughout history and pre-history'.[93] Part of the reason for this, North explains, is that we live in a 'world we are continually altering' – 'a world of continuous novel change'; and, when faced with 'true novelty … we have uncertainty and we simply do not know what the outcomes may be'.[94] In his study of the politics of international relations, Robert Jackson makes a related point:

Human behaviour cannot be predicted scientifically because humans have minds, and because they can make up their minds and change their minds concerning the basic question of how they wish to live. They can be quite unpredictable in doing that. They have fertile imaginations.[95]

Choice

The standard economic conception of choice is hugely productive of definitive analytical answers but, when applied to real-life situations, risks being both anaemic in conception and superhuman in the demands it makes. It is anaemic because it appears to drain choice of its indeterminacy by assuming that there is normally only one right answer – an optimal response that an actor must choose if he is rational. A decision can often seem to resemble, in Shackle's words, 'the empty and determinate upshot of a confrontation of the individual's endowment of tastes and his historically given and in some way fully known circumstances'.[96] At the same time, the standard economic conception of choice is superhuman, because it asks too much of the imaginative and computational capacities of individual actors. Kenneth Boulding has underlined the implausibility that even in straight-forward market situations (for example, choosing between different types of fruit) economic agents can scan all the relevant alternative combinations, and rank them in order of utility, so that an optimal choice presents itself given the prices and resources available. As he puts it: 'Alternatives do not usually have the courtesy to parade themselves in rank order on the drill ground of the imagination.'[97] When it comes to more complex market situations, standard economics is on yet weaker ground in assuming that individuals are able to construct complete 'indifference maps' across the range of possible trade-offs between conflicting options; for there are obvious difficulties in specifying all the possible consequences of choosing each option, and determining the probabilities and subjective value that should attach to them. Furthermore, an equilibrium model of market valuations assumes, in Shackle's words, that all the relevant choices of all market participants can, in some sense, be 'pre-reconciled' and 'simultaneous'.[98]

It is important to acknowledge that in the modern *Game Theory* version of Rational Choice Theory, the strategic interaction of one 'player' and another is made central to the analysis, and subtle versions of it are at pains to introduce time and uncertainty into the equation. Nevertheless, each player is still generally assumed to be playing a 'game' in which she (like the theorist) can calculate (or learn) the optimal course of action at each stage, given the strategies being pursued by the other players, in a process of rational deduction from the given rules of the game. These rules pre-determine the number and character of the players, the set of strategies available to each player, the pay-offs for each strategy, the information available and so on.[99] As Colin Crouch puts it, 'Actors are attributed with a clear maximising objective ("winning" the game) and are required to use prescribed means (the rules of the game) to reach it … But the environment defined by the game is a totally determined structure; the participants have no chance to change it.'[100]

Economists do not, of course, believe that their standard economic and Game Theory models describe exactly how ordinary individuals actually choose. They merely assume that their formalised abstractions capture what Bruce Lyons calls 'the fundamental forces at work',[101] and that deviations from predicted behaviour will tend either to be random or to diminish over time as economic agents learn the ropes. This assumption looks hard to defend, however, whenever the uncertainty faced is so severe that economic agents have no way even in theory of specifying the rules of the game (and so identifying, for example, the complete set of alternative strategies and their respective pay-offs). Such uncertainty is likely to be endemic wherever creativity and novelty abound – that is, where the rules, pay-offs and available strategies are constantly being revised, and where the sequels of choice involve a complex sequence of inventive move and counter-move by an indeterminate number of other players. For example, it may be fair to assume, as Crouch does, that individuals 'operate in a permanent dilemma between following the rules of the institution within which they operate and challenging, breaking, innovating against, those rules'.[102] Where this is indeed the case, we clearly need an alternative model of choice – one that accords a central role to the imagination.

Lyons points out that in practice imagination is involved in most cases of choice simply in visualising 'the problem requiring a decision', in selecting its essential parameters out of the mass of data available, and in comparing the likely alternative 'scenarios'.[103] This is a creative process in itself and one that inevitably introduces some indeterminacy. In real life, choice rarely involves a set of options that comes fully specified and available without effort and selection on our part. Instead, we have to construct the parameters of choice with the help of our imagination. The emphasis placed in modern behavioural economics on 'framing effects' that influence the value we attribute to particular options at the time of decision should also alert us to the role of imagination (as well as of language and metaphor) in colouring the perceptions and analysis that drive human choice.[104]

Shackle, not surprisingly, goes much further than this. Given his emphasis on the radically indeterminate nature of the future yet to be created, he argues that 'choice of conduct is choice amongst things imagined'; for the chooser, there is 'no given and ready-made list of relevant sequels to any one of the rival courses open to him. Such sequels are for him to conceive, to invent.' Choice is, in a very real sense, 'amongst products of imagination and invention'.[105] We are free to invent new options, new possible strategies, and new possible goods to populate the future; and we must also use our imaginations to visualise, and sometimes even invent, the various possible consequences of any decision. Shackle argues that the consequences of action cannot usually be known *ex ante*, since they depend on the creative choices of others or ourselves in the future. As a result, 'the void of time-to-come' can be filled 'only by work of the imagination'.[106] Shackle sums up his position as follows:

Economic choice does not consist in comparing the items in a list, known to be complete, of given fully specified rival and certainly attainable results. It consists in first creating, by conjecture and reasoned imagination on the basis of mere suggestions offered by visible or recorded circumstance, the things on which hope can be fixed. These things, at the time when they are available for choice, are thoughts and even figments.[107]

In terms very reminiscent of Hazlitt, Shackle sees the imagination as working hand in hand with both feeling and rational analysis. He is alive to the fact that the imagined outcomes of choice often inspire in us emotions of hope or 'anticipative satisfaction' that are the instant rewards of personal commitment to a particular action.[108] The choices we make are often aspirational, and the imagined sequels are enjoyed in anticipation. At the same time, Shackle is careful not to deny reason a serious role in the process of choice. Rather, he insists, 'The imagined sequels and their claim to possibility must consult reason at every step.'[109] Reason has a crucial role in determining how feasible or desirable an imagined consequence is likely to be, and in editing the options we imagine we have. Reason alone, though, is not enough: for, in any circumstances where the future may hold in store genuine novelty and surprise that undermine the basis of prediction, reason cannot give us the quantifiable certainties and probabilities that would delimit rational choice. As Shackle puts it: 'Only when novelty is eliminated and all is known can reason be the sole guide of conduct. It is only in the timeless fiction of general equilibrium that reason can prevail alone.'[110]

In Shackle's vision, choice is genuinely creative and 'originative'.[111] It is not, as in Rational Choice Theory, the mere working through of logic and rational calculation in the light of a given goal (optimisation), given preferences, given factors, and given probabilities. Moreover, the creativity of choice comes, according to Shackle, from 'the freedom which uncertainty gives for the creation of *unpredictable hypotheses*'.[112] In other words, it is uncertainty about the future which is, in a very real sense, the locus of our freedom as economic agents. In the world according to Rational Choice Theory and standard economic theory, an economic agent is usually starved of radical uncertainty and is consequently free only to be rational (and optimise) or irrational (and predictably lose out). The right answer is already determined by the pre-specified conditions of choice. Once, however, we realise that the future is uncertain and waiting to be created by the way we (and others) imagine, will and choose it to be, we are liberated from the implicit determinism of perfect rationality and possess the genuine existential freedom that is in reality the main gift of creative markets. As Shackle asked rhetorically: 'Is it not by their access to these creative aspects of their choice of conduct, that we can suppose men to have freedom, without being obliged to deny them the exercise of reason?'[113]

Wordsworth and, later, Jean-Paul Sartre shared the view implicit here that the creative work of the imagination constitutes the very essence of human freedom – that it is the imagination that enables us, in Iris Murdoch's words, to 'break with the given world'.[114] Like most Romantics, however, they were pessimistic about the chances of exercising this freedom of the imagination within the everyday world of commerce and business. Shackle demonstrates how far their pessimism was misplaced. The domain of economics is not one of 'inhuman determinism',[115] as Sartre assumed. It is instead a space for self-expression and creativity, manifested in the ways we imaginatively construct the possible worlds between which we choose.

Expectations

As Hazlitt reminded us, 'all rational and voluntary action … must relate to the future'.[116] Any choice or decision made in an economic or political setting must therefore depend on our expectations of what the future will look like, with or without the action being contemplated. In modern economics, the assumption generally made is that these expectations will on average be correct; they will be 'rational' in the sense that the people concerned will make use of available information to ensure that they do not make systematic errors in their forecasts. In essence, the assumption is that over time economic decision-makers are forced by competitive pressures to correct any systematic bias in the rules of thumb they use to form expectations about the future, so that on average their expectations will be wrong only when the economy is hit by random shocks. In some versions of macroeconomics, the stronger assumption is made that the individuals in an economy will, as a result, have expectations that are in line with the predictions of the particular theory that economists are constructing[117] – an assumption that threatens to introduce a measure of circularity into the microfoundations of those very theories. Nevertheless, the central idea that economic agents will learn to avoid systematic errors in forecasting seems plausible; and it seems to provide a firm rational basis for the formation of expectations, so long as we are dealing with oft-repeated market transactions involving a few readily identifiable variables that behave with a high degree of regularity. The danger comes when this assumption that there is a firm rational basis to expectations is extended to conditions of uncertainty – involving the complex interaction of one-off events, novelty and creative choices.[118] In such situations, the rational avoidance of systematic errors over time is not enough to give us useful expectations about the future yet to be created.

When Keynes sought to explain how the level of investment is affected by interest rates, he emphasised the central importance of the formation of expectations in conditions of uncertainty. In famous passages in chapter 12 of *The General Theory*, he began to unpack the epistemological and psychological reality behind such expectations. Keynes was clear that very often 'our existing knowledge does not provide a sufficient basis for a calculated mathematical expectation', leaving us to fall back on the conventional assumption 'that the existing state of affairs will continue indefinitely, except in so far as we have specific reasons to expect a change'.[119] For this reason, expectations (and the market valuations dependent on them) are, he thought, inevitably subject to the fickle winds of sentiment and rumour;

and we are left to make economic choices 'as best we are able, calculating where we can, but often falling back for our motive on whim or sentiment or chance'.[120]

Shackle shared Keynes' analysis of the slim basis for rational probability-calculating expectations, and sought to emphasise the subversive quality of *The General Theory*: 'Yet the *meaning* is that rational, fully-informed equilibrium is excluded by the denial to us of anything but fragmentary suggestions of what will be the sequel of today's efforts and plans. Expectation is not rational.'[121] For Shackle, however, the uncertain basis of our expectations did not so much leave us prey to whim as free to create visions of how the future could be. In a remarkable parallel with Hazlitt's view that 'The next year, the next hour, the next moment is but a creation of the mind',[122] Shackle sought again and again to stress that 'Tomorrow is a figment', and that our expectations are at once the creation of our imaginations and creative of the future. 'Expectation', he declared, 'is origination'.[123]

Shackle's message is corrosive of any notion that market valuations – when forward-looking – can be stable and correct:

Valuation is expectation. What is vital is that expectations are conjectures, let us say *figments*, resting on elusive, fragmentary and confusing evidence whose interpretation and suggestion can change from moment to moment with no visible cause. Valuation is expectation and expectation is imagination.[124]

The frequent disruption in market valuations is caused, on this view, by 'unaccountable shifts of the expectational kaleidoscope'.[125] It is important to note, however, that the imaginative construction of expectations need be neither fickle nor aimless. As Shackle intimates in his account, imagination is often a consciously directed and highly disciplined, as well as creative, faculty: 'Expectation is not a passive, finished and settled state of thought but an activity of mind which can at no time say that it has completed the imaginative exploitation of its data; for these data are mere fragmentary suggestions in a paradoxically fertile void.'[126] Imagination continuously constructs and builds, as Wordsworth said, from 'least suggestions'; but this compulsion is also disciplined by what Hazlitt called 'a reasoning imagination' that applies the lessons of experience to possible futures being created in the mind.[127]

Collaboration between constructive imagination and reason is clearly essential. For it is only if we stress-test our visions of the future with a rational analysis of their feasibility in the light of our past experience that we can ensure that our imaginative conjectures are 'expectations' of the possible rather than misguided delusions. Furthermore, we live in a world in which our expectations concerning the future need to be guided by an under-standing of what F. W. Scharpf calls the 'social construction of predictabi-lity'; for, as Claus Offe explains, norms and institutions ensure that 'most sources of contingency have been channelled by rules'.[128] In this respect, Shackle exaggerates when he describes the future as a 'void'[129]: it is already part-constructed by the institutional and cultural framework bequeathed by the past and present. But this only serves to underline another crucial function of the imagination in collaboration with reason – namely to help us 'read' and interpret this framework of partial constraints correctly.

If expectations formed in conditions of uncertainty are, at least in part, a function of how we imagine the future might be, and if our economic decisions about how to behave are based on these creative expectations, then – as Dunn has pointed out – there is a clear sense in which our imaginations influence and even create the future.[130] It is in this sense that expectations are 'originative'. Expectations are often self-fulfilling: we create the future as we imagine it to be. Nowhere is this creative and self-fulfilling aspect of expectations more in evidence than in the stock market. As George Soros has written:

The important point is that the future, when it occurs, will have been influenced by the guessing that has preceded it. The guessing finds expression in the stock prices and stock prices have ways of affecting the fundamentals.[131]

Some of the ways in which investors imagine the future are based on so little fact, they are delusional; and, where these delusions are widely shared, consequent stock-market bubbles and crashes can change the future, by altering the price of capital while making or destroying the fortunes of investors. More normally, of course, investor and entrepreneurial expec-tations are only half-created (or half-originated) by imagination – being also half-engineered in the light of such evidence and probability forecasts as are available; but such joint products of imagination and reason (being more plausible) have an even greater habit of creating the future in their own image.

Strategy formation

The final area where Romantic lessons on the nature of imagination can improve the microfoundations of our understanding of economics is in relation to the selection and formation of strategies. Standard economics assumes that all agents employ an overall strategy of optimisation; this assumption, together with the pre-specification of all relevant preferences, endowments and factors, allows for the prediction of behaviour. In Game Theory, too, while the set of feasible strategies available to the players may be quite large, it is generally assumed that a 'Nash equilibrium' will be reached in which each player will select one set of strategies that is her 'best reply' to the (potential) strategies of other players.[132] However, in a world characterised by uncertainty and novelty – where agents are aware that they are operating in a complex, dynamic and constantly changing environment – a notional strategy of optimisation may be as psychologically implausible as it would be meaningless and irrelevant. In such conditions, individuals must, if they are to be effective, imaginatively construct a possible image of their own future that pleases them, and – while constantly adapting it to fit emerging novelty around them – try to realise this image by consistent action. For a true Romantic, of course, this is not a second-best mode of strategy formation made necessary by a sickening degree of uncertainty: it is the free expression of the urge for self-creation – of a determination to forge her own identity by the free choice of a guiding image, in conditions where there is no single rational course of action.

When Brian Arthur made the analogy between the predicament of economic actors and a game of chess, he was emphasising that, despite clear rules, the set of possible moves at the start is effectively endless, and there is no way of calculating an optimising strategy.[133] Waldrop records John Holland making a similar point about complex real-life situations: 'in any real environment, the space of possibilities is so huge that there is no way an agent can find the optimum – or even recognise it. And that's before you take into account the fact that the environment might be changing in unforeseen ways.'[134] When playing the chess game of life, of course, we are helped by being able to supplement the socially formed (institutional) constraints, or rules of the game, with socially learned rules of thumb and norms that guide both our expectations of how others will play and our own choice of strategy. One example of this might be the norm of satisficing (of being content with a good enough result). As Barry Schwartz has argued, in conditions where we are awash with a debilitating number of options, satisficing is often a much more effective strategy for boosting contentment (let alone efficiency) than attempting to maximise or optimise our position.[135] But while such socially learned rules of thumb are certainly useful, there are many occasions when we need to supplement them by using our imagination to create potentially winning strategies.

There are several closely related strategic uses of the imagination. One that is critical to successful strategy formation is a practical version of 'negative capability': this involves being constantly alert to tipping points or sudden changes in the dynamic of the game as it unfolds, and receptive to flashes of insight about new possible moves and new perspectives. To this end, it is critical not to reach a premature conclusion about the situation faced (including the strategies other players are using) or about what strategy should be adopted. As Gareth Morgan puts it in his management bestseller *Images of Organization*, 'Skilled leaders and managers develop the knack of reading situations with various scenarios in mind.' He continues:

> They have a capacity to remain open and flexible, suspending immediate judgements whenever possible, until a more comprehensive view of the situation emerges. They are aware that new insights often arise as one approaches situations from 'new angles' and that a wide and varied reading can create a wide and varied range of action possibilities.[136]

A related function of the imagination is to provide us with an intuitive grasp of any general patterns that are emerging in the way the game is played, and an intuitive sense of when we have hit upon a theoretical framework that rings true as an explanation of what is going on; this can help ensure that any specific strategies and expectations we employ are loosely guided by the most up-to-date working models (or simulations) available. An equally important strategic use of the imagination is the conscious search for new possible strategies – perhaps by engineering the loose juxtaposition of different existing templates of action, and thereby provoking the imaginative growth of new hybrid strategies. A further creative aspect of strategy formation is remaining alert to the possibility of creating new rules of the game that might tip the balance of advantage decisively one way or the other. Economic and political actors are often 'regime-makers' as well as 'regime-takers': they can have a vision for how the rules of the game could be restructured, and develop a strategy designed to ensure that the rules are changed to fit that vision. Finally, the effective player needs to have an imaginative capacity to develop a guiding vision of how she wants to play the game. The vision must not be a detailed route plan that pretends to map out the future exactly and dictate strategy precisely, but rather a powerful image of where the player wants to be (and who she wants to be) that can make it possible to seize any fleeting opportunities to create a future she finds appealing.

CHAPTER 9

Homo romanticus *and other* homines

From the perspective of the social sciences, two species of human being bestride the earth – *homo economicus* (the rational maximiser of utility) and *homo sociologicus* (a social chameleon whose character is determined by its cultural environment). This chapter documents the characteristics of a third equally important denizen of the social world – *homo romanticus* (the self-creating, sentimental, sympathetic and imaginative social animal). It also argues that these three species are rarely found in their pure form. Instead, of course, we usually find *homo sapiens* – endowed with characteristics from all three purebred species in varying proportions to suit different environments. This poses considerable challenges for the social scientist. How are we supposed to decide when (and how far) each set of characteristics is likely to be dominant, and build our explanatory models accordingly? And how far are hybrid models of motivation possible or desirable? This chapter outlines answers to these questions, and indicates ways in which economists can meet the challenges of analysing markets and societies full of individuals who are socially constructed and creative as well as rational.

I *HOMO ECONOMICUS* THROUGH THICK AND THIN

Homo economicus evolved as a discrete analytical species dominating economic discourse from Benthamite utilitarian stock, and was first identified with precision by John Stuart Mill. Mill may have chided Bentham for his 'limited conception' of human motivation – for reducing 'Man, that most complex being', to a simple maximiser of utility or pleasure (subject to constraints), and for ignoring the role played in human affairs by the pursuit of excellence, honour, power and beauty;[1] but when it came to economics and analysing 'the merely *business* part of the social arrangements', Mill was quite content to consider the conduct of man 'solely as a being who desires to possess wealth', and to abstract from all other emotions and motives.

Indeed, he saw economics as delimited by its reliance on the central assumption that an economic actor is 'a being who invariably does that by which he may obtain the greatest amount of necessaries, conveniences, and luxuries, with the smallest quantity of labour and physical self-denial with which they can be obtained in the existing state of knowledge'.[2] Here is the classic rational maximiser of utility who was to become central to standard economics and Rational Choice Theory – someone who strives to maximise his wealth and consumption potential, while minimising both the input of work and the need to sacrifice immediate gratification to meet the demands of the future.

It is easy to underestimate how controversial an assumption this picture of the motivation of economic agents can be. Are wealth or pleasure maximisation, and work aversion, really the central tendencies of economic life? Are personal happiness and wealth the sole values for economic agents, and are they synonymous with each other? Max Weber famously argued in *The Protestant Ethic and the Spirit of Capitalism* that, while the highest goal for the capitalist is 'the earning of more and more money', this is 'combined with the strict avoidance of all spontaneous enjoyment of life', and is pursued with an asceticism and a sense of duty more usually associated with a religious 'calling'.[3] The near-monastic life of some of today's investment bankers – who amass great fortunes but still submit to almost constant work and a regular schedule of calls-to-prayer ('meetings') at all times of day and night as a signal of devotion to their calling, and who practice almost total abstinence from family life or holidays – may suggest that Weber's theory of capitalist motivation has considerable contemporary relevance. There often appear to be no diminishing marginal returns to increased wealth – suggesting that it is wanted for reasons other than material enrichment; and there is often little apparent disinclination to work long hours – again suggesting that hedonism is not at the root of motivation.

In *Unto This Last*, John Ruskin made the related observation that 'a true merchant' does not see his function as maximising profit, but instead devotes all his energies to producing a quality product at 'the cheapest possible price where it is most needed'. To this end, he prioritises 'the perfectness and purity of the thing provided,' and 'faithfulness to engagements' (the latter 'being the real root of all possibilities, in commerce').[4] This important point is echoed more recently in the writings of the business economist John Kay: companies and their employees and directors cannot, if they wish to be successful, simply aim directly to maximise profits or wealth; they must pursue and balance a number of (sometimes contradictory) intermediate goals that may in psychological terms be unrelated to profit maximisation. Indeed, the successful entrepreneur may more often be a perfectionist who takes a pride in the quality of the product, or in opening up a new market, than someone obsessed simply with maximising the size of his pay-packet or the value of his company's shares. As John Kay puts it: 'The businessman whose concern is to build a good business will be more successful than the businessman whose concern is to create shareholder value, and will often be more successful in creating shareholder value.'[5]

None of this would have come as much of a surprise to Mill, or to many in the economics profession since. Faced with clear evidence of motivation in the economic sphere that cannot easily be reduced simply to the maximisation of wealth and consumption (or the minimisation of work), many economists have followed Mill in seeing economics as an 'abstract' science, whose findings are 'true without qualification, only in a case which is purely imaginary'.[6] Walter Bagehot, for example, was adamant that political economy is 'a science of "tendencies" only', modelling 'the result of certain great forces, as if these alone operated'.[7] In particular, he was quite clear that *homo economicus* is merely a convenient abstraction:

More competent persons, indeed, have understood that English Political Economists are not speaking of real men, but of imaginary ones; not of men as we see them, but of men as it is convenient to us to suppose they are.[8]

All science, if it is to progress, necessarily involves simplifying models, and economics is no exception. As Paul Krugman has observed, *homo economicus* may be an 'implausible caricature', but it is also 'a highly productive one, and no useful alternative has yet been found'.[9] So, for example, while it would be difficult to model directly the positive effect of the pride taken by a good business person in developing her product and markets, or in looking after her employees, if it is the case that these attributes do in fact normally help maximise profits, then – for some purposes at least – we can usefully employ a simplified model of profit maximisation to predict outcomes.

Bagehot himself likens the use of *homo economicus* as a simplified model of motivation to considering the operation of forces in the physical world without friction:

If such a simplification is necessary in physical science where the forces are obvious and few, it must much more be necessary in dealing with the science of society, where the forces are, in comparison, very various and difficult to perceive.[10]

Nevertheless, while Bagehot and Mill both agreed that it is useful to focus on the self-interested pursuit of wealth as the main motive of economics, they were equally insistent that simplified abstract models based on this motivational assumption should not be applied to make policy recommendations without very careful consideration being made of other possible relevant and complicating factors.[11] Indeed, Mill was surprisingly optimistic about the possibility of precision when considering the impact of a number of distinct causal factors. The applied economist, he argued, should start with abstract conclusions deduced from the central motivational hypothesis of wealth maximisation, and then add or subtract the effects of other 'disturbing causes':

The disturbing causes have their laws, as the causes which are thereby disturbed have theirs; and from the laws of the disturbing causes, the nature and amount of the disturbance may be predicted *a priori*, like the operation of the more general laws which they are said to modify or disturb, but with which they might more properly be said to be concurrent. The effect of the special causes is then to be added to, or subtracted from, the effect of the general ones.[12]

It remains a contested issue in modern social science how often different motivational impulses do in fact operate concurrently to produce predictable *mixtures* of discrete effects (as Mill assumed), and how often, by contrast, entirely new *compound* motivational tendencies are created when separate tendencies are added together (as Ruskin always assumed).[13] Moreover, Mill's conviction that 'disturbing causes' follow predictive laws of human nature of their own that can be isolated by related social sciences has also proven optimistic: there has not always in practice been much success in other social sciences in producing simple predictive models to sit alongside those based on *homo economicus*. Social analysis remains a messy affair. It is this which has encouraged economists to forget Mill's strictures about treating the results of abstract economic analysis as provisional in an applied setting until other causal factors have been taken into account; and it is this, too, which has encouraged the extension of models based on *homo economicus* to the broader study of politics and society – a move that Mill himself would have deplored.[14]

In modern Rational (and Public) Choice Theory, *homo economicus* is assumed to capture the main motivational tendencies of social and political as well as economic actors. Indeed, Rational Choice Theory represents an attempt to unify the analysis of social interaction under a single all-conquering motivational hypothesis. So, for example, lobby groups (such as farmers' unions) are often analysed with 'rent-seeking' models, which assume that the groups' members are motivated by self-interest to try to harness the government machine to redistribute wealth to themselves from hapless consumers or taxpayers. To this end, it is assumed in these same models that the lobbies try wherever possible to incentivise self-interested bureaucrats and politicians (by means of bribes, campaign finance, or the delivery of votes) to impose high tariffs or quotas (or allow monopolies to develop) that enable the lobbies' members to capture the 'rents' accruing from market inefficiency.[15] Likewise Mancur Olson has used the model of *homo economicus* to explain why certain powerful pressure groups representing concentrated sectoral interests (for example, farm lobbies) exist, while pressure groups representing wider more diffuse interests (for example, consumer groups) tend not to exist. On the assumption that individuals seek only to maximise their own interests, it follows that the pursuit by groups of common interests and collective goals is problematic and vulnerable to *free-riding* by individuals who calculate that they could enjoy the collective good without making a personal contribution. Olson argues that the incentive to free-ride is especially high in large groups where individuals gain only a small fraction of the benefits of their own contribution, and where the costs of establishing effective bargaining procedures to organise (and police) individual contributions are high. By contrast, Olson argues that groups with the means to develop 'selective incentives' (such as specialist insurance or closed-shop arrangements) that give individuals strong incentives to be contributing members, and groups that are small and socially homogeneous enough to find it easy to organise contributions (and sanction free-riding), find it easier to be effective.[16] Olson's theory seems to offer a cogent explanation of why relatively small and narrowly focused special interest groups often have disproportionate ability to further their interests by political lobbying.

Such Rational Choice models can be highly instructive and suggestive. Nevertheless, in their full-blooded form, where they make the substantive and highly contentious assumption that political and bureaucratic motivation is always self-interested (that is, directed at maximising personal wealth), they are also relatively easy to falsify in specific cases. It is simply false that *all* members of *all* pressure groups, and *all* (or even most) bureaucrats and politicians, are out to maximise their 'rents' or wealth. Green Peace activists, for example, are unlikely to see any commercial or environmental benefits accruing to them personally from their contribution to the disruption of whaling or oil exploration, and yet they are notoriously committed and unlikely to free-ride on the contributions of others. Some bureaucrats and politicians are also clearly driven by normative agendas that run directly counter to the assumed goal of self-promotion and personal enrichment. This need not be a problem for Rational Choice models so long as they are not supposed to be universally applicable. Indeed, given the clear predictions that follow from the substantive motivational assumptions on which they are based, it should be possible to analyse the explanatory potential of such models in different conditions, and develop what Green and Shapiro have called 'empirically testable accounts of which domains of politics rational choice theories can be expected to succeed in and why'.[17] As Green and Shapiro also argue, however, in their book *Pathologies of Rational Choice Theory*, this is often not the approach taken by Rational Choice theorists. Instead of sticking to 'thick' versions of the utility maximisation model – where what is meant by 'utility' is clearly specified and all relevant actors are assumed to maximise profits, wealth, or pleasure – so that it is necessary to look for alternative causal explanations where this model fails to explain and predict, many social scientists have instead adopted a 'thin' and flexible version of what constitutes rational choice.[18]

'Thin' accounts of economic and political rationality appear, as Green and Shapiro note, to be much less controversial than thicker versions: by not pre-specifying the nature of the utility to be maximised, they are able to subsume a wider range of motivational impulses into one universal model of behaviour.[19] Indeed, by stipulating that rational agents simply optimise their preferences whatever they happen to be, 'thin' versions of Rational Choice Theory ape the practice in standard neoclassical economics of assuming that rationality need not entail the pursuit of a particular goal (such as wealth or happiness) but merely the ability to rank consistently – and optimise the satisfaction of – preferences determined 'exogenously' (outside the model). In this account, the provenance of preferences is not considered; they are simply taken as 'given', and all that matters is that they can be consistently ordered. Moreover, the precise content of the preferences is taken to be whatever is revealed by the choices that consumers actually make. In the case of our Green Peace activist, the preference revealed might be for kudos among fellow warriors (if this is all he could reasonably expect to achieve) or the furtherance of a strictly normative goal of a world freer from environmental degradation. With such an elastic account of 'utility' (the satisfaction of any preference), all that is left of Mill's *homo economicus* is that the agent is a maximiser, operating on the basis of rational expectations of how best to optimise his preferences within the constraints faced. Of course, without the tendency to maximise and the assumed ability to rank preferences (transitively) and form rational expectations, there would be no tendency to social equilibrium and consequently no basis for precise predictions of social outcomes. It is hardly surprising, therefore, that these formal features are taken by economists to be the irreducible core of *homo economicus*.

Milton Friedman famously defended controversial hypotheses (such as those using the 'thick' account of *homo economicus*) from accusations that their assumptions are clearly unrealistic, by arguing that a theory should be tested not by the realism of its assumptions but by the accuracy of the predictions it allows.[20] Indeed, he went so far as to argue that lack of realism is a positive virtue in a hypothesis (or its assumptions) if conjoined with simplicity and predictive capacity:

Truly important and significant hypotheses will be found to have 'assumptions' that are wildly inaccurate descriptive representations of reality, and, in general, the more significant the theory, the more unrealistic the assumptions (in this sense). The reason is simple. A hypothesis is important if it 'explains' much by little, that is, if it abstracts the common and crucial elements from the mass of complex and detailed circumstances surrounding the phenomena to be explained and permits valid predictions on the basis of them alone.[21]

When considering the 'maximisation-of-returns hypothesis', Friedman readily acknowledged that 'businessmen do not actually and literally solve the system of simultaneous equations in terms of which the mathematical economist finds it convenient to express this hypothesis'; nor do they possess the perfect knowledge of relevant data assumed. Nevertheless, Friedman argued that the hypothesis is validated by seeing that entrepreneurs could not compete and survive for long if they did not in fact learn to behave like this – since systematic failure to optimise would lead them to lose out to those more efficient than themselves.[22] This step in Friedman's argument is dubious: for it essentially assumes that there is an efficient outcome 'out there' to which markets tend. Indeed, Friedman's attempt to validate the assumption of market rationality and a tendency on the part of individuals to maximise returns is dependent on the very general equilibrium model of markets which the assumption is (in turn) used to support. If, on the contrary, markets behave, as Schumpeter and Arthur assume, like dynamic systems that never settle into equilibrium, then it is far from clear that a strategy of maximising efficiency in the short term (by optimising given factors, endowments and preferences) is either possible or desirable. The ability to succeed in creative markets may depend not on efficient optimisation of current endowments but on nurturing the capacity for creativity and adaptability to change.[23] This shows the danger of the backward inference of standard rationality assumptions from the efficient market hypothesis (itself dependent on the 'social physics' metaphor of equilibrium).

Friedman's more general insistence on the primary importance of rigorous empirical testing – designed to judge any explanatory model 'by the precision, scope, and conformity with experience of the predictions it yields'[24] – might seem to provide a better basis for establishing the worth or otherwise of the *homo economicus* assumptions central to Rational Choice

Theory and standard economics. To put it simply, the question is whether empirical tests show that economic and political actors do in fact behave more or less as models using these simplified (and apparently unrealistic) assumptions predict that they should. The problem with this approach is that, unfortunately, there are a number of reasons why testing by economists and social scientists of their own theories is frequently much less rigorous and conclusive than they like to believe. This is crucial: for if testing cannot rigorously establish the relative worth of different simplified assumptions, this would seem to suggest that it may (contrary to Friedman) be wise to rely on the initial plausibility of assumptions as at least one screen for their suitability.

Green and Shapiro argue forcefully that there are four common (often inadvertent) features of Rational Choice analysis that tend to undermine the objectivity and rigour of any actual testing of its hypotheses and assumptions. First, the particular model and assumptions used may bias the interpretation and assessment of evidence: the lens of theory and dominant model (in this case, *homo economicus*) constitute cognitive spectacles that lead to distortion as well as focus in the analyst's vision. As Green and Shapiro put it, all too often Rational Choice analysts allow 'their theoretical commitments to contaminate the sampling of evidence', and they 'dwell on instances of successful prediction'.[25] Moreover, research is usually 'theory driven rather than problem driven, designed more to save or vindicate some variant of rational choice theory rather than to account for any specific set of political phenomena'.[26] In other words, the problems studied are selected as well as framed with the theory in mind, and with a view to bolstering the claims of the dominant paradigm. Some novel ways of avoiding this sort of selection and interpretation bias will be discussed in chapter 10.

A second reason highlighted by Green and Shapiro for shortcomings in the rigour of testing is that inconvenient data and results are sometimes simply ignored and, more frequently, explained away by 'posthoc theory development'. In particular, theory-saving adjustments to the assumptions specified in models are allowed to correct for any prediction failures and to bring the implications of hypotheses in line with outcomes.[27] So, for example, Olson's theory that successful lobby groups usually offer 'selective incentives' (involving material rewards) to encourage participation may be extended to suggest that these can include 'social' selective incentives – in particular, the social kudos flowing from participation.[28] As Green and Shapiro note, the trouble with such an extension is that it blurs the distinction between, on the one hand, a model based on the assumption that all actors are interested only in material self-interest and, on the other hand, an explicitly sociological model that takes account of individuals' sense of belonging to a group or norm-driven behaviour. Indeed, if more and more adjustments to what counts as selective incentives are allowed to explain away most or all instances that seem to disprove Olson's theory, its apparent universality becomes a testament only to theory-saving ingenuity.[29]

A related analytical sleight of hand is endemic to models using the 'thin' version of *homo economicus*: if rationality entails no more than optimising the satisfaction of whatever preferences we happen to have, then most behaviour will count as rational. As Green and Shapiro put it, with ingenuity 'almost any conceivable behavior can be shown to be rational', and 'almost any conceivable political outcome can be shown to result from acts of individual maximization'.[30] Even suicidal commitment to a task becomes maximising behaviour of a perverse sort. Worse still, when the content of preferences is simply revealed by being read off the choices made, it is often impossible to know whether an unexpected outcome is the result of a genuine change in preferences or some irrational failure (or norm-driven refusal) to satisfy particular preferences. The 'thin' version of Rational Choice Theory produces propositions that are so poorly specified as to be largely meaningless, untestable, or even circular. As Bo Rothstein has put it in his discussion of the 'thin' version of the economic approach:

The problem is that, because it has no theory of where preferences come from (of what is 'expected utility' for different actors), it must generally deduce preferences from behaviour: the dependent variable is thus used to explain the independent, which in turn is re-used to explain the same dependent variable.[31]

A final 'pathology' highlighted by Green and Shapiro that reduces the chances of rigorously testing the explanatory efficacy of Rational Choice Theory models based on *homo economicus* is that of systematically ignoring 'competing' or 'alternative' explanations.[32] There are often alternative sufficient explanations of an outcome, and even more often other contributory causes that may be relevant. For example, even if the pattern of lobby pressure may appear to provide a sufficient explanation for the differentiated environmental policy stance of US politicians, we should not ignore the possibility that discourse analysis and interviews would reveal strong normative differences that could provide a competing sufficient explanation of policy differences. Likewise, German firms may have economic incentives to reinforce those institutional settings in their country that support their areas of comparative advantage; but that does not imply that other political and normative factors play no part in the evolution and sustainability of these institutions. All too often economists and political economists hide behind the supposed virtue of economy of hypothesis to restrict their focus to a single explanatory framework and model of motivation. Economy of hypothesis is a recipe for analytical bias and oversimplification, especially in areas where rigorous proof of the validity of hypotheses is in fact impossible.

In summary, it is fair to conclude that *homo economicus* is more likely to be an analytically useful model of motivation in the study of economics or politics if it is in the form of a substantive and fully specified hypothesis that individuals seek to maximise self-interest defined as pleasure or wealth. This hypothesis is clearly plausible in certain circumstances, and is capable of producing predictions of behaviour that can be tested with some degree of rigour. Such a 'thick' version of *homo economicus*, however, is clearly incapable (as Mill well understood) of providing a universal model of behaviour in all social settings. Universality of this sort is, by contrast, the apparent preserve of 'thin' accounts of rationality, but only because they are so flexible and vacuous that they often end up explaining very little – unless supplemented by other models that explain the provenance and content of preferences.

2   *HOMO ECONOMICUS* IN SYMBIOSIS WITH *HOMO ROMANTICUS*

This section analyses how some crucial Romantic lessons about the nature of human motivation relate to the *homo economicus* of standard economics and Rational Choice Theory. The aim is to establish more clearly the limits of applicability of 'thick' models of *homo economicus*, while improving our understanding of what is actually involved in the pursuit of self-interest. At the same time, the aim is to supplement the 'thin', or purely formal, model of Rational Choice with a better understanding of the origin and nature of preferences.

Many of the most important Romantic insights in this area were ably expressed by Hazlitt. In his essay on Bentham in *The Spirit of the Age*, he made two telling and relevant criticisms of the sort of utilitarian thinking that later came to underpin the model of *homo economicus*. First, he criticised Bentham for not making 'sufficient allowance for the varieties of human nature, and the caprices and irregularities of the human will' – in particular, its passions, whims and fancies.[33] In a fascinating discussion of Bentham's theories of crime, punishment and legal reform, Hazlitt took issue with the assumption that even criminals are to be analysed as mere rational utility maximisers who will give up the life of crime if given suitable incentives to do so. Hazlitt argued that the criminal is not typically 'the dupe of ignorance, but the slave of passion, the victim of habit or necessity'.

He continued: 'The charm of criminal life, like that of savage life, consists in liberty, in hardship, in danger, and in the contempt of death, in one word, in extraordinary excitement.'[34] As we shall see later in the chapter, such non-rational facets of character are often just as important in economic as in criminal life; and, whenever they are, models based purely on the motivational hypothesis of rational utility maximisation will give misleading results.

In the same essay, Hazlitt was also critical of Bentham for being too dismissive of the 'collateral aids', the 'rules and principles', and the 'vantage-ground of habit' used by individuals in the moral or practical calculations they make.[35] Utilitarianism demands too much of the cognitive capacity of moral agents (who must calculate all the possible consequences of different candidates for action), just as standard economic models demand too much of the computational capacity of self-interested utility maximisers. In both cases, calculations by real-world actors cannot practically encompass all the relevant factors on each occasion; instead they must be structured and supplemented by rules of thumb and habits. The significance of this is that these rules and habits do not all tend to produce the same rational answers and therefore do not allow us to assume a 'perfect' or 'one-stop' model of rationality or morality; rather the rules and habits are socially constructed and vary in the perspectives they promote, the colouring of data they provide, and the structuring of thought they bestow. The behaviour, thought and, indeed, preferences of individuals are, to some extent at least, socially formed. This insight into the social construction of behaviour and even rationality is embodied in the social sciences in the figure of *homo sociologicus*.

Elsewhere, Hazlitt – like Shackle a century and a half later – underlined the central role played by imagination in guiding action and forming expectations.[36] Both men argued that all rational action designed to promote our self-interest and satisfy our preferences necessarily relates to the future; and this future is, at the moment of decision, partially undetermined and unknowable, since it is still to be created by the original choices we (and others) will make and the new possibilities we (and others) will imagine. From the central importance of creative choice and inherently unpredictable novelty in constructing the future, it follows that the expectations that guide our choices must, in part at least, be the product of imaginative guesswork rather than rational probability estimates. Indeed, Hazlitt saw the future as 'a creation of the mind' – a 'void' until imagination 'impregnates it with life and motion'. He also argued that even the sense of self and personal identity which each of us projects into the future is a figment of the imagination (resembling 'a shadow in the water, a bubble of the brain').[37]

The writings of Hazlitt and Shackle between them have the power to transform the seemingly robust and pedestrian notion of individuals rationally pursuing their own self-interest into a necessarily Romantic and creative activity. To the extent the future is a blank canvas on which our imagination can and must work, even our sense of self going forward, and our conception of its interests, is partially created. The self whose interests we seek to promote must be extended into the future by the good offices of the imagination, since we cannot know for sure what we will be like in future (or even whether we will exist at all). Nor is extension through time the only imaginative extension of the self: it is also (as Hazlitt, Herder and Shelley all emphasised) extended by means of sympathetic imagination to include identification with those around us, and with the society which has in any case partly constituted our identity, our language and our modes of thought. Our identity includes a social dimension as well as being partly socially constructed. Finally, since it is beyond the remit of reason to calculate and predict an uncertain future, we can in the end only imagine the interest that our future (and socially extended) selves will feel for (or objectively have in) the future we are endeavouring to create.[38] Since all purposive action (including investing, saving and training) is undertaken with an eye on the future, and since imagination plays so central a role in our forward-thinking and planning, *homo economicus* seems to mutate before our eyes into *homo romanticus*. He is a visionary catching at shadows – shadows that may or may not be delusional.

In practice, of course, the future is not a total 'void' as Shackle and Hazlitt seemed to suppose. It is in part rationally predictable given observed innate and socially constructed regularities in behaviour (for example, the incidence of young men speeding in cars or dying from drink-related accidents). Very often, too, in any particular market or political situation, the degrees of freedom may be so few, the preferences, endowments and constraints so stable, and the information available from prices and other sources so good, that economic agents are in fact able to form rational expectations and optimise their position. In such constrained circumstances, Rational Choice and standard economic models based on the assumptions of *homo economicus* may work well to explain and predict behaviour; and social outcomes may tend towards a predictable equilibrium because there is at any point only one fully rational course of action – one way of optimising our preferences or maximising our utility within the given constraints. In short, economic agents may indeed (as economists assume) gradually learn how to calculate their best move and behave like *homo economicus*. By contrast, though, *homo economicus* looks to be a very poor hypothesis for understanding and modelling behaviour in conditions of radical uncertainty – when we must imagine the undetermined future and seek to fashion it according to the strategies and visions we create. In such conditions, we cannot assume that economic and political agents will converge on a uniquely rational set of expectations, or be able to adopt optimising strategies. With few relevant pointers to the future from past behaviour, and with new possibilities emerging unpredictably, there may be no stable set of preferences, no *ex ante* definition of what constitutes an optimal move, and no consistent informational feedback to guide the choices individuals make.[39] In short, in such dynamic and uncertain situations, the conditions for *homo economicus* to engage in (and benefit from) predictable optimising behaviour are absent; and we should consequently not expect markets and polities dominated by uncertainty and novelty to tend towards any sort of equilibrium or steady-state.

It is far from clear that most modern economics has fully absorbed this point. Consider an example from state-of-the-art macroeconomics: 'Endogenous Growth Theory' – despite trying to model Schumpeter's creative destruction and the increasing returns to research and development – is still modelled using microfoundations (including *homo economicus*) more suited to General Equilibrium Theory. In their excellent account of Endogenous Growth Theory, Wendy Carlin and David Soskice give us a glimpse of the motivational assumptions made:

Each individual in this economy lives for just one period and aims to maximise their consumption at the end of the period. The decision they face is how to maximise their consumption by making a choice between, on the one hand, working in the intermediate goods sector and receiving a wage of w and, on the other hand, engaging in R&D in the hope of innovating and making monopoly profits. The return from engaging in R&D depends on the probability of success and it is assumed that the investment of q units of labour in R&D leads to a quality improvement with probability λq.[40]

Since the space of possibilities opened up by novelty is often enormous, and since both the pace and the direction of innovation are inherently unpredictable (depending as they do on the vagaries of the imagination and on the intermittent incidence of increasing returns to innovation), it is unclear how individual actors are supposed to go about maximising their consumption potential. Nor is it obvious how their choices can be fully informed by rational probability calculations, when many of the possible outcomes of any decision cannot even be conceived of at the outset. *Homo economicus* – the rational maximiser of utility – seems out of place in the dynamic and uncertain world of creative destruction. The creative entrepreneur is usually someone who combines hard-headed calculation with sometimes disturbing and outlandish visions of possible breakthroughs and pitfalls; she is also endowed with an intuitive sense of where opportunities might lie; and she is often gripped by a consuming passion to win recognition for herself and her company in the battle to succeed. These traits of imagination, intuition and willpower cannot be reduced to a simple principle of maximisation.

At a more general level, standard economics and Rational Choice Theory are too sanguine that the way they define rationality (the main feature of *homo economicus*) is both unproblematic and universally applicable. The supposedly self-evident axioms of rationality they use are designed to ensure that the preferences on which we base decisions are consistent – that is, ordered in rank, and transitive (so that if I prefer A to B and B to C, I also prefer A to C). These axioms, however, begin to look far-fetched as a necessary condition of rationality when we are asked to rank preferences in the light of incommensurable values.[41] This is particularly so if the consistency aspired to is not just at the moment of decision but over an extended period. Consistency in preferences over time is required if revealed preferences and indifference curves at one moment are to be used to predict behaviour in the future; and the assumption of consistency over time appears necessary, too, if any investment in the future (at the expense of present gratification) is ever to be considered optimal or uniquely rational for an individual.[42] Where incommensurable values are involved (for example, autonomy, health and wealth) there is by definition no one uniquely rational trade-off ratio between them; and, in these circumstances, it seems odd to privilege consistency and transitivity of preferences (particularly over time) as a hallmark of rationality. Likewise, where uncertainty, novelty and creative choice abound, it is again unclear why we should privilege the ability to rank preferences in order as central to rationality. For preferences often look towards the uncertain future, where the outcomes of choice are dependent on creativity and choice in the future. In these circumstances, we cannot know what the future will hold, or even be sure that we would like the envisaged future if it comes. In a world where preferences, the implications of choice and the options available are all in a constant state of creative flux, it may hardly be worth our while carefully ordering all our preferences at any moment; and it is certainly unwise to assume that these preferences will remain as ranked for long. This renders the very notion of optimal choice in future-directed action suspect; and it renders forlorn attempts to predict behaviour in uncertain conditions on the basis of indifference curves constructed from preferences revealed at one time.

To be fair to standard economics (and its philosophical parent, utilitarianism), the assumption made in the *homo economicus* model of motivation that individuals seek to maximise utility, wealth, or happiness on the basis of rational assessment of evidence and probability forecasts is not without some basis of fact in human psychology and behaviour. We only have to see people shopping around banks for the best savings rates, or searching for the best school for their children, to know that many of us have a strong disposition towards maximisation and a marked tendency to consult league tables and consumer surveys for information. Where economists go wrong is if they assume that the tendency to maximise utility is ubiquitous (or even always desirable), and if they assume that maximisation and the assessment of probabilities (and other evidence) are pure constructs of reason without input from imagination and sentiment.

Daniel Kahneman and Amos Tversky have done much to alert the economics profession to psychological and behavioural traits displayed by economic agents that suggest the need to make important modifications to the *homo economicus* model.[43] In particular, they have noted that we tend to have greater aversion to losses relative to the status quo than liking for commensurate gains; and, once we possess something, we need to be paid more in compensation to give it up than we would have paid for it before we owned it (the so-called 'endowment effect').[44] These findings are damaging to the standard twin assumptions of a unique market equilibrium and a constant disposition to optimise a given set of stable preferences. Kahneman and Tversky have also highlighted broader 'framing' effects – namely, the influence on our preferences and decisions of the wording or reference points with which we frame (or formulate for others) different options.[45] They have further noted that we tend to overestimate the probability of suffering risks that we (or close acquaintances) have experienced before, even when we are exposed to good statistics on actual probabilities.[46]

These are now generally accepted as important instances of deviation from the pure *homo economicus* assumption that agents objectively optimise their preferences on the basis of the best available information. What is less often noted is that an understanding of the role played by our imaginations may provide a plausible explanation for why these deviations occur, and how to avoid them. It is because it is easier to imagine what it would feel like to be without something we now have than to imagine having something we do not already have that consumers are sometimes more loss-averse than appreciative of prospective gains. Similarly, it is because it is relatively easy to imagine suffering something we have previously witnessed that we tend to be more influenced by personal experience than objective statistics. It is our failure to imagine more creatively things we have not ourselves experienced that makes us have unstable preference in the first case, and fail to make a fully rational assessment of probabilities in the second. In each case, a stronger imagination would make us more likely to behave in line with the *homo economicus* model. When it comes to framing effects, too, imagination plays its part: it is because our analysis of evidence and options is imaginatively coloured and structured by the reference points and language we use that we are prey to others intentionally and unintentionally manipulating the formulations chosen (especially through advertising). We are, though, less likely to be misled if we learn to be openly receptive to a variety of structuring assumptions and creative in our use of different frames, the better to judge their relative worth. Once again, the ability to act rationally and optimise requires a disciplined and active imagination.

In *The Paradox of Choice*, Barry Schwartz points out that maximisation may in any case be an unwise strategy to employ, leading to anxiety and computational overload, wherever consumers are faced with too many options or a burgeoning number of choices; in these cases a strategy of satisficing (being content with a good enough outcome) may be more efficient in terms of time and contentment.[47] Schwartz argues convincingly that, while human consciousness and civilisation have hitherto evolved in ways that helped sort the wood from the trees and save time in the decisions and choices we make – by 'filtering out extraneous information' and restricting the number of options – modern society seems to be reversing this trend.[48] Nowhere is this more evident than on the internet: where a shopper for clothes or holidays would previously have had their options edited by the local shop or travel agent, an almost infinite number of options is now available to everyone on the world-wide web. In such circumstances, maximising in the strict sense – considering all the options available, ranking them and choosing the best one – becomes impossible. Moreover, the economist cannot simply retreat into arguing that, in such cases, satisficing is the new maximising (because of the efficiency costs of extended search). For, as Schwartz points out, maximisation is a 'state of mind' or a disposition, not merely a logical construct or 'measure of efficiency';[49] and, in any particular case, the individual endowed with this maximising disposition has no way of knowing whether the good enough would – all things considered – be better than searching for the best, until he has already considered all the options and every piece of relevant information. In such situations, a learned strategy of satisficing would not only cause problems for economic modellers who assume that consumers always optimise; it would also, Schwartz argues, leave any economic agents still harbouring the underlying disposition to maximise with the emotional cancer of regret or fear of perfection forgone. They could always imagine how much better the options not considered might have been.[50] This brings us back to the role of imagination and sentiment in maximisation.

Maximisation when considered as a psychological disposition involves more than rational calculation, prediction and the optimisation of available endowments and options. It also frequently involves the creation of idealised images of perfection that we then struggle to find or construct in reality. This imaginative creation of idealised images, and the mutation of these images into aspirations, is what drives economic and political agents to create new goods, new technologies and new preferences, and to improve existing institutions. It is also what drives them to search out the best available options in everyday conditions of choice. Every economy and every society needs its maximisers, its dreamers: they may help improve efficiency and certainly promote innovation. But the disposition to maximise comes at a price. For one thing, the idealised images created by our imaginations can be mirages and delusions, and can spur us on to waste our energies and talents. Secondly, the maximiser not only has idealised expectations of the future, but also very often strong idealised counterfactual visions of how the past could have been better had he only tried a bit harder or searched a bit longer. As Schwartz points out, the anticipation or fear of this sort of regret – imagining how we will imagine how much better an alternative could have been – often motivates us to search out more and more options where they exist, and worry about choices to be made, to the point of paralysis.[51] For this reason, a successful society also needs plenty of satisficers – those who can imaginatively construct a stable image of a good enough life and be guided by it. They form the social bedrock of contented and un-neurotic doers that make the world go round. In short, a bounded or constrained imagination can be invaluable; for when the imagination is unleashed and sets to work constructing visions of all possible futures and might-have-beens and all the possibilities of later regret, we are in danger of losing ourselves in a myriad of glittering and frightful possibilities.

3 *HOMO SOCIOLOGICUS*: COHABITING WITH COUSINS

One of the principal weaknesses of the 'thin' account of rationality informing most modern versions of *homo economicus* is that the content of preferences is not stipulated. Preferences are simply assumed to be 'given' or 'revealed' by choice. A complete explanation of social and economic outcomes requires, of course, that we can account for the provenance and nature of preferences and any systematic influences upon them. Many preferences are created by imaginative individuals; but before we analyse more fully the self-creating choice of identity and preferences, it is useful to consider the social construction of other preferences. This involves revisiting briefly some of the lessons of Romantic organicism, and examining the extent to which these are replicated in the model of motivation central to many modern approaches in sociology and political science – that of *homo sociologicus*.

From Herder and Burke onwards, Romantic thinkers focused attention on the role of languages, traditional institutions and inherited norms in structuring individual thought and behaviour. Herder foreshadowed the interest shown by Wittgenstein in the extent to which the socially formed structures of particular languages condition the way we think about the world. For Herder, the educational transmission of language and tradition to the next generation was the means of passing on a 'kinship mode of thought', which allowed for both the 'cumulative progression' of a civilisation and the knitting of individuals 'into the texture of the whole'.[52] Both Burke and Herder emphasised the importance of a national 'spirit' in developing the cohesion and sense of belonging necessary to the organic development of a *Volk* or people; and they underlined the crucial role of inherited institutions and traditions as well as language in embodying this spirit.[53] Individual men and women were seen as quintessentially social constructs – their role, behaviour and thought-processes a function of their place in the whole. Indeed, Herder argued that our very conception of happiness, and the 'manner and measure' of our 'joys and sorrows', are the product of the time and country in which we live.[54]

Translated into the terminology of today's social science, these lessons of Romanticism remain highly pertinent. As Geoffrey Hodgson notes in his critique of the overemphasis in economics on 'market individualism', we need to appreciate the extent to which our understanding and even perception is structured by 'socially acquired cognitive filters'.[55] Socially constructed linguistic rules of classification, inherited myths, and the dominant metaphors, images and narratives of our time all influence the way we see the world; and they structure the way (as economic agents) we analyse data and choose to behave. Moreover, as Hodgson also notes, even our preferences, aspirations and choices are '*partially* constituted and guided by culture and institutions'[56] – shaped by shared norms and institutional contexts. The content of our preferences, the frames of reference of our rational expectations, and the ways in which we formulate the parameters of choice are all products, in part at least, of our social interaction. In the words of Emanuel Adler, 'rational actors live and act in a socially constructed world'.[57]

Even more troubling for those wedded to the individualistic *homo economicus* model of motivation, it is not only the content of our preferences, the nature of our beliefs, and the type of constraints we face that are socially formed: the very logic of motivation may vary with time and place. As North explains, 'The exact mixture between the genetic predispositions and the cultural imperatives is far from resolved'.[58] Unresolved, too, is the relative importance of the underlying logic of rationally optimising whatever preferences we have (usually understood by economists to be an innate universal phenomenon) and various socially constructed and culturally differentiated motivational logics (which in some cases run counter to the logic of maximisation). Following March and Olsen, many Constructivists argue that the specific institutional framework in which individuals are embedded helps form their identities, as well as defining the roles they are expected to play – the 'scripts' they should follow. For example, EU bureaucrats in Brussels may share different constitutive norms from the members of EU farming lobbies; and priests in the Catholic Church may be guided by a different normative logic from London-based investment bankers or Californian hippies. In each case, the particular 'logic of appropriateness' is something which, when identified, can be used to predict behaviour.[59] Here then is a predictive model of motivation to rival *homo economicus* – that of *homo sociologicus*.

The relative analytical strengths and weaknesses of *homo economicus* and *homo sociologicus* are hotly contested. These two rival *homines* – or 'sets of guiding assumptions', as Claus Offe calls them[60] – often appear to be slugging it out in a battle for dominance that rages deep in the traditional heartlands of both economics and sociology. For example, it may be hard to explain the behaviour of firms without reference to distinctive corporate cultures and norms that serve, in the words of Bruce Lyons, to 'modify human behaviour in a group away from the rugged individualism of *Homo economicus* and towards *Homo sociologicus*'; but equally, as Lyons also puts it, '*Homo economicus* is too powerful a beast to tie down for long', and opportunistic behaviour can all too easily resurface to undermine any such cultures.[61] It is becoming increasingly clear that outside certain clear 'reserve areas'[62] where each of the *homines* lives undisturbed, both species of men tend to thrive together; both have an important analytical role to play in explanatory models, and neither of them can be fully reduced to the other. As Albert Weale argues:

Homo economicus and *Homo sociologicus* reflect two aspects of the social world. Just as there is rational strategic calculation in politics and social practices more generally, so there are rule-governed and normative aspects to the economy. We have no theoretical paradigm that adequately integrates the two – nor are we likely to have one.[63]

Advocates of each model of motivation often try to encompass the other within their own set of structural assumptions. For example, champions of *homo sociologicus* may find it tempting to see both the axioms of rationality (that make consistency totemic) and the goals of maximising utility or optimising preferences (normally associated with *homo economicus*) as merely expressions of a socially constructed language and logic of interaction – the fragments of a shattered normative outlook that constitute one particular (presumably Anglo-Saxon) society of shallow maximisers. But such a complete reduction of *homo economicus* to a version of *homo sociologicus* is not plausible: it is clear that the powers of logical deduction and the disposition to optimise are extremely widespread and powerful phenomena in most social settings. Likewise, it may be tempting for proponents of the *homo economicus* model of motivation to go beyond the use of Game Theory and Rational Choice Theory to explain why apparently bizarre social norms are useful in solving coordination problems that would otherwise bedevil self-interested actors, and to assume also that such functionality explains origins and compliance. In other words, it may be tempting to use the microfoundational assumptions of Rational Choice Theory to explain the origins and compliance mechanisms of social norms and institutions, as well as their value to self-interested actors. But, as Offe has argued, just because norms such as keeping promises clearly boost economic efficiency by reducing the transaction costs involved in drawing up and policing legally watertight contracts, this does not mean that 'economising on transaction costs' can be a sufficient 'legitimating and motivating force' to ensure compliance.[64] The norms that drive *homo sociologicus* cannot be reduced to the logic of maximising self-interest without changing behaviour for the worse. Moreover, as Rothstein has articulated clearly, 'establishing a political institution to overcome a collective action problem itself presents a collective action problem'.[65] For example, even if it pays society as a whole to have an institution (or norm) limiting free-riding (say by firms in the provision of training), it is not clear why, on Rational Choice assumptions, individual actors (or firms) would cooperate to set up the institution (or norm) in the first place (given the incentives for free-riding before the institution is in place to sanction such behaviour). *Homo sociologicus* cannot be simply reduced analytically to *homo economicus* any more than vice versa.

In real life, the two *homines* need (and cannot avoid) each other: left to his own devices, *homo economicus* is not socialised enough to be trusted to maximise his own utility (given coordination problems), nor even to know the social meaning of the utility he seeks to maximise; and *homo sociologicus* (as a simple creature of social conditioning) is a prey to the awesome power of rationality and optimisation to disturb the best-laid social structures, and reduce norms to dust, when any new possibilities for opportunistic behaviour emerge. *Homo sociologicus* needs to enlist the help of rational optimisers (as poachers turned gamekeepers) to design institutions that can withstand new opportunities for free-riding on the public good of social norms; just as *homo economicus* needs socially constituted norms and values to avoid market failure and achieve a social ordering of preferences that is not arbitrary.[66]

Homo sociologicus (as normally conceived) has inherited some but not all of the traits of Herder's citizen of the organic *Volk*: what is missing is an understanding that, as well as being socially formed, individuals can often act autonomously, make independent choices, and initiate changes to inherited norms and institutions. The social unit (because it is more than the simple sum of its parts) is an important explanatory force in its own right. But individuals are only partly constituted by society; and they also help form it. In the language of modern *Constructivism*, society and individuals are 'mutually constituted': actors are 'regime-makers' as well as 'regime-takers'.[67] The reason, I believe, that social scientists have generally failed to operationalise models accounting for this self-evident mutual constitution of individual and society is that they tend to think purely in terms of combining the respective logics of *homo sociologicus* and *homo economicus*. The power of rationality and optimisation (belonging to *homo economicus*) can only allow the socialised individual (*homo sociologicus*) to transcend the hand dealt by history to the limited extent of engineering a more efficient use of existing endowments to meet socially given goals. What is normally required to break the seeming circularity of socially formed individuals reforming the society that has formed them, is to admit the role of imagination in creating genuinely novel (exogenous) possibilities that allow us to break free from the implicit determinism of social construction and perfect rationality. In other words, it is *homo romanticus* much more often than *homo economicus* that can explain what Rothstein calls the '*formative moments* of political history', when actors 'change the rules of the game'.[68] These moments happen not only, as Rothstein supposes, when existing institutions 'are so incapacitated as to be unable to handle a new situation.'[69] Creative and imaginative political and economic actors can come up with improvements and new commanding images of a better society at any time; and these can be enacted by means of persuasion or force.

Introducing *homo romanticus* alongside *homo economicus* and *homo sociologicus* – her better established cousins – transforms our understanding of social interaction, and establishes the limits of both these older deterministic models of motivation. It is important to note, however, that *homo romanticus* is as heavily influenced by her cousins as they are by her. Creativity may allow us to transcend our inheritance, and our imaginations may enable us to chart our way through (and exploit) uncertainty; but creativity and imagination are both bounded to some extent by what has been and what is feasible. When we imagine new ideas, we are doing more than rearranging existing mental furniture. Nevertheless, the new original connections are still generally between existing (socially given) ideas; and, however much a new idea may take on a life of its own, it must – if it is to be enacted in the real world – suit its cognitive and social environment and be capable of expression in a language common to others. *Homo romanticus* has no choice but to be schooled by society and to work with instrumental reason, if she is to leave the world of insubstantial dreams. Furthermore, most new ideas are not the product of lone dreamers: they are the social products of institutional contexts – universities, firms, or political parties – where imaginative agents spark off each other and in reaction to unexpected juxtapositions of existing ideas from different sources. Novelty is as much the product of conversation and debate as of imagination; and some forms of social conditioning – some versions of *homo sociologicus* – privilege such creative discussion and debate more than others.

Social scientists need to come to terms with the symbiosis of the three *homines – economicus, sociologicus* and *romanticus*. The symbiosis may be between pure exemplars of each working together. More often, though, each individual actor exhibits traits of all three species in varying proportions. Modern *homo sapiens* has a split personality – at once a calculating optimiser, the creature of social conditioning, and the imaginative creator of new ideas. How we account for this complex motivational reality depends on the way the three traits (or *homines*) interact. Whenever there is a neat division of labour – areas where each of the *homines* thrives on his own, or tasks that each of the traits performs on its own – we can try to develop an analytical approach that demarcates carefully the 'reserve areas' belonging to each type of motivation. In such circumstances, a full explanation may require all three models, but they will be seen as complementary in the insights they bring: *homo romanticus* will explain the creation of new ideas, preferences and institutions; *homo sociologicus* the role of social conditioning and the social construction of preferences; and *homo economicus* the optimisation of given endowments and preferences. All that is required is that the frames of reference of each model are set carefully to reflect the relevant findings of the others – so that *homo economicus* is, for example, optimising socially defined preferences in the light of socially determined and newly created constraints. It becomes much more complex, however, when the discrete logics are seen to operate in exactly the same domain – when, for example, socially constituted normative behaviour (or 'high' politics) competes directly with the opportunistic pursuit of self-interest (or 'low' politics) perhaps in the mind of each individual.[70] For then, we have to establish the relative importance of each motivational logic (perhaps by analysing the discourse used by the relevant agents). We must also be alive to the possibility that the competing motivational logics may interact to form highly specific motivational compounds. For example, a socially constituted goal of spreading political freedom or income equality may compete with the quite different logic of maximising wealth. In such circumstances, there is no single rational trade-off, and no single rational division of labour, between such potentially incommensurable and conflicting motivational logics. Political trade-offs between championing freedom or equality, on the one hand, and maximising prosperity, on the other, are contingent acts of social self-creation.

We will return in chapter 10 to different analytical procedures that may prove useful in these different cases – where there is an easy division of labour between models of motivation, and where there is none. In the meantime, it is helpful to complete our picture of *homo romanticus* by examining further the role of sentiment, sympathy and self-creation.

4 THE ROLE OF SENTIMENT AND SYMPATHY

The Romanticism of Wordsworth, Herder and their followers owed much to the 'cult of sensibility' that preceded it. As Campbell and others have pointed out, the eighteenth century was not a monolithic age of reason, but in many ways also 'the Age of Sentiment'.[71] For example, the Earl of Shaftesbury and later Jean-Jacques Rousseau both championed the view that natural feelings, affections and intuitions are the best sources of morality; and the cult of sensibility they helped to foster attached great value to the spontaneity and authenticity of feelings and the expression of emotion. This focus on sentiment and feelings represented an important counter-weight to the other great eighteenth-century intellectual culture – the obsession with reason and the pursuit of self-interest. Sentiment was even recognised as having considerable significance for the analysis of economic behaviour. Adam Smith, who spent years working on *The Theory of*

Moral Sentiments, was also alive in *The Wealth of Nations* to the role of sentiments in the economy. Indeed, as Emma Rothschild has well documented in her book *Economic Sentiments*, Smith frequently emphasised the 'vexations' and 'emotions'[72] that motivate economic agents: commerce cannot function, in Smith's vision, without 'confidence' and freedom from 'fear' of arbitrary appropriations; and even the motivation to trade and do business is less the function of some assumed rational imperative to maximise than the result of a disposition or 'propensity to truck, barter, and exchange one thing for another'.[73]

Since Smith's time, the importance of sentiments in driving economic behaviour has received relatively little attention from mainstream economists, with the notable exception of John Maynard Keynes. In the famous chapter 12 of *The General Theory*, which analyses the behaviour of investors in conditions of uncertainty, the cool rationality and optimising behaviour of *homo economicus* is little in evidence: instead decisions are driven by 'animal spirits', by 'a spontaneous urge to action', and by 'whim or sentiment'. In Keynes' vision, market valuations are not soundly based on probability-adjusted calculations of prospective yield (since these are usually not possible); rather, valuations are subject to 'waves of optimistic and pessimistic sentiment'.[74] As any investor knows, market confidence (and related economic outcomes) depend as much on the group psychology of hope and fear as on any rational assessment of probabilities. Stock-market bubbles, in particular, are driven by what the former US Federal Reserve chairman Alan Greenspan famously called 'irrational exuberance'. Coleridge used an interesting metaphor for such exuberance in his 'Lay Sermon addressed to the Higher and Middle Classes': he likened the ever-more reckless reliance on credit in bubble conditions to 'Icarian credit', the 'illegitimate offspring of confidence' – a reference to Icarus whose hubristic overconfidence led him to fly so close to the sun that his artificial wings melted. In Coleridge's description of boom and bust, rational 'circumspection' gives way to 'emulous ambition' and 'incaution', and finally to 'a vortex of hopes and hazards, of blinding passions and blind practices', whenever the 'commercial spirit' and 'lust of lucre' are not sufficiently balanced by the correctives of religion.[75] In this account, rationality is not the inalienable right of *homo economicus*, but the fragile product of a necessary balance between a desire for money and moral restraint. Economic rationality – the settled disposition to take account of all factors – comes into play only when avaricious sentiments and wilder emotions are under the governance of a moral compass.

It was Ruskin in *Unto This Last*, who highlighted the crucial role played in economic activity by the nobler sentiments of affection, trust and '*esprit de corps*'. He noted that the most successful firms are those that manage to mobilise these sentiments to their advantage, by giving workers a 'permanent interest in the establishment'. Just as 'a battle has rarely been won unless [the soldiers] loved their general', so 'the largest quantity of work' will be done not for pay but out of affection and loyalty.[76] These sentiments are valuable because they involve the willing suspension by workers of short-term self-interest in order to pool efforts for the common good; in economists' jargon they help solve 'coordination' and 'principal–agent' problems that cannot be solved by *homo economicus* alone. Such useful sentiments, however, need to be nurtured by reciprocal loyalty and consideration by managers – a factor frequently overlooked by modern management theory. Recommended increases in flexibility and short-term efficiency may come at the cost of reduced commitment to staff, with a consequent loss of trust and *esprit de corps* on their part. There is no single correct trade-off between commitment and flexibility for all situations, of course, and in some cases the gain to efficiency from the introduction of short-term contracts, staff reductions, or pay cuts may be worth the loss of cooperative sentiments. But a management approach that undervalues the role played by such sentiments may lead to the wrong trade-off being chosen. All too often, the sacrifice of staff loyalty involved in making reductions to headcount, wages, or job security produces long-term costs to the firm in the form of opportunistic behaviour and lack of commitment by staff that dwarfs short-term efficiency gains. Moreover, these costs may not be adequately controlled by new performance incentives, management targets and tailored contracts. For staff have an information advantage over their employers despite 'big brother' techniques (such as spying on e-mails): if they are not motivated to do their best, employees will find ways to do just enough to avoid sanctions; or they may learn to prioritise marketing their virtues to management over doing the job itself.

An interesting theory in modern economics that recognises these dangers is the 'efficiency wage' hypothesis invented by George Akerlof and Janet Yellen, which helps explain why companies often do not cut wages enough to prevent unemployment at the macroeconomic level. Building on the analogy of 'gift-exchange', Akerlof and Yellen acknowledge the importance of reciprocity and a sense of fair play in inducing sustained effort by employees; and they argue that firms tend to benefit from paying more than the market-clearing wage in times of recession, and suffer poor results if they cut wages below what employees perceive as 'the fair wage'.[77] The reason is that we all prefer to work hard for an employer who treats us well, and tend to become angry and demotivated when working for one we see as acting unfairly or failing to appreciate our efforts. The 'efficiency wage' theory accepts that sentiments of fairness and obligation sometimes play a crucial role in economic motivation and outcomes, and that harnessing these sentiments can be vital to the pursuit of maximum efficiency at company level.

Sentiments also play an important role in the consumer market. Indeed, Campbell went so far as to say that 'consumer behaviour is just as much a matter of emotion and feeling as it is of cognition'.[78] When we buy roses for Valentine's Day, we are often guided by the heart and the symbolic resonance of the intended gift (and the feelings it is expected to engender), rather than by a fine calculation of advantage. Likewise, we project visions of future bliss onto that booked holiday in Venice, and the anticipated bliss produces feelings of pleasure in us now. An economist may insist that such projected and current feelings are part of a good's 'utility' if he wishes, but to do so is to lose the texture of consumer activity. Consumption is as much about Mill's 'imaginative emotion',[79] feelings of self-worth, the pleasure of giving and the thrill of speed, status, or style as about material advantage. A catch-all definition of the 'utility' we are said to pursue obscures the nature and source of value and motivation; and it provides no leverage for understanding and explaining in any detail the patterns of consumption in an economy.

Of all the sentiments that guide behaviour, by far the most important in the philosophy of Adam Smith and many of the Romantics is sympathy. In *The Theory of Moral Sentiments*, Smith highlighted the central role played by sympathy, which he made clear involved both susceptibility to the feelings of others and the ability to imagine ourselves in their predicament. Interestingly, D. D. Raphael argues that Smith saw sympathy more as the basis of our moral judgements than as a motive force in itself.[80] Such sympathy involves what Vivienne Brown has called 'bifocal vision' – imagining first how we would feel in someone else's situation, and then observing this 'as an outsider' in order to form our own judgement.[81] The detail of Smith's theory of sympathy is not important here. What is relevant is his view that sympathetic imaginative identification with the viewpoint and feelings of another (including those of an 'impartial spectator') can be the basis of reasoned judgements; and relevant, too, is the fact that it was by means of the 'sympathetic imagination' that Smith sought, in the words of Abrams, 'to bridge the gap between atomistic individualism … and the possibility of altruism'.[82]

In general terms, sympathy can be seen as either widening the concept of self-interest, by allowing for our interest in (and identification with) the welfare of others, or as providing an important constraint on the pursuit of self-interest more narrowly defined. In the Romantic era that followed Smith, it became a commonplace that human beings are motivated by sympathy for others as well as by self-love. Herder, for example, wrote: 'All the instincts of a living being are reducible to *self-preservation* and *sympathy*. The whole organic structure of man is by superior guidance most carefully adapted to these two basic instincts.'[83] Being a good German, Herder used as his example that human beings possess sympathy and empathy 'to the highest degree' that 'even a tree arouses our sympathy', so that we cannot bear to see it cut down.[84]

Despite its pride of place in his moral philosophy, Smith failed to stress the importance of sympathy to economic behaviour. This was probably because he assumed that sympathy, like benevolence, is too weak a force to be effective in arm's-length market transactions or in the management of an economy as a whole.[85] It is undoubtedly the case that the ability to sympathise (and imaginatively project ourselves into the position of others) tends to evaporate with emotional and physical distance. For Smith, therefore, the social importance of a market was that it allows for mutually advantageous trades without the need for sympathy-induced moral judgements, benevolence, or any other explicitly moral motive. Where Smith missed a trick, however, was in not fully stressing the enormous potential significance of sympathy as a tool of self-interested behaviour in many kinds of economic interaction other than the trading of simple commodities. A good product designer or marketing manager of a consumer-specialty company, for example, empathises with the needs, desires and feelings of (potential) customers and can imagine herself in their shoes. An entrepreneur should not, of course, be so carried away by sympathetic identification with the feelings of others that she forgets her own company's interests; but she should be capable of the sort of 'bifocal vision' Smith posited for the making of moral judgements. In business judgements, entrepreneurs need to see the world from the perspective of client and competitor, the better to judge how to exploit their desires and harness their emotions and feelings.

Hazlitt well understood that our capacity for imaginative projection and identification is not infinite, and that this entails that the 'circle of our affections and duties' cannot extend across the globe.[86] In a modern context, this observation might suggest more than the limits of altruism and moral judgement: it might also suggest where we should expect to find the boundaries of an effective firm (or other organisation). Ronald Coase has argued that the boundary of a firm is set by reference to where the firm structure is more or less effective in reducing the transaction costs of exchange (for example, of labour) relative to arm's-length transactions.[87] Now if Ruskin was right that affections and duty are the most effective means of reducing such transaction costs, it may suggest that the limits of sympathetic identification and affection dictate where the optimal boundary of a firm will be. Firms or other organisations that are so large that employees cannot identify with each other or their bosses (and hence cannot trust them or feel a sense of duty towards them) may be relatively inefficient. Similarly, a firm is likely to have an effective marketing and production strategy only if it is close enough to its customers emotionally and physically to be able to identify with their wishes and needs, and tailor its product range accordingly. In other words, the practical limits of the sympathetic imagination may constitute both the effective boundaries of loyalty within a firm, and the boundaries of a firm's empathetic understanding of its customer base.

5 'SUPERMAN' AND SELF-CREATION IN ECONOMICS

In contrast to the relative certainties and predictability of the world according to *homo sociologicus* (socially structured and constrained) and *homo economicus* (tending to the rational optimisation of given preferences and factors), the world inhabited by *homo romanticus* is apt to be confusing and uncertain: the social constitution of our preferences, and of the roles we play and constraints we face, is only partial and always in flux; there is no way of predicting the future yet to be created by the free and creative choices we make; there is no single rational answer as to what trade-offs we should make between our own conflicting and incommensurable values; and there is no guarantee that we (or other agents) are motivated by rational calculations (even where these are possible) rather than by sentiments and emotions. It is in this very indeterminate state of uncertainty, however, that the seeds of human freedom and greatness lie. There is a danger that, when faced with no single rational or socially constructed answer as to how to proceed, economic agents may, like some of Jean-Paul Sartre's heroes, interpret such freedom as (in Murdoch's words) a form of 'random blundering' – marked by consciousness of the 'absurd emptiness' and occasional 'anguish' of acting for no reasons.[88] But, as Murdoch argues, such a nihilistic response to freedom from the determinism of social conditioning or perfect rationality is not that of 'the full-blooded romantic hero who believes in the reality and importance of his personal struggle'.[89] Indeed, the *homo romanticus* we have identified in economic life revels, as Mill did, in 'the conviction that we have real power over the formation of our own character'.[90] He may also revel, like Byron's heroes, in defying the constraints of convention; and he may take delight, like Nietzsche's Superman, in creating his own set of values and exercising his 'will to power'. Seeing his condition as characterised not so much by a lack of sufficient reasons for action as by a surfeit of conflicting reasons, the response of *homo romanticus* is to shout 'Yes' to life, and welcome the chance to create his own (and others') future according to his own freely chosen vision.

Schumpeter was mistaken when he argued that capitalism is an 'unromantic and unheroic civilisation', with no 'romance' or 'heroism' left, except the waning tendency of the bourgeois entrepreneur to labour hard to establish the capital necessary to bequeath to his children an industrial dynasty or a bourgeois home of a certain size.[91] In fact, the great entrepreneurs of the modern age behave, as often as not, like the quintessential Romantic hero. A few of them, indeed, resemble Nietzsche's Superman: to adapt Nietzsche's famous description, they loath 'the petty virtues, the petty prudences, the sand-grain discretion' of regulators, despise the 'ant-swarm inanity' and 'miserable ease' of the ordinary voter, and are contemptuous of the slave moralities of socialism and the safety net.[92] They see the business world as the perfect stage on which to affirm their unbounded 'will to power' and 'create themselves' as worthy of exceptional recognition and as a law unto themselves.[93] Furthermore, as a number of high-profile corporate failures have shown, such entrepreneurs may (to adapt the words of Byron this time) find that the same impulses that lead them 'To do what few or none would do beside' can, 'in tempting time', mislead their spirits 'equally to crime'.[94] The line between glorious ambition and reckless disregard for the proprieties of law and morality can be as thin in business as in politics or war. Even those many entrepreneurs who avoid the immoral excesses of Byron's darker heroes often resemble, in their restless and indefatigable urge for action, the conquerors and 'founders of sects and systems' described in these lines from Byron's famous *Childe Harold's Pilgrimage*:

> there is a fire
> And motion of the soul which will not dwell
> In its own narrow being, but aspire
> Beyond the fitting medium of desire;
> And, but once kindled, quenchless evermore,
> Preys upon high adventure, nor can tire
> Of aught but rest; a fever at the core,
> Fatal to him who bears, to all who ever bore.[95]

Such a thirst for adventure and challenge is often supplemented in the mind-set of entrepreneurs by an addiction to the intensity and authenticity of a life dedicated to realising their own dreams in the structures they create. As Byron puts it:

> 'Tis to create, and in creating live
> A being more intense, that we endow
> With form our fancy, gaining as we give
> The life we imagine, even as I do now.[96]

Francis Fukuyama, in *The End of History and the Last Man*, argues that Nietzsche was correct to identify 'the desire to be recognised as superior to other people' as a core part of what it is to be human; and societies like the erstwhile communist states, which ignore this fact, do so at their peril, since people 'will rebel at the idea of being undifferentiated members of a universal and homogeneous state'. A successful society, Fukuyama argues, is one that finds sufficient safe (especially economic) 'outlets' for this desire for superior recognition – thereby harnessing it in a 'regulated and sub-limated' form for 'productive uses'. These outlets, he adds, 'serve as grounding wires that bleed off excess energy that would otherwise tear the community apart'.[97] *Homo romanticus* in his extreme form is a dangerous being – prey to delusions, contemptuous of the lessons of history, and desperate to express himself and gain superior recognition by his exploits. A modern society must provide ways of safely channelling the energies of such beings to prevent their expression in ways that could subvert the freedom and security of its citizens. As Fukuyama demonstrates, it is one of the merits of a regulated free-market economy governed by the rule of law that it does just that.

Luckily, there is also a tamer version of the Nietzschean and Byronic hero than we have so far considered; and I would argue that most economic agents in modern economies share traits of this version. In capitalist market economies, most of us seize the opportunity for little acts of self-creation and self-development – trying out a succession of what Mill called 'experiments in living'. It is by our work – the tests we face, the goals we adopt, the unexpected achievements we have – that many of us find out who we are and what we are capable of. It is in our bid to overcome obstacles – tilting at the windmills of unnecessary targets, red tape and prejudice – that we prove ourselves. Whether bureaucrat, investment banker, watercress grower, decorator, engineer, shopkeeper, IT specialist, or teacher, most of us are blessed with chances to excel, to develop, to be recognised, and to win. Indeed, one of the main functions of the economy is to provide us with such opportunities for self-development – each according to her abilities and dreams. Furthermore, consumption, too, has become a means of self-creation and self-expression. Increasingly, we define our identities by the clothes we wear, the cars we drive, the holidays we take. As Campbell argues, we create in our imaginations an 'idealised self-image' of who we want to be and are then forced to act so as to 'bolster and protect' this image.[98] In doing this, we also create specific consumer preferences by projecting onto certain goods an imagined congruence with our idealised image of ourselves: we imagine that by buying that jacket, having that haircut, or choosing that colour scheme we will get closer to the new more perfect life we have already imagined.

We are all driven by a complex mixture of different motivational logics: we are influenced by sentiment and emotion, but also conform, in part at least, to the axioms of rationality and the logic of preference optimisation; and we are socially conditioned – to some extent structured by shared identities, norms and languages. In one sense, the drive for self-creation (associated with *homo romanticus*) is just one more of a long list of logics and motivational drives we must take into account. In another sense, though, the ability to create our own individual image of who we want to be, to shape our own set of preferences, and to act out our own dreams, is the most important aspect of our humanity. For it is this that allows each of us to combine all our complex motivational drivers and incommensurable values into a unique character-defining blend – a set of trade-offs that is an expression of who we are.

CHAPTER 10

Imagination and perspective in economics

Chapters 8 and 9 have examined the crucial part played by the imagination in guiding the behaviour of economic agents, and the significance of creativity for the dynamic structure of markets and economies. This chapter, by contrast, explores the role of imagination in economic analysis itself. Standard economics textbooks rightly emphasise the importance of mathematical modelling and statistical empirical research techniques, but generally give little attention to a number of equally vital roles for the imagination in analytical endeavour. These include imaginative empathy with the human subjects of study and their historically contingent and culture-specific modes of thinking; the creative formation of new systems of thought and new metaphors that can restructure our vision and understanding; the imaginative use of different perspectives and metaphors side-by-side to improve our reading of the multifaceted nature of reality; and an imaginative openness to both unexpected anomalies and the possibility of non-standard readings of reality. To understand why economists need to concern themselves with this sort of analytical imagination and conceptual creativity, it is helpful to focus first on the implications of Romantic theories about the impossibility of objective and unmediated empirical knowledge, and to re-examine, in particular, the role of imagination and language in structuring the world-as-it-appears-to-us.

I AFTER KANT: A DISCONCERTING OR LIBERATING PHILOSOPHY?

The Romantics inherited a recently transformed epistemological landscape. Hume had shown the impossibility of inferring the truth of general explanatory laws governing reality from the sense impressions that impinge upon us. His scepticism cast doubt on our ability to be sure of even Newton's most basic laws – rendering them the mere product of the imaginative projection of belief onto habitual associations of sense impressions and related ideas.[1] Kant had responded by arguing that a basic framework of time and space, as well as other *a priori* interpretative concepts such as causality, are pre-supposed as a necessary condition of our experiencing and understanding reality. Kant was adamant that we cannot have access to the world-*as-it-really-is* (independent of our interpretive structures) but only to the world-*as-it-appears-to-us*; but he argued that at least this world of experience is necessarily organised by certain *a priori* categories and principles that we contribute to it, with this organisation forming a sure foundation for scientific knowledge.[2] Tarnas sums up Kant's revolutionary position as follows:

Without such fundamental frames of reference, such a priori interpretative principles, the human mind would be incapable of comprehending its world. Human experience would be an impossible chaos, an utterly formless and miscellaneous manifold, except that the human sensibility and understanding by their very nature transfigure that manifold into a unified perception, place it in a framework of time and space, and subject it to the ordering principles of causality, substance, and other categories. Experience is a construction of the mind imposed on sensation.[3]

The implications of Kant's philosophy for our understanding of science were enormous. First, as Bryan Magee has explained, Kant underlined that the world we experience '*can never be independent reality*' of the sort that could objectively ground our knowledge. For Magee, 'The error at the heart of the entire empiricist tradition is what you might call the reification of experience, the mistaking of experience for reality';[4] and it is this error which, thanks to Kant and the Romantic thinkers that followed, we no longer have any excuse for making. Secondly, Kant taught us that the world we experience – the world-as-it-appears-to-us – is, in part at least, a creation of the mind: its very order and intelligibility is a function of the mind's capacity to order the chaos of sense impressions into a unified picture or framework of interpretation. Indeed, Kant ascribed an important role to the imagination in structuring our perception and understanding of the world according to both *a priori* interpretive principles and learned empirical concepts. It is the imagination, according to Kant, which synthesises the unstructured sense data we receive and enables us to recognise our experience as something specific by applying to it conceptual images we have constructed.[5]

As we trace the significance of these views for the modern social scientist, we need to explore the ways in which they have been re-interpreted and transformed in the intervening years by Romantic and post-Romantic thinkers, and by scientists themselves. It is important to say at the outset that Kant's particular insistence on there being certain universal interpretative principles with which we necessarily structure the world-as-it-appears-to-us has been less influential than his broader focus on the contribution of the mind to experience. Many modern scientists may accept a sanitised (physiological) version of Kant's belief in necessary conditions of experience to the extent that our brains are hard-wired genetically to process sense data in certain ways. Increasingly, though, the focus has switched to socially conditioned ways of structuring our experience (which may harden with education into semi hard-wired patterns in the brain), and to the scope for creative experimentation with new ways of constructing our experience.

It became a commonplace of Romanticism that observation (or perception) is the joint product of the objects impinging upon our senses and the contribution of our minds in interpreting these stimuli. Herder, for example, argued that a perceptual image is 'the product of an intellectual process; it is the creation of the mind itself in response to the stimuli received by the senses'.[6] Wordsworth, too, saw the mind as half-creating what it sees: the mind is both 'creator' and 'receiver' – 'Working but in alliance with the works/Which it beholds'.[7] In a passage from his *Table Talk*, Coleridge explained beautifully why the mind plays an essential creative role in all empirical observation: he insisted to a young empiricist who believed that all his principles were based on unadorned facts that 'unless he had a principle of selection, he would not have taken notice of those facts upon which he grounded his principle'. Coleridge continued: 'You must have a lantern in your hand to give light, otherwise all the materials in the world are useless, for you cannot find them, and if you could, you could not arrange them.'[8] As Coleridge makes clear, our ability to make sense of the abundant chaos around us depends on our supplying a theoretical and conceptual structure as a framework of interpretation. Over time, most scientists who think upon these matters have come to accept this central truth.

Even at the level of ordinary perception the mind's contributory role is significant. As the famous philosopher of science Thomas Kuhn wrote: 'What a man sees depends both upon what he looks at and also upon what his previous visual-conceptual experience has taught him to see. In the absence of such training there can only be, in William James's phrase, a "bloomin' buzzin' confusion".'[9] Wittgenstein illustrated how dependent our vision is on the learned conceptual structures we apply with his famous duck–rabbit example. The lines he drew are capable of bearing rival interpretations; and whether we see the picture as that of a rabbit or that of a duck depends on the prior held conceptual categories and expectations with which we observe it. We do not normally see the lines as ambiguous raw data and then search for the correct interpretation; instead, based on our experience, we simply see a picture of a duck or a picture of a rabbit. In this sense, perception is unavoidably interpretive: seeing something generally includes seeing it *as something*, and involves (usually unconsciously) the constitutive application by the mind of learned concepts to the objects of experience.[10]

At the level of scientific research, too, we do not have access to uninterpreted raw facts. For the potential field is almost infinite in extent and complexity, and we must order and select the data we consider. As Lionel Robbins insisted (inadvertently echoing Coleridge):

> *no* science really approaches the confusion of experience without a principle of selection – a principle of selection which, in the last analysis, is traceable to consciously formulated hypotheses or unconsciously formulated principles of selection. The idea that you look, so to speak, at something called history with a mind entirely devoid of ideas – to start what Locke calls *tabula rasa* – is nonsense.[11]

There can be no such thing in science (or history) as pure induction from objectively ascertained facts, since the evidence or facts we use are created in our minds by the application of existing theoretical principles of selection and categorisation to the manifold objects of experience. Herein lies a central problem for the scientist (or historian). If we can make sense of the world around us only by ordering it according to the conceptual grids and principles of selection we impose – and if, contrary to Kant, there is nothing universal and necessary about these interpretive principles – how do we avoid serious observational bias in favour of constructing evidence that supports our own prior theoretical schemes? Interestingly, Hazlitt accused Bentham of just such distortionary selectivity: 'He hears and sees only what suits his purpose, or some "foregone conclusion"; and looks out for facts and passing occurrences in order to put them into his logical machinery and grind them into the dust and powder of some subtle theory, as the miller looks out for grist to his mill.'[12] If all observation is focused and structured by the theories and metaphors we use, then the whole empirical basis of science seems in danger of being hopelessly compromised. As Nietzsche exultantly proclaimed, 'facts are precisely what there are not, only interpretations';[13] and if scientific theories cannot be derived by induction from objectively established facts, then these theories, too, are merely (in Nietzsche's words) 'an interpretation and arrangement of the world'.[14]

Many of the Romantics had a special fascination with the role of language in structuring our thought. For example, J. G. Hamann realised (to quote Andrew Bowie's account of his thought) 'that Kant's supposedly universal ways of categorising reality were actually dependent upon particular natural languages', and that 'these languages do not divide up the world in the same manner'.[15] Herder, too, saw language as at once a reflection of the past mental refinement of a particular civilisation and the inherited matrix in which we structure our thoughts.[16] Wittgenstein would many years later follow suit, arguing that our thought is permeated by language, and that the way we experience and understand the world is a function of the structure and rules of the languages we use.[17] Like Herder before him, Wittgenstein saw languages as intimately related to particular 'forms of life', with the meaning of words grounded in shared practices and assumptions.[18] These facets of Romantic thought from Hamann and Herder to Wittgenstein were to have huge implications for the social sciences. For they suggested that we can understand social behaviour and the patterns of thought underlying it only if we understand the languages (and associated social practices and traditions) in which that behaviour and thought is conceived and structured.

Crucially, though, Wittgenstein went beyond insisting that our experience and understanding of the world – the way we divide it up and organise it – is the product of socially agreed rules of use. He also argued that there is no Archimedean point outside language from which we can judge how well particular languages capture the real world: because we cannot escape the structuring role of language altogether, we can never take a neutral reading of the degree of success with which particular languages make sense of the world.[19] This seems to imply that there is no objective way of judging the relative value of different languages (and their conceptual grids). To the extent that this is true, we might seem destined to succumb to a form of cultural or intellectual relativism – to despair about the possibility of establishing the relative usefulness of different natural, theoretical and scientific languages. Indeed, taken to extremes, the Romantic philosophy of language and perspective threatens to lead us into the Post-Modern nightmare of what J. G. Merquior calls a 'free-for-all for warring perspectives': discourses and schemes of interpretation – none of them more valid than any other – battle it out for supremacy, and the 'will to truth' becomes little more than a mask for the 'will to power'.[20] In Merquior's account of Foucault's later thought, for example, theory is no longer 'like a pair of glasses; it is rather like a pair of guns; it does not enable one to see better but to fight better'.[21]

At one level, Foucault's fear of the oppressive dominance of certain 'totalising discourses' and their relationship to power[22] is justified. For our theoretical systems of interpretation affect our actions as well as our beliefs, and have the power to transform social reality and our physical environment. When a discourse becomes dominant, it alters the nature of the society in which we live. Left-wing French phobia of the discourse of neoclassical economics is easily explained. Discourses may in a very real sense construct the reality they purport to interpret. It is for this reason that economics as a discipline is riven by ideologically driven cleavages between different discourses, with their respective merits hotly contested for political as well as scientific reasons. For example, it matters to the way policy-makers think and act whether employment protection and unemployment benefit are seen as 'rigidities' impeding the efficient operation of markets (as in neoclassical discourse) or, alternatively, understood as the pre-requisite for the 'decommodification' of labour (as in Marxist discourse). Different theoretical discourses may imply different visions of how the world works, but they also imply radically different normative outlooks and different policy pronouncements. Keynes understood this perfectly. In the conclusion to *The General Theory*, he wrote:

the ideas of economists and political philosophers, both when they are right and when they are wrong, are more powerful than is commonly understood. Indeed the world is ruled by little else. Practical men, who believe themselves to be quite exempt from any intellectual influences, are usually the slaves of some defunct economist. Madmen in authority, who hear voices in the air, are distilling their frenzy from some academic scribbler of a few years back.[23]

Moreover, Keynes was not afraid to ascribe the popularity of Ricardian economics in ruling circles partly to the fact that 'it could explain much social injustice and apparent cruelty as an inevitable incident in the scheme of progress, and the attempt to change such things as likely on the whole to do more harm than good'.[24] Theoretical discourse, ideology and power are intimately related.

Where the Romantic Economist would take issue with many Post-Modernists (and indeed with Wittgenstein) is in the twin assumptions they make that the incommensurability of different languages renders these languages in some sense mutually unintelligible and that we cannot make any sort of comparison between them in their ability to capture reality. Different natural languages and theoretical discourses or perspectives cannot, it is true, be reduced to one common all-encompassing language, discourse, or perspective without loss of reality-disclosing texture. But such incommensurability in no way precludes us from being 'multilingual', and able to understand each perspective from inside; nor does it preclude us from noting the common conceptual ground between different discourses and, from this shared vantage point, comparing relevant differences. Moreover, while we cannot escape the structuring effect of language altogether, we can switch between different languages (or conceptual structures) and compare their usefulness in disclosing different aspects of reality. We can render mutually intelligible the differences between languages and theoretical discourses in the way they structure our understanding of reality; and we can rationally judge between them (in relation to specific problems) in terms of their explanatory insight, instrumental value and the respective distinctions they allow us to make.[25] In doing this, of course, we cannot simply judge each perspective directly against the world-as-it-is (unmediated by any conceptual scheme); but we can rationally deliberate about which aspects of reality disclosed by various perspectives are important to us; and we can also have an intuition as to whether a particular structure of interpretation captures and explains well those aspects of reality that we have decided are crucial or instead grates with our overall sense of what is going on.

To take a general example, Marshall argued that economic discourse often sows 'confusion' by drawing, and then applying, 'broad artificial lines of division' (such as that between capital and not-capital) which 'cannot be found in real life'.[26] Now, in any particular case, we can make a judgement about the value of such distinctions by comparing the perspectives provided by different disciplinary languages and everyday discourses. This helps establish common ground between them in how they organise and structure our view of what is going on, and also allows us to spot important differences. Experience can then teach us much about which conceptual grid is most useful in a particular situation; and intuition can help us sense whether economics or some alternative discourse better captures the aspects of reality with which we are concerned.

It remains the case, of course, that no discourse or theoretical language can give us an all-encompassing perspective. Reality – in all its unfathomable complexity – is beyond our power to capture. As Iris Murdoch puts it in her description of Sartre's philosophy:

What *does* exist is brute and nameless, it escapes from the scheme of relations in which we imagine it to be rigidly enclosed, it escapes from language and science, it is more than and other than our descriptions of it.[27]

The unending quest to interpret and grasp this brute reality may lead the greatest scientists to think outside and far beyond any existing conceptual framework – 'Voyaging through strange seas of Thought, alone', as Wordsworth said of Newton.[28] A Newton or Einstein may imagine some wholly novel configuration of the world-as-it-appears-to-us, before searching for the metaphors and extensions of language to express it to the rest of us. The new conceptual framework and metaphorical language (in Einstein's case, a four-dimensional space–time continuum 'curved' under the gravitational influence of mass)[29] may then disclose aspects of reality not previously cognitively mapped by anyone else, and make sense of previously unexpected, anomalous and indigestible intrusions of brute reality into the ordered field of our experience. Furthermore, it is my contention that much lesser mortals than Einstein can pursue a tame version of this same quest – by experimenting (in the tradition of Nietzsche) with a whole range of metaphors in the hope of borrowing conceptual structures from related disciplines and sparking new connections between them. For new refinements to the language in which we think can help disclose new and important aspects of reality to us. We will return later in this chapter to the scope in economics for such everyday experimentation with metaphor.

Any social science differs, of course, in one important sense from physics and other natural sciences: it is attempting to interpret a reality constructed by human beings who have already interpreted the world in which they live. Economists, like other social scientists, are seeking to interpret a pre-interpreted world, in which existing socially formed languages and theory-based structures of interpretation have, to some extent at least, structured the beliefs and behaviour of individual agents. For example, whether or not accounting discourse in an economy recognises 'intangible' as well as 'tangible' assets, and whether or not legal discourse distinguishes 'insider' from 'legitimate' trading, affects more than how well these particular discourses disclose aspects of corporate reality; it also implies different normative beliefs and different behaviour – in short, different ways of constructing social reality. When dominant conceptual languages and definitions differ between countries, this implies disjunctions in the very texture of social reality as well as in interpretations of it. Often, of course, the discourses used even within a single society are contested and fragmented, leading to social behaviour that is similarly fragmented and unstable. It follows that one important task for the economist is to be able to read the conflicting and often partially incommensurable discourses that structure social reality; and it is to consideration of ways to meet this challenge of interpreting the interpretations that influence behaviour that I now turn.

2 READING THE INTERPRETATIONS THAT STRUCTURE SOCIAL REALITY

Many modern social scientists – Constructivists in particular – acknowledge that shared languages, traditional outlooks and collective norms shape the perspectives, beliefs and behaviour of individual actors. They also recognise that the institutions, legal systems and foundational texts of a society

embody many of these shared cognitive and normative systems of interpretation and transmit them to the next generation. Indeed, institutions
and traditional narratives help instil in individuals a common sense of
identity and a shared 'logic of appropriateness'[30] that, to some extent at
least, guide the choices they make and provide them with a particular set of
reasons for action. Specific examples are often hard to pin down; but it
seems fairly clear that the American Declaration of Independence's insistence that the 'pursuit of happiness' is an inalienable right (like the US
constitution's enshrinement of the right to bear arms) has served to embody
and transmit a shared vision and set of values that partly constitute today's
American logic of appropriateness. Likewise, structural differences between
national languages – for example, between German (heavy in complex and
aggregative conceptual categories), French (heavy in abstract terms) and
English (uniquely flexible, practical and empirical) – serve both to reflect
and shape differences in the complexion of ideas and the standard cognitive
categories prevalent in these nations.[31]

In an influential essay, 'Interpretation and the Sciences of Man', Charles
Taylor highlighted the central importance of what he calls the 'web of
intersubjective meanings' that provide a people with 'a common language to
talk about social reality and a common understanding of certain norms', as
well as a 'set of common terms of reference'. These intersubjective meanings
constitute 'the social matrix in which individuals find themselves and act',
by embodying 'a certain self-definition, a vision of the agent and his society,
which is that of the society or community'.[32] For Taylor, 'The range of
human desires, feelings, emotions, and hence meanings is bound up
with the level and type of culture, which in turn is inseparable from the
distinctions and categories marked by the language people speak'.[33] As a
result, the art of interpreting the nexus of culture, language and behaviour
becomes a crucial component of social science. Such interpretation, Taylor
believes, must proceed (by analogy to the methods employed by a literary critic
interpreting a text) by highlighting any 'underlying coherence or sense' in the
situation studied.[34] When it comes to explaining patterns of social behaviour,
this involves understanding the specific set of meanings that constitute the
behaviour's significance for the actors concerned. As Taylor puts it, 'We make
sense of action when there is a coherence between the actions of the agent and
the meaning of his situation for him'. Making sense of action in this way
requires a careful 'reading' of the 'common meanings' which help structure
'the meaning of a situation for an agent'; and, crucially, Taylor maintains that,
when we are outside the civilisation concerned, such a reading requires us to
get 'somehow into their way of life, if only in imagination'.[35]

Taylor's emphasis on the importance of 'insight' and 'intuition' in successfully grasping 'the meaning field in question', and thereby reading the intersubjective meanings and practices of a society,[36] is reminiscent of the views of Herder. Herder advocated using a species of historical imagination as a way of empathising with the mind-set of geographically or historically distant civilisations.[37] Like Vico before him, he believed that a historian must, as Tarnas puts it, 'feel himself into the spirit of other ages through an empathetic "historical sense", to understand from within by means of the sympathetic imagination'.[38] Beatrice Webb came to a similar conclusion in the early days of sociology, arguing that 'sympathy' based on the faculty of 'analytical imagination' is crucial to understanding the full variety of human behaviour and motivation.[39] More recently, the classical or 'English School' approach to the study of International Relations has also stressed the importance, as Robert Jackson puts it, of getting '*inside* the subject' – interpreting a situation 'by gaining insight into the mentality of the people involved'.[40] It is a central tenet of the Romantic Economist, too, that analytical use of sympathetic imagination should be recognised as key to successful comparative analysis of different political economies and societies. Without it, we can never hope to get to the bottom of differences in the formation and content of guiding beliefs and preferences. As Taylor argues, the various 'conceptual webs' in which beliefs and preferences are constituted are often 'incommensurable', in the sense that they 'cannot be defined in relation to a common stratum of expressions'.[41] From this it follows that we cannot hope to understand differences in behaviour fully if we insist on operating only within our own, or some notionally universal, 'vocabulary of behaviour'.[42] We must seek to engage empathetically with the language- and culture-specific nuances of meaning and significance attached to action in different countries. Any systematic failure to do this will entail that our explanatory models are largely blind to the significance that the behaviour studied has for the actors concerned.

The analytical imagination required for a successful reading of the diverse interpretations and meanings that structure social reality is a special gift analogous to the unusual ability to be genuinely multilingual. As Taylor acknowledges, we all too often find 'great difficulty grasping definitions whose terms structure the world in ways that are utterly different from, incompatible with, our own'.[43] This raises the question of how we can nurture and develop this imaginative capacity. F. R. Leavis may have applauded Webb for seeing a literary training as a useful qualification for the sociologist – helping to develop the required sensitivity and imaginative openness to a wide variety of ways of life and feeling;[44] but what Webb could not have foreseen is how far the emphasis on mathematical skills in the social sciences of today has come at the expense of a literary training for most in the field. An alternative solution is to recommend that social scientists, including economists, should always take the time to go at least partially native in the society or economy they study – so that they have the chance to learn the collective narratives, neuroses, ideologies and psychological scars that influence behaviour. It is not possible, for example, to explain the specific transition path taken by each Central or Eastern European country from communism to market-based democracy since 1989 without understanding the very particular and localised impact of diverse twentieth-century historical events and narratives upon their collective modes of interpretation. Nor is it possible to explain fully the resilience of 'co-determination' mechanisms in the German corporate governance system without understanding the particular cultural and historical resonances that such close cooperation between management and workforce has for Germans, and without understanding the complex interdependence between this feature of corporate governance and so much else of significance in the German social economy.[45]

It should be emphasised that imaginative empathy with the society being studied – understanding the meaning and significance of behaviour 'from the inside' – is in no way a replacement for (nor antipathetic to) criticism 'from the outside'. As Adam Smith well understood, sympathetic imagination can be the basis of reasoned judgement precisely because it allows for what Vivienne Brown calls 'bifocal vision' – understanding from the inside and then judging from the outside.[46] The discourse used by Germans may be incommensurable in some respects with the discourse normally used by a British social scientist – requiring a sustained effort of internalisation and interpretation; but this does not make it difficult (once both discourses have been mastered) to isolate and analyse mutually intelligible differences between them, and then assess the impact of such differences. Furthermore, while it is not legitimate when explaining behaviour to ignore the local and cultural construction of both meaning and reasons for action, it is perfectly legitimate to complement this internal perspective with an alternative external or theoretical one. For example, while a local culturally aware perspective may explain action in the terms in which the agents themselves understand their own behaviour, a Rational Choice perspective may quite legitimately underline the functional impact (positive or negative) of that same behaviour. So, we may explain why religious groups originating in the Middle East avoid eating pork in terms of deeply entrenched cultural and religious beliefs, while at the same time analysing these traditional norms in terms of the functional rationale of avoiding a meat that can be dangerous in hot climates.

Since theoretical discourses can themselves have strongly constitutive effects on social reality, one important task for an economist seeking to explain economic behaviour in a specific country is to read and analyse the impact of the particular political-economy discourse that has structured the policy choices concerned. So, while a neoclassical economist may want to use her own theoretical perspective to analyse the impact of Scandinavian welfare states on market efficiency, she can account for the policy and behaviour choices actually made in these countries only by understanding the quite different discourse (centred on the concept of the 'decommodification' of labour')[47] in which the relevant local actors tend to structure their beliefs. In many societies, of course, the issue of which theoretical discourse should dominate is hotly contested – with sudden changes in intellectual fashion leading to dislocations in the theoretical structuring of observation, analysis and policy. This, too, must be the focus of our attention when explaining behaviour.

The emphasis by Taylor and others on society-wide webs of intersubjective meanings tends to obscure the equally crucial impact of intellectual specialisation in fragmenting discourse between those operating in different disciplinary and policy fields. As the renowned physicist David Bohm has pointed out, this fragmentation has, at the level of a society as a whole, had the effect of 'breaking the field of awareness into disjoint parts, whose deep unity can no longer be perceived'.[48] When policy-makers and analysts study the reasons why joined-up thinking is so difficult in dealing with many of the great interdependent issues that now face us (for example, in relation to global warming), they need to take into account the fragmentation of vision and incommensurability of conceptual frameworks implied by the increasing specialisation of discourses within economics and other sciences. Very often the cognitive dissonance between those operating in different policy fields is startlingly large. In some multicultural countries, there may also, of course, be a similar dissonance of outlook and perspective between different ethnic and linguistic groups. This, too, complicates the task of all social scientists, including economists, who want to model behaviour.

3 KUHN, IMAGINATION AND THE NATURE OF PARADIGMS

Thomas Kuhn, perhaps the most influential philosopher of science in the twentieth century, incorporated many aspects of Romantic epistemology in his theories – in particular an emphasis on the structuring role of prior theoretical beliefs in observation and analysis, and an insistence on the incommensurability of different theoretical discourses. Kuhn's theory of 'paradigms' and the nature of the shifts between them is of particular relevance to our consideration of the methodological importance in economics of both imagination and creative experimentation with different perspectives and metaphors.

Kuhn argued that scientists operate within the mental framework provided by paradigms. He defined a 'paradigm' as a 'family-resemblance' group of 'various research problems and techniques', a 'set of recurrent and quasi-standard illustrations of various theories', and a 'core of solved problems', learned models and shared practices. For Kuhn, a paradigm is not a definitive 'body of rules and assumptions' but a fully internalised intellectual culture – a discourse absorbed by education and training.[49] He argued that such paradigms guide the prosecution of all 'normal science'. Normal science in turn consists not in the formation of radically new theories but instead in 'mopping-up operations' – matching facts to existing theory and further articulating theory to resolve 'residual ambiguities' and already identified problems. As such, the 'enterprise seems an attempt to force nature into the preformed and relatively inflexible box that the paradigm supplies'.[50] Kuhn is careful to acknowledge the essential and positive role played by paradigms – focusing and directing research, providing researchers with a common intellectual language, and ensuring that they do not need to reinvent the conceptual and technical wheel each time. Paradigms provide scientists with a cognitive 'map'; and 'since nature is too complex and varied to be explored at random, that map is as essential as observation and experiment to science's continuing development'. Paradigms enable scientists in analytical terms to see the wood for the trees, and to isolate theoretically significant facts from empirical noise or insignificant anomalies.[51]

The beneficial effects of paradigms are, however, closely linked to the costs of the cognitive constraints they imply. In particular, the theoretical structuring of observations – the fact that different paradigms cause scientists to see the world differently – ensures that paradigms tend to be intellectually self-reinforcing. Scientists operating within them often fail to see what does not fit their theoretical expectations, and their area of investigative focus is in any case highly restricted to problems for which the paradigm is suited.[52] As Kuhn himself put it, the awareness of significant paradigm-challenging anomalies tends to emerge 'only with difficulty, manifested by resistance, against a background provided by expectation. Initially, only the anticipated and usual are experienced even under circumstances where anomaly is later to be observed.' This observational bias is partly offset, as Kuhn admits, by the precision of observational expectations cast by sophisticated paradigms, which helps throw any anomalies that are observed into sharp relief.[53] Nevertheless, scientists operating within a paradigm often remain resistant to wholesale paradigm change for two further reasons highlighted by Kuhn. First, when significant anomalies are recognised, the instinct of scientists is to adjust their working set of theories and assumptions 'so that the anomalous has become the expected', rather than challenge their whole conceptual framework. The result of this theory mending is usually an increased complexity in standard models and a 'proliferation of versions of a theory' – with sometimes so many ad hoc adjustments to theory that 'the rules of normal science become increasingly blurred'.[54] Secondly, there is a cultural inertia and resistance to radical theory change implied by the increasing 'paraphernalia of specialisation' – specialist journals, societies and academic departments – and by the fact that most scientific articles are written only with a specialist audience of paradigm-believers in mind. Kuhn argues that because the scientist is generally 'working only for an audience of colleagues, an audience that shares his own values and beliefs', he 'can take a single set of standards for granted'. Moreover, he adds, 'the insulation of the scientific community from society permits the individual scientist to concentrate his attention upon problems that he has good reason to believe he will be able to solve'.[55]

In considering the relevance of Kuhn's theory to the social sciences, it is useful to start by re-examining Rational Choice Theory – undoubtedly the dominant paradigm of modern political economy. The 'pathologies' in the conduct of research within this paradigm that Green and Shapiro have enumerated chime very closely indeed with Kuhn's concerns. These include most research being 'theory driven rather than problem driven', evidence being 'selected and tested in a biased fashion', a tendency to explain away inconvenient data by 'posthoc theory development', and a systematic failure to consider 'competing' or 'alternative' explanatory frameworks. Perhaps most telling of all is Green and Shapiro's focus on the tendency to water down and adjust the specification of what counts as rational utility-maximising behaviour in Rational Choice Theory models to the point where 'almost any conceivable behaviour can be shown to be rational'.[56] On this account, Rational Choice Theory does indeed bear the hallmarks of Kuhn's description of a mature paradigm – complete with the theoretical construction and selection of evidence and problems, the prevalence of theory-saving adjustments, and the proliferation of types of Rational Choice model.

There are a number of respects in which the whole academic structure of the modern social sciences conforms to Kuhn's picture. As David Colander has observed in *The Lost Art of Economics*, the institutional incentives of the economics' profession, in particular, ensure that most researchers concentrate on what he calls 'microdisagreements' as opposed to 'macrodisagreements' – with the latter defined as those that might 'significantly change their analysis'.[57] The structural incentives to stay within the bounds of Kuhn's 'normal science' include, Colander argues, 'tenure and quantitative publication requirements based upon rankings of journals', which militate against research on problems that cannot be resolved within the confines of short specialist journal articles.[58] The academic journals concerned operate with strong normative criteria, judging submissions on their use of state-of-the-art models and techniques from within the paradigm; and they tend to judge iconoclastic attacks on the paradigm as a whole as insufficiently specified. It is possible, of course, to overstate this culture of conformity: since many academics are measured in performance terms on the number of citations of their work, there are benefits to being an outrageous academic outlier who must always be cited or quoted if only as a straw man in more conformist articles. Nevertheless, many researchers can identify with Colander's diagnosis.

One of the most striking, but also potentially misleading, aspects of Kuhn's theory is his argument that a paradigm 'shift' in response to a paradigm 'crisis' is a sudden, once-for-all, and 'unstructured event like the gestalt switch', brought about by 'flashes of intuition' that present us with a new way of looking at the world and solve some of our most pressing analytical puzzles.[59] The reason that Kuhn is convinced that paradigm shifts are sudden and 'irreversible' – no less than 'scientific revolutions' – is that he sees paradigms as 'incommensurable' with one another: those operating within different paradigms see the world differently and have such different 'criteria determining the legitimacy both of problems and of proposed solutions' that they are 'always slightly at cross-purposes'. Kuhn assumes that this incommensurability entails constraints on the mutual intelligibility of paradigms and, consequently, the need for something like a 'conversion' experience to occur before a switch is made.[60]

At one level, Kuhn is clearly right (and completely in line with Romantic theory) to emphasise that flashes of intuition are often needed to create new paradigms – new ways of arranging and seeing the world. David Bohm has written in a similar vein of the scientist assimilating experience into a 'coherent totality' of harmony and beauty – '*discovering* oneness and totality in nature' – by *creating* 'new overall structures of ideas', in a sudden 'flash of understanding' and '*imaginative insight*' that resolves previous confusion and contradiction.[61] Bohm's language echoes Coleridge's repeated stress on the role of the imagination as a 'synthetic' faculty or power that can 'by a sort of *fusion*' produce 'out of many things ... a oneness'.[62] Coleridge's own subtle analysis of the imagination, however, led him to focus not only on sudden flashes of inspiration, but also on the willed and conscious exploration of new ways of seeing – the directed search for new connections and new metaphors. Coleridge always saw the imagination as acting in concert with reason and under the direction of the will.[63] This suggests one set of criticisms of Kuhn's theory: first, he seems to underestimate our ability to make deliberate and rationally guided efforts – not least by experimenting with different metaphors – to spark the intuitive jumps necessary to create new theory. And, secondly, he overstates how unusual or exceptional is the generation of completely novel ideas and conceptions. New and original ways of thinking – in the sense of new connections, new hypotheses and new perspectives – may appear at all levels of research, and are the potential prize of any imaginative thinker. They need not be merely the product of once-in-a-lifetime 'gestalt' switches.

A related criticism of Kuhn's theory concerns his belief that paradigms are serial and that shifts between them involve an irreversible process of conversion. Kuhn did stress (in the 1969 postscript to his original book) that he saw the incommensurability of paradigms as neither precluding communication between those involved in different paradigms, nor preventing scientists from having '*good* reasons' to change paradigms. He remained convinced, however, that the genuine adoption of a new paradigm requires a conversion (or internalisation of outlooks and vocabulary) that is difficult to achieve and unlikely once achieved to be reversed – a process akin, in short, to going 'native'.[64] This may sometimes be true. In general, though, Kuhn overstates the difficulty of scientists (whether as individuals or in teams) being, as it were, 'multilingual' – in the sense of being genuinely at home in two or more paradigms at once. Certainly at the level of different theoretical approaches (such as Rational Choice Theory and Constructivism) *within* each of the broad social science disciplines (economics, sociology, political science and so on), there is usually enough conceptual and technical common ground to make it feasible to consider the different approaches from the 'inside' and decide which one to use. What is more, the success of some interdisciplinary organisations, such as the Santa Fe Institute in New Mexico,[65] suggests that conversation even between disciplines as different as economics, physics and biology can be straightforward enough to produce new insights.

Kuhn is indeed correct to maintain that different paradigms or theoretical outlooks are incommensurable in the sense that they cannot all be conflated into one super-paradigm, and that switching from one to another entails 'losses as well as gains' in terms of vision and analysis.[66] But such incommensurability is not a necessary barrier to having two or more paradigm structures at our disposal at one time and being able to switch back and forth between them; nor, as Charles Sabel has pointed out, does it preclude the intellectually nimble from understanding the mutually intelligible differences between the ways these paradigms structure problems, evidence and outlook, and hence learning how to exploit whichever is best in a particular situation.[67] Indeed, I would argue that the very incommensurability of paradigms – the fact that each one shows us different aspects of reality and provides relatively more or less analytical traction with particular problems – entails that the scientist should aim, wherever possible, to examine his area of research from the perspective of more than one paradigm. If we want to understand our complex and multifaceted world, we need to have a multifaceted intellectual approach, based on a conversation between academic disciplines and paradigms. We need to think inside and outside the intellectual box provided by any one paradigm. Being ready to switch cognitive spectacles in this way is a necessary part of any reasoned and open-minded analysis of the world around us. In particular, we need to view the world from different angles if we wish to make informed choices about which problems require our attention and which paradigms seem best placed to help us solve them. For all the subtlety of Kuhn's theory, it seems both to overstate the theoretical difficulties of such a multi-paradigm approach and to underestimate the need for it.

One advantage of multi-paradigm vision is that it can help us resolve the problem of anomalies with greater ease than Kuhn allows. Kuhn's argument that different paradigms structure the vision of scientists differently so that they 'see different things when they look from the same point in the same direction' is his most telling: but, as he himself acknowledges, this theoretical construction of observation does not imply that scientists 'can see anything they please'.[68] As Wordsworth would say, scientists only *half-create* the evidence they work with. At times, we do not observe what we expect to see, and we observe what we do not expect to see. Brute reality constrains our ability to read any particular order into the world; indeed, it has a habit of spoiling the best-laid systems of interpretation. Kuhn, though, argues that normally, thanks to paradigm inertia, scientists are resistant to acknowledging these anomalies, and attempt to explain away those they do acknowledge by making minor adjustments to the existing paradigm. In his account, it is only when anomalies build up to an intolerable degree that a 'paradigm crisis' is triggered and a whole new explanatory framework may be accepted. In practice, however, scientists have it in their power, even within the ordinary course of their work, to detect and overcome the theoretical biasing of observations and interpretations.[69] The contention of the Romantic Economist is that this can best be achieved by engaging in multi-paradigm vision – by looking with the help of several cognitive lenses – and trying out different ways of mapping and categorising our experience and then judging between them. In this way, the scientist can render himself relatively open to registering anomalies – aspects of reality that do not fit into his normal scheme of interpretation; and he can proactively choose which among several existing paradigms best reveal and make sense of aspects and problems important to him.

4 THE CREATIVE USE OF METAPHOR

Before we consider the practical research implications of multi-paradigm vision further, it is worth re-examining a more general technique for changing the way we see and understand the world, namely the creative use of metaphor. Experimentation with metaphor plays two related functions that are central to the project of the Romantic Economist. First, it can add new depth to our vision and alert us to previously hidden aspects of reality; in this role it often enables us to escape the confines of paradigm-bound perception and interpretation. Secondly, it can suggest new ways of developing the theoretical texture of economics and related social sciences, by providing us with alternative ways to model and structure our analysis. The incorporation of new metaphors may help a paradigm evolve, but it may also sometimes lead to a paradigm shift.

When Wordsworth spoke of 'the modifying powers of the imagination' – its capacity to present familiar things in a new light – he explicitly linked these powers to the use of metaphor.[70] Applying words (and their associated images and resonances) from one context to an object in another context was one of the techniques perfected by Wordsworth to allow his poetry, in the words of Coleridge, to awaken 'the mind's attention from the lethargy of custom'.[71] Metaphor can play a similar role in shaking us out of habitual ways of seeing within economics or any other discipline. As I. A. Richards once said, metaphor is a 'transaction between contexts'.[72] Its use involves experimenting with changes to the conceptual grid with which we observe and interpret reality, by borrowing elements of the standard grid used in one context and applying them to another context. For example, if we call labour 'a commodity', it reveals new aspects and new interrelationships that we might not have noticed before, such as the fact that the value of labour is measured in terms of the price it can fetch on the world market and is (in this respect) like the value of any other traded good. Metaphor can be seen as a sort of filter or lens through which we look at something; and using a metaphor for the first time, or changing metaphors, can change our way of seeing. In his famous book on the role of metaphor in understanding the organisation and management of businesses, Gareth Morgan gives the following example from physics of metaphors altering what we see:

When scientists study light as a wave it reveals itself as a wave. When it is studied as a particle, it reveals itself as a particle. Both tendencies or qualities co-exist. The metaphor that the scientist uses to study these latent tendencies *shapes* what he or she sees.[73]

Abrams made the important distinction between merely illustrative metaphors or analogies and those that are 'constitutive' in the sense that 'they yield the ground plan and essential structural elements' of a theory. While illustrative metaphors may help develop an existing theory or paradigm, constitutive metaphors may enable us to create a substantially new one. Moreover, new constitutive metaphors restructure more than theory itself; they also provide us with a new framework for collecting and interpreting evidence. For, as Abrams put it, constitutive metaphors 'select and mould those "facts" which a theory comprehends. For facts are *facta*, things made as much as things found, and made in part by the analogies through which we look at the world as through a lens.'[74] So, for example, this book has shown how we can access different aspects of socio-economic reality – and refashion our picture of that reality and the very facts at our disposal – by using organic metaphors (borrowed from biology) instead of the 'social physics'[75] and mechanical (equilibrium-based) metaphors that normally structure standard economics.

Metaphors are often as constitutive of social reality as they are of theory and theory-laden observation. For in guiding our theoretical outlooks and beliefs, metaphors have the power to transform the way we behave. When we see the Earth as 'Mother' or as 'inherited capital', it may cause us to focus on the care we should take to honour and preserve something that is both precious and (unless wantonly squandered) capable of providing for future generations. When we see markets as dynamic organisms rather than as mechanical systems tending to equilibrium, it may focus our attention on policies needed to improve innovation and adaptation to the unexpected rather than on measures to improve efficiency in a static allocation sense. Likewise, Morgan gives many examples of how management practices are shaped and reshaped by the metaphors used to think about companies – as machines, organisms, or cultures:

The metaphors and ideas through which we 'see' and 'read' situations influence how we act. Managers who see organisations in a mechanistic way have a tendency to 'mechanise'. Those dominated by a cultural lens tend to act in a way that shapes and reshapes culture. Favoured metaphors tend to trap us in specific modes of action.[76]

It is for this reason that, if we want to analyse and predict social, economic, or corporate behaviour, we need to 'read' the metaphors constituting the dominant discourse of the main actors involved.

There are, of course, several dangers with using metaphor to structure theory, vision and practice. First, as Morgan argues, by focusing our attention on certain aspects, a metaphor '*always* creates distortions' as well as insight; in other words, 'the way of seeing created through a metaphor becomes a way of *not* seeing'.[77] So, for example, Shackle has shown that because standard economic theories are shaped by 'schemes of thought' related to 'celestial mechanics' – that is, given a shape 'derived from other contexts' and 'devised for other questions' – they disclose a measure of intelligible and predictable order in apparent chaos only at the cost of making us blind to the central importance of uncertainty and imagination in economic behaviour. Discussing the formation of economic theory, Shackle adds:

The procedure of invention was often to accept some such self-suggesting analogy and make the economic questions fit it; not to ask what is peculiar and essential in economic questions, what is the essential nature of the world to which those questions belong. Thus economic theory took on a character belonging to the manipulable, calculable, external world of *things*, not the world of the conscious mind in its eternal station on the edge of the void of time.[78]

Given such potential distortions, and the losses as well as gains in focus implied by the use of any metaphor, it follows that it is essential for us always to be aware of the structuring impact that particular metaphors impose on our theories or vision.

Such awareness of the impact of metaphors is, however, rendered difficult by the fact that frequently repeated metaphors tend to harden into elements of the unconscious structuring of our vision and understanding of the world, and become part of the very fabric of our everyday language and specialist discourse. For this reason, we are often blind to the distortions of vision they imply. As Abrams argues, because metaphor (even when no longer consciously recognised as such) 'is an inseparable element of all discourse', we need to uncover the influence of these 'more or less submerged conceptual models'.[79] Accordingly, I would argue that one of the central tasks of the Romantic Economist is to carry out a version of Derrida's project of textual 'deconstruction'[80] – to unmask the unconscious structuring impact of the metaphors prevalent in the various social science paradigms and discourses relevant to economics. For only by becoming aware of this influence can we render mutually intelligible the differences in vision implied by one paradigm and another and understand their respective insights and distortions. Such deconstruction is not made any easier, of course, by the fact that much of the metaphorical structuring of economics is buried in the implicit rather than explicit assumptions of its mathematical models.

Given that economics, like all other languages and discourses, is largely constituted by the metaphors embedded within it, economists should not be shy of experimenting with metaphor. Such experimentation is not a frivolous or unscientific act of rhetorical distortion, but an effective vehicle for jolting us into new ways of looking at familiar material by trying out alternative perspectives derived from apparently remote discourses or disciplines. Metaphor is one of the main tools of theoretical imagination and lateral thinking, and is a crucial factor in the development of theory. One economist to recognise this is Brian Arthur, who is quoted by Waldrop as saying: 'Nonscientists tend to think that science works by deduction ... But actually science works mainly by metaphor.'[81] Arthur and his colleagues at the Santa Fe Institute have promoted the application of metaphors derived from non-linear biological and meteorological systems to the study of economies and markets. Perhaps the most important lesson to be drawn, though, from Waldrop's account of this work at Santa Fe relates to the conditions needed to foster such metaphorical experimentation and interdisciplinary cross-pollination.[82] Creative thinking is encouraged by an environment (not typically found in university departments) where academics are given the intellectual space and leisure to think originally, with the help of a bracing blend of discipline-based excellence and anarchic disregard for cognitive boundaries. In particular, a forum that allows for the constant juxtaposition of perspectives from very different sources is likely to be the most suggestive of the new illustrative and constitutive metaphors that may form the next generation of vision-enhancing models or paradigms.

5 ROMANTIC POINTERS TO BEST RESEARCH PRACTICE

The remainder of this chapter outlines some general intellectual and procedural approaches to economics research that seem to flow from the Romanticism-inspired analysis on the nature of the imagination and the role of perspective and language presented in this book. These approaches may succeed in helping economists and other social scientists enjoy the benefits of using ever-more specialised techniques within academic paradigms, while at the same time avoiding some of the costs of that specialisation in terms of either distortion of vision or bias in the collection of evidence and formulation of problems.

Analytical negative capability

One useful intellectual technique for researchers is an analytical version of Keats' 'negative capability' – an imaginative and un-proscriptive receptiveness to new theoretical perspectives and unexpected evidence from the senses. Keats emphasised the importance for the creative artist of being open to new ideas and not rushing to impose one favoured interpretation. He described this aspect of imagination as '*negative capability*: that is, when man is capable of being in uncertainties, mysteries, doubts, without any irritable reaching after fact and reason'.[83] Coleridge sometimes spoke in similar terms. For him, one of the things that differentiated an imaginative approach from mere mechanical 'understanding' is the capacity of the mind to remain suspended between different ways of looking at the world: 'As soon as it is fixed on one image, it becomes understanding; but while it is unfixed and wavering between them, attaching itself permanently to none, it is imagination.'[84]

Many modern scientists now implicitly recognise that a version of negative capability is just as necessary to their trade as it is to that of the poets. Scientists, too, must accept doubt and lay themselves open to both the promptings of their unconscious and the awareness of empirical anomalies. They must remain receptive to alternative perspectives and avoid encasing their analysis too soon in the cognitive straitjacket of one paradigm. As Bohm put it after a lifetime in science: 'real perception that is capable of seeing something new and unfamiliar requires that one be attentive, alert, aware, and sensitive.' For Bohm, originality in science requires 'that a person shall not be inclined to impose his preconceptions on the fact as he sees it'; and it presupposes a 'creative state of mind that is generally sensitive to the differences that always exist between the observed fact and *any* preconceived ideas, however noble, beautiful, and magnificent they may seem to be'.[85]

Acute sensitivity to anomaly and receptiveness to alternative perspectives in this passive sense is not, however, sufficient (as Coleridge understood) for either good poetry or good science. There is also a need for constant consciously directed experimentation with different perspectives. Observation must always be selective and interpretive if it is to make any sense of the infinite chaos around us. We cannot simply access by some open intuition a pure unmediated and complete set of empirical data and use it to suggest and correct theories; rather we must observe and construct our picture of the world with the help of prior principles of selection, categorisation and organisation. But, since no such perspective gives us a complete picture or an all-encompassing interpretation, the more theoretical and metaphorical perspectives we expose ourselves to, the more aspects and interpretations of reality we can tap into, and the more potential anomalies in relation to our own preferred theory we may become aware of. This is where creative experimentation with different meta-phors and paradigms comes in.

Multi-paradigm scan of research problems and questions

Every researcher knows that the foundation of good research is a careful assessment of the nature of the problem and a careful formulation of the questions to be answered. As the discussion of Kuhn and metaphors has shown, however, this initial assessment of a field of research is usually structured by the paradigm or dominant metaphor with which we (con-sciously or unconsciously) structure our vision. In other words, we tend to frame and scan the available evidence and formulate the riddles to be solved in the light of the standard hypotheses, theoretical expectations and con-ceptual grid that we have internalised through operating within one para-digm or metaphor-constituted language. This tendency to theoretical bias in the initial reading of evidence and definition of research questions is endemic to all research[86] – particularly when conducted by those with heavy sunk costs in particular modelling techniques. As Paul Krugman has noted:

> once you have a model, it is essentially impossible to avoid seeing the world in terms of that model – which means focusing on the forces and effects your model can represent and ignoring or giving short shrift to those it cannot. The result is that the very act of modelling has the effect of destroying knowledge as well as creating it. A successful model enhances our vision, but it also creates blind spots, at least at first.[87]

John Stuart Mill well understood this danger of looking at particular cases with preconceived templates of understanding in mind: 'such is the nature of the human understanding,' he wrote, 'that the very fact of atten-ding with intensity to one part of a thing, has a tendency to withdraw the attention from the other parts'.[88] The solution Mill proposed for an analyst engaged in applied research (directed at explaining real-world as opposed to abstract theoretical problems) was as follows:

He can do no more than satisfy himself that he has seen all that is visible to any other persons who have concerned themselves with the subject. For this purpose he must endeavour to place himself at their point of view, and strive earnestly to see the object as they see it.[89]

Mill is here advocating an early version of what in today's terminology might be called a multi-paradigm scan or audit of a research field; and this forms a central part of the methodological armoury of the Romantic Economist.

As Kuhn constantly reminds us, 'there is no such thing as research in the absence of any paradigm'.[90] We cannot make progress in research without the cognitive maps and the theoretical and methodological tools embodied in paradigms. Moreover, while Kuhn exaggerated the problems of interna- lising two or more paradigms, it is clearly difficult for a researcher to operate within the framework of a number of paradigms at the same time through- out a research project. What I am suggesting here recognises this; but it also recognises the truth of Kuhn's description of the self-reinforcing nature of paradigm-based vision – in particular, the tendency to overlook or explain away anomalies and the equally distorting tendency to address only those problems that the paradigm is suited to explain. My contention is that we can derive the benefits of operating within paradigms without incurring all the costs if we learn to escape the confines of single-paradigm vision at two key stages in research – the initial reading of the situation to be analysed and the final audit of research results. It is the initial reading with which we are concerned here.

Since unmediated and unbiased perception is impossible, there is no definitive and fully objective way of establishing the practical problems we face (or the distortions of reality imposed by the particular models, metaphors, or paradigms we use). As Karl Popper recognised, 'Observation is always selective', because the scientific observations we make at each stage of analysis presuppose 'a frame of reference: a frame of expectations: a frame of theories'.[91] Schumpeter did posit the existence of a 'preanalytical cognitive act' that could supply the 'raw material' for a radically new theoretical approach; and he thought that this sort of preanalytical vision could 're-enter the history of every established science each time somebody teaches us to *see* things in a light of which the source is not to be found in the facts, methods, and results of the pre-existing state of the science'. Schumpeter, however, believed that such preanalytical vision tends to be 'ideological almost by definition';[92] in other words, it remains selective but on an ideological rather than theoretical basis. The challenge for the Romantic Economist in seeking to generate a more genuinely open-minded initial assessment of a field of research is therefore considerable: it involves finding a method that harnesses (rather than tries vainly to rise above) the necessary selectivity and prior structuring of all perception and analysis, and one that does not merely substitute ideological for theoretical prejudice. This can be achieved, I would argue, by engaging in a systematic attempt to look at (and interpret) a situation serially from a variety of discrete metaphorical or paradigm-based perspectives. What I am suggesting is not a conflation or confusion of perspectives, but a disciplined exercise of the imagination designed to assess a situation from different perspectives and with the help of different cognitive maps. Only then can we become aware of aspects of the situation that would have eluded us if operating solely within one paradigm or metaphorical scheme – aspects which may have an important bearing on the nature of the problem being studied.

Good practice requires that at the initial assessment and problem-definition phase of research we move back and forth between perspectives, and remain open to different structuring metaphors and paradigms. Being careful to avoid tribal loyalty to the constitutive metaphors, hypotheses and models of just one paradigm, we should be happy at this stage to switch between alternative focus-enhancing conceptual structures, and see the world from the perspective of several paradigms. Morgan maintains that a similar open-minded and multi-perspective assessment is needed before a manager can evaluate a corporate and business situation, and decide how to act. Arguing that an 'effective diagnostic reading' depends on 'an ability to play with multiple insights', Morgan continues:

> In a way, the metaphors, theories, and frames through which we implicitly scan the situations that we are trying to understand act as a kind of 'radar' or 'homing device' that draws our attention toward key features of a situation.[93]

In the same way, by making use of several different paradigms or metaphor-based approaches, social scientists can avoid undue selectivity and distortion in their initial assessment, while simultaneously benefiting from the focus provided by each paradigm or metaphor to discern key aspects of a situation. Such an approach requires versatility, of course, and there are limits to how many paradigms even the best-educated researcher can be conversant with. This problem can be ameliorated, though, by working in research teams that contain a variety of specialists sharing enough conceptual common ground to be able to hunt as an analytical pack.

Initial fluidity and openness in the characterisation of a situation – thanks to an organised exercise of imagination in switching between different cognitive spectacles – can help ensure that we do not prematurely define the exact nature of the research problem. The problem should dictate the theory used to analyse it and not the other way round; and this can happen only if our assessment and formulation of the problem is not dependent on the selective vision of one theory. This leaves open the question, however, of how we decide eventually on an agreed working definition of the problem – one that takes account of the frequently incommensurable aspects revealed by different paradigms. I would argue that what is needed here is a reasoned debate in the minds of researchers about which aspects of a situation are most salient from a practical or theoretical point of view, and which aspects have a good preliminary claim to be potentially causally relevant variables. This debate can build on the common ground between all perspectives on how to characterise the situation, and then make a judgement about how to balance the mutually intelligible differences between the aspects highlighted by different perspectives in the light of our academic and practical interests. There is never one obviously correct way to formulate a research problem; but there are apparent problems that dissolve when looked at from a different perspective, and problems that emerge from a multi-paradigm scan with enhanced definition and urgency.

The nature of a research problem is not, of course, only a function of our reading of relevant aspects of social reality: it is also a function of our analytical purpose. It is helpful here to distinguish schematically between three types of research in economics and political economy. First, some 'pure science' researchers are not aiming to explain particular cases but rather to develop a model that hypothesises certain causal relationships between variables (such as wage bargaining systems and inflation).[94] These researchers may initially be interested only in the logical relationships within their model, with a view to creating more robust hypotheses. Secondly, other researchers (or the same researchers at a different stage) are primarily interested in using a model as what Sutton calls a 'diagnostic tool'[95] – to unearth systematic tendencies, or 'systematic fragments' of social reality, if they exist. It is in this applied application of pure models – or in the attempt to test their status as encapsulations of law-like systematic tendencies in the real world – that the greatest dangers of theory-soaked observation and paradigm-driven formulation of problems occur. The good researcher needs to take great care neither to overstylise actual situations nor to ignore complicating factors just because they fail to fit her model; she must instead make a broad assessment of all potentially causally relevant aspects of the situations considered. The third type of research is different again: it is not geared to developing pure models or discerning systematic fragments of social reality as a whole; instead, it aims to explain one contingent particular – one specific compound of general tendencies and contingent events in all its multifaceted complexity. This involves necessarily taking a multi-paradigm look at what might be called a 'holistic fragment' of reality, and making a judgement about the relative importance of the different aspects or logics highlighted by different perspectives, in order to create a 'narrative' of events.[96] Some economists would argue that such a narrative is not 'science' but 'history'. If so, more economists need to do history if their subject is to be relevant to the large areas of messy reality where a number of incommensurable aspects and contingent events are causally relevant.

Disciplined eclecticism: choice of theory driven by nature of problem

When an initial multi-paradigm scan of a situation is complete – and the nature of a problem has been given a working definition based on an exercise of reasoned judgement about the likely relative importance of the various potential causally relevant or practically pertinent aspects revealed – it is time to choose the paradigms or theories most suited to deepen our analysis. Here it is important to remember that the incommensurability of different paradigms (and the fact that none gives complete insight) does not prevent there being good reasons to choose one over another. We can render mutually intelligible the different aspects of reality that the respective analytical tools and conceptual grids of each paradigm are suited to uncover and explain; and on the basis of this variation we can choose the theory or paradigm best able to solve the particular problem.

In advocating that research should in this sense be 'problem-driven' rather than 'theory-driven', I am taking a position argued for compellingly by Green and Shapiro, Colander and others.[97] Indeed, it might seem far from controversial that, unless the problem studied is purely in the realm of abstract theory, a preliminary assessment of potential causally or practically relevant aspects of a situation should determine which paradigm is likely to be most pertinent to further research. Nevertheless, to many economists and Rational Choice theorists, the idea that they should use different paradigms to solve different types of problems smacks of a woolly eclecticism. As a result, it is important to emphasise that the methodological eclecticism I am suggesting here is disciplined in three ways: first, it is disciplined in the way it links the choice of theory in each case to the results of a multi-paradigm scan used to determine the nature of the situation studied and the working definition of the analytical or practical problem requiring a solution; secondly, it is disciplined in its use of experience and logic to define a set of criteria for theory selection that make clear the conditions in which certain paradigms, models, or sets of assumptions can be expected to work; and, thirdly, it is disciplined by virtue of keeping paradigms carefully discrete and not attempting the sort of general synthesis of different paradigms that is a recipe for conceptual confusion.

In his famous essay on economic methodology, Milton Friedman argued for the need to find 'criteria for determining what abstract model it is best to use for particular kinds of problems', and to explore 'what features of the problem or of the circumstances have the greatest effect on the accuracy of the predictions yielded by a particular model or theory'.[98] Similarly, Green and Shapiro argue for 'an empirically testable account of the conditions' in which various Rational Choice Theory models apply.[99] Such scientific precision is laudable where possible; but it often eludes us where the number of variables involved makes testing difficult, or where the predictive capacity of the models in question is not high. (Complexity models, for example, do not allow for spot predictions, because of the prevalence of increasing returns and threshold effects.) In these cases, a mixture of analytical experience and logic can help define a working set of criteria for theory selection. For example, if there is strong *prima facie* evidence that the identities and norms constituting our interests and preferences are fixed, there is a much greater chance that Rational Choice models (taking these interests and preferences as *given*) will explain and predict well than if a multi-paradigm scan of the situation suggests that value contestation is playing an important role. In the latter case, there may be a need for discourse analysis of the different norms and identities of key players. Likewise, where there is strong initial evidence that a number of incommensurable and incompatible goals or values are considered important by the key actors in a policy dilemma, there are strong reasons to use a multi-goal approach when constructing a cost-benefit analysis – one that makes explicit the need for value weighting decisions rather than burying them in the catch-all language of utility.[100] Similarly, if a multi-paradigm audit reveals that a situation is characterised by the wholesale creation of new goods and opportunities, it makes little sense to treat such creativity as 'exogenous' in an equilibrium model, or to treat uncertainty as a minor problem in modelling terms. In these circumstances, it is much more logical to bring the motivational model of *homo romanticus* into play at the level of microfoundations, and to model markets and economies at the macro-level as dynamic and organic systems.

Where a multi-paradigm scan suggests that certain aspects of a situation are dominant, and where these aspects correspond closely to the 'reserve area' in which our *ex ante* definition of the criteria for theory selection suggests that a particular model or theory works well, disciplined eclecticism is straightforward. Much more often, of course, the initial audit of a problem will reveal a concurrence of different causal factors (or aspects) in a given situation. In these cases, we need to decide whether we can discern a neat division of labour between the factors – for example, social conditioning defining the content of preferences but leaving intact the tendency on the part of individuals to optimise the satisfaction of *given* preferences. Where there is such a division of labour, we can use different models (for example based on *homo sociologicus* and *homo economicus*) side-by-side, with the frames of reference of each model set to reflect the relevant findings of the other. If, on the other hand, there is no neat division of labour – for example, if norms conflict with the optimisation of preferences across the board – then we may need to carry a multi-paradigm approach into our detailed analysis stage. At times, we may be lucky enough to uncover some systematic interaction between aspects previously revealed and considered only in separate paradigms, and this may form the basis of a new synthetic model or paradigm. Much more often, however, there is no such systematic interaction (for example between altruistic norms and self-interest) and we are instead faced in each case with a specific compound of interacting social tendencies, perhaps laced with highly contingent events and dominant individual personalities. In these cases, we need a less scientific sort of joint venture between different paradigms to disclose how the different aspects interact with each other. Such a joint venture can produce a more holistic look at the particular case and help construct a narrative of events.

A joint venture between different paradigms to uncover and explain the different aspects of a contingent particular – to construct a narrative account of a holistic fragment of reality – is different from the disciplined use of paradigms on their own, or side-by-side, to diagnose systematic tendencies across many cases or to model the systematic interaction of (or division of labour between) these tendencies. But such a joint venture can still be disciplined in the sense of not involving a confusion of different paradigms. Each paradigm tends to give most analytical leverage and observational focus when used in its pure form. As a result, those wishing to arrive at a more holistic understanding of a particular case need to avoid the conflation of discrete paradigms; instead, they should be aiming at a one-off imaginative synthesis of findings derived from using discrete paradigm discourses to construct a narrative of a specific situation.[101] This sort of imaginative synthesis of insights from a range of different perspectives is generally possible, of course, only in relation to a particular situation; and, for this reason, it should not be confused with the creation of a new synthetic paradigm.

As Kuhn suggested, genuinely new synthetic paradigms that have wide application are few and far between; and, even when they are created, they do not succeed in synthesising every potentially important perspective into one super-perspective capable of encompassing all aspects of social or physical reality. The goal of the perfect paradigm or metaphorical schema is a mirage. As a result, while the creation of a new synthetic paradigm occasionally plays a dramatic role in scientific advance, this is normally less important than learning how to get the most out of the different paradigms we already have available – by using them singly, side-by-side, or in specific joint ventures, as the problem demands.

Post-analytical audit

The final element of good practice suggested by the themes we have considered is the post-analytical auditing of research results. However careful we are to be open-minded in defining a research problem, and however disciplined in choosing the theoretical approach most appropriate to the problem so defined, the danger remains that our research results will fail to capture all the causally relevant aspects of a situation (or unwittingly distort our picture of those aspects we do capture). Indeed, the Romantic Economist would argue that we should always treat the results of empirical research as provisional. This is principally because the paradigms and hypotheses we employ in conducting research necessarily result in selective vision and cause us unwittingly to read structures and distinctions into reality that may not actually be there. As Wordsworth warned (in a fragment quoted by Warnock):

> In weakness we create distinctions, then
> Believe that all our puny boundaries are things
> Which we perceive and not which we have made:[102]

Our empirical findings are part-constructed by the theory we use. Research results are the creative union between the theoretical framework (or metaphors) we apply and the real world impinging on our senses. In *Middlemarch*, George Eliot described this creative process (in relation to Lydgate's medical research) as 'that delightful labour of the imagination which is not mere arbitrariness, but the exercise of disciplined power – combining and constructing with the clearest eye for probabilities and the fullest obedience to knowledge'. But Eliot recognised that this imaginative enterprise must also comprise a second aspect, with the researcher 'in yet more energetic alliance with impartial Nature, standing aloof to invent tests by which to try its own work'.[103] It is this capacity to stand back and judge our own attempts to frame and explain aspects of reality that is crucial to any scientist who, like Lydgate, is 'enamoured of that arduous invention which is the very eye of research, provisionally framing its object and correcting it to more and more exactness of relation'.[104] For this reason, I would suggest that researchers need to develop a scientific version of the 'impartial spectator' that Adam Smith posits for the formation of ethical judgements: they need to imagine how a spectator who is impartial between theoretical paradigms would view both their research findings and the assumptions and categories they applied to get to them. If the imagined impartial spectator – carrying out a multi-paradigm audit of her own – can, for example, point to anomalies or causally important aspects of reality that the researchers' particular theoretical framework and empirical findings do not encompass, they should be ready to admit this to themselves and others in the presentation of their results. The impartial analytical spectator can also help scientists to make a reasoned judgement about whether they need to amend their theory or consider some alternative conceptual grids (or paradigms) in order to encompass the full panoply of causally relevant aspects of which they are now aware.

Mill – as so often the prophet of a more Romantic approach – stressed the importance of being impartial critics of our own research and open to the need for further analysis:

> All that we can do more, is to endeavour to be impartial critics of our own theories, and to free ourselves, as far as we are able, from that reluctance from which few inquirers are altogether exempt, to admit the reality or relevancy of any facts which they have not previously either taken into, or left a place open for in, their systems.[105]

The impartial critic to be found in every good researcher who seeks to apply theory to practice must, Mill argued, 'carefully watch the result of every experiment, in order that any residuum of facts which his principles did not lead him to expect, and do not enable him to explain, may become the subject of a fresh analysis'.[106]

A complete post-analytical audit should ideally encompass more than an impartial receptiveness to anomalies requiring further explanation. It should involve switching back (at the end of research carried out using a particular paradigm) to alternative cognitive spectacles supplied by other paradigms, with two specific purposes in mind: first, to see whether from these perspectives it appears we may have massaged (or unduly selected) data to fit our particular theory; and, secondly to highlight any overlooked alternative explanations of the problem studied, which might suggest that our findings – while plausible in themselves – may not be the whole story.

In reality, of course, a researcher cannot be expected to redo his analysis *ad infinitum* from the perspective of one paradigm after another. Instead, what is essential is that his results and theoretical assumptions are presented in an accessible enough way that others in the broader research community can audit them from the perspective of their respective disciplines. What is needed, in other words, is an open research society in which those working in each discipline lay their research findings and methods open to scrutiny by other minds using different cognitive spectacles. For this to happen, it is necessary that specialists, wherever possible, translate their work back into what Wordsworth called the 'language really used by men';[107] only this can ensure that research findings, and the limiting cognitive assumptions and categories used to produce them, are accessible to those operating in different paradigms rather than hidden in mutually unintelligible specialist jargon and equations. Helping in this way to facilitate others from a broad range of backgrounds to audit our own research is the mark of a good scientist. It is equally important that research conclusions routinely include a proactive and disciplined summary of all the potential causally relevant aspects of the situation studied which the researcher's own pre- and post-analytical audits have suggested may not be adequately captured or explained by the paradigms or models used. Indeed, in a world where policy-makers and entrepreneurs rely on economic research to inform their decisions, such openness about the limitations of the research perspective or models used becomes a moral as well as a professional duty.

CHAPTER 11

The Romantic Economist: conclusion

Throughout this book I have borrowed conceptual frameworks, metaphors and ideas from the field of Romantic philosophy and literature, and used them to articulate criticisms of standard economics and formulate amendments to this rationalist discipline. I have argued that lessons from Romanticism can perform two vital functions for economics.

First, they can suggest new ways of understanding and carrying out the business of economics. By underlining that we never have unmediated access to reality in all its multifaceted complexity, the Romantics taught us that we half-create what we see, and that we can never entirely escape the role of perspective and language in structuring our thought. They also stressed the power of the imagination in helping us see the world in a new light. One of the principal duties of the Romantic Economist is to help social scientists face up to how far their observation of data and formulation of research problems and conclusions is structured by the formal models and language they use. Another is to develop methodological and analytical techniques that can enable open-minded and creative use of different perspectives and paradigms at key stages in analysis, so that researchers can avoid having their vision entirely constrained by the dominant paradigm in which they work. In particular, I have argued that there is an important role for multi-perspective scans of data at the initial problem-definition phase of research, combined with disciplined eclecticism designed to ensure that the choice of theory or model is driven by this initial assessment of the problem. Likewise, a post-analytical audit is needed to render research results open to scrutiny from a wide range of perspectives. The aim throughout is to derive the benefits of paradigm focus without suffering the costs of being locked into one paradigm. In addition, the Romantic Economist has a crucial role to play in creating new generations of formal (and less formal) models that can develop the theoretical texture of economics, by consciously experimenting with metaphors and assumptions drawn from Romanticism. This is the creative counterpart to the other important bread-and-butter work of the

Romantic Economist – deconstructing and analysing the largely unconscious metaphors (derived from physics) that currently structure standard economics.

The second broad function that lessons from Romanticism can perform for economics is to suggest new ways of understanding socio-economic reality itself. They can open our eyes to how far economies, and the societies in which they are embedded, are creative and dynamic systems in which individuals are driven by imagination and sentiment as well as rational optimisation. By preferring organic to mechanical metaphors, and hence focusing on the self-reinforcing mutual interdependence of individuals and the societies that form (and are formed by) them, the Romantics taught us that both history and creative interaction matter to the development of social economies; and they underlined that the beliefs and behaviour of individuals are, at least in part, socially formed. Above all, of course, the Romantics stressed the central role of the imagination in creating and envisioning the future, and in forging our own identities and aims out of the incommensurable and conflicting values and discourses we face. It follows that the most important duty of the Romantic Economist is to develop new substantive models and microfoundations for understanding how creative (but historically situated) economies, and the imaginative (but partly socially formed) agents within them, behave. I have argued that this involves developing organic models of the self-reinforcing interdependence of institutions, languages, norms and individual creativity or choice; nurturing our ability to read the different mutually intelligible discourses and cultures that structure the meaning (to the actors concerned) of social and economic behaviour; focusing on the impact of incommensurable values – not least in ensuring that there is often no single right answer (or optimal trade-off) for economic actors and policy-makers; and, finally, articulating the motivational model of *homo romanticus* – the agent who is self-creative, sympathetic and driven by sentiments or dreams, and who uses her imagination to create, and chart a way through, the unknowable future. In short, the goal of the Romantic Economist must be to build on recent innovations along these lines from within economics, and further revitalise the discipline by equipping economists with a new set of guiding metaphors and grounding assumptions.

This chapter gives only the briefest summary of these lessons from Romanticism and the consequent panoply of techniques and models at the disposal of the Romantic Economist. Its principal aim is to draw together linked answers to a series of organising questions that can help delineate the scope and significance of the more Romantic approaches to economics outlined throughout the book. These questions are: first, what Romantic theory tells us about the status of the standard formal models at the centre of modern economics; secondly, whether more Romantic approaches to economics should be seen as replacing or rather as complementing standard economics; thirdly, whether these Romantic approaches can represent a coherent paradigm of their own; and, finally, what the main political and corporate policy implications are of adopting the techniques and models championed by the Romantic Economist.

Economics often seems to resemble what Wordsworth, describing the charms of abstract mathematical geometry, called 'an independent world/Created out of pure Intelligence'.[1] Consider, for example, General Equilibrium Theory as formalised by Kenneth Arrow and Gerard Debreu in the 1950s – a logical construct of great mathematical beauty that, by assuming away the problems of creativity, externalities and increasing returns, proves (within the terms of the theory) that there is an equilibrium or optimal solution to which all markets tend, given an initial set of endowments, preferences and goods. The theory was never intended to represent economic reality, of course, not least because the real world is in fact rife with the very externalities, increasing returns and uncertainty born of creativity that the theory assumes away, and because there is no way of developing the complete futures markets the theory posits.[2] General Equilibrium Theory exemplifies economics as 'an *abstract science*' – one that, in Mill's words, reasons like geometry from assumed hypotheses or premises, its conclusions 'true without qualification, only in a case which is purely imaginary'.[3] As Shackle has observed, the choice of such an axiomatic, or hypothetical, method of reasoning as a central plank of economics 'was a bold and a surprising stroke'; it enables economics to 'study in outline, by means of an imposed simplicity and precision, some aspects of a subject-matter which in the fullness of its unabstracted nature involves a vast richness of intricate and yet essential detail'.[4]

Formal or abstract models are valuable because they elucidate the frequently counter-intuitive implications of a set of assumptions; but the logical deductions that comprise the results of such analysis are only as true (in describing the real world) as the assumptions on which they are based. Bagehot pointed out that such an abstract form of economics has as its object 'to work out and ascertain the results of certain great forces, as if these alone operated, and as if nothing else had any effect in the matter'; but since, 'in matter of fact, many other forces have an effect, the computed results of the larger isolated forces will never exactly happen'.[5] Robbins, who famously defined the economic method as 'an instrument for "shaking out" all the implications of given suppositions', also underlined that the economic laws so established are only true *ceteris paribus*; and, he added, 'Of course, if other things do not remain unchanged, the consequences predicted do not necessarily follow.'[6] The true importance of the *ceteris paribus* clause in models – of assuming that 'other things' remain equal and can safely be ignored – becomes apparent only when the models are applied to the study of messy reality. As Mill was always careful to insist (and wise economists since remember), when economics is applied to policy, there is an overriding need to put into the equation (metaphorically or otherwise) any 'disturbing causes', even if this means being conversant with other sciences or disciplines.[7]

The argument developed in this book suggests that, wherever formal economic models are based on the standard twin assumptions of a tendency to equilibrium and individuals rationally optimising their preferences, consideration of the *ceteris paribus* clause in these models is at once more crucial and more problematic than generally assumed. An audit of the *cetera* is crucial because they are so often not equal when we are studying dynamic markets and the multifaceted nature of real-world social economies. New complications and contingent factors tend to limit the universality and applicability of the conclusions of a standard formal model wherever individual creativity, self-creating choice between incommensurable values, or the particular history of a socio-economic organism play a significant role. The predictions that flow from such a model concerning the impact of changing one factor (for example, the price of goods or amount of investment) are valid only if, among other things, there are no concurrent changes in ways of thinking and no technological or preference innovation; it is only if there are no new dreams, no new products and no new conceptual categories that the predicted result will happen. It is a central tenet of the Romantic Economist that in a world of imaginative and creative agents the *ceteris paribus* clause in standard models is often overladen.

At the same time, assessing the *cetera*, or other factors, that matter is problematic because the models we use structure and distort our vision. The assumptions and hypotheses on which models are built influence the focus of research and the interpretation of data, by structuring the definition of problems and the principles of data selection. The more awesome a model's algebra, the stronger is its rhetorical influence on our definition and assessment of 'other factors'. An invented system or model may act as what Sutton calls a 'diagnostic tool' for teasing out 'systematic influences' or tendencies in the world we analyse;[8] but as well as focusing our attention in this way, a model will also, as Mill was aware, divert our attention away from complicating factors unless we are very careful.[9] For this reason, the Romantic Economist advocates a systematic attempt to vary the hypotheses by which we select and interpret data at least initially, and champions the open-minded use of different models or theories to highlight as many crucial aspects of the situation or problem studied as possible. Only this multi-perspective approach can ensure that the *cetera* (or other possible complicating factors) excluded from a particular model do not get re-engineered or explained away in line with the structuring principles of that model; and only this approach can ensure that the 'objective' testing of hypotheses is not marred by bias in the selection of data and a systematic tendency to ignore competing explanations. One of the principal lessons of Romantic philosophy is that we must be alert to the troublesome nature of the interface between theory and observation of data. We must be creative in using different theories to structure our vision, so that we become aware of any observational or conceptual bias, and alive to different aspects of reality.

In the language of Romanticism, all economic models – indeed, all paradigms – are fragments in the search for a unified understanding. The Romantics valued fragments as self-sufficient but inevitably provisional encapsulations of some aspect of the world. For them, the virtue of fragments was that, while striving for completeness, they simultaneously acknowledge limitation, thereby advertising the essential predicament of human thought. In this way, they leave open the promise that the juxtaposition of different fragments might suggest the more unified vision that has so far eluded us.[10] The theoretical systems and models invented by the greatest minds in economics should, I would argue, be seen as resembling Romantic fragments: for they, too, create an ordered vision that is complete and systematic in one sense, while necessarily partial and provisional in other respects. General Equilibrium Theory and Rational Choice models, for example, both succeed in capturing the tendency to efficient optimisation of given endowments and preferences that is a very real aspect of both markets and strategic interaction in the political sphere; but while they seek to represent this tendency as a complete explanatory system, the *ceteris paribus* clause should advertise loudly and clearly that the findings of these models are always provisional. Such theoretical fragments may succeed in capturing a systematic tendency or fragment of reality but they provide us only with what Mill called 'half-truths':[11] the tendencies unearthed and modelled have merely provisional status. The Rational Choice paradigm and standard economic models (resting on the assumption that individuals optimise their preferences) may be among the greatest and most illuminating of intellectual fragments, but we must always remember that they are only fragments. They cannot provide us with complete vision; and the tendencies they reveal are abstracted from complicating factors. We need to remain constantly alert to the constraints on vision implied by any model or paradigm, and to the possibility that in any particular case it abstracts from, or ignores, something vital that may in fact corrupt or counter the tendencies revealed.

This leaves the essential question of how we can build a more unified vision out of the fragments at our disposal. Mill was always sanguine about our ability simply to add together the various causal tendencies revealed by different sciences.[12] He believed that if a model's 'assumption is correct as far as it goes, and differs from the truth no otherwise than as a part differs from the whole, then the conclusions which are correctly deduced from the assumption constitute *abstract* truth; and when completed by adding or subtracting the effect of the non-calculated circumstances, they are true in the concrete, and may be applied to practice'.[13] Sadly, of course, social science is rarely as straightforward as Mill implies. Different causes and different aspects of reality revealed by different models and paradigms do not just neatly add up. Very often a systematic fragment or half-truth is not even half-true when other factors are taken into account. While there is sometimes a neat division of labour between causal tendencies, and sometimes a stable and predictable interaction between them, more often than not the compound effect of the interaction of different systematic tendencies is the result of a one-off contingent self-creative choice between incommensurable logics on the part of the actors concerned (perhaps influenced by other highly contingent factors).[14] Moreover, the specific tendency isolated by any one model may not exist at all in circumstances different from those assumed. For example, Lyons argues that Game Theory models which assume 'an idealised world of complete information' can be defended on the grounds that 'a certain amount of abstraction' is needed 'in order to bring out the fundamental forces at work'; however, as he also suggests, this defence looks less compelling if the results of such analysis are in fact totally invalidated in many conditions of less than complete information.[15] The Romantic Economist would argue that this is indeed the case: the fundamental forces at work in carefully defined stable environments where actors know the pay-offs and strategies available are just not the same as those operating in more common highly fluid and dynamic situations where new options and strategies are continually being invented. The tendency to optimise is a fruitless strategy in conditions of uncertainty created by radical innovation.

It is the central epistemological lesson of Romanticism that we need different cognitive spectacles (or different models used as diagnostic tools) to reveal different aspects of reality. No one explanatory system or conceptual grid can make sense of all the incommensurable aspects of socio-economic reality. Tarnas argues that this lesson is now widely absorbed:

In virtually all contemporary disciplines, it is recognised that the prodigious complexity, subtlety, and multivalance of reality far transcend the grasp of any one intellectual approach, and that only a committed openness to the interplay of many perspectives can meet the extraordinary challenges of the postmodern era.[16]

At times, such interplay of different perspectives can give us a fleeting glimpse of the full complexity and multifaceted nature of socio-economic reality. This may happen during an initial multi-paradigm scan of a situation pending our provisional reading of the situation and choice of the appropriate systematic approach to study it. Moreover, even at the detailed analytical stage we may be able to focus on all the various aspects of a particular situation – and capture a holistic fragment of reality – by using our judgement to create an imaginative synthesis of findings derived from using discrete paradigms side-by-side to construct a narrative of the particular situation. But such relatively unified analytical vision is impossible to systematise or maintain at the general level. Political economy is necessarily suffused as much as Romantic poetry with the sense of fleeting visions of unity now lost forever. The imaginative analyst may sometimes ape the poet in seeking to represent what Abrams calls 'plenary fact from which science, for its special purposes, pulls out a limited number of stable, and, therefore, manageable attributes'.[17] But in the end there is a choice to be made – between the holistic narrative of the particular and the systematic and quintessentially scientific encapsulation of a widespread but hypothetical tendency.

As this book has emphasised, standard economics and Rational Choice Theory have never been monolithic paradigms, impervious to all Romantic criticism of their focus on narrow motivational models (borrowed from utilitarianism) and equilibrium analysis (borrowed from nineteenth-century physics). For example, Endogenous Growth Theory attempts to build Schumpeter's creative destruction (as well as increasing returns to learning and innovation) into models using standard motivational assumptions; while in some 'thin' versions of Rational Choice Theory, the 'utility' being maximised by rational agents is redefined as the satisfaction of whatever preferences their choices reveal them to have – a wide enough definition to allow *homo economicus* to resemble *homo romanticus* in some respects.[18] Indeed, so ingenious has been the theory mending within these paradigms that they begin to resemble Kuhn's description of mature paradigms: with so many adjustments to the basic model, any apparent fit with all aspects of reality (including creativity and sentiment) has come at the cost of theoretical complexity, loss of clarity and even some lack of internal consistency.[19] To use the same examples, 'thin' versions of Rational Choice Theory often produce propositions that are so poorly specified in content terms as to be largely meaningless, untestable and even circular; while Endogenous Growth Theory clings to rational expectations- and maximisation-based microfoundations that sit oddly with attempts to model the dynamic and uncertain impact of innovation and novelty.[20] It would, however, be wrong to anticipate on this basis one of Kuhn's paradigm crises and an imminent irreversible shift away from standard economics and Rational Choice Theory. For what is required is not a wholesale once-for-all paradigm shift to a new superior paradigm (nor, indeed, endless attempts to amend the standard paradigm) to cope with as much as possible of the Romantic critique. Instead, we need to be ready to use different paradigms side-by-side; and we need to develop new models based more fully on lessons from Romanticism as a complement to standard models.

There is, of course, no universal answer as to whether it is better to amend and even jettison a paradigm or instead use it in its pure form alongside an alternative framework. But it is worth remembering that economics gained as well as lost much by abstracting from the concerns of Romanticism: it gained extraordinary rigour and focus at the cost of separation from a more holistic vision of reality. This is why the general presumption of the Romantic Economist is in favour of exploiting multiple perspectives serially as the problem demands, so that we can enjoy the benefits of specialist focus and conceptual rigour without incurring all the attendant costs of restricted vision and observational bias. Rather than yearning for an impossible-to-achieve unified but systematic vision, we should avail ourselves of the cognitive order provided by discrete and sharply defined models and systems, while preserving the freedom that comes from thinking outside the box by switching between models and paradigms. For example, the standard paradigm of neoclassical economics is still unsurpassed in revealing and explaining the allocative-efficiency aspects of markets in situations where preferences, goods and incentives are relatively stable. There is no need to replace or drastically amend this model simply because alternative Complexity models are also required to reveal and explain the self-organising and dynamic aspects of market behaviour in situations where the presence of increasing returns, high barriers to entry, constant innovation and self-reinforcing standard-setting prevent any tendency to a unique equilibrium. In order to cater for both types of situation, we need to adopt a policy of 'horses for courses' – that is, having several models at our disposal and choosing the one most suited to the particular problem we are trying to solve.

It is for these reasons that the Romantic Economist advocates a twin-track approach: first, complementing standard economics with models that work better when dealing with certain types of problem; and, secondly, bolstering the effectiveness of both standard and more Romantic models by defining carefully the limits of their applicability. It is only by defining the extent of their remit that we can get the most out of the systematic models or fragments at our disposal. As Bagehot said when seeking to elucidate boundaries of applicability for the standard version of 'English Political Economy' of his time, 'We shall then find that our Political Economy is not a questionable thing of unlimited extent, but a most certain and useful thing of limited extent'.[21] Defining such boundaries will make it easier for an active conversation between different disciplines and paradigms to achieve a clear division of labour between their respective models. It will also make it easier to set up specific interdisciplinary joint ventures in relation to specific problems. So we may want to employ Rational Choice Theory to explain the functionality of a specific institutional configuration, while using a Constructivist approach to unearth its social meaning in terms of dominant norms, discourses and identities, before complementing this analysis with an organic model that underlines any mutual complementarities between different parts of the overall institutional configuration.

Many economists may say that this is all very well, but that whenever less formal models are used (and whenever *homo economicus* is replaced by *homo sociologicus* or *homo romanticus*) it stops being economics. Some indeed may not even allow that a substantive focus on institutions and norms is any business of economics. It is worth remembering that, for all his Romantic leanings, Mill was adamant that the discipline of economics is delimited by certain *a priori* hypotheses and methods, together with a substantive focus on wealth creation. Mill was equally clear, however, that the 'art' of *applied* economics must necessarily involve a wider focus and the use of many distinct sciences.[22] Since, in practice, even 'pure' economists in today's world usually want to be useful, and since they generally supplement the *a priori* assumptions and hypotheses in their models with specific allowance for particular factors from contingent reality, I would argue that economics has little choice but to come to terms, one way or another, with other disciplines and broader aspects of our humanity. Whether this broader focus is, in definitional terms, seen as part of economics or as part of an associated interdisciplinary endeavour is perhaps immaterial. What matters is that practising economists take on board a more Romantic approach to methodology and epistemology, and complement their focus on optimisation within a framework of constraints and incentives with an interest in the more Romantic (creative, social and incommensurable) attributes of economic life.

In some senses, this broader approach may appear to be a return to something closer to the older more eclectic economics of Adam Smith. As Emma Rothschild has made clear, Smith operated in 'an earlier and less bounded scene, in which the territory of economic life extends in all directions', and his political economy was still much broader in technique and focus than today's science.[23] Crucially, however, the approach I am arguing for in this book is a version of Smith's political economy that is updated in one important respect: while still being imaginative and open-minded about which explanatory system to use and which aspects of economic life to focus upon, the Romantic Economist advocates a disciplined eclecticism that tries to capitalise on the benefits of modern disciplinary focus. Such a Romantic but disciplined redefinition of 'political economy' to suit the *post*-Post-Modern era differs radically, of course, from the tendency in recent years to use the term 'political economy' to designate more narrowly the application of Rational Choice models to the study of politics.[24] The political economy engaged in by the Romantic Economist is the study of the intersection of economic, political and social aspects of reality, with the help of a disciplined dialectic between different perspectives designed to ensure that the choice of method to be used is driven by an open-minded assessment of the nature of the problems to be solved.

The Romantic Economist does not share Nietzsche's total mistrust of systematisers. It is not ' the will to a system'[25] in itself that is misguided, but rather the will to establish the supremacy – and believe in the sufficiency – of *one* system. The Romantic Economist is happy to celebrate the achievements of standard economics, with its law-like tendencies and its formal models – while at the same time insisting that such a systematic approach can provide only partial and provisional encapsulations of economic reality. The Romantic Economist assumes that we need to employ a number of different (more or less systematic) forms of analysis if we can hope to capture the multivalence of socio-economic reality. While sharing economists' normal prejudice in favour of mathematical precision and rigour where this is appropriate, the Romantic Economist recognises that much of our economic analysis is concerned with particular historically conditioned and creatively dynamic situations where it is less appropriate. In these cases, we need lower (less scientific) standards of explanation, less formal models and softer modes of analysis; and we may need to be content to provide *post hoc* narratives told in the tooled language of several discrete disciplines, together with useful simulations of general patterns. Economists, like the economic actors they study, need to combine reason with imagination: they need to combine deductive logic and probabilistic analysis, on the one hand, with cultural empathy, analytical open-mindedness, imaginative leaps and a willingness to see the world from a variety of perspectives, on the other.

Turning to the question of whether the more Romantic approaches to economics outlined in this book could represent a coherent paradigm of their own, it is worth recalling Kuhn's own characterisation of what constitutes the coherence of a scientific paradigm. Kuhn thought that the various aspects of a paradigm could not generally be reduced to a 'full set of rules'; instead, 'the various research problems and techniques' and the standard illustrations and assumptions making up a paradigm form a 'natural family' – 'constituted by a network of overlapping and crisscross resemblances'.[26] An acute reader may remember that I argued earlier in the book that the term 'Romantic' is a 'family resemblance' word in the Wittgensteinian sense, and that the various doctrines and assumptions associated with Romanticism consequently form what Kuhn (inspired by Wittgenstein) calls a 'natural family'.[27] I backed this claim by demonstrating a number of suggestive and, in some cases, logically necessary links between different ideas associated with Romanticism; and I argued that there is also a mutually reinforcing interdependence between many of the different lessons to be drawn from Romanticism, such that each one of them is more obviously valid if the others are held to be important. I concluded that there is more coherence to the Romantic critique of rationalism than is often assumed. For, while we do not need to accept all aspects of the *corpus* of ideas posthumously labelled 'Romantic' to accept any one aspect of it, each aspect is generally more compelling in self-reinforcing combination with others.[28] From this it would seem to follow that there may be, likewise, a strong 'family resemblance' and self-reinforcing coherence to the various Romanticism-inspired suggestions in this book for new models, microfoundations and grounding assumptions designed to improve our substantive understanding of economic reality.

Does such a 'family resemblance' between its different aspects imply that a version of the Romantic Economics set out in this book could form a new paradigm of its own to rival the coherence, vitality and insight-generation of standard economics? Or do we merely have fragments that are at most suggestive of a more unified and holistic approach to political economy? It is certainly true that much remains to be done to operationalise and develop the new methods, techniques and assumptions proposed here before they are likely to be widely adopted. Nevertheless, I would maintain that they do together represent a serious candidate to become a paradigm in their own right in due course. There is a set of important linkages between the various factors identified as limiting the applicability of the standard paradigm of neoclassical economics – linkages which are best explained by seeing them in the context of the two-hundred-year-old dialectic between Romantic and rationalist thinkers. Moreover, the self-reinforcing interdependence between the different assumptions, metaphors and models promoted by the Romantic Economist is matched by similarly strong links between the political and corporate policy implications of adopting them. It is with a brief summary of these policy implications, and the links between them, that the book concludes.

Many Romantics were fascinated by the role of language and cultural tradition in structuring our thought and interpretation of events, and hence our actions. They showed that specific national languages, traditional outlooks and shared norms play a significant part in shaping the perspectives, beliefs and behaviour of individual actors. If this is true in economic as well as purely social situations, it follows that it is important for economists no less than other social scientists to develop the ability to 'read' the different incommensurable but mutually intelligible discourses that structure our views of the world. Such readings require a degree of imaginative empathy that is, I have argued, a central analytical tool in all good comparative analysis of different economies and societies. Moreover, this ability to read and intuitively grasp cultural, linguistic and conceptual grids that are different from our own is also an important commercial weapon for companies in the fight for new export markets.

The structuring role played by language (as well as by foundational narratives and constitutions) is a central aspect of an organicist understanding of social reality. The organic metaphor championed by Romantics such as Herder, Burke and Coleridge can be applied by modern social scientists to capture the dynamic interdependence of social actors with each other and with the society that forms them, and to model the spontaneous self-organising development of society as a whole. The pattern of development of an organic social whole is a function not only of the creative choices made by individuals within it, but also of the self-reinforcing complementarities that do or do not exist in that society between its 'genetic' inheritance (in terms of institutions and cultural or cognitive norms) and the interests and capacities of its citizens. In an organicist vision of the world, history, culture and institutions matter to outcomes as much as the rationality and creativity of individuals. Small events in a nation's history can have a significant long-term impact on its development; and the behaviour of individuals cannot be predicted (if at all) except in the context of their interrelationship with the rest of society. Some aspects of an organic approach can be modelled mathematically in terms of modern Complexity models: these show that systems characterised by increasing returns can display dynamic self-organisation in conditions where the rules of the game constrain degrees of freedom sufficiently to pattern behaviour but not enough to lock it into one determinate outcome. Such models can be used to underline the importance of thresholds effects and unpredictable (non-linear) reactions to small events in markets, economies and ecosystems.

There are several direct implications of an organicist approach for both economic analysis and for economic and corporate policy. The interdependence of all the parts of an organism with each other, and of each organism with other organisms, makes it very difficult to isolate, or control for, particular variables and so test for precise causal linkages. Moreover, the prevalence of mutual complementarities and increasing returns makes precise *ex ante* prediction of the impact of specific changes an almost hopeless task. In these conditions, we must learn to beware economists bearing long-term predictions, and beware politicians or company directors bearing five-year plans; and we must learn instead to use organic (or Complexity) models and simulations to guide us in the imaginative task of reading patterns in social and economic reality as they unfold. An organic understanding of the importance of increasing returns, and of the hand played by history and inherited institutions in structuring beliefs and behaviour, should also alert us to the dangers inherent in radical reforms promising a clean sweep of the past – a *tabula rasa*. Given the complex organic interdependence of the different elements making up each society, economy, or company, we generally need to undertake piecemeal reforms; and, while doing so, we need at all times to be imaginatively receptive to possible triggers or unexpected events that may tip us onto a whole new social, economic, or corporate trajectory.

The lessons of organicism for economics and policy-makers are strongly linked with another key plank of Romantic Economics – a central focus on the role of imagination and creativity. Given their emphasis on increasing returns and the often large and unpredictable impact of small changes in conditions, organicism and its modern cousin Complexity Theory seem to imply the need for a radical reformulation of the standard microfoundations of economics – towards a much greater role for imagination and creative choice in strategy formation, and away from rational expectations and calculations of how to optimise given preferences and endowments. The central fact of radical uncertainty in complex creative systems implies that imagination must play as significant a role as reason in both structuring the choices individuals make and in forming the expectations and strategies that guide their behaviour. It is, of course, imagination, creativity and choice that are themselves partly responsible for making the future unknowable by injecting novelty and surprise into the equations of life. Indeed, imagination is central to the dynamic development of organic social and economic entities. It is the creative imagination of the individual actor that is usually the source of evolutionarily significant mutations in the DNA of a social organism; and it is the imagination of *homo romanticus* (more often than the capacity of *homo economicus* to optimise the efficient use of given endowments) that allows individuals and society as a whole to break free from the implicit determinism of social construction.[29]

An organicist approach is also strongly linked to two other lessons from Romanticism for economics. First, it underlies the strong emphasis by many Romantics on the importance of nation states, and nationally specific as opposed to universal models of behaviour and templates for action. With so much of our cognitive development, our social and economic behaviour, and even our capacity for innovation and creativity, conditioned by national institutions, norms and education systems, it follows that we cannot fully understand patterns of economic behaviour and specialisation without considering the role of nation states. Secondly, social organicism in the tradition of Herder helps highlight the anthropological fact that there is no universal system of values, but rather a whole host of different socially agreed solutions to the problem of how to balance conflicting and incommensurable values.

The Romantics almost all rejected utilitarianism for its inadequate model of human motivation – for reducing human beings to 'pleasure machines' who decide how to act solely by reference to what is expected to maximise their own pleasure, utility, or wealth; and they focused instead on the role of sympathy, imagination and sentiment. But their quarrel with utilitarianism went deeper than that. They asserted time and again the intrinsic value of love, beauty, freedom and human life – values that are neither directly commensurable with pleasurable feelings (or material wealth) nor in many cases even compatible with them. This constitutes one of the most important lessons to be derived from Romanticism: values are not (contrary to utilitarianism) all commensurable according to a single unit of account, and there is therefore no single right answer as to how we should balance the conflicting demands they make upon us. Individuals and nations must constantly make self-creating or self-defining choices between values; and, although they make these choices for reasons, there are no uniquely rational solutions to the dilemmas they face.

This has several important implications for economists and policy-makers alike. In particular, if choices about what relative weighting to assign to incommensurable values or goals cannot be decided by reference to one ultimate scale of value, and if the decisions made necessarily define our collective identities, it makes little sense for public policy-makers to sub-contract these value decisions to the weightings implied in catch-all variables like GDP; and it may be similarly unwise simply to bury them in the assumed 'willingness-to-pay' calculations of standard cost-benefit analysis. Instead, it is preferable to make explicit the need for identity-defining political choices of how we wish to balance different incommensurable goals (such as freedom, equality, natural beauty and average wealth), while supporting these choices by detailed analysis of the implications of alternative value weighting decisions.[30] Furthermore, if individual actors must constantly decide their own trade-offs between incommensurable values in the everyday market decisions they make, and if there is no uniquely rational answer for each individual as to what those trade-offs should be, it is not clear why we should privilege the consistency of preferences as a hall-mark of economic rationality; nor is it obvious that we should expect revealed indifference curves to provide a good basis for predicting consumer behaviour.[31] The moral indeterminacy implied by value pluralism translates in practice into indeterminacy of consumer preferences and a further reason to expect market instability.

It is perhaps only the 'two cultures' divide identified by C. P. Snow[32] that can fully explain the mystery of why most economists (and, indeed, most poets) have overlooked the supreme importance of creativity and imagination in economic activity and business. Indeed, the most important attribute of capitalist economies is the constant scope they provide for technological and product innovation, and also for the creation of new desires, new dreams and new identities. This makes strange the emphasis placed by economists on reason over imagination, and even stranger the obsessive focus of many policy-makers on maximising efficiency in a static allocation sense. They forget what Schumpeter well understood, that – in a world of 'creative destruction' – our capacity to innovate and make the right moves in the endless battle to create the next generation of dominant goods and technologies is far more important in the long run than the efficient allocation of today's resources.[33] Policy-makers may need to focus more on nurturing each nation's capacity to innovate and adapt successfully to constant change than on boosting the efficiency of production in the short term. Moreover, politicians would do well to recognise that the main social value of markets in advanced economies may no longer be their ability to engineer increases in wealth, but rather the opportunities they offer individual citizens to develop their own potential, express their identity, and create their own future. Increasingly, we define our identities by the jobs that we choose to do and the goods that we choose to buy; and, where we are able to do so, we choose jobs and goods that match our idealised visions of the way we wish to live our lives. It is for this reason, of course, that companies wanting to identify emerging consumer trends and create new markets must learn to empathise with consumers' dreams, while constantly inventing novel outlets for self-expression.

Our education systems also need to reflect the importance of imagination, creativity and sympathy to economic success. P. B. Shelley wrote: 'A man, to be greatly good, must imagine intensely and comprehensively';[34] and this is true well beyond the confines of morality and poetry. Indeed, the Romantic Economist would argue that imagination is equally a prerequisite for someone to become a good economist or scientist, a successful entrepreneur, a wise policy-maker, or even to function as a modern self-creating consumer. There is a danger in this rationalist age that we undervalue the importance in our education system of developing children's capacity to be creative and imaginative. Reading novels or poetry, and interpreting civilisations distant from our own in time, geography, or culture, may be as important to economic success as developing our capacity to do mathematics and conduct controlled experiments; and creative thinking exercises and learning how to harness our imaginations in the production of art may also provide us with essential life-skills. For it is the ability to imagine ourselves in other people's shoes, and read their concerns and their dreams, that makes us both good members of society and good entrepreneurs. It is our analytical imagination that enables us to grasp the conceptual schemes and norms of remote societies and render them intelligible enough that we can learn from them and engage with them constructively. It is in our imaginative capacity to think outside the box, make new connections and, in Wordsworth's words, 'build up greatest things/From least suggestions'[35] that the extraordinary innovative potential of mankind resides. It is the imagination's genius for constructing and visualising possible futures that enables us to make choices; and it is its ability to develop in each of us a guiding vision of how we wish to live our lives that can set us free. None of this is antithetical to reason. Imagination and reason are our two greatest gifts, and they must work hand in hand. Indeed, as Wordsworth said, imagination is in many ways only 'another name for … clearest insight, amplitude of mind, / And reason in her most exalted mood'.[36]

Notes

CHAPTER 1

1. Snow, C. P., *The Two Cultures and the Scientific Revolution*, Cambridge University Press, 1959, p. 4.
2. Shackle, G. L. S., *Epistemics and Economics – A Critique of Economic Doctrines* (originally published in 1972), Transaction Publishers, 1992, preface, p. xiv.
3. Hazlitt, William, *An Essay on the Principles of Human Action* (originally published in 1805), reprinted in *The Selected Writings of William Hazlitt*, ed. Duncan Wu, vol. 1, Pickering & Chatto, 1998, pp. 3–82.
4. Ruskin, John, *Unto this Last* (originally published in 1862), ed. Clive Wilmer, Essay 1, Penguin Classics, 1985, pp. 179.
5. Leavis, F. R., commenting on and quoting from Beatrice Webb's *My Apprenticeship* (1883), 'Introduction', in *Mill on Bentham and Coleridge*, Chatto & Windus, 1950, pp. 24–6.
6. Smith, Adam, *History of Astronomy*, in *Essays on Philosophical Subjects* (originally published in 1795), ed. W. P. D. Wightman and J. C. Bryce, Oxford University Press, 1980; extract quoted in Fleischacker, Samuel, *On Adam Smith's Wealth of Nations – A Philosophical Companion*, Princeton University Press, 2004, p. 21.
7. Heinzelman, Kurt, *The Economics of the Imagination*, University of Massachusetts Press, 1980, pp. 9, 11, 50.
8. McCloskey, D. N., *The Rhetoric of Economics*, 2nd edn., University of Wisconsin Press, 1998, pp. xiv, 40.
9. Ortony, Andrew, article on 'Metaphor', in *The Oxford Companion to the Mind*, ed. Richard L. Gregory, Oxford University Press, 1987, p. 478f.
10. Norris, Christopher, *Derrida*, Fontana, 1987, pp. 20–2.
11. See the literary criticism discussion in Abrams, M. H., *The Mirror and the Lamp – Romantic Theory and the Critical Tradition*, Oxford University Press, 1953, pp. 6–29.
12. Mill, J. S., essay on 'Bentham' (originally published in 1838), in *Mill on Bentham and Coleridge*, ed. F. R. Leavis, *op. cit.*, p. 39.
13. Drolet, Michael, 'Introduction', in *The Postmodernism Reader – Foundational Texts*, Routledge, 2004, pp. 20, 25.
14. Stiglitz, Joseph E., 'Whither Reform? Ten Years of the Transition', Keynote Address, Annual World Bank Conference on Development Economics, 1999;

reproduced as chapter 4 in *The Rebel Within*, ed. Ha-Joon Chang, Wimbledon Publishing Company, 2001, pp. 127–71.

15. Coleman, William Oliver, *Economics and its Enemies – Two Centuries of Anti-Economics*, Palgrave Macmillan, 2002, p. 220f.

16. Dasgupta, Partha, 'Modern Economics and its Critics', chapter 3 in *Fact and Fiction in Economics: Models, Realism and Social Construction*, ed. Uskali Mäki, Cambridge University Press, 2002, p. 57.

17. Coyle, Diane, *The Soulful Science – What Economists Really Do and Why It Matters*, Princeton University Press, 2007, p. 1.

18. Schumpeter, Joseph A., *History of Economic Analysis*, George Allen & Unwin, 1954, p. 10.

19. See, for example, Caporaso, James A. and Levine, David P., *Theories of Political Economy*, Cambridge University Press, 1992, pp. 126–58.

20. Kuhn, Thomas S., *The Structure of Scientific Revolutions*, 3rd edn., University of Chicago Press, 1996, p. 68f.

21. *Ibid.*, *passim*. For a further discussion of this point, see chapter 10 of *The Romantic Economist* (pp. 270, 271f. and nn. 60, 66).

22. Wordsworth, William, *The Prelude* (1805), book XII, lines 77f., 205f., ed. E. de Selincourt, Oxford University Press, 1960. See an excellent discussion of this passage in Connell, Philip, *Romanticism, Economics and the Question of 'Culture'*, Oxford University Press, 2001, pp. 44f., 49–52.

23. Mill, J. S., essay on 'Coleridge' (originally published in 1840), in *Mill on Bentham and Coleridge*, *op. cit.*, p. 155.

24. Wordsworth, William, 'Lines Written a Few Miles above Tintern Abbey', in *Lyrical Ballads*, 1798, line 25f., reprinted in *Romanticism – An Anthology*, 2nd edn., ed. Duncan Wu, Blackwell, 1998, p. 266. For a discussion of the 'great divide' between a Romantic and rationalist outlook, see chapter 2 of *The Romantic Economist* (pp. 31–56).

25. See the discussion in Butler, Marilyn, *Romantics, Rebels and Reactionaries – English Literature and its Background (1760–1830)*, Oxford University Press, 1981, pp. 1–10; and Day, Aidan, *Romanticism*, Routledge, 1996, pp. 82–8.

26. Abrams, M. H., *The Mirror and the Lamp*, *op. cit.*, p. 100.

27. Butler, Marilyn, *op. cit.*, p. 184.

28. Kuhn, Thomas S., *op. cit.*, p. 45. For a further discussion of Wittgenstein's 'family resemblance' theory of the meaning of words, and relevant references, see chapter 4 of *The Romantic Economist* (p. 87 and n. 11).

29. Berlin, Isaiah, *The Roots of Romanticism*, ed. Henry Hardy, Chatto & Windus, 1999, *passim*.

30. Coleridge, Samuel Taylor, *Biographia Literaria* (originally published in 1817), chapter IX, ed. J. Shawcross, Oxford, 1907, vol. I, p. 98.

31. Abrams, M. H., *The Mirror and the Lamp*, *op. cit.*, p. 100.

32. Day, Aidan, *op. cit.*, pp. 38, 76f.

33. Wordsworth, William, *Preface* to the *Lyrical Ballads*, 1800 and 1802 amendment, in Wordsworth, William and Coleridge, Samuel Taylor, *Lyrical Ballads*, ed. R. L. Brett and A. R. Jones, Methuen, 1963, p. 254.

34. *Ibid.*, pp. 249, 252f.; and Wordsworth, William, *The Prelude* (1805), book X, lines 843f., book XI, lines 131, 159, ed. E. de Selincourt, *op. cit.*

35. Wordsworth, William, *Preface* to the *Lyrical Ballads*, *op. cit.*, p. 238.

36. Wordsworth, William, 'Preface to Poems' (1815), in *Romanticism – An Anthology*, ed. Duncan Wu, *op. cit.*, p. 413; and 'Lines Written a Few Miles above Tintern Abbey', *op. cit.*, line 106f.

37. Wordsworth, William, *Preface* to the *Lyrical Ballads*, *op. cit.*, pp. 238–40, 244f., 255.

38. Waldrop, M. Mitchell, *Complexity – The Emerging Science at the Edge of Order and Chaos*, Penguin, 1994, p. 49.

39. Hazlitt, William, *The Spirit of the Age*, essay on 'Jeremy Bentham' (1825 edn.), The Wordsworth Trust, 2004, p. 99.

40. See the discussion in Connell, Philip, *op. cit.*, p. 230.

41. Marshall, Alfred, Letter to Arthur Lyon Bowley, 21 February 1901; Letter to Arthur Lyon Bowley, 3 March 1901 – Letters 634, 637, in *The Correspondence of Alfred Marshall*, ed. J. K. Whitaker, Cambridge University Press, 1996, vol. 2, pp. 300f., 305f.

42. Marshall, Alfred, Letter to Arthur Lyon Bowley, 27 February 1906, Letter 840 in *The Correspondence of Alfred Marshall*, *op. cit.*, vol. 3, p. 130.

43. Marshall, Alfred, *Principles of Economics*, preface to First Edition (1890), Macmillan, 1927, pp. x–xi.

44. Pigou, A. C., *Alfred Marshall and Current Thought* – Lecture on Mathematical Methods, Macmillan, 1953, p. 7.

45. *Ibid.*, p. 10.

46. Marshall, Alfred, *Principles of Economics*, preface to Eighth Edition (1920), Macmillan, 1927, p. xiv.

47. Friedman, Milton, 'The Methodology of Positive Economics', from *Essays in Positive Economics*, University of Chicago Press, 1953; reproduced as chapter 9 in *The Philosophy of Economics – An Anthology*, 2nd edn., ed. Daniel M. Hausman, Cambridge University Press, 1994, pp. 180–213.

48. Krugman, Paul, *Development, Geography, and Economic Theory*, MIT Press, 1997, p. 79f.

49. Abrams, M. H., *The Mirror and the Lamp*, *op. cit.*, pp. 57–69. For a full discussion of Romantic epistemology and the creative nature of perception, see chapter 4 of *The Romantic Economist* (pp. 103–5, 106 and nn. 80–83, 89).

50. Abrams, M. H., *The Mirror and the Lamp*, *op. cit.*, p. 31.

51. Tabb, William K., *Reconstructing Political Economy – The Great Divide in Economic Thought*, Routledge, 1999, p. 27f.

52. Waldrop, M. Mitchell, *op. cit.*, p. 150f.

53. McCloskey, D. N. *op. cit.*, pp. 37, 40–2, 44f.

54. Coleridge, Samuel Taylor, passage quoted in Abrams, M. H., *The Mirror and the Lamp*, *op. cit.*, p. 35.

55. Carlyle, Thomas, *Signs of the Times* (originally published in 1829), reprinted in *Critical and Miscellaneous Essays*, vol. 2, James Fraser, 1840, pp. 274f., 292.

56. Mirowski, Philip, *More Heat than Light – Economics as Social Physics, Physics as Nature's Economics*, Cambridge University Press, 1989, pp. 224, 240 and *passim*.

57. Coleridge, Samuel Taylor, 'Lay Sermon addressed to the Higher and Middle Classes' (1817), reprinted in *Biographia Literaria and Two Lay Sermons*, George Bell & Son, 1898, p. 426.

58. Schumpeter, Joseph, *History of Economic Analysis*, *op. cit.*, p. 27.

59. Friedman, Milton, *op. cit.*, p. 183f.

60. Schumpeter, Joseph, *History of Economic Analysis*, *op. cit.*, p. 7.

61. Colander, David, *The Lost Art of Economics – Essays on Economics and the Economics Profession*, Edward Elgar, 2001, pp. 57f., 129f.

CHAPTER 2

1. Keats, John, *Lamia* (originally published in 1819), part II, line 234f., reprinted in *Romanticism – An Anthology*, 2nd edn., ed. Duncan Wu, Blackwell, 1998, p. 1078.

2. Mill, J. S., essay on 'Bentham' (originally published in 1838), in *Mill on Bentham and Coleridge*, ed. F. R. Leavis, Chatto & Windus, 1950, p. 40.

3. Mill, J. S., essay on 'Coleridge' (originally published in 1840), in *Mill on Bentham and Coleridge*, *op. cit.*, p. 101.

4. Mill, J. S., 'Bentham', *op. cit.*, p. 40.

5. *Ibid.*, pp. 63, 70.

6. Mill, J. S., 'Coleridge', *op. cit.*, pp. 100, 107.

7. Mill, J. S. 'Bentham', *op. cit.*, p. 66f.

8. *Ibid.*, pp. 82, 73.

9. Mill, J. S., 'Coleridge', *op. cit.*, pp. 121, 123f., 129.

10. *Ibid.*, pp. 129, 132, 144, 148.

11. Connell, Philip, *Romanticism, Economics and the Question of 'Culture'*, Oxford University Press, 2001, p. 145f.

12. Mill, J. S., 'Bentham', *op. cit.*, p. 48; and 'Coleridge', *op. cit.*, p. 130.

13. Mill, J. S. 'Bentham', *op. cit.*, p. 59.

14. *Ibid.*, pp. 61, 74.

15. Webb, Beatrice, *My Apprenticeship* (1883), quoted and discussed in Leavis, F. R., 'Introduction', in *Mill on Bentham and Coleridge*, *op. cit.*, pp. 24–6.

16. Mill J. S., 'Bentham', *op. cit.*, p. 95.

17. *Ibid.*, pp. 64, 65; and Mill, J. S., 'Coleridge', *op. cit.*, p. 133.

18. Mill, J. S., 'Bentham', *op. cit.*, p. 65; and 'Coleridge', *op. cit.*, pp. 102, 104.

19. Leavis, F. R., 'Introduction', in *Mill on Bentham and Coleridge*, *op. cit.*, p. 8.

20. Mill, J. S., 'Coleridge', *op. cit.*, p. 104.

21. See the discussion in Stafford, William, *John Stuart Mill*, Macmillan, 1998, pp. 35–7; and in Skorupski, John, *The Cambridge Companion to Mill*, Cambridge University Press, 1998, p. 535.

22. Mill, J. S., 'Coleridge', *op. cit.*, p. 105.

23. *Ibid.*, p. 117.

24. *Ibid.*, p. 107f.

25. Mill, J. S., *Autobiography* (originally published in 1873), Penguin, 1989, p. 112.

26. *Ibid.*, pp. 115, 117f., 121, 127.

27. *Ibid.*, pp. 118, 121, 123.

28. *Ibid.*, p. 121.

29. *Ibid.*, p. 117.

30. *Ibid.*, p. 123.

31. Stafford, William, *op. cit.*, p. 35.

32. *Ibid.*, p. 44.

33. Mill, J. S., *Autobiography*, *op. cit.*, p. 130f.

34. *Ibid.*, pp. 125–27.

35. Mill, J. S., 'Coleridge', *op. cit.* p. 113.

36. Snow, C. P., *The Two Cultures and the Scientific Revolution*, Cambridge University Press, 1959, p. 9f.

37. Tarnas, Richard, *The Passion of the Western Mind – Understanding the Ideas that have Shaped our World View*, Ballantine Books, 1993, pp. 375, 377.

38. Connell, Philip, *op. cit.*, p. 73f.

39. Hume, David, *A Treatise of Human Nature* (1740), Part III, section 14; see especially *David Hume on Human Nature and the Understanding*, ed. Anthony Flew, Macmillan, 1962, p. 210f. See also Magee, Bryan, *The Great Philosophers – An Introduction to Western Philosophy*, BBC Books, 1987, for a discussion on Hume with John Passmore, p. 148f.; and Warnock, Mary, *Imagination*, Faber & Faber, 1976, p. 23f.

40. Rothschild, Emma, *Economic Sentiments – Adam Smith, Condorcet, and the Enlightenment*, Harvard University Press, 2001, chapter 7 and esp. p. 212.

41. Berlin, Isaiah, *The Roots of Romanticism*, ed. Henry Hardy, Chatto & Windus, 1999, p. 1.

42. See, for example, Day, Aidan, *Romanticism*, Routledge, 1996, *passim*; and Beer, John, 'Fragmentations and Ironies', in *Questioning Romanticism*, ed. John Beer, Johns Hopkins University Press, 1995, p. 238f.

43. Wordsworth, William, *Preface* to the *Lyrical Ballads*, 1800 and 1802 amendment, in Wordsworth, William and Coleridge, Samuel Taylor, *Lyrical Ballads*, ed. R. L. Brett and A. R. Jones, Methuen, 1963, p. 254; *The Prelude* (1850), book III, lines 59–63, ed. J. Wordsworth, M. H. Abrams and S. Gill, W. W. Norton, 1979, p. 95; *The Prelude* (1805), book X, lines 807–11, 823, 840–9, and book XII, lines 69–219, ed. E. de Selincourt, Oxford University Press, 1960, pp. 199f., 220–4. See also the discussion of *The Prelude* book XII passage in Connell, Philip, *op. cit.*, pp. 41–62; and the discussion of Wordsworth's attitude to science in Abrams, M. H., *The Mirror and the Lamp*, Oxford University Press, 1953, p. 309.

44. Connell, Philip, *op. cit.*, chapter 1.

45. Coleridge, Samuel Taylor, 'Lay Sermon addressed to the Higher and Middle Classes' (originally published in 1817), reprinted in *Biographia Literaria and Two Lay Sermons*, George Bell & Son, 1898, pp. 418f., 422, 425; and see the discussion in Connell, Philip, *op. cit.*, pp. 156–59.

46. See, for example, Coleridge, Samuel Taylor, *Biographia Literaria* (originally published in 1817), chapter XIV, ed. J. Shawcross, Oxford University Press, 1907, vol. II, p. 12.

47. de Quincey, Thomas, *The Logic of Political Economy* (1844), in *The Collected Writings of Thomas de Quincey*, ed. David Masson, vol. IX, Adam & Charles Black, 1890, p. 118f.; and see the discussion in McDonagh, Josephine, *De Quincey's Disciplines*, Oxford University Press, 1994, pp. 45f., 53f., 58–65.

48. For a fuller discussion of 'Christian Political Economy', see chapter 3 of *The Romantic Economist* (pp. 65f. and nn. 22–25); and Waterman, A. M. C., *Revolution, Economics and Religion: Christian Political Economy, 1798–1833*, Cambridge University Press, 1991, *passim*.

49. Blake, William, *Laocoon*, aphorisms 17, 19 (1665, 666), quoted in Berlin, Isaiah, *op. cit.*, p. 50; and Burke, Edmund, *Reflections on the Revolution in France* (originally published in 1790), extract quoted from Connell, Philip, *op. cit.*, p. xiii.

50. Coleridge, Samuel Taylor, *Table Talk* (originally published in 1835), extract quoted in Williams, Raymond, *Culture and Society: 1780–1950*, Chatto & Windus, 1958, p. 58; and Wordsworth, William, *Ecclesiastical Sonnets*, 3.43, extract quoted in Coleman, William Oliver, *Economics and its Enemies – Two Centuries of Anti-Economics*, Palgrave Macmillan, 2002, p. 114; and Wordsworth, William, 'To the Utilitarians', extract quoted in Connell, Philip, *op. cit.*, p. xiii, 22.

51. Macaulay, Thomas Babington, review in *Edinburgh Review* (January 1830) of Southey's 'Colloquies on the Progress and Prospects of Society', quoted in Connell, Philip, *op. cit.*, p. 4.

52. Shelley, P. B., *A Defence of Poetry* (originally published in 1840), extracts reprinted in *Romanticism – An Anthology*, 2nd edn., ed. Duncan Wu, *op. cit.*, pp. 944–6, 951–3, 956; and see the discussion of Thomas Love Peacock's 'The Four Ages of Poetry' (1820), and Shelley's response, in Connell, Philip, *op. cit.*, pp. 212–14, 228.

53. Connell, Philip, *op. cit.*, p. 11.

54. *Ibid.*, pp. 12, 191.

55. Carlyle, Thomas, *Signs of the Times* (originally published in 1829), reprinted in *Critical and Miscellaneous Essays*, vol. 2, James Fraser, 1840, pp. 274, 276f., 283f., 292.

56. *Ibid.*, p. 292: 'We are but fettered by chains of our own forging, and which ourselves also can rend asunder. This deep, paralysed subjection … comes not from Nature, but from our own unwise mode of *viewing* Nature … If Mechanism, like some glass bell, encircles and imprisons us; … – yet the bell is but of glass; "one bold stroke to break the bell in pieces, and thou art delivered!"' See the further discussion of this passage in chapter 1 of *The Romantic Economist* (p. 24).

57. Snow, C. P., *The Two Cultures and the Scientific Revolution*, Cambridge University Press, 1959, pp. 3f., 12, 15, 17 and *passim*.

58. Mason, John Hope, *The Value of Creativity – The Origins and Emergence of a Modern Belief*, Ashgate, 2003, pp. 4f., 6 and *passim*.

59. *Ibid.*, p. 232; and Fukuyama, Francis, *The End of History and the Last Man*, Penguin, 1992, *passim*.

60. Winch, Donald, 'Political Economy', chapter 33 in *An Oxford Companion to the Romantic Age – British Culture 1776–1832*, ed. Iain McCalman, Oxford University Press, 1999, p. 319.

61. Mill, J. S., *Autobiography, op. cit.* p. 117; and Gray, John, *Mill on Liberty – A Defence*, 2nd edn., Routledge, 1996, esp. pp. 35, 38f.

62. See the discussion in Gray, John, *Mill on Liberty – A Defence, op. cit.*, p. 70f.

63. Mill, J. S., *Utilitarianism* (originally published in 1861), ed. Mary Warnock, William Collins & Sons, 1962, p. 258f.; and see the discussion in Gray, John, *Mill on Liberty – A Defence, op. cit.*, p. 45f.; and in Gray, John, *Two Faces of Liberalism*, Polity Press, 2000, p. 58f.

64. Roll, Eric, *A History of Economic Thought*, 5th edn., Faber & Faber, 1992, p. 325.

65. Mill, J. S., 'Essay on the Definition of Political Economy; and on the Method of Investigation Proper to it' (originally published in 1830), as Essay V in Mill, J. S., *Essays on Some Unsettled Questions of Political Economy*, 3rd edn., Longmans, Green & Co., 1877, p. 137f.

66. *Ibid.*, p. 139.

67. *Ibid.*, p. 140; and Mill, J. S., essay on 'Bentham' (ed. F. R. Leavis), *op. cit.*, p. 73.

68. Mill, J. S., *Autobiography, op. cit.*, p. 178f.; and see Hollander, Samuel, *The Economics of John Stuart Mill*, vol. I, University of Toronto Press, 1985, pp. 134–6.

69. Mill, J. S., 'Essay on the Definition of Political Economy', *op. cit.*, p. 144f.

70. Mill J. S., *Autobiography, op. cit.*, p. 178f.

71. Mill, J. S., 'Essay on the Definition of Political Economy', *op. cit.*, p. 155.

72. *Ibid.*, pp. 153f., 156f.

73. See the discussion of this point in Robbins, Lionel, *A History of Economic Thought – The LSE Lectures*, ed. Steven G. Medema and Warren J. Samuels, Princeton University Press, 1998, Lecture 23, p. 224.

74. Mill, J. S., 'Essay on the Definition of Political Economy', *op. cit.*, p. 151.

75. Ruskin, John, *Unto this Last* (originally published in 1862), Essay 1, ed. Clive Wilmer, Penguin, 1985, p. 167.

76. *Ibid.*, p. 168.

CHAPTER 3

1. Tabb, William K., *Reconstructing Political Economy – The Great Divide in Economic Thought*, Routledge, 1999, pp. 5f., 18f.

2. *Ibid.*, pp. 6, 12 and *passim*; and, for a discussion of the 'social physics' metaphor, see Mirowski, Philip, *More Heat than Light – Economics as Social Physics, Physics as Nature's Economics*, Cambridge University Press, 1989, *passim*.

3. Tabb, William K., *op. cit.*, pp. 37, 50f.

4. See the discussion of the 'Adam Smith problem', in Tabb, William K., *op. cit.*, p. 37; Brown, Vivienne, *Adam Smith's Discourse – Canonicity, Commerce and Conscience*, Routledge, 1994, p. 1f.; and Bronk, Richard, *Progress and the Invisible Hand – The Philosophy and Economics of Human Advance*, Little Brown, 1998, p. 89f.

5. Fleischacker, Samuel, *On Adam Smith's Wealth of Nations – A Philosophical Companion*, Princeton University Press, 2004, p. 46; and see the discussion in Raphael, D. D., *Adam Smith*, Oxford University Press, 1985, pp. 29–35.

6. Smith, Adam, *An Inquiry into the Nature and Causes of the Wealth of Nations* (originally published in 1776), I.ii, ed. Kathryn Sutherland, Oxford University Press, 1993, p. 22; and see the discussion in Bronk, Richard, *Progress and the Invisible Hand*, *op. cit.*, pp. 90f., 182.

7. Raphael, D. D., *op. cit.*, p. 93f.; and Fleischacker, Samuel, *op. cit.*, pp. 90f., 95f.

8. Rothschild, Emma, *Economic Sentiments – Adam Smith, Condorcet, and the Enlightenment*, Harvard University Press, 2001, p. 1f. and chapter 1.

9. Smith, Adam, *The Wealth of Nations*, IV.ii, *op. cit.*, pp. 289, 291f.

10. See the discussion in Bronk, Richard, *Progress and the Invisible Hand*, *op. cit.*, pp. 92, 107.

11. Rothschild, Emma, *op. cit.*, pp. 116, 138, 144.

12. Smith, Adam, *The Wealth of Nations*, IV.ix, *op. cit.*, p. 391f.

13. *Ibid.*, IV.ii, III.iv, IV.vii, I.viii, I.ii, pp. 290, 272, 350, 66, 343, 21; and Smith, Adam, *The Theory of Moral Sentiments*, VI.i.3, quoted in the notes on p. 519 of *The Wealth of Nations*, *op. cit.*

14. Wordsworth, William, *The Prelude* (1805), book X, line 808f., ed. E. de Selincourt, Oxford University Press, 1960.

15. Rothschild, Emma, *op. cit.*, p. 224. See a more extended discussion of the importance of sympathy and empathy to economic actors in chapter 9 of *The Romantic Economist* (p. 251f. and n. 85).

16. Smith, Adam, 'History of Astronomy', in *Essays on Philosophical Subjects* (originally published in 1795), ed. W. P. D. Wightman and J. C. Bryce, Oxford University Press, 1980; extracts quoted in Fleischacker, Samuel, *op. cit.*, pp. 21, 32.

17. Fleischacker, Samuel, *op. cit.*, pp. 20, 33–44; and Smith, Adam, *The Wealth of Nations*, I.viii, IV.v, *op. cit.*, pp. 73, 334.

18. See the discussion of Jean-Baptiste Say in Drolet, Michael, *Tocqueville, Democracy and Social Reform*, Palgrave Macmillan, 2003, pp. 43; Tabb, William K., *op. cit.*, p. 65f.; and Roll, Eric, *A History of Economic Thought*, 5th edn., Faber & Faber, 1992, p. 169f.

19. Backhouse, Roger E., *The Penguin History of Economics*, Penguin, 2002, pp. 137f., 140; and see also the discussion in Roll, Eric, *op. cit.*, pp. 165–7; and in Tabb, William K., *op. cit.*, p. 53f.

20. Schumpeter, Joseph, *History of Economic Analysis*, George Allen & Unwin, 1954, p. 472f.; the key passage is quoted in Tabb, William K., *op. cit.*, p. 56.

21. See the discussion of Malthus in Waterman, A. M. C., *Revolution, Economics and Religion: Christian Political Economy, 1798–1833*, Cambridge University Press, 1991, pp. 5–7 and chapter 2, esp. pp. 15, 38–42.

22. Waterman, A. M. C., *op. cit.*, chapter 2 (esp. p. 51), and chapter 4 (esp. pp. 136–44); and Malthus, Robert, *An Essay on the Principle of Population* (originally published in 1798), ed. Anthony Flew, Penguin, 1970, chapter 5, pp. 97–100.

23. Malthus, Robert, *A Summary View of the Principle of Population* (originally published in 1830), in ed. Anthony Flew, *An Essay on the Principle of Population*, *op. cit.*, p. 271f.
24. Waterman, A. M. C., *op. cit.*, pp. 10–14, 206–8, 244, 259f.
25. See the discussion in chapter 7 of *The Romantic Economist* (pp. 186f., 189f. and nn. 50–51, 54–55).
26. Keynes, John Maynard, essay on 'Thomas Robert Malthus', reproducing and commenting on Ricardo's letter to Malthus, dated 24 January 1817, and Malthus' letter to Ricardo, dated 26 January 1817, chapter 12 in *The Collected Writings of John Maynard Keynes*, vol. X, Macmillan, 1972, pp. 94–101.
27. *Ibid.*, p. 97f.; and Keynes, John Maynard, 'A Tract on Monetary Reform' (1923), chapter 3 in *The Collected Writings of John Maynard Keynes*, vol. IV, Macmillan, 1971, p. 65.
28. See the discussion of Walras in Backhouse, Roger E., *op. cit.*, pp. 170–72; and of Arrow and Debreu in Bronk, Richard, *Progress and the Invisible Hand*, *op. cit.*, p. 107f.
29. See the discussion of Marshall in Backhouse, Roger E., *op. cit.*, p. 179; and in Roll, E., *op. cit.*, p. 363.
30. Marshall, Alfred, *Principles of Economics*, Preface to First Edition (1890); and Preface to Eighth Edition (1920), Macmillan, 1927, pp. vii, xivf.
31. Backhouse, Roger E., *op. cit.*, p. 180.
32. Marshall, Alfred, *Principles of Economics*, Preface to Eighth Edition, *op. cit.*, p. xv.
33. Shackle, G. L. S., *Epistemics and Economics – A Critique of Economic Doctrines* (originally published in 1972), Transaction Publishers, 1992, p. 4.
34. Veblen, Thorstein, 'The Limitations of Marginal Utility', *Journal of Political Economy*, 17 (1909); reproduced as chapter 6 in *The Philosophy of Economics – An Anthology*, 2nd edn., ed. Daniel M. Hausman, Cambridge University Press, 1994, pp. 143–56.
35. Schumpeter, Joseph A., *Capitalism, Socialism and Democracy* (originally published in 1943), Routledge, 1994, chapter 6 (n. 5), p. 77, chapter 7, pp. 82–4.
36. See Gamble, Andrew, *Hayek – The Iron Cage of Liberty*, Polity Press, 1996, pp. 38, 67–9; Buchanan, James M. and Vanberg, Viktor J., 'The Market as a Creative Process', *Economics and Philosophy*, 7 (1991), p. 184, reproduced as chapter 18 in *The Philosophy of Economics – An Anthology*, ed. Daniel M. Hausman, *op. cit.*, n. 33, p. 333; and Backhouse Roger, E., *op. cit.*, p. 278f.
37. Arthur, W. Brian, 'Positive Feedbacks in the Economy', *Scientific American*, February 1990, p. 85; and see Waldrop, M. Mitchell, *Complexity – The Emerging Science at the Edge of Order and Chaos*, Penguin, 1994, *passim*.
38. Shackle, G. L. S., *op. cit.*, *passim*.
39. Keynes, John Maynard, *The General Theory of Employment, Interest and Money* (originally published in 1936), in *The Collected Writings of John Maynard Keynes*, vol. VII, Macmillan, 1973, chapter 12, esp. pp. 149, 161.
40. See the discussion on Menger in Backhouse, Roger E., *op. cit.* pp. 174–77.

41. Roll, Eric, *op. cit.*, p. 281f.; see also the discussion of Schmoller and the Historical School in Backhouse, Roger E., *op. cit.*, p. 173f.; Tabb, William K., *op. cit.*, p. 114; and Keynes, John Neville, *The Scope and Method of Political Economy*, 3rd edn., Macmillan, 1904, p. 24f.

42. Backhouse, Roger E., *op. cit.*, pp. 177, 183.

43. Keynes, John Neville, *op. cit.*, pp. 15f., 31–6, 55f., 61f., 63–5.

44. Colander, David, *The Lost Art of Economics – Essays on Economics and the Economics Profession*, Edward Elgar, 2001, pp. 19–33, 162f.; and Keynes, John Neville, *op. cit.*, p. 19.

45. Say, Jean-Baptiste, 'Discours préliminaire', passage quoted in Rothschild, Emma, *op. cit.*, p. 248.

46. Robbins, Lionel, *An Essay on the Nature and Significance of Economic Science*, 2nd edn., Macmillan, 1935, extracts reprinted as chapter 3 in *The Philosophy of Economics – An Anthology*, ed. Daniel M. Hausman, *op. cit.*, p. 89.

47. Marshall, Alfred, Inaugural Lecture, extract quoted in J. M. Keynes' essay on 'Alfred Marshall', in *The Collected Writings of John Maynard Keynes*, vol. X, *op. cit.*, p. 196; and Sutton, John, *Marshall's Tendencies – What Can Economists Know?*, MIT Press, 2000, pp. 4, 16.

48. Robbins, Lionel, *op. cit.*, pp. 85, 102, 105.

49. Sen, Amartya, *On Ethics and Economics*, Blackwell, 1987, pp. 4–7 and *passim*.

50. For a fuller discussion of this so-called 'potential Pareto improvement' and of cost-benefit analysis in general, see chapter 7 of *The Romantic Economist* (pp. 188–90 and nn. 52–55).

51. Schumpeter, Joseph, *History of Economic Analysis*, *op. cit.*, chapter 2, pp. 12–24; and for a discussion of Weber, see Tabb, William K., *op. cit.*, p. 116.

52. See, for example, Backhouse, Roger E., *op. cit.*, p. 311.

53. Mirowski, Philip, *More Heat than Light – Economics as Social Physics, Physics as Nature's Economics*, Cambridge University Press, 1989, *passim*. See also the discussion of Mirowski and the 'social physics' metaphor in chapter 1 of *The Romantic Economist* (p. 24 and n. 56).

54. Mirowski, Philip, *op. cit.*, p. 219f., quotation from Léon Walras' *Elements of Pure Economics* and the general discussion on Walras.

55. Pareto, Vilfredo, 'On the Economic Phenomenon', passage quoted in Mirowski, Philip, *op. cit.*, p. 221.

56. Mirowski, Philip, *op. cit.*, p. 224f. on 'Fisher's Translations', quoted from Fisher, Irving, *Mathematical Investigations in the Theory of Value and Prices*, Yale University Press, 1925, pp. 85f.

57. Backhouse, Roger E., *op. cit.*, pp. 191–94.

58. Backhouse, Roger, E., *op. cit.*, p. 248f. (on Tinbergen) and p. 258f. (on Samuelson).

59. See Coleman, William Oliver, *Economics and its Enemies – Two Centuries of Anti-Economics*, Palgrave Macmillan, 2002, *passim*, esp. pp. 220–34. On page 8f., Coleman defines a past critic as objectively 'anti-economics' if his theories did not contribute in some form or other to the further development of the current version of the paradigm, and as 'subjectively' so if they were intended to be destructive of the mainstream tradition within economics. This is a good

example of the general mind-set of the discipline in relation to its harshest critics.

60. Colander, David, *op. cit.*, p. 156f.

61. For a discussion on 'imperfect information', see Stiglitz, Joseph, *Principles of Micro-Economics*, 2nd edn., W. W. Norton, 1997, chapter 18, pp. 430–37.

62. For a discussion on 'Endogenous Growth Theory', see Carlin, Wendy and Soskice, David, *Macroeconomics: Imperfections, Institutions and Policies*, Oxford University Press, 2006, chapter 14, pp. 529–59.

63. For a discussion on 'hysteresis', see Bronk, Richard, *Progress and the Invisible Hand*, *op. cit.*, pp. 195–97.

64. See an example of this in Carlin, Wendy and Soskice, David, *op. cit.*, pp. 543–46.

65. See an example of this in Carlin, Wendy and Soskice, David, *op. cit.*, pp. 563–73.

66. For a summary of the "Varieties of Capitalism' approach, see Hall, Peter and Soskice, David (eds.), *Varieties of Capitalism – The Institutional Foundations of Comparative Advantage*, Oxford University Press, 2001, chapter 1, pp. 1–68; and see the discussion in chapter 6 of *The Romantic Economist* (pp. 158–68).

67. For an example of this definition of 'political economy', see Caporaso, James A. and Levine, David D., *Theories of Political Economy*, Cambridge University Press, 1992, chapter 6, pp. 126–28.

68. For an introduction to 'Constructivism', see Adler, Emanuel, 'Constructivism and International Relations', chapter 5 in *Handbook of International Relations*, ed. W. Carlsnaes *et al.*, Sage, 2002, pp. 95–118; and see the discussion in chapter 5 of *The Romantic Economist* (p. 135).

CHAPTER 4

1. Butler, Marilyn, *Romantics, Rebels and Reactionaries – English Literature and its Background (1760–1830)*, Oxford University Press, 1981, p. 2.

2. For a discussion of John Gibson Lockhart's use of this distinction in his articles for *Blackwood's Edinburgh Magazine*, see Connell, Philip, *Romanticism, Economics and the Question of 'Culture'*, Oxford University Press, 2001, pp. 188–90.

3. For a discussion of the views of Blake and Wollstonecraft on repressive institutions of the day, see Day, Aidan, *Romanticism*, Routledge, 1996, pp. 23–6.

4. For a discussion of A. W. Schlegel's famous lectures on the classical versus romantic style and on organic versus mechanical metaphors, see Day, Aidan, *op. cit.*, p. 82f. (especially his quotation from René Wellek); and see Beer, John, 'Fragmentations and Ironies', in *Questioning Romanticism*, ed. John Beer, Johns Hopkins University Press, 1995, pp. 244–46. For a discussion and references on F. Schlegel's use of fragments and articulation of 'Romantic Irony', see later in this chapter of *The Romantic Economist* (pp. 108–10 and nn. 93–102).

5. For a discussion of the Christian and neo-Platonic aspect of German Idealism (and its influence on Coleridge), see Hedley, Douglas, *Coleridge, Philosophy and Religion – Aids to Reflection and the Mirror of the Spirit*, Cambridge University Press, 2000, pp. 4–6; and for a discussion of Schelling, in particular, see Warnock, Mary, *Imagination*, Faber & Faber, 1976, p. 69f.

6. Despite his late date, I follow Bertrand Russell and Richard Tarnas in seeing Friedrich Nietzsche as an honorary member of the Romantic movement (broadly defined), or at least as representing the crucial link between Romanticism and its Post-Modern legacy; see Russell, Bertrand, *A History of Western Philosophy*, George Allen & Unwin, 1946, p. 789; and Tarnas, Richard, *The Passion of the Western Mind – Understanding the Ideas that have Shaped our World View*, Ballantine Books, 1993, pp. 368–71.

7. For a discussion and references on C. P. Snow's 'two culture divide', see chapter 2 of *The Romantic Economist* (p. 48 and n. 57).

8. Lovejoy, A. O., 'On the Discrimination of Romanticisms', from *Essays in the History of Ideas*, Johns Hopkins University Press, 1948, reprinted in *English Romantic Poets – Modern Essays in Criticism*, ed. M. H. Abrams, Oxford University Press, 1975, p. 8.

9. Beer, John, 'Introduction', in *Questioning Romanticism, op. cit.*, p. xiii.

10. Berlin, Isaiah, *The Roots of Romanticism*, ed. Henry Hardy, Chatto & Windus, 1999, pp. 15f., 134, 137f. and *passim*.

11. For a discussion of the 'family resemblance' theory of meaning of words, see Wittgenstein, Ludwig in *The Wittgenstein Reader*, ed. Anthony Kenny, Blackwell, 1994, p 48f.; and Magee, Bryan, *The Great Philosophers – An Introduction to Western Philosophy*, BBC Books, 1987, discussion on Wittgenstein with John Searle, p. 328f.; and Kuhn, Thomas S., *The Structure of Scientific Revolutions*, 3rd edn., University of Chicago Press, 1996, p. 45.

12. See the excellent discussion in Barnard, F. M., *Herder's Social and Political Thought – From Enlightenment to Nationalism*, Oxford University Press, 1965, p. 36f. and *passim*; and Barnard, F. M., 'Introduction', in *J. G. Herder on Social and Political Culture*, Cambridge University Press, 1969, p. 31f.

13. Herder, J. G., *Ideas for a Philosophy of the History of Mankind* (originally published in 1791), extracts trans. F. M. Barnard, in *J. G. Herder on Social and Political Culture, op. cit.*, p. 324f.; and see the discussion in Barnard, F. M., *Herder's Social and Political Thought, op. cit.*, pp. 54–71, 102.

14. Herder, J. G., *Ideas for a Philosophy of the History of Mankind, op. cit.*, pp. 270, 304; and see the discussion in Barnard, F. M., *Herder's Social and Political Thought, op. cit.*, pp. 37, 54f.; and in Drolet, Michael, 'Introduction', in *The Postmodernism Reader – Foundational Texts*, Routledge, 2004, p. 13.

15. Berlin, Isaiah, *op. cit.*, p. 124; and Burke, Edmund, 'Speech on Moving the Resolutions for Conciliation with the Colonies' (1775), quoted in Whale, John, *Imagination Under Pressure, 1789–1832*, Cambridge University Press, 2000, p. 32; and see the discussion of Burke's *Reflections on the Revolution in France* (originally published in 1790) in Day, Aidan, *op. cit.*, p. 13f.

16. See the excellent discussion of Burke's distrust of abstract rational analysis, and of his appreciation of the role of civic imagination 'in support of a specific national identity', in Whale, John, *op. cit.*, pp. 31f., 38–40.

17. See the discussion of Burke in Day, Aidan, *op. cit.*, p. 13f.; and in *An Oxford Companion to the Romantic Age – British Culture 1776–1832*, ed. Iain McCalman, Oxford University Press, 1999, p. 437; and for a discussion of Burke's influence

on Hayek, Popper and other opponents of both shock therapy and radical blueprints for change, see Gamble, Andrew, *Hayek – The Iron Cage of Liberty*, Polity Press, 1996, p. 34; and Stiglitz, Joseph E., 'Whither Reform? Ten Years of the Transition', Keynote Address, Annual World Bank Conference on Development Economics, 1999, reproduced as chapter 4 in *The Rebel Within*, ed. Ha-Joon Chang, Wimbledon Publishing Company, 2001, p. 153f. For a discussion of Herder's aversion to rapid change, see Barnard, F. M., *Herder's Social and Political Thought, op. cit.*, p. 83f.

18. Coleridge, Samuel Taylor, *On the Constitution of the Church and State* (originally published in 1830), ed. John Barrell, J. M. Dent & Sons, 1972, pp. 91, 37, 16, 34.

19. Coleridge, Samuel Taylor, 'Lay Sermon addressed to the Higher and Middle Classes' (originally published in 1817), reprinted in *Biographia Literaria and Two Lay Sermons*, George Bell & Son, 1898, p. 425f.; and see the discussion in Connell, Philip, *op. cit.*, pp. 156–59.

20. Herder, J. G., *Ideas for a Philosophy of the History of Mankind, op. cit.*, p. 263.

21. Barnard, F. M., *Herder's Social and Political Thought, op. cit.*, pp. 57–9, 141f.

22. Herder, J. G., *Ideas for a Philosophy of the History of Mankind, op. cit.*, p. 300; and *Essay on the Origin of Language* (originally published in 1772), extracts trans. F. M. Barnard, in *J. G. Herder on Social and Political Culture, op. cit.*, pp. 163–65.

23. Gray, John, *Two Faces of Liberalism*, Polity Press, 2000, pp. 34f., 40.

24. See the discussion of Herder's belief that each nation creates 'its own peculiar image of *Humanität*' as part of 'national self-determination', in Barnard, F. M., *Herder's Social and Political Thought, op. cit.*, p. 97f.; and the discussion of his rejection of a linear conception of progress in *ibid.*, p. 131.

25. Berlin, Isaiah, 'The Apotheosis of the Romantic Will', in *The Crooked Timber of Humanity – Chapters in the History of Ideas*, ed. Henry Hardy, John Murray, 1990, p. 224.

26. Lockridge, Laurence S., *The Ethics of Romanticism*, Cambridge University Press, 1989, p. 143.

27. Coleridge, Samuel Taylor, 'The Statesman's Manual' (originally published in 1816), appendix C, reprinted in *Biographia Literaria and Two Lay Sermons, op. cit.*, p. 346.

28. Hazlitt, William, *An Essay on the Principles of Human Action* (originally published in 1805), reprinted in *The Selected Writings of William Hazlitt*, ed. Duncan Wu, Pickering & Chatto, 1998, vol. 1, fn. on p. 14f.; and see the discussion of this passage in Lockridge, Laurence, *op. cit.*, p. 343.

29. Shelley, P. B., *A Defence of Poetry* (originally published in 1840), extracts reprinted in *Romanticism – An Anthology*, 2nd edn., ed. Duncan Wu, Blackwell, 1998, p. 951f.; and see the discussion of this passage in Lockridge, Laurence, *op. cit.*, p. 324f.

30. Wordsworth, William, *Ecclesiastical Sonnets*, 3.43, quoted in Coleman, William Oliver, *Economics and its Enemies – Two Centuries of Anti-Economics*, Palgrave Macmillan, 2002, p. 114.

31. Berlin, Isaiah, *The Roots of Romanticism, op. cit.*, p. 136f.

32. Blake, William, extracts from 'Milton' (composed 1803–8), reproduced in *Romanticism – An Anthology*, ed. Duncan Wu, *op. cit.*, p. 120, as well as in the hymn, 'And did those feet in ancient time'.

33. Wordsworth, William, *Preface* to the *Lyrical Ballads*, 1800, in Wordsworth, William and Coleridge, Samuel Taylor, *Lyrical Ballads*, ed. R. L. Brett and A. R. Jones, Methuen, 1963, p. 243.

34. Wordsworth, William, 'The world is too much with us' (from *Poems in Two Volumes*, 1807), reprinted in *Romanticism – An Anthology*, ed. Duncan Wu, *op. cit.*, p. 372.

35. Wordsworth, William, 'Lines Written a Few Miles above Tintern Abbey' (from *Lyrical Ballads*, 1798), line 25f., reprinted in *Romanticism – An Anthology*, ed. Duncan Wu, *op. cit.*, p. 265f.

36. Mill, J. S., *Principles of Political Economy*, IV.6.2 (originally published in 1848), ed. Jonathan Riley, Oxford University Press, 1994, p. 128f.; see the discussion of this passage in Bronk, Richard, *Progress and the Invisible Hand – The Philosophy and Economics of Human Advance*, Little Brown, 1998, p. 166f.

37. Bate, Jonathan, *The Song of the Earth*, Picador, 2000, p. 123.

38. See the discussion of this utilitarian assumption in Bronk, Richard, *Progress and the Invisible Hand, op. cit.*, p. 104.

39. Coleridge, Samuel Taylor, Letter to Wordsworth, 1815, passage quoted in Abrams, M. H., *The Mirror and the Lamp – Romantic Theory and the Critical Tradition*, Oxford University Press, 1953, p. 170.

40. Carlyle, Thomas, *Signs of the Times* (originally published in 1829), reprinted in *Critical and Miscellaneous Essays*, vol. 2, James Fraser, 1840, pp. 277f., 281.

41. Coleridge, Samuel Taylor, passage quoted in Whale, John, *op. cit.*, p. 169.

42. Coleridge, Samuel Taylor, *Biographia Literaria*, chapter XIV (originally published in 1817), ed. J. Shawcross, Oxford, 1907, vol. II, p. 12.

43. Hazlitt, William, *The Spirit of the Age*, 2nd edn. (originally published in 1825), essay on 'Jeremy Bentham', The Wordsworth Trust, 2004, pp. 89f., 92.

44. Hazlitt, William, passage quoted in Abrams, M. H., *The Mirror and the Lamp*, *op. cit.*, p. 141.

45. Hazlitt, William, passage quoted (from essay 'On Poetry in General'), in Abrams, M. H., *The Mirror and the Lamp, op. cit.*, p. 142.

46. Mill, J. S., *Autobiography* (originally published in 1873), Penguin, 1989, pp. 118f., 123; see the discussion in chapter 2 of *The Romantic Economist*, (pp. 38–9).

47. Herder, J. G., *Ideas for a Philosophy of the History of Mankind, op. cit.*, p. 311; and Barnard, F. M., *Herder's Social and Political Thought, op. cit.*, pp. 39–44.

48. Herder, J. G., *Ideas for a Philosophy of the History of Mankind, op. cit.*, pp. 260, 301.

49. Coleridge, Samuel Taylor, *Biographia Literaria*, chapter XIV, ed. J. Shawcross, *op. cit.*, vol. II, p. 12. For a discussion of the organicist view of the mind explicit in this passage and elsewhere in Coleridge, see Abrams, M. H., *The Mirror and the Lamp, op. cit.*, pp. 169–75. Notwithstanding the neo-Platonic idealism

associated, here and elsewhere, with Coleridge's understanding of the role of the imagination as fusing together sensible particulars and different faculties into '*ideal* perfection', Coleridge draws simultaneously on the power of organic metaphors to describe the complex workings of the mind – workings that this and many other passages so subtly evoke. For a full discussion of Coleridge's organicism, see Armstrong, Charles I., *Romantic Organicism – From Idealist Origins to Ambivalent Afterlife*, Palgrave Macmillan, 2003, chapter 4, esp. p. 51f.

50. Coleridge, Samuel Taylor, *Biographia Literaria*, chapter XVIII, ed. J. Shawcross, *op. cit.*, vol. II, p. 65.
51. Herder, J. G., *Ideas for a Philosophy of the History of Mankind*, *op. cit.*, p. 264.
52. *Ibid.*, pp. 317, 268f.
53. *Ibid.*, p. 269.
54. Nietzsche, Friedrich, extract from *The Gay Science* (originally published in 1882), in *A Nietzsche Reader*, sel. and trans. R. J. Hollingdale, Penguin, 1977, p. 237.
55. Nietzsche, Friedrich, *The Twilight of the Idols* (originally published in 1889), trans. Anthony M. Ludovici, George Allen & Unwin, 1911, p. 5.
56. Nietzsche, Friedrich, *Notes on 'Thus Spake Zarathustra'*, No. 45, appended to *The Twilight of the Idols*, trans. Anthony M. Ludovici, *op. cit.*, p. 269.
57. Nietzsche, Friedrich, extract from *Thus Spake Zarathustra*, part IV (originally published in 1892), in *A Nietzsche Reader*, sel. and trans. R. J. Hollingdale, *op. cit.*, p. 243.
58. Nietzsche, Friedrich, *The Twilight of the Idols*, trans. A. M. Ludovici, *op. cit.*, p. 2.
59. Nietzsche, Friedrich, extract from *Thus Spake Zarathustra*, part IV, trans. R. J. Hollingdale, *op. cit.*, p. 244.
60. Byron, Lord George, *Child Harold's Pilgrimage*, Canto III, Stanza 45 (originally published in 1816), reprinted in 'The Oxford Authors' *Byron*', ed. Jerome J. McGann, Oxford University Press, 1986, p. 117.
61. Byron, Lord George, extract from *Lara* (originally published in 1814), verse 18, reprinted in 'The Oxford Authors' *Byron*', *op. cit.*, p. 251.
62. *Ibid.*
63. Warnock, Mary, *Imagination*, *op. cit.*, pp. 73f., 76, 107f.
64. Wordsworth, William, *The Prelude* (1805), book VI, lines 525f. ed. E. de Selincourt, Oxford University Press, 1960, p. 99.
65. Wordsworth, William, *The Prelude* (1850), book VI, line 594, ed. J. Wordsworth, M. H. Abrams and S. Gill, W. W. Norton, 1979, p. 217.
66. Wordsworth, William, *The Prelude* (1805), book XIII, lines 41–44, 56–59, 62–65, ed. E. de Selincourt, *op. cit.*, p. 230.
67. Coleridge, Samuel Taylor, *Biographia Literaria*, chapter XIV, ed. J. Shawcross, *op. cit.*, vol. II, p. 12.
68. Coleridge, Samuel Taylor, 'Lecture on Romeo and Juliet' (9 December 1811), reprinted in *Imagination in Coleridge*, ed. John Spencer Hill, Macmillan, 1978, p. 81.
69. Keats, John, 'Letter to George and Tom Keats', 21 December 1817, extract reprinted in *Romanticism – An Anthology*, ed. Duncan Wu, *op. cit.*, p. 1019.

70. Coleridge, Samuel Taylor, *Biographia Literaria*, chapter XIII, ed. J. Shawcross, *op. cit.*, vol. I, p. 202.

71. Hill, John Spencer (ed.), *Imagination in Coleridge*, Macmillan, 1978, pp. 21f., 127.

72. Coleridge, Samuel Taylor, 'The Statesman's Manual', *op. cit.*, p. 321.

73. Berlin, Isaiah, *The Crooked Timber of Humanity*, *op. cit.*, p. 82.

74. Wordsworth, William, 'The Tables Turned', line 28 (from *Lyrical Ballads*, 1798), reprinted in *Romanticism – An Anthology*, ed. Duncan Wu, *op. cit.*, p. 260. The passage is discussed in Abrams, M. H., *The Mirror and the Lamp*, *op. cit.*, p. 309; and in Berlin, Isaiah, *The Roots of Romanticism*, *op. cit.*, p. 120.

75. Berlin, Isaiah, *The Roots of Romanticism*, *op. cit.*, p. 120.

76. Shelley, P. B., *A Defence of Poetry* (originally published in 1840), extracts reprinted in *Romanticism – An Anthology*, ed. Duncan Wu, *op. cit.*, p. 949.

77. Hazlitt, William, *An Essay on the Principles of Human Action* (1805), reprinted in *The Selected Writings of William Hazlitt*, ed. Duncan Wu, *op. cit.*, vol. 1, p. 3.

78. Hazlitt, William, from *Complete Works*, ed. P. P. Howe and J. M. Dent, vol. IX.58, passage quoted in Lockridge, Laurence, *op. cit.*, p. 344; and see *An Essay on the Principles of Human Action*, *op. cit.*, p. 9 and *passim*.

79. Wordsworth, William, *The Prelude* (1805), book V, lines 372, 380–8, ed. E. de Selincourt, *op. cit.*, p. 77.

80. Hume, David, *A Treatise of Human Nature*, part III, section 14; see especially *David Hume on Human Nature and the Understanding*, ed. Anthony Flew, Macmillan, 1962, p. 210f. See also the discussion of Hume in Magee, Bryan, *The Great Philosophers*, *op. cit.*, discussion on Hume with John Passmore, pp. 148–53; in Tarnas, Richard, *The Passion of the Western Mind*, *op. cit.*, pp. 337–40; and in Warnock, Mary, *Imagination*, *op. cit.*, pp. 23–5.

81. See the discussion of Kant in Kemp, John, *The Philosophy of Kant*, Thoemmes Press, 1995, pp. 21–5; in Magee, Bryan, *The Great Philosophers*, *op. cit.*, discussion with Geoffrey Warnock, pp. 174–80; in Tarnas, Richard, *The Passion of the Western Mind*, *op. cit.*, pp. 343–7; and in Warnock, Mary, *Imagination*, *op. cit.*, pp. 26–31, 42.

82. Tarnas, Richard, *The Passion of the Western Mind*, *op. cit.*, p. 345.

83. See the discussion in Kemp, John, *The Philosophy of Kant*, *op. cit.*, p. 21; and in Warnock, Mary, *Imagination*, *op. cit.*, pp. 27–31.

84. See the discussion in Magee, Bryan, *The Great Philosophers*, *op. cit.*, discussion on Kant with Geoffrey Warnock, pp. 174, 178.

85. Magee, Bryan, *Confessions of a Philosopher – A Journey Through Western Philosophy*, Phoenix, 1997, p. 460. See also the discussion in Warnock, Mary, *Imagination*, *op. cit.*, pp. 66–8; and in Berlin, Isaiah, *The Roots of Romanticism*, *op. cit.*, p. 97f.

86. For a discussion of the Christian aspect of German Idealism, see Hedley, Douglas, *Coleridge, Philosophy and Religion*, *op. cit.*, pp. 4–6.

87. Coleridge, Samuel Taylor, *Biographia Literaria*, chapter XIII, ed. J. Shawcross, *op. cit.*, vol. I, p. 202.

88. Wordsworth, William, *The Prelude* (1805), book II, lines 271–5, ed. E. de Selincourt, *op. cit.*, p. 27.

89. Wordsworth, William, 'Lines Written a Few Miles above Tintern Abbey' (from *Lyrical Ballads*, 1798), line 106f:

> … of all the mighty world
> Of eye and ear (both what they half-create
> And what perceive) –

reprinted in *Romanticism – An Anthology*, ed. Duncan Wu, *op. cit.*, p. 268.

90. *Ibid.*, lines 94–97, 101–03.

91. Coleridge, Samuel Taylor, Notebook entry, March 1808, in *Coleridge's Notebooks – A Selection*, ed. Seamus Perry, Oxford University Press, 2002, no. 451, p. 101. See also the discussion in Perry's introduction, p. viif.

92. Beer, John, 'Fragmentations and Ironies', in *Questioning Romanticism, op. cit.*, p. 258f.

93. Schlegel, Friedrich, quoted in 'Friedrich Schlegel and Novalis', by Ernst Behler, in *A Companion to Continental Philosophy*, ed. Simon Critchley and William R. Schroeder, Blackwell, 1998, p. 78.

94. Friedrich, Caspar David, *The Wanderer above the Sea of Mist* (or 'Wanderer über dem Nebelmeer'), 1817, from the Hamburger Kunsthalle; and Friedrich, Caspar David, *On a Sailing Boat*, 1818, The Hermitage, reproduced in *German Art for Russian Imperial Palaces, 1800–1850*, Hermitage Rooms at Somerset House, 2002, p. 64.

95. Schlegel, Friedrich, *Critical Fragments* (originally published in 1797): Fragment 108, quoted in 'Friedrich Schlegel and Novalis', by Ernst Behler, *op. cit.*, p. 80f.

96. Schlegel, Friedrich, *Athenaeum Fragments* (originally published in 1798): Fragment 53, quoted in Beer, John, 'Fragmentations and Ironies', *op. cit.*, p. 251.

97. Schlegel, Friedrich, *Athenaeum* Fragment 206, quoted in Armstrong, Charles I., *Romantic Organicism, op. cit.*, p. 44.

98. Armstrong, Charles I, *Romantic Organicism, op. cit.*, p. 43.

99. Schlegel, Friedrich, *Ideas* (originally published in the last volume of the *Athenaeum* in 1800), fragment quoted in 'Friedrich Schlegel and Novalis', by Ernst Behler, *op. cit.*, p. 81.

100. Berlin, Isaiah, *The Roots of Romanticism, op. cit.*, p. 105.

101. Armstrong, Charles I., *Romantic Organicism, op. cit.*, p. 44.

102. Bowie, Andrew, *From Romanticism to Critical Theory – The Philosophy of German Literary Theory*, Routledge, 1997, p. 85.

103. Hedley, Douglas, *op. cit.*, pp. 91–3.

104. See n. 22 above for references.

105. Nietzsche, Friedrich, passage quoted in Tarnas, Richard, *The Passion of the Western Mind, op. cit.*, p. 370.

106. Nietzsche, Friedrich, extract from *Beyond Good and Evil* (originally published in 1886), in *A Nietzsche Reader*, sel. and trans. R. J. Hollingdale, *op. cit.*, p. 63.

107. Nietzsche, Friedrich, extract from *The Gay Science*, in *A Nietzsche Reader*, *op. cit.*, p. 69.

108. See discussion in Drolet, Michael (ed.), *The Postmodernism Reader – Foundational Texts*, Routledge, 2004, pp. 18–26; and in Merquior, J. G., *Foucault*, Fontana Press, 1985, pp. 35–8, 84.

109. Shackle, G. L. S., *Epistemics and Economics – A Critique of Economic Doctrines* (originally published in 1972), Transaction Publishers, 1992, p. 48f.

110. Schumpeter, Joseph A., *Capitalism, Socialism and Democracy* (originally published in 1943), Routledge, 1994, p. 82f.

111. Schlegel, Friedrich, extract from *Studien des Klassichen Altertums*, 98, quoted in Armstrong, Charles I, *Romantic Organicism*, *op. cit.*, p. 43.

112. Schlegel, Friedrich, *Athenaeum* Fragment 206, quoted in Armstrong, Charles I., *op. cit.*, p. 44.

113. MacIntyre, Alasdair, *After Virtue – A Study in Moral Theory*, Duckworth, 1981, pp. 1–3, 239.

114. Schumpeter, Joseph A., *A History of Economic Analysis*, George Allen & Unwin, 1954, p. 29.

115. Mirowski, Philip, *More Heat than Light – Economics as Social Physics, Physics as Nature's Economics*, Cambridge University Press, 1989, p. 392.

116. Coleridge, Samuel Taylor, *Biographia Literaria*, chapter XIII, ed. J. Shawcross, *op. cit.*, vol. I, p. 200.

CHAPTER 5

1. For a general introduction to Herder's organicism, see Barnard, F. M., *Herder's Social and Political Thought – From Enlightenment to Nationalism*, Oxford University Press, 1965, p. 36f. and *passim*; and Barnard, F. M., 'Introduction', in *J. G. Herder on Social and Political Culture*, Cambridge University Press, 1969, p. 31f.; and Abrams, M. H., *The Mirror and the Lamp – Romantic Theory and the Critical Tradition*, Oxford University Press, 1953, p. 204f.

2. Herder, J. G., *Ideas for a Philosophy of the History of Mankind* (originally published in 1791); extracts trans. F. M. Barnard, in *J. G. Herder on Social and Political Culture*, *op. cit.*, pp. 259f., 275.

3. Coleridge, Samuel Taylor, extract from *Aids to Reflection*, quoted in Abrams, M. H., *op. cit.*, p. 171.

4. Coleridge, Samuel Taylor, extract from *Theory of Life*, quoted in Abrams, M. H., *op. cit.*, p. 174.

5. See the discussion in Abrams, M. H., *op. cit.*, pp. 172f., 213.

6. Herder, J. G., *Ideas for a Philosophy of the History of Mankind*, *op. cit.*, p. 282.

7. *Ibid.*, p. 290f.

8. *Ibid.*, p. 295.

9. *The Independent*, 16 January 2006, articles by Michael McCarthy and James Lovelock, to mark the publication of Lovelock, James, *The Revenge of Gaia*, Penguin, 2006.

10. Herder, J. G., *Ideas for a Philosophy of the History of Mankind*, *op. cit.*, pp. 282, 304, 300, 313; and *Essay on the Origin of Language* (1772), extracts trans. F. M. Barnard, in *J. G. Herder on Social and Political Culture*, *op. cit.*, p. 163.

11. Herder, J. G., *Essay on the Origin of Language*, *op. cit.*, pp. 157, 163.

12. See the discussion in chapter 3 of *The Romantic Economist* (p. 73 and n. 41).

13. 'Comparative statics' was formalised as a method by Paul Samuelson in *Foundations of Economic Analysis*, Harvard University Press, 1947, pp. 7–20 and *passim*. The method analyses the impact of changing one particular parameter within a given set of conditions as a shift in the equilibrium outcome. See also the discussion in Sutton, John, *Marshall's Tendencies – What Can Economists Know?* MIT Press, 2000, p. 13f.

14. Keynes, John Neville, *The Scope and Method of Political Economy*, 3rd edn., Macmillan, 1904, pp. 145–9.

15. Tabb, William K., *Reconstructing Political Economy – The Great Divide in Economic Thought*, Routledge, 1999, p. 104f.

16. Marshall, Alfred, *Principles of Economics*, Eighth Edition, book IV, chapter 13, Macmillan, 1927, p. 315f.

17. *Ibid.*, book IV, chapter 10, p. 271f.; and see the discussion in Krugman, Paul, *Development, Geography, and Economic Theory*, MIT Press, 1997, p. 49f.

18. Schumpeter, Joseph A., *Capitalism, Socialism and Democracy*, Routledge, 1994, p. 79.

19. *Ibid.*, chapter 7, p. 82f.

20. *Ibid.*, p. 83f.

21. *Ibid.*, p. 83.

22. Skidelsky, Robert, *John Maynard Keynes, Volume Two – The Economist as Saviour, 1920–1937*, Macmillan, 1992, p. 412f.; and Keynes, John Maynard, essay on 'Francis Ysidro Edgeworth', in *The Collected Writings of John Maynard Keynes*, vol. X, Macmillan, 1972, p. 262.

23. For a discussion on the theory of 'externalities', see Bronk, Richard, *Progress and the Invisible Hand – The Philosophy and Economics of Human Advance*, Little Brown, 1998, pp. 145–50.

24. Krugman, Paul, *Development, Geography, and Economic Theory*, *op. cit.*, p. 51f.

25. For a discussion of Endogenous Growth Theory, see Carlin, Wendy and Soskice, David, *Macroeconomics: Imperfections, Institutions and Policies*, Oxford University Press, 2006, chapter 14, pp. 529–59.

26. See, for example, Carlin Wendy and Soskice, David, *op. cit.*, p. 545f.

27. For details of the research programme of the Santa Fe Institute, see website www.santafe.edu.

28. Arthur, W. Brian, 'Positive Feedbacks in the Economy', *Scientific American*, February 1990, pp. 80–2.

29. *Ibid.*, p. 80.

30. *Ibid.*, p. 85.

31. *Ibid.*, p. 85.

32. Waldrop, M. Mitchell, *Complexity – The Emerging Science at the Edge of Order and Chaos*, Penguin, 1994, pp. 18, 30–1, 36, 38, 252.

33. *Ibid.*, p. 119.

34. *Ibid.*, pp. 277–80, 292–4.

35. Coleridge, Samuel Taylor, Letter to Wordsworth 1815, passage quoted in Abrams M. H., *op. cit.*, p. 170; and see the discussion of Coleridge's objection to mechanical models of the mind in chapter 4 of *The Romantic Economist* (p. 95 and n. 39).

36. Waldrop, M. Mitchell, *op. cit.*, p. 280, reporting spoken views of Christopher G. Langton.

37. Waldrop, M. Mitchell, *op. cit.*, esp. p. 294, discussing the views of physicist Doyne Farmer; Farmer suggests that, while the Soviet Union under Stalin was an example of insufficient degrees of freedom leading to stasis, the post-1991 collapse of the Soviet Union afforded examples of the opposite extreme – anarchy and chaos.

38. Waldrop, M. Mitchell, *op. cit.*, p. 255, reporting spoken views of John H. Holland.

39. Friedman, Milton, 'The Methodology of Positive Economics', from *Essays in Positive Economics*, University of Chicago Press, 1953; reproduced as chapter 9 in *The Philosophy of Economics – An Anthology*, 2nd edn., ed. Daniel M. Hausman, Cambridge University Press, 1994, p. 181.

40. I am indebted to David Bowers, my erstwhile colleague at Merrill Lynch, both for showing how this can be done to great effect, and for stressing the importance of 'trip-wires'.

41. Waldrop, M. Mitchell, *op. cit.*, pp. 150, 253, reporting spoken views of W. Brian Arthur.

42. Grayling, A. C., *Wittgenstein – A Very Short Introduction*, Oxford University Press, 2001, p. 79; see also the discussion of Wittgenstein in Magee, Bryan, *The Great Philosophers – An Introduction to Western Philosophy*, BBC Books, 1987, discussion with John Searle, pp. 327–39.

43. Grayling, A. C., *op. cit.*, p. 97.

44. Taylor, Charles, 'Interpretation and the Sciences of Man', *Review of Metaphysics*, 25 (1971); reproduced as chapter 13 in *Readings in the Philosophy of Social Science*, ed. Michael Martin and Lee C. McIntyre, MIT Press, 1994, pp. 194, 195, 197, 199 and *passim*.

45. *Ibid.*, pp. 199, 203.

46. For a discussion of different versions of Rational Choice Theory, see chapter 9 of *The Romantic Economist* (pp. 228–30).

47. For an introduction to 'Constructivism', see Adler, Emanuel, 'Constructivism and International Relations', chapter 5 in *Handbook of International Relations*, ed. W. Carlsnaes *et al.*, Sage, 2002, pp. 95–118; and Checkel, Jeffrey T., 'The Constructivist Turn in International Relations Theory', Review Article, *World Politics*, 50(2), 1998, pp. 324–48.

48. Adler, Emanuel, *op. cit.*, p. 104.

49. For a full discussion of Herder on 'historical imagination' and Beatrice Webb on 'analytical imagination,' see chapter 10 of *The Romantic Economist* (p. 265f. and nn. 37–39, 44).

50. Burke, Edmund, 'Speech on Moving the Resolutions for Conciliation with the Colonies' (1775), quoted in Whale, John, *Imagination Under Pressure, 1789–1832*, Cambridge University Press, 2000, p. 32.

51. For a discussion of Burke's philosophy, see Whale, John, *op. cit.*, chapter 1, pp. 19–41; Berlin, Isaiah, *The Roots of Romanticism*, Chatto & Windus, 1999, pp. 124f.; and *An Oxford Companion to the Romantic Age – British Culture 1776–1832*, ed. Iain McCalman, Oxford University Press, 1999, pp. 435–7.

52. Keynes, J. M., *The General Theory of Employment, Interest and Money* (originally published in 1936), *The Collected Writings of John Maynard Keynes*, vol. VII, Macmillan, 1973, pp. 149, 152, 154, 161.

53. For a discussion of the role of institutions in 'guiding and forming expectations' and further examples, see Arrow, Kenneth J., 'The Place of Institutions in the Economy: A Theoretical Perspective', in *The Institutional Foundations of East Asian Economic Development*, ed. Y. Hayami and M. Aoki, Macmillan, 1998; reproduced as chapter 3 in *Readings in Political Economy*, ed. Kaushik Basu, Blackwell, 2003, p. 29.

54. Veblen, Thorstein, 'The Limitations of Marginal Utility', *Journal of Political Economy*, 17 (1909); reproduced as chapter 6 in *The Philosophy of Economics – An Anthology*, ed. Daniel M. Hausman, *op. cit.*, pp. 148, 149, 150.

55. North, Douglass C., *Understanding the Process of Economic Change*, Princeton University Press, 2005, pp. 24, 27, 61f. and *passim*.

56. *Ibid.*, p. 69, quoting from Donald, Merlin, *Origins of the Modern Mind: Three Stages in the Evolution of Culture and Cognition*, Harvard University Press, 1991, p. 14. See also Waldrop, M. Mitchell, *Complexity, op. cit.*, p. 146, where John Holland makes a similar point: 'The brain will continually strengthen or weaken myriad connections between its neurons as an individual learns from his or her encounters with the world.' Holland sees the brain as a 'complex adaptive system'.

57. Hodgson, Geoffrey M., *Economics and Utopia – Why the Learning Economy is not the End of History*, Routledge, 1999, p. 70.

58. North, Douglass C., *op. cit.*, p. 22 (on the consequences of 'uncertainty in a non-ergodic world') and p. 62.

59. Hodgson, Geoffrey, *op. cit.*, p. 60.

60. Herder, J. G., *Ideas for a Philosophy of the History of Mankind, op. cit.*, p. 282; and see the discussion in Barnard, F. M., *Herder's Social and Political Thought, op. cit.*, pp. 164–6 and *passim*. Coleridge held a similar view on the equal importance of component parts and organic whole: see Abrams, M. H., *The Mirror and the Lamp, op. cit.*, p. 220f., for a discussion of the poet's definition of 'the Beautiful' as an organic whole in which 'the *many*, still seen as many, becomes one'. Coleridge's insistence that a work of art is 'rich in proportion to the variety of parts which it holds in unity' is a characteristically strong statement of his view that the value and strength of the organic whole is dependent on it containing a plurality and diversity of individual components. Social organisms are no different.

61. Checkel, Jeffrey T., *op. cit.*, pp. 340–42 and *passim*.

62. Crouch, Colin, *Capitalist Diversity and Change – Recombinant Governance and Institutional Entrepreneurs*, Oxford University Press, 2005, pp. 23f., 63–6 and *passim*.

63. Boulding, Kenneth E., *The Image – Knowledge in Life and Society*, Ann Arbor Paperbacks (University of Michigan Press), 1961, chapter 5, esp. p. 64.
64. *Ibid.*, p. 76.
65. Arrow, Kenneth J., 'The Place of Institutions in the Economy', *op. cit.*; reproduced in *Readings in Political Economy*, ed. Kaushik Basu, *op. cit.*, p. 31f. For a contrary view that sees mutation analogy as inappropriate, see North, Douglass C., *op. cit.*, p. 66. North stresses the importance in economic evolution and selection mechanisms of intentionality and beliefs – factors that have no corollary in biological evolution.
66. Arrow, Kenneth, J., *Social Choice and Individual Values*, John Wiley & Sons, 1951. For a discussion of what is now known as Arrow's 'impossibility' theorem, see Caporaso, James A. and Levine, David P., *Theories of Political Economy*, Cambridge University Press, 1992, p. 136f.; and Sen, Amartya, 'Rationality and Social Choice', *American Economic Review*, 85 (1995), reproduced as chapter 16 in *Readings in Political Economy*, ed. Kaushik Basu, *op. cit.*, pp. 264–90.
67. Barnard, F. M., *Herder's Social and Political Thought, op. cit.*, p. 126.
68. For a discussion of 'interlocking complementarities', see Soskice, David, 'Divergent Production Regimes', chapter 4 in *Continuity and Change in Contemporary Capitalism*, ed. Herbert Kitschelt *et al.*, Cambridge University Press, 1999, p. 109f. And for a general introduction to the Varieties of Capitalism approach, see this article (pp. 101–34); and *Varieties of Capitalism – The Institutional Foundations of Comparative Advantage*, ed. Peter A. Hall and David Soskice, Oxford University Press, 2001, chapter 1, pp. 1–68.
69. See the discussion in chapter 6 of *The Romantic Economist* (pp. 158–68).
70. Coase, Ronald H., 'The Nature of the Firm' (1937); reproduced as chapter 2 in *The Nature of the Firm: Origins, Evolution, and Development*, ed. Oliver E. Williamson and Sidney G. Winter, Oxford University Press, 1991. See also the discussion in Backhouse, Roger E., *The Penguin History of Economics*, Penguin, 2002, pp. 317–19.
71. Kay, John A., *The Business of Economics*, Oxford University Press, 1996, pp. 89–99, esp. p. 95.
72. Carlyle, Thomas, *Past and Present* (1843): 'We have profoundly forgotten everywhere that *Cash-payment* is not the sole relation of human beings', passage quoted in Ferguson, Niall, *The Cash Nexus*, Allen Lane, 2001, p. vii.
73. *Financial Times*, 9 February 2005, 'Why top performers hit bottom when they change jobs', by Michael Skapinker, discussing research by Boris Groysberg and Ashish Nanda of Harvard Business School.
74. Morgan, Gareth, *Images of Organization*, Sage, 2006, esp. chapters 3, 5, 10. See also chapter 10 of *The Romantic Economist* (pp. 274f., 280 and nn. 73, 76f., 93), for a discussion of Morgan's methodological emphasis on the importance of 'metaphorical thinking' and being open to the insights provided by different metaphors.
75. Morgan, Gareth, *op. cit.*, chapter 2 and p. 69. See also Taylor, F. W., *Principles of Scientific Management*, Harper & Row, 1911.

76. Morgan, Gareth, *op. cit.*, pp. 40, 43, 142 and chapters 3, 5, *passim*. Morgan's definition of the 'organismic' metaphor is narrower than the conception of organicism found in Burke, Herder and other Romantic writers. Morgan separates out the use of 'open systems', 'ecology' and other related biological metaphors from the application of the metaphor of 'culture' or metaphors borrowed from Complexity Theory. All three of these metaphor types are subsumed in the definition of organicism (and the organic metaphor) used in *The Romantic Economist*.

77. For a canonical statement of the 'Washington consensus' approach to transition reforms, see *From Plan to Market*, World Development Report, 1996, Oxford University Press, 1996, chapters 1–2.

78. Stiglitz, Joseph E., 'Whither Reform? Ten Years of the Transition', Keynote Address, Annual World Bank Conference on Development Economics, 1999; reproduced as chapter 4 in *The Rebel Within*, ed. Ha-Joon Chang, Wimbledon Publishing Company, 2001, esp. pp. 153f., 136f.

79. *Ibid.*, p. 137.

80. Herder, J. G., quoted in Barnard, F. M., *Herder's Social and Political Thought*, *op. cit.*, p. 83.

81. Gamble, Andrew, *Hayek – The Iron Cage of Liberty*, Polity Press, 1996, p. 34.

82. *Ibid.*, p. 187f.

83. Gray, John, *Hayek on Liberty*, 3rd edn., Routledge, 1998, p. 153.

84. See the discussion in Gamble, Andrew, *op. cit.*, pp. 38, 189; and Hodgson, Geoffrey, *op. cit.*, pp. 90–3.

85. Berlin, Isaiah, *The Roots of Romanticism, op. cit.*, p. 126; and Rothschild, Emma, *Economic Sentiments – Adam Smith, Condorcet, and the Enlightenment*, Harvard University Press, 2001, p. 63f.

86. Hall, Peter A. and Soskice, David, *Varieties of Capitalism, op. cit.*, p. 37 and *passim*; and see the discussion of their theory in chapter 6 of *The Romantic Economist* (p. 161f.).

87. Marx, Karl, *Das Kapital, vol. 1*, passage quoted by Tabb, William K., *Reconstructing Political Economy, op. cit.*, p. 233.

88. Marx, Karl and Engels, Frederick, *Manifesto of the Communist Party* (originally published in 1848), Progress Publishers (Moscow), 1977, p. 46.

CHAPTER 6

1. Hume, David, quotation from *An Inquiry Concerning Human Understanding* (1777), in Coleman, William Oliver, *Economics and its Enemies – Two Centuries of Anti-Economics*, Palgrave Macmillan, 2002, p. 67.

2. See the discussion in Bronk, Richard, *Progress and the Invisible Hand – The Philosophy and Economics of Human Advance*, Little Brown, 1998, p. 60.

3. Herder, J. G., quoted in Barnard, F. M., *Herder's Social and Political Thought – From Enlightenment to Nationalism*, Oxford University Press, 1965, p. 81.

4. Herder, J. G., *Ideas for a Philosophy of the History of Mankind* (originally published in 1791), extracts trans. F. M. Barnard, in *J. G. Herder on Social and Political Culture*, Cambridge University Press, 1969, p. 311.

5. See the discussion in Barnard, F. M., *Herder's Social and Political Thought*, *op. cit.*, pp. 60–2, 99f.

6. Herder, J. G., quoted in Barnard, F. M., *Herder's Social and Political Thought*, *op. cit.*, p. 102.

7. Berlin Isaiah, *The Crooked Timber of Humanity – Chapters in the History of Ideas*, ed. Henry Hardy, John Murray, 1990, p. 224.

8. Gray, John, *False Dawn – The Delusions of Global Capitalism*, Granta Books, 1998, pp. 2–3, 101; and see the discussion in Gray, John, *Enlightenment's Wake – Politics and Culture at the Close of the Modern Age*, Routledge, 1995, p. 65.

9. Gray, John, *Two Faces of Liberalism*, Polity Press, 2000, p. 24.

10. See the discussion of Montesquieu in Berlin, Isaiah, *The Roots of Romanticism*, ed. Henry Hardy, Chatto & Windus, 1999, p. 30f.

11. See the discussion in Sutton, John, *Marshall's Tendencies – What can Economists Know?*, MIT Press, 2000, pp. 4f., 16.

12. Dasgupta, Partha, 'Modern Economics and its Critics', chapter 3 in *Fact and Fiction in Economics: Models, Realism and Social Construction*, ed. Uskali Mäki, Cambridge University Press, 2002, p. 77, with embedded quotation ('fired in the same crucible') from Goody, Jack, *The East in the West*, Cambridge University Press, 1996.

13. See the discussion and references in chapter 5 of *The Romantic Economist* (p. 146 and n. 85).

14. See the discussion in chapter 2 of *The Romantic Economist* (p. 54 and n. 73 and *passim*).

15. Mill, J. S., essay on 'Bentham' (originally published in 1838), in *Mill on Bentham and Coleridge*, ed. F. R. Leavis, Chatto & Windus, 1950, p. 82.

16. Mayall, James, *Nationalism and International Society*, Cambridge University Press, 1990, p. 2.

17. See the discussion of Fichte in Berlin, Isaiah, *The Roots of Romanticism*, *op. cit.*, p. 95f.

18. Müller, Adam, quoted in Roll, Eric, *A History of Economic Thought*, 5th edn., Faber & Faber, 1992, p. 199.

19. See the discussion in Roll, Eric, *op. cit.*, pp. 197f., 202; and in Berlin, Isaiah, *The Roots of Romanticism*, *op. cit.*, p. 126.

20. Herder, J. G., *Ideas for a Philosophy of the History of Mankind*, extracts trans. F. M. Barnard, *op. cit.*, pp. 284, 285–7, 305 and *passim*.

21. See the discussion in Henderson, W. O., *Friedrich List: Economist and Visionary 1789–1846*, Frank Cass, 1983, pp. 55–70.

22. Herder, J. G., *Essay on the Origin of Language* (originally published in 1772), extracts trans. F. M. Barnard, in *J. G. Herder on Social and Political Culture*, *op. cit.*, p. 173f.

23. See the discussion of Muller in Roll, Eric, *op. cit.*, p. 201; and in Greenfeld, Liah, *The Spirit of Capitalism – Nationalism and Economic Growth*, Harvard University Press, 2001, p. 198f.

24. Roll, Eric, *op. cit.*, p. 199.

25. See the discussion of Bruno Hildebrand in Coleman, William Oliver, *op. cit.*, p. 72.

26. For a similar position taken recently in relation to social sciences in general, see the discussion of Charles Taylor in chapter 5 of *The Romantic Economist* (p. 134 and n. 45). Taylor stressed the dangers of taking US/UK discourse and behaviour types as the basis of a supposedly universal analytical language of social behaviour.

27. Bagehot, Walter, 'The Postulates of English Political Economy', in his posthumous *Economic Studies*, ed. R. H. Hutton, Longmans, Green & Co., 2nd edn., 1888, p. 16.

28. 'Romantic Economics': this term is used by Berlin in *Roots of Romanticism*, *op. cit.*, p. 126 to include Fichte and List among others. However, Roll, *op. cit.*, p. 204, argues that List should not be seen as belonging to the same posthumously defined movement as Fichte and Müller, given List's more liberal politics and his fascination with modern industry. I have followed Berlin's classification because List's rejection of cosmopolitanism and his focus on the productive powers of a nation clearly owe much to liberal versions of Romantic organicism.

29. See Henderson, W. O., *op. cit.*, *passim*.

30. *Ibid.*, pp. 146, 150.

31. List, Friedrich, *The National System of Political Economy*, 1841, trans. S. S. Lloyd, Longmans, Green & Co., 1922; the extract is quoted in Greenfeld, Liah, *op. cit.*, p. 205; and see the discussion in Roll, Eric, *op. cit.*, p. 205.

32. Greenfeld, Liah, *op. cit.*, p. 204.

33. List, Friedrich, *Outlines of American Political Economy*, 1827, extract quoted in Henderson, W. O., *op. cit.*, p. 146.

34. Henderson, W. O., *op. cit.*, pp. 160, 167f., 177f.

35. See the discussion of Endogenous Growth Theory in chapter 5 of *The Romantic Economist* (p. 127 and n. 25).

36. See the discussion in Henderson, W. O., *op. cit.*, pp. 150–2, 176–9 and *passim*.

37. See the discussion of Development Economics and Gunnar Myrdal's works, in particular, in Coleman, William Oliver, *op. cit.*, p. 81f.; and in Krugman, Paul, *Development, Geography, and Economic Theory*, MIT Press, 1997, pp. 6f., 23–7.

38. See for example, Arthur, W. Brian, 'Positive Feedbacks in the Economy', *Scientific American*, February 1990, p. 84 and *passim*.

39. See the discussion of the Historical School in chapter 3 of *The Romantic Economist* (p. 73 and n. 41); and in Coleman, William Oliver, *op. cit.* p. 71f.

40. Veblen, Thorstein, 'The Limitations of Marginal Utility', *Journal of Political Economy*, 17 (1909); reproduced as chapter 6 in *The Philosophy of Economics – An Anthology*, 2nd edn., ed. Daniel M. Hausman, Cambridge University Press, 1994, esp. p. 149.

41. Schumpeter, Joseph, *History of Economic Analysis*, George Allen & Unwin, 1954, p. 34.

42. See Porter, Michael E., *The Competitive Advantage of Nations*, Macmillan, 1990; Albert, Michel, *Capitalism Against Capitalism*, Whurr Publishers, 1993; and Crouch, Colin and Streek, Wolfgang (eds.), *Political Economy of Modern Capitalism – Mapping Convergence and Diversity*, Sage, 1997.

43. Hall, Peter A. and Soskice, David, 'Introduction', in *Varieties of Capitalism – The Institutional Foundations of Comparative Advantage*, Oxford University Press, 2001, pp. 1–68.

44. For the research papers of the Wissenschaftszentrum in Berlin, see www.wzb. eu/default.en.asp.

45. Hall, Peter A. and Soskice, David, *op. cit.*, p. 4.

46. This point is well made by Howell, Chris, 'Varieties of Capitalism: And Then There Was One?', *Comparative Politics*, 36(1) (October 2003), pp. 103–24.

47. Hall, Peter A. and Soskice, David, *op. cit.* pp. 5–7.

48. *Ibid.*, p. 46.

49. For a discussion of 'asymmetric information' problems leading to 'thin' markets (and George Akerlof's famous example of the used car market), see Stiglitz, Joseph E., *Principles of Micro-Economics*, 2nd edn., W. W. Norton, 1997, pp. 433–5.

50. For an excellent discussion of 'hold-up problems' and the relevance of other 'market failures' to a comparative analysis of different market and non-market 'coordination mechanisms', see CPB Netherlands Bureau for Economic Policy Analysis, *Challenging Neighbours – Rethinking German and Dutch Economic Institutions*, Springer-Verlag, 1997, chapter 2, esp. p. 50f.

51. See Bronk, Richard, 'Which Model of Capitalism?', *OECD Observer*, 221/222, Summer 2000, p. 13.

52. For a discussion of 'network reputational monitoring', see Hall, Peter A. and Soskice, David, *op. cit.*, p. 22f.

53. Ricardo, David, *The Principles of Political Economy and Taxation* (originally published in 1817), reprinted in *The Works and Correspondence of David Ricardo*, ed. Piero Sraffa, vol. 1, Cambridge University Press, 1951, p. 132; the passage is quoted in Mayall, James, *op. cit.*, p. 159.

54. For an introductory discussion of Ricardo's theory, see Bronk, Richard, *Progress and the Invisible Hand*, *op. cit.*, p. 206f.

55. Hall, Peter A. and Soskice, David, *op. cit.*, p. 37.

56. *Ibid.*, pp. 41–4.

57. Soskice, David, 'Divergent Production Regimes: Coordinated and Uncoordinated Market Economies in the 1980s and 1990s', chapter 4 in *Continuity and Change in Contemporary Capitalism*, ed. Herbert Kitschelt, *et al.*, Cambridge University Press, 1999, p. 113f.

58. Hall, Peter A. and Soskice, David, *op. cit.*, p. 38f. For a fuller discussion of the distinction between 'radical' and 'incremental' innovation, see Lundvall, Bengt-Åke, chapter 3 in *National Systems of Innovation – Towards a Theory of Innovation and Interactive Learning*, ed. Bengt-Åke Lundvall, Pinter, 1995, esp. pp. 57–9.

59. Johnson, Björn, 'Institutional Learning', chapter 2 in *National Systems of Innovation*, *op. cit.*, p. 29.

60. Hall, Peter A. and Soskice, David, *op. cit.*, p. 39.

61. Lundvall, Bengt-Åke, 'Introduction', in *National Systems of Innovation*, *op. cit.*, p. 9.

62. Hodgson, Geoffrey M., *Economics and Utopia – Why the Learning Economy is not the End of History*, Routledge, 1999, p. 57f.

63. See the discussion of Schumpeter in chapter 5 of *The Romantic Economist* (p. 123f. and nn. 19, 21).

64. Soskice, David, 'Divergent Production Regimes', in Herbert Kitschelt *et al.* (eds.), *op. cit.*, p. 109.

65. Hall, Peter A. and Soskice, David, *op. cit.*, p. 17.

66. *Ibid.*, p. 27.

67. See the discussion of Herder in chapter 4 of *The Romantic Economist* (p. 88f. and n. 13).

68. Bronk, Richard, 'Which Model of Capitalism?', *op. cit.*, p. 14f.

69. *Ibid.*, p. 15.

70. Hall, Peter A. and Soskice, David, *op. cit.*, p. 60. See also *ibid.*, p. 57, for the discussion of a related reason to expect trade to 'reinforce differences in national institutional frameworks': Hall and Soskice argue that firms engage in a sort of *'institutional arbitrage'* by switching different parts of their production to different nations in order to make use of the various institutional resources on offer.

71. See discussion of Marx in chapter 5 of *The Romantic Economist* (p. 147f. and n. 88).

72. Kitschelt, Herbert, Lange, Peter, Marks, Gary, and Stephens, John D., 'Convergence and Divergence in Advanced Capitalist Democracies', chapter 15 in Herbert Kitschelt *et al.* (eds.), *Continuity and Change in Contemporary Capitalism*, *op. cit.*, p. 440. These authors acknowledge that 'each set of institutions and actors has its own "bounded rationality"'.

73. Boulding, Kenneth E., *The Image – Knowledge in Life and Society*, Ann Arbor Paperbacks (University of Michigan Press), 1961, p. 64f.; see the discussion of Boulding's views in chapter 5 of *The Romantic Economist* (p. 140 and n. 63f.)

74. Coleridge, Samuel Taylor, *On the Constitution of the Church and State* (originally published in 1830), ed. John Barrell, J. M. Dent & Sons, 1972, p. 91. Coleridge thought of the 'Idea of a Constitution' as 'the informing principle' of a nation's 'coherence and unity'.

75. See the discussion of Burke in chapter 4 of *The Romantic Economist* (p. 89 and n. 15).

76. Howell, Chris, 'Varieties of Capitalism: And Then There Was One?', *op. cit.*, pp. 110, 112.

77. This point is well made by Rothstein, Bo, 'Political Institutions: An Overview', chapter 4 in *A New Handbook of Political Science*, ed. Robert E. Goodin and Hans-Dieter Klingemann, Oxford University Press, 1996, pp. 156–60. For a fuller discussion of the collective action problems inherent in any attempt to establish cooperative institutions, and the vulnerability of all collective action to 'free-riding', see the discussion in chapter 9 of *The Romantic Economist* (pp. 229, 244 and nn. 16, 64, 65).

78. Hall, Peter A. and Soskice, David, *op. cit.*, p. 63f. For a further discussion of the relationship between institutional complementarities and change, see 'Introduction', in *Beyond Varieties of Capitalism – Conflict, Contradiction,*

and Complementarities in the European Economy, ed. Bob Hancké, Martin Rhodes and Mark Thatcher, Oxford University Press, 2007, pp. 6, 10–13.

79. See Berger, Suzanne, 'Introduction', in *National Diversity and Global Capitalism*, ed. Suzanne Berger and Ronald Dore, Cornell University Press, 1996, p. 23.

80. Hancké, Bob and Goyer, Michel, 'Degrees of Freedom: Rethinking the Institutional Analysis of Economic Change', chapter 3 in *Changing Capitalisms? – Internationalisation, Institutional Change and Systems of Economic Organisation*, ed. G. Morgan, R. Whitley and E. Moen, Oxford University Press, 2005, pp. 53–7 (esp. pp. 53, 60, 71). Colin Crouch makes a similar argument in his book, *Capitalist Diversity and Change – Recombinant Governance and Institutional Entrepreneurs*, Oxford University Press, 2005, pp. 23f., 85–7 and *passim*. Crouch argues that 'institutional entrepreneurs' may 'carry out costed searches into alternative paths concealed within their own past experience' (p. 23f.), and then recombine these inherited but previously 'dormant resources' into new configurations. For Crouch, acknowledgement that economic behaviour is path-dependent need not involve denying that 'alternatives exist somewhere within agents' repertoires' (p. 87) – alternatives that may have fallen into disuse but are not beyond reach.

81. See the discussion of Complexity Theory in chapter 5 of *The Romantic Economist* (pp. 129, 131 and nn. 32, 37).

82. Hancké, Bob and Goyer, Michel, *op. cit.*, pp. 58–60. See also the discussion in chapter 5 of *The Romantic Economist* (p. 140f. and nn. 63–66); and in chapter 9 of *The Romantic Economist* (p. 245f. and nn. 67, 68) on the importance of the imaginative intuition and lateral thinking of *homo romanticus* in enabling societies to break free from the implicit determinism of either social construction or rational optimisation.

83. Herder, J. G., *Essay on the Origin of Language*, extracts trans. F. M. Barnard, *op. cit.*, p. 170.

84. See discussion in Barnard, F. M., *Herder's Social and Political Thought, op. cit.*, pp. 118f., 130f.

85. Herder, J. G., *Essay on the Origin of Language*, extracts trans. F. M. Barnard, *op. cit.*, p. 173f.

86. Sabel, Charles F., 'Intelligible Differences: On Deliberate Strategy and the Exploration of Possibility in Economic Life', *Rivista Italiana degli Economisti*, I, 1996, pp. 55–80; also available at www2.law.columbia.edu/sabel/papers.

87. See, for example, the discussion of the Structural Impediment Initiative and the EU's mutual recognition agenda in Berger, Suzanne, 'Introduction', in *National Diversity and Global Capitalism, op. cit.*, pp. 14–16.

88. Howell, Chris, *op. cit.*, p. 117.

89. Berger, Suzanne, 'Globalization and Politics', *Annual Review of Political Science*, 3, 2000, p. 59; also available as MIT IPC Globalization Working Paper 00–005.

90. Gray, John, *Two Faces of Liberalism, op. cit.*, p. 24.

CHAPTER 7

1. For this distinction and much of the rest of my thinking on incommensurable values, I am indebted to the ground-breaking treatment of the topic in Gray, John, *Two Faces of Liberalism*, Polity Press, 2000, pp. 4f., 34–68.

2. For a discussion of the link between economics and utilitarianism, see Bronk, Richard, *Progress and the Invisible Hand – The Philosophy and Economics of Human Advance*, Little Brown, 1998, pp. 100f., 105–13, 222–7.

3. 'Pareto efficiency' – where no one could be better off without someone else being worse off – is, of course, a quite different goal from the pure utilitarian goal of maximising the utility or happiness of the greatest number. This is because the market pursuit of an efficient outcome through mutually advantageous transactions does not in itself allow for redistribution of initial endowments (i.e. making someone worse off), even if that would maximise happiness overall. See discussion of this point in Bronk, Richard, *Progress and the Invisible Hand, op. cit.*, pp. 106–8.

4. Shackle, G. L. S., *Epistemics and Economics – A Critique of Economic Doctrines* (originally published in 1972), Transaction Publishers, 1992, p. 9.

5. *Ibid.*, p. 10.

6. Bentham, Jeremy, *An Introduction to the Principles of Morals and Legislation* (originally published in 1789), W. Pickering, 1823, vol. 1, pp. 1–5.

7. Bentham, Jeremy, *The Rationale of Reward*, Robert Heward, 1830, p. 206; the passage is quoted in Whale, John, *Imagination Under Pressure, 1789–1832 – Aesthetics, Politics and Utility*, Cambridge University Press, 2000, p. 107.

8. Coleridge, Samuel Taylor, 'The Statesman's Manual' (originally published in 1816); and Hazlitt, William, *An Essay on the Principles of Human Action* (originally published in 1805). For the full references and related discussion, see chapter 4 of *The Romantic Economist* (p. 92 and nn. 27, 28).

9. Hazlitt, William, 'On Reason and Imagination', Essay V in *The Plain Speaker*, in *The Collected Works of William Hazlitt*, ed. A. R. Waller and A. Glover, J. M. Dent & Co., 1903, vol. XII, pp. 47–50; the passages are quoted and discussed in Whale, John, *op. cit.*, p. 133.

10. Lockridge, Laurence S., *The Ethics of Romanticism*, Cambridge University Press, 1989, pp. 142f., 145.

11. See the discussion in Bowie, Andrew, *From Romanticism to Critical Theory – The Philosophy of German Literary Theory*, Routledge, 1997, pp. 50, 308 (n. 43).

12. Coleridge, Samuel Taylor, 'Lay Sermon addressed to the Higher and Middle Classes' (originally published in 1817): for full reference and the related discussion, see chapter 4 of *The Romantic Economist* (p. 90 and n. 19).

13. See the discussion of Kant in Warnock, Mary, *Imagination*, Faber & Faber, 1976, p. 63. And for an example of Wordsworth's view of the symbolic value of natural beauty and the sublime, see Wordsworth, William, *The Prelude* (1805), book VI, lines 556–72, ed. E. de Selincourt, Oxford University Press, 1960, p. 100.

14. Mill, J. S., *Autobiography* (originally published in 1873): for the full reference and discussion, see chapter 2 of *The Romantic Economist* (p. 38 and nn. 25, 28).

15. See the discussion in Stafford, William, *John Stuart Mill*, Macmillan, 1998, p. 91f.; and in Gray, John, *Mill on Liberty: A Defence*, 2nd edn., Routledge, 1996, p. 45f.

16. Mill, J. S., *Utilitarianism* (1861), ed. M. Warnock, William Collins & Sons, 1962, p. 259.

17. For a further discussion of these points, see Gray, John, *Mill on Liberty – A Defence, op. cit.*, esp. pp. 141f., 144.

18. Gray, John, *Two Faces of Liberalism, op. cit.*, p. 41.

19. *Ibid.*, p. 8.

20. See the discussion in Barnard, F. M., *Herder's Social and Political Thought – From Enlightenment to Nationalism*, Oxford University Press, 1965, p. 97f.

21. *Ibid.*, pp. 110, 130f.

22. Berlin, Isaiah, 'The Apotheosis of the Romantic Will' in *The Crooked Timber of Humanity – Chapters in The History of Ideas*, ed. Henry Hardy, John Murray, 1990, p. 224; and *The Roots of Romanticism*, Chatto & Windus, 1999, pp. 65–7.

23. Gray, John, *Two Faces of Liberalism, op. cit.*, p. 65.

24. Nietzsche, Friedrich, extract from *The Gay Science* (1882), in *A Nietzsche Reader*, sel. and trans. R. J. Hollingdale, Penguin, 1977, p. 237. See also the discussion in chapter 4 of *The Romantic Economist* (p. 97 and nn. 54, 55); and in Gray, John, *Two Faces of Liberalism, op. cit.*, pp. 62f., 65f.

25. Schwartz, Barry, *The Paradox of Choice – Why More is Less*, HarperCollins, 2004, p. 42.

26. *Ibid.*, p. 67.

27. Gray, John, *Two Faces of Liberalism, op. cit.*, pp. 48–52.

28. Taylor, Charles, 'Interpretation and the Sciences of Man', *Review of Metaphysics*, 25 (1971); reproduced as chapter 13 in *Readings in the Philosophy of Social Science*, ed. Michael Martin and Lee C. McIntyre, MIT Press, 1994, p. 209.

29. See the discussion in chapter 10 of *The Romantic Economist* (p. 265 and nn. 38–40), and in chapter 6 of *The Romantic Economist* (p. 168 and n. 85).

30. Gray, John, *Two Faces of Liberalism, op. cit.*, pp. 48–50.

31. *Ibid.*, p. 45.

32. See Layard, Richard, *Happiness – Lessons from a New Science*, Allen Lane, 2005, *passim*.

33. See the discussion of the distinction between 'formal' and 'substantive' theories of welfare or well-being, and the reasons why economists often prefer the former, in Hausman, Daniel M. and McPherson, Michael S., *Economic Analysis and Moral Philosophy*, Cambridge University Press, 1996, p. 72f.

34. See the discussion in Bronk, Richard, *Progress and the Invisible Hand, op. cit.*, p. 118f.

35. Shackle, G. L. S., *Epistemics and Economics, op. cit.*, pp. 38–40.

36. See the discussion in Bronk, Richard, *Progress and the Invisible Hand, op. cit.*, pp. 120–4.

37. *Ibid.*, p. 126f.

38. Todaro, Michael P., *Economic Development*, 5th edn., Longman, 1994, p. 142f.

39. *Ibid.*, p. 145.
40. See the discussion of 'poverty-weighted' and 'equal-weights' indices in Todaro, Michael P., *op. cit.*, p. 162f.
41. *Ibid.*
42. For details of the *Human Development Index*, see annual United Nations Human Development Reports, or visit http://hdr.undp.org/en/statistics/data.
43. Jacobs, Michael, *The Green Economy – Environment, Sustainable Development and the Politics of the Future*, Pluto Press, 1991, p. 240f.
44. Keynes, John Neville, *The Scope and Method of Political Economy*, 3rd edn., Macmillan, 1904, p. 60. See also the discussion of Robbins in chapter 3 of *The Romantic Economist* (p. 76 and n. 48).
45. See the discussion in Sen, Amartya, *On Ethics and Economics*, Blackwell, 1987, esp. pp. 30–8.
46. See the discussion in Hausman, Daniel M. and McPherson, Michael S., *Economic Analysis and Moral Philosophy*, *op. cit.*, esp. p. 44.
47. Sen, Amartya, *On Ethics and Economics*, *op. cit.*, p. 4f.
48. See the discussion in Bronk, Richard, *Progress and the Invisible Hand*, *op. cit.*, p. 99f.
49. Friedman, Milton, 'The Methodology of Positive Economics', from *Essays in Positive Economics*, University of Chicago Press, 1953; reproduced as chapter 9 in *The Philosophy of Economics – An Anthology*, 2nd edn., ed. Daniel M. Hausman, Cambridge University Press, 1994, p. 181f.
50. Robbins, Lionel, *An Essay on the Nature and Significance of Economic Science*, 2nd edn., Macmillan, 1935, extracts reprinted as chapter 3 in Hausman, Daniel M. (ed.), *The Philosophy of Economics*, *op. cit.*, pp. 84f., 102.
51. *Ibid.*, pp. 102f., 105.
52. For a general introduction to cost-benefit analysis, and for a discussion of the specific distinction between '*actual* Pareto improvements' (and efficiency) and '*potential* Pareto improvements' (and efficiency) – the so-called 'Kaldor–Hicks criterion' – see Boardman, Anthony E., Greenberg, David H., Vining, Aidan R. and Weimer, David L., *Cost-Benefit Analysis: Concepts and Practice*, Prentice Hall, 1996, pp. 28–33.
53. Hausman, Daniel, M. and McPherson, Michael S., *Economic Analysis and Moral Philosophy*, *op. cit.*, p. 97f.
54. Weimer, David L. and Vining, Aidan R., *Policy Analysis: Concepts and Practice*, 2nd edn., Prentice Hall, 1992, pp. 212–36.
55. *Ibid.*, p. 217.
56. Robbins, Lionel, *An Essay on the Nature and Significance of Economic Science*, *op. cit.*, p. 99f.
57. *Ibid.*, pp. 87, 89.
58. *Ibid.*, p. 87.
59. Gray, John, *Two Faces of Liberalism*, *op. cit.*, p. 18.
60. Boulding, Kenneth E., 'Economics as a Moral Science', *American Economic Review*, March 1969, p. 1f. The passage is quoted in Tabb, William K., *Reconstructing Political Economy – The Great Divide in Economic Thought*, Routledge, 1999, p. 120.

CHAPTER 8

1. Herder, J. G., *Ideas for a Philosophy of the History of Mankind* (originally published in 1791), extracts trans. F. M. Barnard, in *J. G. Herder on Social and Political Culture*, Cambridge University Press, 1969, p. 301.

2. Coleridge, Samuel Taylor, extract from 1818 lecture quoted in Whale, John, *Imagination Under Pressure, 1789–1832 – Aesthetics, Politics and Utility*, Cambridge University Press, 2000, p. 166.

3. Coleridge, Samuel Taylor, extract from 'Lecture on the Slave Trade' (June 1795), reprinted in Hill, John Spencer, *Imagination in Coleridge*, Macmillan, 1978, p. 27.

4. Bronowski, J., *The Ascent of Man*, BBC Books, 1973, p. 56.

5. Shelley, P. B., *A Defence of Poetry* (originally published in 1840), extract reprinted in *Romanticism – An Anthology*, 2nd edn., ed. Duncan Wu, Blackwell, 1998, p. 949.

6. Coleridge, Samuel Taylor, Notebook entry, 25 January 1811, reprinted in *Coleridge's Notebooks – A Selection*, ed. Seamus Perry, Oxford University Press, 2002, no. 514, p. 122.

7. Arnold, Matthew, extract from 'The Function of Criticism at the Present Time' (1864), quoted in Mason, John Hope, *The Value of Creativity – The Origins and Emergence of a Modern Belief*, Ashgate, 2003, p. 198.

8. For a discussion of C. P. Snow's *The Two Cultures*, and of Mason's characterisation and explanation of the 'puzzle' that creativity – despite emerging as a value at the beginning of the scientific and industrial revolutions – came to be seen as having 'nothing to do with technology or economics' (Mason, John Hope, *op. cit.*, p. 5f.), see chapter 2 of *The Romantic Economist* (esp. pp. 48–50 and nn. 57–59).

9. Buchanan, James M. and Vanberg, Viktor J., 'The Market as a Creative Process', *Economics and Philosophy*, 7 (1991); reproduced as chapter 18 in *The Philosophy of Economics – An Anthology*, 2nd edn., ed. Daniel M. Hausman, Cambridge University Press, 1994, pp. 315–35.

10. Shackle, G. L. S., *Epistemics and Economics – A Critique of Economic Doctrines* (originally published in 1972), Transaction Publishers, 1992, p. xiv.

11. Waldrop, M. Mitchell, *Complexity – The Emerging Science at the Edge of Order and Chaos*, Penguin, 1994, p. 30 (reporting the thoughts of W. Brian Arthur).

12. Whale, John, *op. cit.*, p. 9.

13. Wittgenstein, Ludwig, passage from *Philosophical Investigations*, quoted in Warnock, Mary, *Imagination*, Faber & Faber, 1976, p. 158.

14. See the discussion of Wittgenstein's theory of 'family resemblance' words, and relevant references, in chapter 1 of *The Romantic Economist* (p. 14 and n. 28) and chapter 4 of *The Romantic Economist* (p. 87 and n. 11).

15. Warnock, Mary, *op. cit.*, p. 35.

16. Coleridge, Samuel Taylor, *Biographia Literaria* (originally published in 1817), chapter XIII, ed. J. Shawcross, Oxford University Press, 1907, vol. I, p. 202. See also Wordsworth, William, 'Lines Written a Few Miles above Tintern Abbey',

line 106f., (from *Lyrical Ballads*, 1798), reprinted in *Romanticism – An Anthology*, 2nd edn., ed. Duncan Wu, *op. cit.*, p. 268; and Hill, John Spencer, *op. cit.*, p. 127 for a discussion of Coleridge's view of 'seeing as making'.

17. For a further discussion of Kant's theories, and useful references, see chapter 4 of *The Romantic Economist* (p. 104f. and nn. 81, 82, 83).

18. Warnock, Mary, *op. cit.*, pp. 10, 29.

19. Wordsworth, William, *Preface* (1802) to Wordsworth, William and Coleridge, Samuel Taylor, *Lyrical Ballads*, ed. R. L. Brett and A. R. Jones, Methuen, 1963, p. 238.

20. Abrams, M. H., *The Mirror and the Lamp – Romantic Theory and the Critical Tradition*, Oxford University Press, 1953, pp. 57–69.

21. Murdoch, Iris, 'The Darkness of Practical Reason', Review article in *Encounter*, July 1966, reprinted in Murdoch, Iris, *Existentialists and Mystics – Writings on Philosophy and Literature*, ed. Peter Conradi, Chatto & Windus, 1997, p. 199.

22. Wordsworth, William, *The Prelude* (1805), book XI, line 258, ed. E. de Selincourt, Oxford University Press, 1960, p. 213.

23. Mill, J. S., *Autobiography* (originally published in 1873), Penguin, 1989, p. 123.

24. Hazlitt, William, *An Essay on the Principles of Human Action* (1805), reprinted in *The Selected Writings of William Hazlitt*, ed. Duncan Wu, vol. 1, Pickering & Chatto, 1998, pp. 3, 20, 22.

25. *Ibid.*, p. 27f.

26. *Ibid.*, p. 8f.

27. *Ibid.*, pp. 12, 20f., 37.

28. BBC R4, *In Our Time*, 28 November 2002. This stimulating discussion between Melvyn Bragg and Susan Stuart, Steven Mithen and Semir Zeki influenced my thinking in this paragraph. See also the interesting introductory discussion in Howkins, John, *The Creative Economy – How People Make Money from Ideas*, Penguin, 2001, pp. 4–8, 14–18, 119.

29. Herder, J. G., *Ideas for a Philosophy of the History of Mankind*, extracts trans. F. M. Barnard, *op. cit.*, p. 301.

30. Coleridge, Samuel Taylor, *Biographia Literaria*, chapter XIII, ed. J. Shawcross, *op. cit.*, vol. I, p. 202.

31. Coleridge, Samuel Taylor, extracts from *The Watchman* (25 March 1796), and from a 'Lecture on Romeo and Juliet' (9 December 1811), in Hill, John Spencer, *op. cit.*, pp. 28, 81.

32. Coleridge, Samuel Taylor, *Biographia Literaria*, chapters XIV, XXII, ed. J. Shawcross, *op. cit.*, vol. II, pp. 12, 123.

33. Keats, John, 'Letter to George and Tom Keats', 21 December 1817, extract reprinted in *Romanticism – An Anthology*, ed. Duncan Wu, *op. cit.*, p. 1019. See also the discussion in *Romanticism – An Anthology*, *op. cit.*, p. 1011.

34. Keats, John, 'Letter to George and Tom Keats', *op. cit.*, p. 1019.

35. Shelley, P. B., *A Defence of Poetry*, extracts reprinted in *Romanticism – An Anthology*, ed. Duncan Wu, *op. cit.*, p. 949.

36. Hazlitt, William, *The Spirit of the Age*, 2nd edn. (originally published in 1825), essay on 'Mr. Coleridge', The Wordsworth Trust, 2004, p. 122.

37. Coleridge, Samuel Taylor, *Biographia Literaria*, chapter XIV, ed. J. Shawcross, *op. cit.*, vol. II, p. 12.

38. Wordsworth, William, *The Prelude* (1805), book XIII, lines 98–102, ed. E. de Selincourt, *op. cit.*, p. 231.

39. Murdoch, Iris, 'The Darkness of Practical Reason', *op. cit.*, p. 198f.

40. de Bono, Edward, article on 'Lateral Thinking', in *The Oxford Companion to the Mind*, ed. Richard L. Gregory, Oxford University Press, 1987, p. 428f.

41. See chapter 4 of *The Romantic Economist* (p. 110f. and nn. 102, 103) for a discussion of the use made by Schlegel, Coleridge and Bacon of an unsystematic juxtaposition of fragments and aphorisms as a means of prompting new insights.

42. Coleridge, Samuel Taylor, *Biographia Literaria*, chapter VII, ed. J. Shawcross, *op. cit.*, vol. I, p. 85f.

43. Holmes, Richard, *Coleridge – Darker Reflections*, HarperCollins, 1998, p. 397f.

44. Wordsworth, William, *The Prelude* (1850), book VI, lines 594f., ed. J. Wordsworth, M. H. Abrams and S. Gill, W. W. Norton, 1979, p. 217.

45. Schlegel, A. W., extract from Berlin Lectures (1801–4), quoted in Abrams, M. H., *The Mirror and the Lamp, op. cit.*, p. 213.

46. See Coleridge, Samuel Taylor, *Biographia Literaria*, chapter XIII, ed. J. Shawcross, *op. cit.*, vol. I, p. 202; and the excellent discussion of this passage in Holmes, Richard, *op. cit.*, p. 411. See also the discussion in Abrams M. H., *The Mirror and the Lamp, op. cit.*, p. 173f.

47. Coleridge, Samuel Taylor, extract from *Notebooks* (April 1811), reprinted in Hill, John Spencer, *op. cit.*, p. 73; and *Biographia Literaria*, chapter XIII, ed. J. Shawcross, *op. cit.*, vol. I, p. 202. See also the discussion in Hill, John Spencer, *op. cit.*, p. 1f. and *passim*; and in McFarland, Thomas, *Originality and Imagination*, Johns Hopkins University Press, 1985, pp. 108–18.

48. Coleridge, Samuel Taylor, *Biographia Literaria*, chapter XIII, ed. J. Shawcross, *op. cit.*, vol. I, p. 202.

49. Howkins, John, *op. cit.*, p. 5f.

50. See Hodgkiss, Philip, *The Making of the Modern Mind – The Surfacing of Consciousness in Social Thought*, The Athlone Press, 2001, p. 10.

51. Weimer, David L. and Vining, Aidan R., *Policy Analysis: Concepts and Practice*, 2nd edn., Prentice Hall, 1992, pp. 202, 241f.

52. Howkins, John, *op. cit.*, p. 16f.

53. Hazlitt, William, *An Essay on the Principles of Human Action, op. cit.*, pp. 19, 21.

54. Lockridge, Laurence S., *The Ethics of Romanticism*, Cambridge University Press, 1989, p. 343.

55. Wordsworth, William, *The Prelude* (1805), book XIII, lines 167–70, ed. E. de Selincourt, *op. cit.*, p. 233.

56. *Ibid.*, book VI, lines 538–42, ed. E. de Selincourt, *op. cit.*, p. 100.

57. Wordsworth, William, 'Lines written a Few Miles above Tintern Abbey', lines 48f., 94–103 in *Romanticism – An Anthology*, ed. Duncan Wu, *op. cit.*, pp. 266–8.

58. Howkins, John, *op. cit.*, p. 15.

59. Waldrop, M. Mitchell, *op. cit.*, p. 133.

60. Berlin, Isaiah, *The Roots of Romanticism*, ed. Henry Hardy, Chatto & Windus, 1999, pp. 119–21.
61. Schumpeter, Joseph A., *Capitalism, Socialism and Democracy* (originally published in 1943), Routledge, 1994, pp. 77, 82.
62. *Ibid.*, p. 83.
63. *Ibid.*, pp. 77, 83.
64. *Ibid.*, p. 84.
65. See the discussion and references in chapter 6 of *The Romantic Economist* (p. 162f. and nn. 58, 60–2).
66. See the discussion in Johnson, Björn, 'Institutional Learning', chapter 2 in *National Systems of Innovation*, ed. Bengt-Åke Lundvall, Pinter, 1995, p. 29.
67. Hodgson, Geoffrey, M., *Economics and Utopia – Why the Learning Economy is not the End of History*, Routledge, 1999, p. 49.
68. Buchanan, James M. and Vanberg, Viktor J., 'The Market as a Creative Process', *op. cit.*
69. *Ibid.*, pp. 319–23.
70. *Ibid.*, p. 326f.
71. *Ibid.*, p. 333 (n. 33). See also Hayek, Friedrich A., 'Competition as a Discovery Procedure', in *New Studies in Philosophy, Politics, Economics and the History of Ideas*, by F. A. Hayek, University of Chicago Press, 1978, pp. 179–90. And for an introductory discussion of Hayek's views on the market as a 'spontaneous order' and a 'discovery procedure', see Gamble, Andrew, *Hayek – The Iron Cage of Liberty*, Polity Press, 1996, pp. 38, 67f.; and Backhouse, Roger E., *The Penguin History of Economics*, Penguin, 2002, p. 278f.
72. Buchanan, James M. and Vanberg, Viktor J., *op. cit.*, p. 323.
73. *Ibid.*, pp. 315–17.
74. See the discussion and references in chapter 5 of *The Romantic Economist* (pp. 128–32 and nn. 28–40).
75. Buchanan, James M. and Vanberg, Viktor J., *op. cit.*, p. 327.
76. *Ibid.*, p. 318.
77. Shackle, G. L. S., *Epistemics and Economics*, *op. cit.*, p. 23.
78. *Ibid.*, p. 4.
79. *Ibid.*, p. 26.
80. Hodgson, Geoffrey, M., *op. cit.*, p. 76f.
81. Campbell, Colin, *The Romantic Ethic and the Spirit of Modern Consumerism*, Blackwell, 1987, pp. 6–8 and *passim*.
82. *Ibid.*, pp. 86–90 and *passim*.
83. Brown S., Doherty, A. M. and Clarke, B., *Romancing the Market*, Routledge, 1998, p. 12.
84. Rifkin, Jeremy, *The End of Work*, G. P. Putnam & Sons, 1995, p. 20.
85. Buchanan, James J. and Vanberg, Viktor, J., *op. cit.*, p. 327f. See also the interesting discussion on the relative merits of these three different characterisations of markets in Lyons, Bruce, 'Risk, Ignorance and Imagination', chapter 4 in *The Theory of Choice – A Critical Guide*, ed. S. Heap, M. Hollis, B. Lyons, R. Sugden and A. Weale, Blackwell, 1992, pp. 51–61.

86. Krugman, Paul, *Development, Geography, and Economic Theory*, MIT Press, 1997, pp. 76–8.
87. For an introductory discussion of Frank Knight's work, see Backhouse, Roger E., *op. cit.*, p. 202f.
88. Keynes, John Maynard, *The General Theory of Employment, Interest and Money* (originally published in 1936), in *The Collected Writings of John Maynard Keynes*, vol. VII, Macmillan, 1973, pp. 149, 161.
89. Dunn, Stephen P., 'Keynes and Transformation', chapter 13 in *The Philosophy of Keynes's Economics: Probability, Uncertainty and Convention*, ed. Jochen Runde and Sohei Mizuhara, Routledge, 2003, pp. 170–81, esp. p. 177f.
90. Shackle, G. L. S., *Imagination and the Nature of Choice*, Edinburgh University Press, 1979, pp. 52f., 55f.
91. *Ibid.*, pp. 9, 27.
92. Shackle, G. L. S., *Epistemics and Economics*, *op. cit.*, p. 123.
93. North, Douglass C., *Understanding the Process of Economic Change*, Princeton University Press, 2005, p. 14.
94. *Ibid.*, pp. 16, 21.
95. Jackson, Robert, *The Global Covenant: Human Conduct in a World of States*, Oxford University Press, 2000, p. 72.
96. Shackle, G. L. S., *Imagination and the Nature of Choice*, *op. cit.*, p. 51.
97. Boulding, Kenneth E., *The Image – Knowledge in Life and Society*, Ann Arbor Paperbacks (University of Michigan Press), 1961, p. 83f.
98. Shackle, G. L. S., *Epistemics and Economics*, *op. cit.*, p. 120.
99. For a good introduction to Game Theory, see Lyons, Bruce, 'Game Theory', chapter 7 in *The Theory of Choice*, *op. cit.*, pp. 93–129.
100. Crouch, Colin, *Capitalist Diversity and Change – Recombinant Governance and Institutional Entrepreneurs*, Oxford University Press, 2005, p. 19.
101. Lyons, Bruce, 'Game Theory', in *The Theory of Choice*, *op. cit.*, p. 120.
102. Crouch, Colin, *op. cit.*, p. 19.
103. Lyons, Bruce, 'Game Theory', in *The Theory of Choice*, *op. cit.*, pp. 127–9.
104. See, for example, Rabin, Matthew, 'Psychology and Economics', *Journal of Economic Literature*, XXXVI (March 1998), pp. 36–8. For a further discussion of 'framing effects' and the research of Daniel Kahneman and Amos Tversky in particular, see chapter 9 of *The Romantic Economist* (p. 239f. and nn. 43–46).
105. Shackle, G. L. S., *Epistemics and Economics*, *op. cit.*, pp. 122, 366, 364.
106. Shackle, G. L. S., *Imagination and the Nature of Choice*, *op. cit.*, p. 8.
107. Shackle, G. L. S., *Epistemics and Economics*, *op. cit.*, p. 96.
108. Shackle, G. L. S., *Imagination and the Nature of Choice*, *op. cit.*, p. 44f.
109. *Ibid.*, p. 56f.
110. Shackle, G. L. S., *Epistemics and Economics*, *op. cit.*, p. 96.
111. Shackle, G. L. S., *Imagination and the Nature of Choice*, *op. cit.*, *passim*.
112. Shackle, G. L. S., *Decision, Order and Time in Human Affairs*, Cambridge University Press, 1961, p. 6; passage quoted in Lyons, Bruce, 'Risk Ignorance and Imagination', in *The Theory of Choice*, *op. cit.*, p. 56.
113. Shackle, G. L. S., *Epistemics and Economics*, *op. cit.*, p. 131.

114. See Wordsworth, William, *The Prelude* (1805), book XIII, lines 120–43, ed. E. de Selincourt, *op. cit.*, p. 232f. See also Murdoch, Iris, *Sartre: Romantic Rationalist*, Vintage 1999, p. 96.

115. Murdoch, Iris, *Sartre: Romantic Rationalist*, *op. cit.*, p. 112.

116. Hazlitt, William, *An Essay on the Principles of Human Action*, *op. cit.*, p. 8.

117. See the discussion in Carlin, Wendy and Soskice, David, *Macroeconomics: Imperfections, Institutions and Policies*, Oxford University Press, 2006, p. 565 – including a quotation from John Muth.

118. See the discussion in North, Douglass C., *op. cit.*, p. 23f.; and Waldrop, M. Mitchell, *op. cit.*, p. 271.

119. Keynes, John Maynard, *The General Theory*, *op. cit.*, p. 152.

120. *Ibid.*, p. 163.

121. Shackle, G. L. S., *Epistemics and Economics*, *op. cit.*, preface, p. xvii.

122. Hazlitt, William, *Collected Works*, ed. P. P. Howe, J. M. Dent, vol. IX.58; the passage is quoted in Lockridge, Laurence S., *op. cit.*, p. 344. For a discussion of a later part of the same passage – with its further parallels with Shackle's characterisation of the future as 'the void of time-to-come' (*Imagination and the Nature of Choice*, *op. cit.*, p. 8) waiting to be filled by the imagination, see chapter 4 of *The Romantic Economist* (p. 103 and n. 78).

123. Shackle, G. L. S., *Epistemics and Economics*, *op. cit.*, preface, p. xv.

124. *Ibid.*, p. 8.

125. *Ibid.*, p. 8f.

126. *Ibid.*, p. 366.

127. For a further discussion of these quotations from Wordsworth and Hazlitt, and relevant references, see *The Romantic Economist*, above (p. 202 and n. 38, and p. 205f. and n. 53f.). See also the discussion of Shackle's 'reasoned imagination' – another echo of Hazlitt, in *The Romantic Economist*, above (p. 218f. and nn. 107, 109).

128. Offe, Claus, 'Political Economy: Sociological Perspectives', chapter 29 in *A New Handbook of Political Science*, ed. Robert E. Goodin and Hans-Dieter Klingemann, Oxford University Press, 1998, p. 682 (includes an embedded quotation from Scharpf, F. W., 'Games (Real) Actors may Play: The Problem of Mutual Predictability', *Rationality and Society*, 4 (1990), pp. 471–94).

129. Shackle, G. L. S., *Epistemics and Economics*, *op. cit.*, p. 3 and *passim*.

130. Dunn, Stephen P, *op. cit.*, p. 170.

131. Soros, George, *The Crisis of Global Capitalism: Open Society Endangered*, Little Brown, 1998, p. 49.

132. For an introductory explanation of a 'Nash equilibrium', see Lyons, Bruce, 'Game Theory', in *The Theory of Choice*, *op. cit.*, p. 101.

133. Waldrop, M. Mitchell, *op. cit.*, p. 150f., reporting spoken words of W. Brian Arthur. See the discussion in chapter 5 of *The Romantic Economist* (p. 132 and n. 41).

134. Waldrop, M. Mitchell, *op. cit.*, p. 254, reporting spoken views of John H. Holland.

135. Schwartz, Barry, *The Paradox of Choice – Why More is Less*, HarperCollins, 2004, pp. 77–96.

136. Morgan, Gareth, *Images of Organization*, Sage, 2006, p. 3f.

CHAPTER 9

1. Mill, J. S., essay on 'Bentham' (originally published in 1838), in *Mill on Bentham and Coleridge*, ed. F. R. Leavis, Chatto & Windus, 1950, pp. 63, 67f.

2. *Ibid.*, p. 73; and Mill, J. S., 'Essay on the Definition of Political Economy; and on the Method of Investigation Proper to it' (originally published in 1830), as Essay V in Mill, J. S., *Essays on Some Unsettled Questions of Political Economy*, 3rd edn., Longmans, Green & Co., 1877, pp. 137, 144.

3. Weber, Max, *The Protestant Ethic and the Spirit of Capitalism* (originally published in English in 1930), Routledge, 1992, p. 53f.

4. Ruskin, John, *Unto this Last* (originally published in 1862), ed. Clive Wilmer, Penguin, 1985, p. 178.

5. Kay, John, *The Business of Economics*, Oxford University Press, 1996, p. 86.

6. Mill, J. S., 'Essay on the Definition of Political Economy', *op. cit.*, p. 145.

7. Bagehot, Walter, 'The Preliminaries of Political Economy', in his posthumous *Economic Studies*, ed. R. H. Hutton, Longmans, Green & Co., 2nd edn., 1888, p. 76.

8. Bagehot, Walter, 'The Postulates of English Political Economy', in *Economic Studies, op. cit.*, p. 5.

9. Krugman, Paul, *Development, Geography, and Economic Theory*, MIT Press, 1997, p. 78.

10. Bagehot, Walter, 'The Preliminaries of Political Economy', *op. cit.*, p. 74f.

11. See *ibid.*, p. 77f.; and see Mill, J. S., *Autobiography* (originally published in 1873), Penguin, 1989, p. 179.

12. Mill, J. S., 'Essay on the Definition of Political Economy', *op. cit.*, p. 151.

13. See the discussion of Ruskin (and references) in chapter 2 of *The Romantic Economist* (p. 55 and n. 75).

14. See the discussion of Mill (and references) in chapter 2 of *The Romantic Economist* (p. 53 and n. 67f).

15. See the discussion of 'rent-seeking' in Mueller, Dennis C., *Public Choice II*, Cambridge University Press, 1989, pp. 38, 229–46.

16. Olson, Mancur, *The Logic of Collective Action*, Harvard University Press, 1965. For a good introduction to Olson's theory, see Olson, Mancur, *The Rise and Decline of Nations: Economic Growth, Stagflation, and Social Rigidities*, Yale University Press, 1982, chapter 2, esp. pp. 21, 29f.

17. Green, Donald P. and Shapiro, Ian, *Pathologies of Rational Choice Theory – A Critique of Applications in Political Science*, Yale University Press, 1994, p. 192.

18. *Ibid.*, pp. 17–19.

19. *Ibid.*, p. 18.

20. Friedman, Milton, 'The Methodology of Positive Economics', from *Essays in Positive Economics*, University of Chicago Press, 1953; reproduced as chapter 9 in *The Philosophy of Economics – An Anthology*, 2nd edn., ed. Daniel M. Hausman, Cambridge University Press, 1994, pp. 187f., 206.

21. *Ibid.*, p. 188.

22. *Ibid.*, p. 193.

23. See the discussion (and references) in chapter 8 of *The Romantic Economist* (pp. 207f., 209, 210 and nn. 61, 63f., 73–75).

24. Friedman, Milton, 'The Methodology of Positive Economics', *op. cit.*, p. 181.

25. Green, Donald P. and Shapiro, Ian, *op. cit.*, p. 42f.

26. *Ibid.*, p. 6.

27. *Ibid.*, pp. 34–8.

28. See, for example, Olson, Mancur, *The Rise and Decline of Nations*, *op. cit.*, p. 23f.

29. See the discussion in Green, Donald P. and Shapiro, Ian, *op. cit.*, p. 87f.

30. *Ibid.*, p. 187.

31. Rothstein, Bo, 'Political Institutions: An Overview', chapter 4 in *A New Handbook of Political Science*, ed. Robert E. Goodin and Hans-Dieter Klingemann, Oxford University Press, 1998, p. 148.

32. Green, Donald P. and Shapiro, Ian, *op. cit.*, pp. 6, 37, 109 and *passim*.

33. Hazlitt, William, *The Spirit of the Age*, 2nd edn. (originally published in 1825), essay on 'Jeremy Bentham', The Wordsworth Trust, 2004, p. 92.

34. *Ibid.*, pp. 96–8.

35. *Ibid.*, p. 93.

36. See the discussion of Hazlitt and Shackle (and references) in chapter 8, of *The Romantic Economist* (pp. 200, 215f., 218f., 221 and nn. 24–27, 90–92, 105–13, 122–27).

37. Hazlitt, William, from *Collected Works*, ed. P. P. Howe, J. M. Dent, vol. IX.58; the passage is quoted in Lockridge, Laurence S., *The Ethics of Romanticism*, Cambridge University Press, 1989, p. 344.

38. The concept of 'interest' contained in 'self-interest' is ambiguous between 'of interest to me emotionally' and 'objectively in my interest'. For our purposes, however, all that is relevant is that imagination plays a role in our envisaging our future interests, in either sense of the word, when the future is genuinely uncertain.

39. See the discussion of this point in North, Douglass C., *Understanding the Process of Economic Change*, Princeton University Press, 2005, pp. 20–4. See also the discussion of suitable microfoundations for economics in conditions of uncertainty, in chapter 8 of *The Romantic Economist* (pp. 214–24).

40. Carlin, Wendy and Soskice, David, *Macroeconomics: Imperfections, Institutions and Policies*, Oxford University Press, 2006, p. 545f.

41. See the discussion in chapter 7 of *The Romantic Economist* (pp. 190–5).

42. See the discussion of consistency 'at one time' and 'over a period', in Hollis, Martin, 'Autonomy', chapter 6 in *The Theory of Choice – A Critical Guide*, ed. S. Heap, M. Hollis, B. Lyons, R. Sugden and A. Weale, Blackwell, 1992, pp. 75–9.

43. See, for example, Kahneman, Daniel and Tversky, Amos, 'Choices, Values, and Frames', *American Psychologist*, 39(4) (1984), reprinted as chapter 1 in *Choices, Values, and Frames*, ed. Daniel Kahneman and Amos Tversky, Cambridge University Press, 2000, pp. 1–16.

44. See the good discussion in Rabin, Matthew, 'Psychology and Economics', *Journal of Economic Literature*, XXXVI (March 1998), p. 13f.

45. *Ibid.*, p. 36f.; and see Kahneman, Daniel and Tversky, Amos, *op. cit.*, p. 9f.

46. See the discussion in Rabin, Matthew, *op. cit.*, p. 30f.
47. Schwartz, Barry, *The Paradox of Choice – Why More is Less*, HarperCollins, 2004, pp. 3–5, 77–86 and *passim*.
48. *Ibid.*, p. 23.
49. *Ibid.*, p. 90; and p. 79 (discussing Herbert Simon's view that 'satisficing *is*, in fact, the maximising strategy').
50. *Ibid.*, pp. 147f., 152–4.
51. *Ibid.*, p. 147f.
52. Herder, J. G., *Essay on the Origin of Language* (originally published in 1772), extracts trans. F. M. Barnard, in *J. G. Herder on Social and Political Culture*, Cambridge University Press, 1969, p. 163.
53. For a discussion of Burke's views on the constitutive role of institutions, see chapter 5 of *The Romantic Economist* (p. 135f. and n. 50f. for relevant references). See also the discussion of Herder's views in Barnard, F. M., *Herder's Social and Political Thought – From Enlightenment to Nationalism*, Oxford University Press, 1965, p. 141f.
54. Herder, J. G., *Ideas for a Philosophy of the History of Mankind*, extracts trans. F. M. Barnard, in *J. G. Herder on Social and Political Culture*, *op. cit.*, p. 307f.
55. Hodgson, Geoffrey M., *Economics and Utopia – Why the Learning Economy is not the End of History*, Routledge, 1999, p. 71.
56. *Ibid.*, p. 72.
57. Adler, Emanuel, 'Constructivism and International Relations', chapter 5 in *Handbook of International Relations*, ed. W. Carlsnaes *et al.*, Sage, 2002, p. 103.
58. North, Douglass C., *op. cit.*, p. 30.
59. See the discussion of the 'logic of appropriateness', in Rothstein, Bo, *op. cit.*, p. 147f.; and in Checkel, Jeffrey T., 'The Constructivist Turn in International Relations Theory', Review Article, *World Politics*, 50(2), 1998, p. 330. For a canonical expression, see March, James G. and Olsen, Johan P., *Rediscovering Institutions: The Organisational Basis of Politics*, Free Press, 1989, pp. 23, 160–2.
60. Offe, Claus, 'Political Economy: Sociological Perspectives', in *A New Handbook of Political Science*, *op. cit.*, p. 675.
61. Lyons, Bruce, 'Organisations', chapter 10 in *The Theory of Choice*, *op. cit.*, pp. 167–9.
62. For the notion of 'reserve areas', I am indebted to Williams, Raymond, *Culture and Society: 1780–1950*, Chatto & Windus, 1958, p. 67.
63. Weale, Albert, '*Homo economicus, Homo sociologicus*', chapter 5 in *The Theory of Choice*, *op. cit.*, p. 71.
64. Offe, Claus, *op. cit.*, p. 687.
65. Rothstein, Bo, *op. cit.*, p. 158.
66. For a discussion of Kenneth Arrow's 'Impossibility Theorem' and the role of social institutions in providing for a consistent social ordering of preferences (and relevant references), see chapter 5 of *The Romantic Economist* (p. 141 and n. 66).
67. For a discussion of the views of Herder and the Constructivists on the 'mutual constitution' of society and individuals, see chapter 5 of *The Romantic Economist* (p. 139f. and n. 60f.). See also, Offe, Claus, *op. cit.*, p. 679.

68. Rothstein, Bo, *op. cit.*, p. 159.
69. *Ibid.*
70. See, for example, the discussion of 'high' and 'low' politics in the process of EU enlargement in Baldwin, R. E., 'The Eastern Enlargement of the European Union', *European Economic Review*, 39, 1995, pp. 474–81.
71. Campbell, Colin, *The Romantic Ethic and the Spirit of Modern Consumerism*, Blackwell, 1987, p. 138.
72. Rothschild, Emma, *Economic Sentiments – Adam Smith, Condorcet, and the Enlightenment*, Harvard University Press, 2001, p. 224 and *passim*.
73. Smith, Adam, *An Inquiry into the Nature and Causes of the Wealth of Nations*, (originally published in 1776) V.iii and I.ii, ed. Kathryn Sutherland, Oxford University Press, 1993, pp. 459f., 21.
74. Keynes, John Maynard, *The General Theory of Employment, Interest and Money* (originally published in 1936), in *The Collected Writings of John Maynard Keynes*, vol. VII, Macmillan, 1973, pp. 161, 163, 154.
75. Coleridge, Samuel Taylor, 'Lay Sermon addressed to the Higher and Middle Classes' (originally published in 1817), in *Biographia Literaria and Two Lay Sermons*, George Bell & Sons, 1898, pp. 418f., 422–5.
76. Ruskin, John, *Unto this Last*, *op. cit.*, pp. 170, 172f.
77. Akerlof, George A. and Yellen, Janet L., 'The Fair Wage–Effort Hypothesis and Unemployment', *Quarterly Journal of Economics*, 105(2) (May 1990), pp. 255–83. See also the discussion of this theory in Rabin, Matthew, 'Psychology and Economics', *op. cit.*, p. 23f.; and Coyle, Diane, *The Soulful Science – What Economist Really Do and Why It Matters*, Princeton University Press, 2007, pp. 123, 134.
78. Campbell, Colin, *op. cit.*, p. 48.
79. Mill, J. S., *Autobiography*, *op. cit.*, p. 123.
80. Raphael, D. D., *Adam Smith*, Oxford University Press, 1985, pp. 29–31.
81. Brown, Vivienne, *Adam Smith's Discourse – Canonicity, Commerce and Conscience*, Routledge, 1994, pp. 69–72.
82. Abrams, M. H., *The Mirror and the Lamp – Romantic Theory and the Critical Tradition*, Oxford University Press, 1953, p. 332.
83. Herder, J. G., *Ideas for a Philosophy of the History of Mankind*, *op. cit.*, p. 268.
84. *Ibid.*, p. 269.
85. See the discussion in Fleischacker, Samuel, *On Adam Smith's Wealth of Nations – A Philosophical Companion*, Princeton University Press, 2004, pp. 85–96; and in Raphael, D. D., *op. cit.*, p. 93f.
86. Hazlitt, William, *The Spirit of the Age*, essay on 'Jeremy Bentham', *op. cit.*, p. 94.
87. Coase, Ronald H., 'The Nature of the Firm' (1937); reproduced as chapter 2 in *The Nature of the Firm: Origins, Evolution, and Development*, ed. Oliver E. Williamson and Sidney G. Winter, Oxford University Press, 1991. For a brief introduction to Coase's theory, see Backhouse, Roger E., *The Penguin History of Economics*, Penguin, 2002, p. 318f.
88. Murdoch, Iris, *Sartre: Romantic Rationalist*, Vintage, 1999, pp. 86f., 103f.

89. *Ibid.*, pp. 107, 112.
90. Mill, J. S. *Autobiography*, *op. cit.*, p. 135.
91. Schumpeter, Joseph A., *Capitalism, Socialism and Democracy* (originally published in 1943), Routledge, 1994, p. 160.
92. Phrases selected from Nietzsche, Friedrich, *Thus Spoke Zarathustra*, part IV, (1885), extract reprinted in *A Nietzsche Reader*, ed. and trans. R. J. Hollingdale, Penguin, 1977, p. 243. See the discussion of the full quotation in chapter 4 of *The Romantic Economist* (p. 98).
93. See the discussion on Nietzsche (and relevant reference) in chapter 4 of *The Romantic Economist* (p. 97 and n. 54).
94. Phrases selected from Byron, Lord George, *Lara* (originally published in 1814), stanza 18, lines 54f., extract reprinted in 'The Oxford Authors' *Byron*', ed. Jerome J. McGann, Oxford University Press, 1986, p. 251.
95. Byron, Lord George, *Childe Harold's Pilgrimage*, Canto III.42 (originally published in 1816), reprinted in 'The Oxford Authors' *Byron*', *op. cit.*, p. 116.
96. *Ibid.*, Canto III.6, p. 105.
97. Fukuyama, Francis, *The End of History and the Last Man*, Penguin, 1992, pp. 182, 314–16.
98. Campbell, Colin, *op. cit.*, p. 214.

CHAPTER 10

1. For relevant references and further discussion of Hume, see chapter 4 of *The Romantic Economist* (p. 104 and n. 80).
2. For relevant references and further discussion of Kant, see chapter 4 of *The Romantic Economist* (pp. 104–6 and nn. 81, 84).
3. Tarnas, Richard, *The Passion of the Western Mind – Understanding the Ideas that have Shaped our World View*, Ballantine Books, 1993, p. 344.
4. Magee, Bryan, *Confessions of a Philosopher – A Journey Through Western Philosophy*, Phoenix, 1997, p. 190.
5. See the discussion in Warnock, Mary, *Imagination*, Faber & Faber, 1976, pp. 27–31.
6. Herder, J. G., *Ideas for a Philosophy of the History of Mankind* (originally published in 1791), extracts trans. in F. M. Barnard, *J. G. Herder on Social and Political Culture*, Cambridge University Press, 1969, p. 276.
7. Wordsworth, William, *The Prelude* (1805), book II, lines 271f., ed. E. de Selincourt, Oxford University Press, 1960, p. 27; and see also 'Lines Written a Few Miles above Tintern Abbey' (from *Lyrical Ballads*, 1798), lines 106–8, reprinted in *Romanticism – An Anthology*, 2nd edn., ed. Duncan Wu, Blackwell, 1998, p. 268.
8. Coleridge, Samuel Taylor, *Table Talk*, 21 September 1830, reprinted in 'The Oxford Authors' *Samuel Taylor Coleridge*', ed. H. J. Jackson, Oxford University Press, 1985, p. 596.
9. Kuhn, Thomas S., *The Structure of Scientific Revolutions*, 3rd edn., University of Chicago Press, 1996, p. 113.

10. Wittgenstein, Ludwig, *Philosophical Investigations II*, trans. G. E. M. Anscombe (originally published in 1953), Blackwell, 2001, pp. 165–8. See also the discussion in Warnock, Mary, *op. cit.*, pp. 183–95.

11. Robbins, Lionel, *A History of Economic Thought – The LSE Lectures*, ed. Steven G. Medema and Warren J. Samuels, Princeton University Press, 1998, p. 250.

12. Hazlitt, William, *The Spirit of the Age*, 2nd edn. (originally published in 1825), essay on 'Jeremy Bentham', The Wordsworth Trust, 2004, p. 91.

13. Nietzsche, Friedrich, passage quoted in Tarnas, Richard, *op. cit.*, p. 370.

14. Nietzsche, Friedrich, extract from *Beyond Good and Evil* (originally published in 1886), in *A Nietzsche Reader*, sel. and trans. R. J. Hollingdale, Penguin, 1977, p. 63: 'It is perhaps just dawning on five or six minds that physics too is only an interpretation and arrangement of the world …'

15. Bowie, Andrew, *From Romanticism to Critical Theory – The Philosophy of German Literary Theory*, Routledge, 1997, p. 60.

16. See Herder, J. G., *Essay on the Origin of Language* (originally published in 1772), extracts trans. in F. M. Barnard, *J. G. Herder on Social and Political Culture*, *op. cit.*, pp. 158f., 163f.

17. See the excellent introductory discussion of this aspect of Wittgenstein's philosophy in Magee, Bryan, *The Great Philosophers – An Introduction to Western Philosophy*, BBC Books, 1987, discussion with John Searle, pp. 326f., 334f.

18. See the discussion in Grayling, A. C., *Wittgenstein – A Very Short Introduction*, Oxford University Press, 2001, p. 96f.

19. See the discussion in Magee, Bryan, *The Great Philosophers*, discussion with John Searle, *op. cit.*, p. 331f.

20. Merquior, J. G., *Foucault*, Fontana Press, 1985, pp. 74, 84.

21. *Ibid.*, p. 85.

22. See the discussion of Foucault in Drolet, Michael, 'Introduction', in *The Postmodernism Reader – Foundational Texts*, Routledge, 2004, p. 20.

23. Keynes, John Maynard, *The General Theory of Employment, Interest and Money*, in *The Collected Writings of John Maynard Keynes*, vol. VII, Macmillan, 1973, p. 383.

24. *Ibid.*, p. 33.

25. See the interesting discussion of these issues in Grayling, A. C., *op. cit.*, pp. 119–22; and in Sabel, Charles F., 'Intelligible Differences: On Deliberate Strategy and the Exploration of Possibility in Economic Life', *Rivista Italiana degli Economisti*, I, 1996, pp. 55-80; also available at www2.law.columbia.edu/sabel/papers.

26. Marshall, Alfred, *Principles of Economics*, Preface to First Edition (1890), Macmillan, 1927, p. ix.

27. Murdoch, Iris, *Sartre: Romantic Rationalist*, Vintage, 1999, p. 42.

28. Wordsworth, William, *The Prelude* (1850), book III, line 63, ed. J. Wordsworth, M. H. Abrams and S. Gill, W. W. Norton, 1979, p. 95.

29. See Bronk, Richard, *Progress and the Invisible Hand – The Philosophy and Economics of Human Advance*, Little Brown, 1998, p. 78.

30. For a discussion of James G. March, Johan P. Olsen and others on the 'logic of appropriateness', and for relevant references, see chapter 9 of *The Romantic*

Economist (p. 243 and n. 59); and for a discussion and relevant references on Constructivism, see chapter 5 of *The Romantic Economist* (p. 135 and nn. 47, 48).

31. I am indebted to Liv Borg, who has studied and worked in all three languages, for an interesting discussion on this topic.

32. Taylor, Charles, 'Interpretation and the Sciences of Man', *Review of Metaphysics*, 25 (1971); reproduced as chapter 13 in *Readings in the Philosophy of Social Science* ed. Michael Martin and Lee C. McIntyre, MIT Press, 1994, pp. 197, 195, 206.

33. *Ibid.*, p. 188.

34. *Ibid.*, p. 181f.

35. *Ibid.*, p. 186f.

36. *Ibid.*, p. 207.

37. See the discussion in Berlin, Isaiah, *The Crooked Timber of Humanity – Chapters in the History of Ideas*, ed. Henry Hardy, John Murray, 1990, p. 82.

38. Tarnas, Richard, *op. cit.*, p. 369.

39. Webb, Beatrice, *My Apprenticeship*, extract quoted in Leavis, F. R., 'Introduction', in *Mill on Bentham and Coleridge*, Chatto & Windus, 1950, p. 25f.

40. Jackson, Robert, *The Global Covenant: Human Conduct in a World of States*, Oxford University Press, 2000, p. 71.

41. Taylor, Charles, *op. cit.*, p. 209.

42. *Ibid.*, p. 199. See the further discussion of Taylor's views on this point in chapter 5 of *The Romantic Economist* (p. 134 and n. 45).

43. Taylor, Charles, *op. cit.*, p. 208.

44. Leavis, F. R., *Mill on Bentham and Coleridge, op. cit.*, p. 25f.

45. See the further discussion of national models of capitalism in chapter 6 of *The Romantic Economist, passim*.

46. Brown, Vivienne, *Adam Smith's Discourse – Canonicity, Commerce and Conscience*, Routledge, 1994, pp. 69–72. For a further discussion on Adam Smith's sympathetic imagination, see chapter 9 of *The Romantic Economist* (p. 250 and nn. 80, 81).

47. See the discussion in Esping-Anderson, Gøsta, *The Three Worlds of Welfare Capitalism͵* Polity Press, 1990, *passim*.

48. Bohm, David, *On Creativity*, Routledge, 1996, p. 76.

49. Kuhn, Thomas S., *The Structure of Scientific Revolutions, op. cit.*, pp. 43–6.

50. *Ibid.*, pp. 24f., 27, 34.

51. *Ibid.*, pp. 15f., 19f., 64f., 109.

52. *Ibid.*, pp. 24f., 111f. and *passim*.

53. *Ibid.*, p. 64f.

54. *Ibid.*, pp. 53, 71, 83.

55. *Ibid.*, pp. 19, 164.

56. Green, Donald P. and Shapiro, Ian, *Pathologies of Rational Choice Theory – A Critique of Applications in Political Science*, Yale University Press, 1994, pp. 6, 34, 37, 187. For a full discussion and examples of these points, see chapter 9 of *The Romantic Economist* (pp. 232–4 and nn. 25–32).

57. Colander, David, *The Lost Art of Economics – Essays on Economics and the Economics Profession*, Edward Elgar, 2001, p. 128.

58. *Ibid.*, pp. 129f., 3–6.

59. Kuhn, Thomas S., *op. cit.*, pp. 122f., 150.

60. *Ibid.*, pp. 109, 111f., 148, 150, 152, 204 and *passim*.

61. Bohm, David, *op. cit.*, pp. 3, 8, 39, 54.

62. Coleridge, Samuel Taylor, *Biographia Literaria* (originally published in 1817), chapter XIV, ed. J. Shawcross, Oxford, 1907, vol. II, p. 12; and Notebook entry, March 1808, in *Coleridge's Notebooks – A Selection*, ed. Seamus Perry, Oxford University Press, 2002, no. 451, p. 101.

63. See Coleridge, Samuel Taylor, *Biographia Literaria*, chapter XIV, ed. J. Shawcross, *op. cit.*, vol. II, p. 12; and see the discussion in chapter 8 of *The Romantic Economist* (pp. 202–4 and nn. 37–43).

64. Kuhn, Thomas, S., *op. cit.*, pp. 198f., 203f.

65. For details of the research programme and history of the Santa Fe Institute, see www.santafe.edu; and the discussion in Waldrop, M. Mitchell, *Complexity – The Emerging Science at the Edge of Order and Chaos*, Penguin, 1994; and chapter 5 of *The Romantic Economist* (pp. 128–31 and nn. 27–38).

66. Kuhn, Thomas S., *op. cit.*, p. 167.

67. Sabel, Charles F., *op. cit.*, *passim*.

68. Kuhn, Thomas S., *op. cit.*, p. 150.

69. See the interesting discussion on this in Martin, Michael, 'Taylor on Interpretation and the Sciences of Man', chapter 17 in *Readings in the Philosophy of Social Science*, *op. cit.*, pp. 266–8.

70. Wordsworth, William, *Preface* to *Poems* (1815), in *Romanticism – An Anthology*, ed. Duncan Wu, *op. cit.*, p. 413.

71. Coleridge, Samuel Taylor, *Biographia Literaria*, chapter XIV, ed. J. Shawcross, *op. cit.*, vol. II, p. 6.

72. Richards, I. A., *The Philosophy of Rhetoric*, Oxford University Press, 1936; the passage is quoted in McCloskey, D. N., *The Rhetoric of Economics*, 2nd edn., University of Wisconsin Press, 1998, p. 42.

73. Morgan, Gareth, *Images of Organization*, Sage, 2006, p. 339.

74. Abrams, M. H., *The Mirror and the Lamp – Romantic Theory and the Critical Tradition*, Oxford University Press, 1953, p. 31.

75. See Mirowski, Philip, *More Heat than Light – Economics as Social Physics, Physics as Nature's Economics*, Cambridge University Press, 1989, *passim*; and see the discussion in chapter 1 of *The Romantic Economist* (p. 24 and n. 56) and chapter 3 of *The Romantic Economist* (p. 78f. and nn. 53–58).

76. Morgan, Gareth, *op. cit.*, p. 340.

77. *Ibid.*, p. 4f.

78. Shackle, G. L. S., *Epistemics and Economics – A Critique of Economic Doctrines* (originally published in 1972), Transaction Publishers, 1992, p. 3f.

79. Abrams, M. H., *The Mirror and the Lamp*, *op. cit.*, p. 31.

80. See the discussion in Norris, Christopher, *Derrida*, Fontana, 1987, pp. 18–27.

81. Waldrop, M. Mitchell, *op. cit.*, p. 327.

82. *Ibid.*, *passim*.
83. Keats, John, 'Letter to George and Tom Keats', 21 December 1817, extract reprinted in *Romanticism – An Anthology*, ed. Duncan Wu, *op. cit.*, p. 1019; and see the discussion in chapter 8 of *The Romantic Economist* (p. 201f. and nn. 33, 34).
84. Coleridge, Samuel Taylor, extract from a 'Lecture on Romeo and Juliet' (9 December 1811), reprinted in Hill, John Spencer (ed.), *Imagination in Coleridge*, Macmillan, 1978, p. 81.
85. Bohm, David, *op. cit.*, pp. 4f., 23.
86. For an interesting discussion and some examples of the impact of 'initial hypotheses' on the interpretation of evidence and problems, see Rabin, Matthew, 'Psychology and Economics', *Journal of Economic Literature*, XXXVI (March 1998), pp. 26–8.
87. Krugman, Paul, *Development, Geography, and Economic Theory*, MIT Press, 1997, p. 71f.
88. Mill, J. S., 'Essay on the Definition of Political Economy; and on the Method of Investigation Proper to it' (originally published in 1830), as Essay V in Mill, J. S., *Essays on Some Unsettled Questions of Political Economy*, 3rd edn., Longmans, Green, & Co., 1877, p. 153.
89. *Ibid.*, p. 161.
90. Kuhn, Thomas S., *op. cit.*, p. 79.
91. Popper, Karl R., *Conjectures and Refutations – The Growth of Scientific Knowledge*, Routledge, 1963, p. 46f.
92. Schumpeter, Joseph, *History of Economic Analysis*, George Allen & Unwin, 1954, p. 41f.
93. Morgan, Gareth, *op. cit.*, p. 357f.
94. See, for example, Calmfors, Lars and Drifill, John, 'Centralisation of Wage Bargaining and Macro-Economic Performance', *Economic Policy*, 6 (April 1988), pp. 13–61.
95. Sutton, John, *Marshall's Tendencies – What Can Economists Know?*, MIT Press, 2000, p. 16; and see the discussion in chapter 3 of *The Romantic Economist* (p. 75 and n. 47).
96. See, for example, Innes, Abby, *Czechoslovakia – The Short Goodbye*, Yale University Press, 2001, pp. 40–2. This book uses a number of different 'exploratory theories' to examine the reasons behind the break-up of Czechoslovakia, thereby constructing an exemplary political-science narrative of a particular event (or, in my terminology, a 'holistic fragment').
97. See Green, Donald P. and Shapiro, Ian, *op. cit.*, p. 203f. and *passim*; and Colander, David, *op. cit.*, p. 56.
98. Friedman, Milton, 'The Methodology of Positive Economics', from *Essays in Positive Economics*, University of Chicago Press, 1953; reproduced as chapter 9 in *The Philosophy of Economics – An Anthology*, 2nd edn., ed. Daniel M. Hausman, Cambridge University Press, 1994, 207f.
99. Green, Donald P. and Shapiro, Ian, *op. cit.*, p. 97.
100. See the discussion in chapter 7 of *The Romantic Economist* (p. 189f. and n. 54f.).

101. See Innes, Abby, *op. cit.*, *passim*, for an example of what I call 'a one-off imaginative synthesis of findings derived from using discrete paradigm discourses to construct a narrative of a specific situation'.

102. Wordsworth, William, 'Fragment', dated by E. de Selincourt as 1798–1800, reproduced in Warnock, Mary, *Imagination*, *op. cit.*, p. 125.

103. Eliot, George, *Middlemarch* (originally published in 1871), Penguin, 1965, chapter 16, p. 193f.

104. *Ibid.*, p. 194.

105. Mill, J. S., 'Essay on the Definition of Political Economy', *op. cit.*, p. 159f.

106. *Ibid.*, p. 158f.

107. Wordsworth, William, *Preface* to the *Lyrical Ballads*, 1802 amendment, in Wordsworth, William and Coleridge, Samuel Taylor, *Lyrical Ballads*, ed. R. L. Brett and A. R. Jones, Methuen, 1963, p. 238. See the discussion of Wordsworth and Marshall's views on this subject in chapter 1 of *The Romantic Economist* (pp. 16f., 18f. and nn. 37f., 42f.).

CHAPTER 11

1. Wordsworth, William, *The Prelude* (1805), book VI, lines 186f., ed. E. de Selincourt, Oxford University Press, 1960, p. 90.

2. See the introductory discussion of General Equilibrium Theory in Backhouse, Roger E., *The Penguin History of Economics*, Penguin, 2002, pp. 254–62; and in Bronk, Richard, *Progress and the Invisible Hand – The Philosophy and Economics of Human Advance*, Little Brown, 1998, p. 107f.

3. Mill, J. S., 'Essay on the Definition of Political Economy; and on the Method of Investigation Proper to it' (originally published in 1830), as Essay V in Mill, J. S., *Essays on Some Unsettled Questions of Political Economy*, 3rd edn., Longmans, Green & Co., 1877, pp. 143–5.

4. Shackle, G. L. S., *Epistemics and Economics – A Critique of Economic Doctrines* (originally published in 1972), Transaction Publishers, 1992, p. 38.

5. Bagehot, Walter, 'The Preliminaries of Political Economy', in his posthumous *Economic Studies*, ed. R. H. Hutton, 2nd edn., Longmans, Green & Co., 1888, p. 76.

6. Robbins, Lionel, *An Essay on the Nature and Significance of Economic Science*, 2nd edn., Macmillan, 1935, extracts reprinted as chapter 3 in Hausman, Daniel M. (ed.), *The Philosophy of Economics, An Anthology*, 2nd edn., Cambridge University Press, 1994, p. 96f.

7. Mill, J. S., 'Essay on the Definition of Political Economy', *op. cit.*, p. 150f.

8. Sutton, John, *Marshall's Tendencies – What Can Economists Know?*, MIT Press, 2000, p. 16.

9. Mill, J. S., 'Essay on the Definition of Political Economy', *op. cit.*, p. 153f.

10. See the discussion of the Romantic attitude to fragments in chapter 4 of *The Romantic Economist* (pp. 108–10, 113 and nn. 95–99, 101–2, 112).

11. Mill, J. S., essay on 'Bentham' (originally published in 1838), in *Mill on Bentham and Coleridge*, ed. F. R. Leavis, Chatto & Windus, 1950, p. 64f.; and see the

discussion of Mill's views on 'half-truths' and 'systematic half-thinkers' in chapter 2 of *The Romantic Economist* (p. 34f. and nn. 17, 18, 19).

12. See the discussion in chapter 2 of *The Romantic Economist* (p. 55 and nn. 74, 75) and chapter 9 of *The Romantic Economist* (p. 228 and nn. 12–14).

13. Mill, J. S., 'Essay on the Definition of Political Economy', *op. cit.*, p. 149.

14. See the discussion in chapter 9 of *The Romantic Economist* (p. 246f.) and chapter 10 of *The Romantic Economist* (p. 284).

15. Lyons, Bruce, 'Game Theory', chapter 7 in *The Theory of Choice – A Critical Guide*, ed. S. Heap, M. Hollis, B. Lyons, R. Sugden and A. Weale, Blackwell, 1992, p. 120f.

16. Tarnas, Richard, *The Passion of the Western Mind – Understanding the Ideas that Have Shaped our World View*, Ballantine Books, 1993, p. 404.

17. Abrams, M. H., *The Mirror and the Lamp – Romantic Theory and the Critical Tradition*, Oxford University Press, 1953, p. 316f.

18. For a discussion of Endogenous Growth Theory, see chapter 5 of *The Romantic Economist* (p. 127 and nn. 25, 26); and for a discussion of 'thin' versions of Rational Choice Theory, see chapter 9 of *The Romantic Economist* (pp. 230, 233 and nn. 18f., 30).

19. Kuhn, Thomas S., *The Structure of Scientific Revolutions*, 3rd edn., University of Chicago Press, 1996, p. 68f. and *passim*; and see the discussion of Kuhn's theory in chapter 1 of *The Romantic Economist* (p. 10 and n. 20) and chapter 10 of *The Romantic Economist* (p. 269 and nn. 54, 56).

20. See the discussion in chapter 9 of *The Romantic Economist* (pp. 233, 237 and nn. 30–31, 40).

21. Bagehot, Walter, 'The Postulates of English Political Economy', in *Economic Studies*, *op. cit.*, p. 21.

22. Mill, J. S., 'Essay on the Definition of Political Economy', *op. cit.*, pp. 137–44, 151f.

23. Rothschild, Emma, *Economic Sentiments – Adam Smith, Condorcet, and the Enlightenment*, Harvard University Press, 2001, p. 218.

24. For a discussion of different ways of conceptualising 'political economy', and the modern tendency to use the term to describe the application of economic method (especially Rational Choice assumptions) to the study of politics, see Caporaso, James A. and Levine, David, P., *Theories of Political Economy*, Cambridge University Press, 1992, chapter 6, esp. pp. 126–8.

25. Nietzsche, Friedrich, *The Twilight of the Idols* (originally published in 1889), trans. Anthony M. Ludovici, George Allen & Unwin, 1911, p. 5; and see the discussion of the whole maxim in chapter 4 of *The Romantic Economist* (p. 97 and n. 55).

26. Kuhn, Thomas S., *op. cit.*, pp. 43–6; and see the discussion in chapter 10 of *The Romantic Economist* (p. 268 and n. 49).

27. Kuhn, Thomas S., *op. cit.*, p. 45; and see the discussion in chapter 1 of *The Romantic Economist* (p. 14 and n. 28) and chapter 4 of *The Romantic Economist* (p. 87 and n. 11).

28. See the discussion in chapter 4 of *The Romantic Economist* (p. 87).

29. See the discussion in chapter 5 of *The Romantic Economist* (p. 140) and chapter 9 of *The Romantic Economist* (p. 245).

30. For a discussion of the problems with both GDP measures and standard cost-benefit analysis and of some possible replacements, see chapter 7 of *The Romantic Economist* (pp. 182–5, 188–90 and nn. 34–43, 52–55).

31. For a discussion of the impact of incommensurable values on the meaningfulness of indifference curves and the consistency requirements of economic rationality, see chapter 7 of *The Romantic Economist* (pp. 190–5).

32. Snow, C. P., *The Two Cultures and the Scientific Revolution*, Cambridge University Press, 1959, *passim*; and see the discussion in chapter 2 of *The Romantic Economist* (p. 48 and n. 57).

33. Schumpeter, Joseph A., *Capitalism, Socialism and Democracy* (originally published in 1943), Routledge, 1994, pp. 82–4; and see the discussion in chapter 8 of *The Romantic Economist* (p. 207f. and nn. 62–64).

34. Shelley, P. B., *A Defence of Poetry* (originally published in 1840), extract reprinted in *Romanticism – An Anthology*, 2nd edn., ed. Duncan Wu, Blackwell, 1998, p. 949.

35. Wordsworth, William, *The Prelude* (1805), book XIII, line 98f., ed. E. de Selincourt, *op. cit.*, p. 231.

36. *Ibid.*, book XIII, lines 169f., ed. E. de Selincourt, *op. cit.*, p. 233.

Bibliography

Abrams, M. H., *The Mirror and the Lamp – Romantic Theory and the Critical Tradition*, Oxford University Press, 1953

(ed.), *English Romantic Poets – Modern Essays in Criticism*, Oxford University Press, 1975

Adler, Emanuel, 'Constructivism and International Relations', chapter 5 in *Handbook of International Relations*, ed. W. Carlsnaes *et al.*, Sage, 2002

Akerlof, George A. and Yellen, Janet L., 'The Fair Wage–Effort Hypothesis and Unemployment', *Quarterly Journal of Economics*, 105(2) (May 1990), pp. 255–83

Albert, Michel, *Capitalism Against Capitalism*, Whurr Publishers, 1993

Armstrong, Charles I., *Romantic Organicism – From Idealist Origins to Ambivalent Afterlife*, Palgrave Macmillan, 2003

Arrow, Kenneth, J., *Social Choice and Individual Values*, John Wiley & Sons, 1951

'The Place of Institutions in the Economy: A Theoretical Perspective', in *The Institutional Foundations of East Asian Economic Development*, ed. Y. Hayami and M. Aoki, Macmillan, 1998; reproduced as chapter 3 in *Readings in Political Economy*, ed. Kaushik Basu, Blackwell, 2003

Arthur, W. Brian, 'Positive Feedbacks in the Economy', *Scientific American*, February 1990, pp. 80–5

Backhouse, Roger E., *The Penguin History of Economics*, Penguin, 2002

Bagehot, Walter, 'The Preliminaries of Political Economy' and 'The Postulates of English Political Economy', in his posthumous *Economic Studies*, ed. R. H. Hutton, 2nd edn., Longmans, Green & Co., 1888

Baldwin, R. E., 'The Eastern Enlargement of the European Union', *European Economic Review*, 39, 1995, pp. 474–81

Barnard, F. M., *Herder's Social and Political Thought – From Enlightenment to Nationalism*, Oxford University Press, 1965

(trans.), *J. G. Herder on Social and Political Culture*, Cambridge University Press, 1969

Basu, Kaushik (ed.), *Readings in Political Economy*, Blackwell, 2003

Bate, Jonathan, *The Song of the Earth*, Picador, 2000

Beer, John, 'Fragmentations and Ironies', in *Questioning Romanticism*, ed. John Beer, Johns Hopkins University Press, 1995

Begg, David, Fischer, Stanley and Dornbusch, Rudiger, *Economics*, 4th edn., McGraw-Hill, 1994

Behler, Ernst, 'Early German Romanticism: Friedrich Schlegel and Novalis', chapter 4 in *A Companion to Continental Philosophy*, ed. Simon Critchley and William R. Schroeder, Blackwell, 1998

Bentham, Jeremy, *An Introduction to the Principles of Morals and Legislation* (originally published in 1789), W. Pickering, 1823

The Rationale of Reward, Robert Heward, 1830

Berger, Suzanne, 'Introduction', in *National Diversity and Global Capitalism*, ed. Suzanne Berger and Ronald Dore, Cornell University Press, 1996

'Globalization and Politics', *Annual Review of Political Science*, 3, 2000, p. 59; also available as MIT IPC Globalization Working Paper 00–005

Berlin, Isaiah, *The Crooked Timber of Humanity – Chapters in the History of Ideas*, ed. Henry Hardy, John Murray, 1990

The Roots of Romanticism, ed. Henry Hardy, Chatto & Windus, 1999

Blake, William, 'Milton' (composed 1803–8), extract reproduced in *Romanticism – An Anthology*, ed. Duncan Wu, Blackwell, 1998, p. 120

Boardman, Anthony E., Greenberg, David H., Vining, Aidan R. and Weimer, David L., *Cost-Benefit Analysis: Concepts and Practice*, Prentice Hall, 1996

Bohm, David, *On Creativity*, Routledge, 1996

Boulding, Kenneth E., *The Image – Knowledge in Life and Society*, Ann Arbor Paperbacks (University of Michigan Press), 1961

Bowie, Andrew, *From Romanticism to Critical Theory – The Philosophy of German Literary Theory*, Routledge, 1997

Bronk, Richard, *Progress and the Invisible Hand – The Philosophy and Economics of Human Advance*, Little Brown, 1998

'Which Model of Capitalism?', *OECD Observer*, 221/222, Summer 2000, pp. 12–15

Bronowski, J., *The Ascent of Man*, BBC Books, 1973

Brown, S., Doherty, A. M. and Clarke, B., *Romancing the Market*, Routledge, 1998

Brown, Vivienne, *Adam Smith's Discourse – Canonicity, Commerce and Conscience*, Routledge, 1994

Buchanan, James M. and Vanberg, Viktor J., 'The Market as a Creative Process', *Economics and Philosophy*, 7 (1991); reproduced as chapter 18 in *The Philosophy of Economics – An Anthology*, 2nd edn., ed. Daniel M. Hausman, Cambridge University Press, 1994

Burke, Edmund, *Reflections on the Revolution in France* (originally published in 1790), ed. L. G. Mitchell, Oxford University Press, 1993

'Speech on Moving the Resolutions for Conciliation with the Colonies' (1775), extract quoted in Whale, John, *Imagination Under Pressure, 1789–1832*, Cambridge University Press, 2000, p. 32

Butler, Marilyn, *Romantics, Rebels and Reactionaries – English Literature and its Background (1760–1830)*, Oxford University Press, 1981

Byron, Lord George, *Childe Harold's Pilgrimage*, Canto III (originally published in 1816), reprinted in 'The Oxford Authors' *Byron*', ed. Jerome J. McGann, Oxford University Press, 1986

Lara (originally published in 1814), extracts reprinted in 'The Oxford Authors' *Byron*', ed. Jerome J. McGann, Oxford University Press, 1986

Calmfors, Lars and Drifill, John, 'Centralisation of Wage Bargaining and Macro-Economic Performance', *Economic Policy* 6 (April 1988), pp. 13–61

Campbell, Colin, *The Romantic Ethic and the Spirit of Modern Consumerism*, Blackwell, 1987

Caporaso, James A. and Levine, David P., *Theories of Political Economy*, Cambridge University Press, 1992

Carlin, Wendy and Soskice, David, *Macroeconomics: Imperfections, Institutions and Policies*, Oxford University Press, 2006

Carlsnaes, W. *et al.* (eds.), *Handbook of International Relations*, Sage, 2002

Carlyle, Thomas, *Signs of the Times* (originally published in 1829), reprinted in *Critical and Miscellaneous Essays*, vol. 2, James Fraser, 1840

Chang, Ha-Joon (ed.), *The Rebel Within*, Wimbledon Publishing Company, 2001

Checkel, Jeffrey T., 'The Constructivist Turn in International Relations Theory', Review Article, *World Politics*, 50(2), 1998, pp. 324–48

Coase, Ronald H., 'The Nature of the Firm' (1937); reproduced as chapter 2 in *The Nature of the Firm: Origins, Evolution, and Development*, ed. Oliver E. Williamson and Sidney G. Winter, Oxford University Press, 1991

Colander, David, *The Lost Art of Economics – Essays on Economics and the Economics Profession*, Edward Elgar, 2001

Coleman, William Oliver, *Economics and its Enemies – Two Centuries of Anti-Economics*, Palgrave Macmillan, 2002

Coleridge, Samuel Taylor, 'Lay Sermon addressed to the Higher and Middle Classes' (originally published in 1817), and 'The Statesman's Manual' (originally published in 1816), reprinted in *Biographia Literaria and Two Lay Sermons*, George Bell & Son, 1898

    Biographia Literaria (originally published in 1817), ed. J. Shawcross, vols. I and II, Oxford, 1907

    On the Constitution of the Church and State (originally published in 1830), ed. John Barrell, J. M. Dent & Sons, 1972

    'Lecture on Romeo and Juliet' (9 December 1811), and 'Lecture on the Slave Trade' (June 1795), extracts reprinted in Hill, John Spencer (ed.), *Imagination in Coleridge*, Macmillan, 1978, pp. 81f., 27f.

    Table Talk (originally published in 1835), extracts reprinted in 'The Oxford Authors' *Samuel Taylor Coleridge*', ed. H. J. Jackson, Oxford University Press, 1985, pp. 590–603

    'Dejection: An Ode', 'A Letter to Sara Hutchinson', and 'Kubla Khan', in *Selected Poems*, ed. Richard Holmes, Penguin, 1996

    Notebooks, extracts reprinted in *Coleridge's Notebooks – A Selection*, ed. Seamus Perry, Oxford University Press, 2002

Connell, Philip, *Romanticism, Economics and the Question of 'Culture'*, Oxford University Press, 2001

Coyle, Diane, *The Soulful Science – What Economists Really Do and Why It Matters*, Princeton University Press, 2007

CPB Netherlands Bureau for Economic Policy Analysis, *Challenging Neighbours – Rethinking German and Dutch Economic Institutions*, Springer-Verlag, 1997

Critchley, Simon and Schroeder, William R. (eds.), *A Companion to Continental Philosophy*, Blackwell, 1998

Crouch, Colin, *Capitalist Diversity and Change – Recombinant Governance and Institutional Entrepreneurs*, Oxford University Press, 2005

Crouch, Colin and Streek, Wolfgang (eds.), *Political Economy of Modern Capitalism – Mapping Convergence and Diversity*, Sage, 1997

Dasgupta, Partha, 'Modern Economics and its Critics', chapter 3 in *Fact and Fiction in Economics: Models, Realism and Social Construction*, ed. Uskali Mäki, Cambridge University Press, 2002

Day, Aidan, *Romanticism*, Routledge, 1996

de Bono, Edward, article on 'Lateral Thinking', in *The Oxford Companion to the Mind*, ed. Richard L. Gregory, Oxford University Press, 1987, p. 428f.

de Quincey, Thomas, *The Logic of Political Economy* (1844), in *The Collected Writings of Thomas de Quincey*, ed. David Masson, vol. IX, Adam & Charles Black, 1890

Donald, Merlin, *Origins of the Modern Mind: Three Stages in the Evolution of Culture and Cognition*, Harvard University Press, 1991

Drolet, Michael, *Tocqueville, Democracy and Social Reform*, Palgrave Macmillan, 2003
   (ed.) *The Postmodernism Reader – Foundational Texts*, Routledge, 2004

Dunn, Stephen P., 'Keynes and Transformation', chapter 13 in *The Philosophy of Keynes's Economics: Probability, Uncertainty and Convention*, ed. Jochen Runde and Sohei Mizuhara, Routledge, 2003

Eliot, George, *Middlemarch* (originally published in 1871), Penguin, 1965

Esping-Anderson, Gøsta, *The Three Worlds of Welfare Capitalism*, Polity Press, 1990

Ferguson, Niall, *The Cash Nexus*, Allen Lane, 2001

Fisher, Irving, *Mathematical Investigations in the Theory of Value and Prices*, Yale University Press, 1925

Fleischacker, Samuel, *On Adam Smith's Wealth of Nations – A Philosophical Companion*, Princeton University Press, 2004

Friedman, Milton, 'The Methodology of Positive Economics', from *Essays in Positive Economics*, University of Chicago Press, 1953; reproduced as chapter 9 in *The Philosophy of Economics – An Anthology*, 2nd edn., ed. Daniel M. Hausman, Cambridge University Press, 1994

Fukuyama, Francis, *The End of History and the Last Man*, Penguin, 1992
   Trust – The Social Virtues and the Creation of Prosperity, Penguin, 1996

Gamble, Andrew, *Hayek – The Iron Cage of Liberty*, Polity Press, 1996

Gerrard, Bill, 'Keynesian Uncertainty: What do we Know?', chapter 19 in *The Philosophy of Keynes's Economics: Probability, Uncertainty and Convention*, ed. Jochen Runde and Sohei Mizuhara, Routledge, 2003

Goodin, Robert E. and Klingemann, Hans-Dieter (eds.), *A New Handbook of Political Science*, Oxford University Press, 1998

Gray, John, *Enlightenment's Wake – Politics and Culture at the Close of the Modern Age*, Routledge, 1995
   Mill on Liberty – A Defence, 2nd edn., Routledge, 1996
   False Dawn – The Delusions of Global Capitalism, Granta Books, 1998

Hayek on Liberty, 3rd edn., Routledge, 1998

Two Faces of Liberalism, Polity Press, 2000

Grayling, A. C., *The Quarrel of the Age: The Life and Times of William Hazlitt*, Phoenix Press, 2001

Wittgenstein – A Very Short Introduction, Oxford University Press, 2001

Green, Donald P. and Shapiro, Ian, *Pathologies of Rational Choice Theory – A Critique of Applications in Political Science*, Yale University Press, 1994

Greenfeld, Liah, *The Spirit of Capitalism – Nationalism and Economic Growth*, Harvard University Press, 2001

Gregory, Richard L. (ed.), *The Oxford Companion to the Mind*, Oxford University Press, 1987

Hall, Peter A. and Soskice, David (eds.), *Varieties of Capitalism – The Institutional Foundations of Comparative Advantage*, Oxford University Press, 2001

Hancké, Bob and Goyer, Michel, 'Degrees of Freedom: Rethinking the Institutional Analysis of Economic Change', chapter 3 in *Changing Capitalisms? – Internationalisation, Institutional Change and Systems of Economic Organisation*, ed. G. Morgan, R. Whitley and E. Moen, Oxford University Press, 2005

Hancké, Bob, Rhodes, Martin and Thatcher, Mark (eds.), *Beyond Varieties of Capitalism – Conflict, Contradiction, and Complementarities in the European Economy*, Oxford University Press, 2007

Hausman, Daniel M. (ed.), *The Philosophy of Economics – An Anthology*, 2nd edn., Cambridge University Press, 1994

Hausman, Daniel M. and McPherson, Michael S., *Economic Analysis and Moral Philosophy*, Cambridge University Press, 1996

Hayek, Friedrich A., 'Competition as a Discovery Procedure', in *New Studies in Philosophy, Politics, Economics and the History of Ideas*, by F. A. Hayek, University of Chicago Press, 1978

Hazlitt, William, 'On Reason and Imagination', Essay V in *The Plain Speaker*, in *The Collected Works of William Hazlitt*, ed. A. R. Waller and A. Glover, vol. XII, J. M. Dent & Co., 1903

An Essay on the Principles of Human Action (originally published in 1805), reprinted in *The Selected Writings of William Hazlitt*, ed. Duncan Wu, vol. 1, Pickering & Chatto, 1998, pp. 3–82

The Spirit of the Age, 2nd edn. (originally published in 1825), essays on 'Jeremy Bentham' and 'Mr. Coleridge', The Wordsworth Trust, 2004

Heap, S., Hollis, M., Lyons, B., Sugden, R. and Weale, A. (eds.), *The Theory of Choice – A Critical Guide*, Blackwell, 1992

Hedley, Douglas, *Coleridge, Philosophy and Religion – Aids to Reflection and the Mirror of the Spirit*, Cambridge University Press, 2000

Heinzelman, Kurt, *The Economics of the Imagination*, University of Massachusetts Press, 1980

Henderson, W. O., *Friedrich List: Economist and Visionary 1789–1846*, Frank Cass, 1983

Herder, J. G., *Essay on the Origin of Language* (originally published in 1772), extracts trans. F. M. Barnard, in *J. G. Herder on Social and Political Culture*, Cambridge University Press, 1969

Ideas for a Philosophy of the History of Mankind (originally published in 1791), extracts trans. F. M. Barnard, in *J. G. Herder on Social and Political Culture*, Cambridge University Press, 1969

Hill, John Spencer (ed.), *Imagination in Coleridge*, Macmillan, 1978

Hodgkiss, Philip, *The Making of the Modern Mind – The Surfacing of Consciousness in Social Thought*, The Athlone Press, 2001

Hodgson, Geoffrey M., *Economics and Utopia – Why the Learning Economy is not the End of History*, Routledge, 1999

Hollander, Samuel, *The Economics of John Stuart Mill*, vol. I, University of Toronto Press, 1985

Hollingdale, R. J. (trans. and ed.), *A Nietzsche Reader*, Penguin, 1977

Hollis, Martin, 'Autonomy', chapter 6 in *The Theory of Choice – A Critical Guide*, ed. S. Heap, M. Hollis, B. Lyons, R. Sugden and A. Weale, Blackwell, 1992

Holmes, Richard, *Coleridge – Darker Reflections*, HarperCollins, 1998

Howell, Chris, 'Varieties of Capitalism: And Then There Was One?', *Comparative Politics*, 36(1) (October 2003), pp. 103–24

Howkins, John, *The Creative Economy – How People Make Money from Ideas*, Penguin, 2001

Hume, David, *An Inquiry Concerning Human Understanding* (1777), and extracts from *A Treatise of Human Nature* (1740), reprinted in *David Hume on Human Nature and the Understanding*, ed. Anthony Flew, Macmillan, 1962

Innes, Abby, *Czechoslovakia – The Short Goodbye*, Yale University Press, 2001

Jackson, Robert, *The Global Covenant: Human Conduct in a World of States*, Oxford University Press, 2000

Jacobs, Michael, *The Green Economy – Environment, Sustainable Development and the Politics of the Future*, Pluto Press, 1991

Johnson, Björn, 'Institutional Learning', chapter 2 in *National Systems of Innovation*, ed. Bengt-Åke Lundvall, Pinter, 1995

Kahneman, Daniel and Tversky, Amos, 'Choices, Values, and Frames', *American Psychologist*, 39(4) (1984), reprinted as chapter 1 in *Choices, Values, and Frames*, ed. Daniel Kahneman and Amos Tversky, Cambridge University Press, 2000

Kay, John A., *The Business of Economics*, Oxford University Press, 1996

Keats, John, *Lamia* (originally published in 1819), reprinted in *Romanticism – An Anthology*, 2nd edn., ed. Duncan Wu, Blackwell, 1998, pp. 1064–79

'Letter to George and Tom Keats', 21 December 1817, extract reprinted in *Romanticism – An Anthology*, 2nd edn., ed. Duncan Wu, Blackwell, 1998, p. 1019

Kemp, John, *The Philosophy of Kant*, Thoemmes Press, 1995

Kenny, Anthony (ed.), *The Wittgenstein Reader*, Blackwell, 1994

Kermode, Frank, *Romantic Image*, Routledge, 2002

Keynes, John Maynard, 'A Tract on Monetary Reform' (1923), chapter 3 in *The Collected Writings of John Maynard Keynes*, vol. IV, Macmillan, 1971

Essay on 'Thomas Robert Malthus', essay on 'Alfred Marshall' and essay on 'Francis Ysidro Edgeworth', chapters 12, 14, 16, in *The Collected Writings of John Maynard Keynes*, vol. X, Macmillan, 1972

The General Theory of Employment, Interest and Money (originally published in 1936), in *The Collected Writings of John Maynard Keynes*, vol. VII, Macmillan, 1973

Keynes, John Neville, *The Scope and Method of Political Economy*, 3rd edn., Macmillan, 1904

Kitschelt, Herbert, Lange, Peter, Marks, Gary and Stephens, John D., 'Convergence and Divergence in Advanced Capitalist Democracies', chapter 15 in *Continuity and Change in Contemporary Capitalism*, ed. Herbert Kitschelt *et al.*, Cambridge University Press, 1999

Krugman, Paul, *Development, Geography, and Economic Theory*, MIT Press, 1997

Kuhn, Thomas S., *The Structure of Scientific Revolutions*, 3rd edn., University of Chicago Press, 1996

Layard, Richard, *Happiness – Lessons from a New Science*, Allen Lane, 2005

Leavis, F. R. (ed.), *Mill on Bentham and Coleridge*, Chatto & Windus, 1950

Levinson, Marjorie, *The Romantic Fragment Poem – A Critique of a Form*, University of North Carolina Press, 1986

List, Friedrich, *Outlines of American Political Economy*, 1827, extracts quoted in Henderson, W. O., *Friedrich List: Economist and Visionary 1789–1846*, Frank Cass, 1983, pp. 145–55

The National System of Political Economy, 1841, trans. S. S. Lloyd, Longmans, Green & Co., 1922, extracts quoted in Greenfeld, Liah, *The Spirit of Capitalism – Nationalism and Economic Growth*, Harvard University Press, 2001, pp. 201–6

Little, I. M. D., *Ethics, Economics, and Politics – Principles of Public Policy*, Oxford University Press, 2002

Lockridge, Laurence S., *The Ethics of Romanticism*, Cambridge University Press, 1989

Lovejoy, A. O., 'On the Discrimination of Romanticisms', from *Essays in the History of Ideas*, Johns Hopkins University Press, 1948, reprinted in *English Romantic Poets – Modern Essays in Criticism*, ed. M. H. Abrams, Oxford University Press, 1975, pp. 3–24

Lovelock, James, *The Revenge of Gaia*, Penguin, 2006

Lundvall, Bengt-Åke, chapters 1, 3 in *National Systems of Innovation – Towards a Theory of Innovation and Interactive Learning*, ed. Bengt-Åke Lundvall, Pinter, 1995

Lyons, Bruce, 'Risk, Ignorance and Imagination', 'Game Theory' and 'Organisations', chapters 4, 7, 10 in *The Theory of Choice – A Critical Guide*, ed. S. Heap, M. Hollis, B. Lyons, R. Sugden and A. Weale, Blackwell, 1992

MacIntyre, Alasdair, *After Virtue – A Study in Moral Theory*, Duckworth, 1981

Magee, Bryan, *The Great Philosophers – An Introduction to Western Philosophy*, BBC Books, 1987

Confessions of a Philosopher – A Journey Through Western Philosophy, Phoenix, 1997

Mäki, Uskali (ed.), *Fact and Fiction in Economics: Models, Realism and Social Construction*, Cambridge University Press, 2002

Malthus, Robert, *An Essay on the Principle of Population* (originally published in 1798), and *A Summary View of the Principle of Population* (originally published in 1830), ed. Anthony Flew, Penguin, 1970

    Letter to David Ricardo, 26 January 1817; extract reprinted in Keynes, John Maynard, essay on 'Thomas Robert Malthus', in *The Collected Writings of John Maynard Keynes*, vol. X, Macmillan, 1972, p. 97f.

March, James G. and Olsen, Johan P., *Rediscovering Institutions: The Organisational Basis of Politics*, Free Press, 1989

Marshall, Alfred, *Principles of Economics*, Eighth Edition (including Preface to First Edition, 1890), Macmillan, 1927

    Inaugural Lecture, extract quoted in Keynes, John Maynard, essay on 'Alfred Marshall', in *The Collected Writings of John Maynard Keynes*, vol. X, Macmillan, 1972, p. 196

    Letter to Arthur Lyon Bowley, 21 February 1901; Letter to Arthur Lyon Bowley, 3 March 1901; Letter to Arthur Lyon Bowley, 27 February 1906, Letters 634, 637, 840, in *The Correspondence of Alfred Marshall*, ed. J. K. Whitaker, vols. 2, 3, Cambridge University Press, 1996

Martin, Michael, 'Taylor on Interpretation and the Sciences of Man', chapter 17 in *Readings in the Philosophy of Social Science*, ed. Michael Martin and Lee C. McIntyre, MIT Press, 1994

Martin, Michael and McIntyre, Lee, C. (eds.), *Readings in the Philosophy of Social Science*, MIT Press, 1994

Marx, Karl and Engels, Frederick, *Manifesto of the Communist Party* (originally published in 1848), Progress Publishers (Moscow), 1977

Mason, John Hope, *The Value of Creativity – The Origins and Emergence of a Modern Belief*, Ashgate, 2003

Mayall, James, *Nationalism and International Society*, Cambridge University Press, 1990

McCalman, Iain (ed.), *An Oxford Companion to the Romantic Age – British Culture 1776–1832*, Oxford University Press, 1999

McCloskey, D. N., *The Rhetoric of Economics*, 2nd edn., University of Wisconsin Press, 1998

McDonagh, Josephine, *De Quincey's Disciplines*, Oxford University Press, 1994

McFarland, Thomas, *Originality and Imagination*, Johns Hopkins University Press, 1985

Merquior, J. G., *Foucault*, Fontana Press, 1985

Mill, John Stuart, 'Essay on the Definition of Political Economy; and on the Method of Investigation Proper to it' (originally published in 1830), as Essay V in Mill, J. S., *Essays on Some Unsettled Questions of Political Economy*, 3rd edn., Longmans, Green & Co., 1877

    Essay on 'Bentham' (originally published in 1838), and essay on 'Coleridge' (originally published in 1840), in *Mill on Bentham and Coleridge*, ed. F. R. Leavis, Chatto & Windus, 1950

    Utilitarianism (originally published in 1861), ed. Mary Warnock, William Collins & Sons, 1962

Autobiography (originally published in 1873), Penguin, 1989

On Liberty (originally published in 1859), in *On Liberty and Other Essays*, ed. John Gray, Oxford University Press, 1991

Principles of Political Economy (originally published in 1848), ed. Jonathan Riley, Oxford University Press, 1994

Mirowski, Philip, *More Heat than Light – Economics as Social Physics, Physics as Nature's Economics*, Cambridge University Press, 1989

Morgan, Gareth, *Images of Organization*, Sage, 2006

Morgan, G., Whitley, R. and Moen, E. (eds.), *Changing Capitalisms? – Internationalisation, Institutional Change and Systems of Economic Organisation*, Oxford University Press, 2005

Mueller, Dennis C., *Public Choice II*, Cambridge University Press, 1989

Murdoch, Iris, 'The Darkness of Practical Reason', Review article in *Encounter*, July 1966, reprinted in Murdoch, Iris, *Existentialists and Mystics – Writings on Philosophy and Literature*, ed. Peter Conradi, Chatto & Windus, 1997, pp. 193–202

Sartre: Romantic Rationalist, Vintage, 1999

Nietzsche, Friedrich, *The Twilight of the Idols* (originally published in 1889), and *Notes on 'Thus Spake Zarathustra'*, trans. Anthony M. Ludovici, George Allen & Unwin, 1911

Extracts from *Beyond Good and Evil* (originally published in 1886), *The Gay Science* (originally published in 1882) and *Thus Spake Zarathustra*, part IV (originally published in 1892), in *A Nietzsche Reader*, sel. and trans. R. J. Hollingdale, Penguin, 1977

Norris, Christopher, *Derrida*, Fontana, 1987

North, Douglass C., *Understanding the Process of Economic Change*, Princeton University Press, 2005

Offe, Claus, 'Political Economy: Sociological Perspectives', chapter 29 in *A New Handbook of Political Science*, ed. Robert E. Goodin and Hans-Dieter Klingemann, Oxford University Press, 1998

Olson, Mancur, *The Logic of Collective Action*, Harvard University Press, 1965

The Rise and Decline of Nations: Economic Growth, Stagflation, and Social Rigidities, Yale University Press, 1982

Ormorod, Paul, *The Death of Economics*, Faber & Faber, 1994

Ortony, Andrew, article on 'Metaphor', in *The Oxford Companion to the Mind*, ed. Richard L. Gregory, Oxford University Press, 1987, pp. 478–81

Paulin, Tom, *The Day-Star of Liberty – William Hazlitt's Radical Style*, Faber & Faber, 1998

Pigou, A. C., *Alfred Marshall and Current Thought* – Lecture on Mathematical Methods, Macmillan, 1953

Popper, Karl R., *Conjectures and Refutations – The Growth of Scientific Knowledge*, Routledge, 1963

Porter, Michael E., *The Competitive Advantage of Nations*, Macmillan, 1990

Rabin, Matthew, 'Psychology and Economics', *Journal of Economic Literature*, XXXVI (March 1998), pp. 11–46

Raphael, D. D., *Adam Smith*, Oxford University Press, 1985

Ricardo, David, *On the Principles of Political Economy and Taxation* (originally published in 1817), reprinted in *The Works and Correspondence of David Ricardo*, ed. Piero Sraffa, vol. 1, Cambridge University Press, 1951

Letter to Robert Malthus, 24 January 1817, extract reprinted in Keynes, John Maynard, essay on 'Thomas Robert Malthus', in *The Collected Writings of John Maynard Keynes*, vol. X, Macmillan, 1972, p. 97

Rifkin, Jeremy, *The End of Work*, G. P. Putnam & Sons, 1995

Robbins, Lionel, *An Essay on the Nature and Significance of Economic Science*, 2nd edn., Macmillan, 1935, extracts reprinted as chapter 3 in *The Philosophy of Economics – An Anthology*, 2nd edn., ed. Daniel M. Hausman, Cambridge University Press, 1994

A History of Economic Thought – The LSE Lectures, ed. Steven G. Medema and Warren J. Samuels, Princeton University Press, 1998

Roll, Eric, *A History of Economic Thought*, 5th edn., Faber & Faber, 1992

Rothschild, Emma, *Economic Sentiments – Adam Smith, Condorcet, and the Enlightenment*, Harvard University Press, 2001

Rothstein, Bo, 'Political Institutions: An Overview', chapter 4 in *A New Handbook of Political Science*, ed. Robert E. Goodin and Hans-Dieter Klingemann, Oxford University Press, 1998

Runde, Jochen and Mizuhara, Sohei (eds.), *The Philosophy of Keynes's Economics: Probability, Uncertainty and Convention*, Routledge, 2003

Ruskin, John, *Unto this Last* (originally published in 1862), ed. Clive Wilmer, Penguin, 1985

Russell, Bertrand, *A History of Western Philosophy*, George Allen & Unwin, 1946

Sabel, Charles F., 'Intelligible Differences: On Deliberate Strategy and the Exploration of Possibility in Economic Life', *Rivista Italiana degli Economisti*, I, 1996, pp. 55-80; also available at www2.law.columbia.edu/sabel/papers

Samuelson, Paul Anthony, *Foundations of Economic Analysis*, Harvard University Press, 1947

Schlegel, Friedrich, Fragment 53 from *Athenaeum Fragments* (originally published in 1798), quoted in Beer, John, 'Fragmentations and Ironies', in *Questioning Romanticism*, ed. John Beer, Johns Hopkins University Press, 1995, p. 251

Fragment 108 from *Critical Fragments* (originally published in 1797), and a fragment from *Ideas* (originally published in the last volume of the *Athenaeum*, 1800), quoted in 'Friedrich Schlegel and Novalis', by Ernst Behler, in *A Companion to Continental Philosophy*, ed. Simon Critchley and William R. Schroeder, Blackwell, 1998, p. 80f.

Athenaeum fragment 206, and extract from *Studien des Klassischen Altertums*, 98, quoted in Armstrong, Charles I., *Romantic Organicism – From Idealist Origins to Ambivalent Afterlife*, Palgrave Macmillan, 2003, p. 43f.

Schumpeter, Joseph A., *History of Economic Analysis*, George Allen & Unwin, 1954

Capitalism, Socialism and Democracy (originally published in 1943), Routledge, 1994

Schwartz, Barry, *The Paradox of Choice – Why More is Less*, HarperCollins, 2004

Sen, Amartya, *On Ethics and Economics*, Blackwell, 1987

'Rationality and Social Choice', *American Economic Review*, 85 (1995); reproduced as chapter 16 in *Readings in Political Economy*, ed. Kaushik Basu, Blackwell, 2003

Shackle, G. L. S., *Decision, Order and Time in Human Affairs*, Cambridge University Press, 1961

Imagination and the Nature of Choice, Edinburgh University Press, 1979

Epistemics and Economics – A Critique of Economic Doctrines (originally published in 1972), Transaction Publishers, 1992

Shelley, Percy Bysshe, *A Defence of Poetry* (originally published in 1840), extracts reprinted in *Romanticism – An Anthology*, 2nd edn., ed. Duncan Wu, Blackwell, 1998, pp. 944–56

Skidelsky, Robert, *John Maynard Keynes, Volume Two – The Economist as Saviour, 1920–1937*, Macmillan, 1992

Skorupski, John, *The Cambridge Companion to Mill*, Cambridge University Press, 1998

Smith, Adam, *The Theory of Moral Sentiments* (originally published in 1759), ed. D. D. Raphael and A. L. Macfie, Oxford University Press, 1976

An Inquiry into the Nature and Causes of the Wealth of Nations (originally published in 1776), ed. Kathryn Sutherland, Oxford University Press, 1993

'History of Astronomy', in *Essays on Philosophical Subjects* (originally published in 1795), ed. W. P. D. Wightman and J. C. Bryce, Oxford University Press, 1980, extracts quoted in Fleischacker, Samuel, *On Adam Smith's Wealth of Nations – A Philosophical Companion*, Princeton University Press, 2004, pp. 21, 32

Snow, C. P., *The Two Cultures and the Scientific Revolution*, Cambridge University Press, 1959

Soros, George, *The Crisis of Global Capitalism: Open Society Endangered*, Little Brown, 1998

Soskice, David, 'Divergent Production Regimes: Coordinated and Uncoordinated Market Economies in the 1980s and 1990s', chapter 4 in *Continuity and Change in Contemporary Capitalism*, ed. Herbert Kitschelt *et al.*, Cambridge University Press, 1999

Stafford, William, *John Stuart Mill*, Macmillan, 1998

Stiglitz, Joseph E., *Principles of Micro-Economics*, 2nd edn., W. W. Norton, 1997

'Whither Reform? Ten Years of the Transition', Keynote Address, Annual World Bank Conference on Development Economics, 1999; reproduced as chapter 4 in *The Rebel Within*, ed. Ha-Joon Chang, Wimbledon Publishing Company, 2001

Sutton, John, *Marshall's Tendencies – What Can Economists Know?* MIT Press, 2000

Tabb, William K., *Reconstructing Political Economy – The Great Divide in Economic Thought*, Routledge, 1999

Tarnas, Richard, *The Passion of the Western Mind – Understanding the Ideas that have Shaped our World View*, Ballantine Books, 1993

Taylor, Charles, 'Interpretation and the Sciences of Man', *Review of Metaphysics*, 25 (1971); reproduced as chapter 13 in *Readings in the Philosophy of Social Science*, ed. Michael Martin and Lee C. McIntyre, MIT Press, 1994

Todaro, Michael P., *Economic Development*, 5th edn., Longman, 1994

United Nations Development Program, *Human Development Report 1996*, Oxford University Press; for recent years, see http://hdr.undp.org/en

Veblen, Thorstein, 'The Limitations of Marginal Utility', *Journal of Political Economy*, 17 (1909); reproduced as chapter 6 in *The Philosophy of Economics – An Anthology*, 2nd edn., ed. Daniel M. Hausman, Cambridge University Press, 1994

Waldrop, M. Mitchell, *Complexity – The Emerging Science at the Edge of Order and Chaos*, Penguin, 1994

Warnock, Mary, *Imagination*, Faber & Faber, 1976

Waterman, A. M. C., *Revolution, Economics and Religion: Christian Political Economy, 1798–1833*, Cambridge University Press, 1991

Weale, Albert '*Homo economicus, Homo sociologicus*', chapter 5 in *The Theory of Choice – A Critical Guide*, ed. S. Heap, M. Hollis, B. Lyons, R. Sugden and A. Weale, Blackwell, 1992

Webb, Beatrice, *My Apprenticeship* (1883), extracts quoted in Leavis, F. R., 'Introduction', in *Mill on Bentham and Coleridge*, Chatto & Windus, 1950, pp. 18–29

Weber, Max, *The Protestant Ethic and the Spirit of Capitalism* (originally published in English in 1930), Routledge, 1992

Weimer, David L. and Vining, Aidan R., *Policy Analysis: Concepts and Practice*, 2nd edn., Prentice Hall, 1992

Whale, John, *Imagination Under Pressure, 1789–1832 – Aesthetics, Politics and Utility*, Cambridge University Press, 2000

Williams, Raymond, *Culture and Society: 1780–1950*, Chatto & Windus, 1958

Winch, Donald, 'Political Economy', chapter 33 in *An Oxford Companion to the Romantic Age – British Culture 1776–1832*, ed. Iain McCalman, Oxford University Press, 1999

Wittgenstein, Ludwig, *Philosophical Investigations*, trans. G. E. M. Anscombe (originally published in 1953), Blackwell, 2001

Wordsworth, William, *The Prelude* (1805), ed. E. de Selincourt, Oxford University Press, 1960

   Preface to the *Lyrical Ballads*, 1800, and 1802 amendment, in Wordsworth, William and Coleridge, Samuel Taylor, *Lyrical Ballads*, ed. R. L. Brett and A. R. Jones, Methuen, 1963, pp. 235–66

   'Fragment', dated by E. de Selincourt as 1798–1800, reproduced in Warnock, Mary, *Imagination*, Faber & Faber, 1976, p. 125

   The Prelude (1850), ed. J. Wordsworth, M. H. Abrams and S. Gill, W. W. Norton, 1979

   'Lines Written a Few Miles above Tintern Abbey', and 'The Tables Turned' (from *Lyrical Ballads*, 1798), reprinted in *Romanticism – An Anthology*, 2nd edn., ed. Duncan Wu, Blackwell, 1998, pp. 260f., 265–9

   Preface to *Poems* (1815), reprinted in *Romanticism – An Anthology*, 2nd edn., ed. Duncan Wu, Blackwell, 1998, pp. 411–14

'The world is too much with us' (from *Poems in Two Volumes*, 1807), reprinted in *Romanticism – An Anthology*, 2nd edn., ed. Duncan Wu, Blackwell, 1998, p. 372

World Bank, *From Plan to Market*, World Development Report, 1996, Oxford University Press, 1996

Wu, Duncan (ed.), *Romanticism – An Anthology*, 2nd edn., Blackwell, 1998

Index

Bold type represents the page numbers of key entries.